Clarity PPM Fundamentals

Rama Velpuri and Arpit Das

Apress®

Clarity PPM Fundamentals

Copyright © 2011 by CA, Inc. All rights reserved. All trademarks, trade names, service marks and logos referenced herein belong to their respective companies.

The information in this publication could include typographical errors or technical inaccuracies, and the authors assume no responsibility for its accuracy or completeness. The statements and opinions expressed in this book are those of the authors and are not necessarily those of CA Technologies. ("CA"). CA may make modifications to any CA product, software program, method or procedure described in this publication at any time without notice.

Any reference in this publication to third-party products and websites is provided for convenience only and shall not serve as the authors' endorsement of such products or websites. Your use of such products, websites, any information regarding such products or any materials provided with such products or on such websites shall be at your own risk.

To the extent permitted by applicable law, the content of this book is provided "AS IS" without warranty of any kind, including, without limitation, any implied warranties of merchantability, fitness for a particular purpose, or non-infringement. In no event will the authors or CA be liable for any loss or damage, direct or indirect, arising from or related to the use of this book, including, without limitation, lost profits, lost investment, business interruption, goodwill or lost data, even if expressly advised in advance of the possibility of such damages. Neither the content of this book nor any software product referenced herein serves as a substitute for your compliance with any laws (including but not limited to any act, statute, regulation, rule, directive, standard, policy, administrative order, executive order, and so on (collectively, "Laws") referenced herein or otherwise. You should consult with competent legal counsel regarding any such Laws.

All rights reserved. No part of this work may be reproduced or transmitted in any form or by any means, electronic or mechanical, including photocopying, recording, or by any information storage or retrieval system, without the prior written permission of the copyright owner and the publisher.

ISBN-13 (pbk): 978-1-4302-3557-6

ISBN-13 (electronic): 978-1-4302-3558-3

Trademarked names, logos, and images may appear in this book. Rather than use a trademark symbol with every occurrence of a trademarked name, logo, or image we use the names, logos, and images only in an editorial fashion and to the benefit of the trademark owner, with no intention of infringement of the trademark.

The use in this publication of trade names, trademarks, service marks, and similar terms, even if they are not identified as such, is not to be taken as an expression of opinion as to whether or not they are subject to proprietary rights.

President and Publisher: Paul Manning
Lead Editor: Jeffrey Pepper
Technical Reviewers: Debroop Dasgupta and Ponniah Rajagopal
Editorial Board: Steve Anglin, Mark Beckner, Ewan Buckingham, Gary Cornell, Morgan Ertel, Jonathan Gennick, Jonathan Hassell, Robert Hutchinson, Michelle Lowman, Matthew Moodie, Jeff Olson, Jeffrey Pepper, Douglas Pundick, Ben Renow-Clarke, Dominic Shakeshaft, Matt Wade, Tom Welsh
Coordinating Editor: Jennifer L. Blackwell, Rita Fernando
Copy Editor: Kim Wimpsett
Compositor: Apress Production (Christine Ricketts)
Formatter: Nancy Wright
Indexer: Kumar Dhaneesh
Cover Designer: Anna Ishchenko

Distributed to the book trade worldwide by Springer Science+Business Media, LLC., 233 Spring Street, 6th Floor, New York, NY 10013. Phone 1-800-SPRINGER, fax (201) 348-4505, e-mail orders-ny@springer-sbm.com, or visit www.springeronline.com.

For information on translations, please e-mail rights@apress.com, or visit www.apress.com.

Apress and friends of ED books may be purchased in bulk for academic, corporate, or promotional use. eBook versions and licenses are also available for most titles. For more information, reference our Special Bulk Sales–eBook Licensing web page at www.apress.com/bulk-sales.

The information in this book is distributed on an "as is" basis, without warranty. Although every precaution has been taken in the preparation of this work, neither the author(s) nor Apress shall have any liability to any person or entity with respect to any loss or damage caused or alleged to be caused directly or indirectly by the information contained in this work.

To our parents

Contents at a Glance

Contents v
Foreword vi
About the Authors vii
About the Technical Reviewers viii
Acknowledgements ix
Preface x
Part 1: CA Clarity PPM Fundamentals 1
Chapter 1: Introduction to CA Clarity PPM 3
Chapter 2: CA Clarity PPM in Use 25
Chapter 3: An Overview of CA Clarity PPM 59
Part 2: CA Clarity PPM Modules 99
Chapter 4: CA Clarity PPM Components: Project Management Module 101
Chapter 5: CA Clarity PPM Components: Resource Management 125
Chapter 6: CA Clarity PPM Components: Time Management 143
Chapter 7: CA Clarity PPM Components: Financial Management 161
Chapter 8: Demand Management 191
Chapter 9: Portfolio Management 209
Chapter 10: Process Management 225
Part 3: CA Clarity PPM Utilities 237
Chapter 11: CA Clarity PPM Organizational Breakdown Structure 239
Chapter 12: CA Clarity PPM Security 269
Chapter 13: CA Clarity PPM Components: Prepackaged Work Products 291
Index 319

Contents

Contents at a Glance iv
Foreword vi
About the Authors vii
About the Technical Reviewers viii
Acknowledgements ix
Preface x

Part 1: CA Clarity PPM Fundamentals 1

Chapter 1: Introduction to CA Clarity PPM 3
  What Is CA Clarity PPM? 3
    CA Clarity IT Portfolio Manager 5
    CA Clarity IT Financial Manager 6
    CA Clarity BRM 6
    CA Clarity PPM 7
    CA Clarity Resource Manager 7
    CA Clarity Project Manager 8
    CA Clarity Demand Manager 8
    CA Clarity Project Financial Manager 9
    CA Clarity Process Manager 9
  Why Use CA Clarity PPM? 10
    The Challenges 10
    CA Clarity PPM Provides Visibility for Effective Project Management 13
    Benefits of Integrating Clarity PPM with External Systems 17
  Who Uses CA Clarity PPM? 17

The Public Sector and Utilities Companies	18
The Professional Services Companies	19
The Financial Sector Companies	20
The Oil and Gas Industry	21
The Entertainment Industry	22
Summary	24

Chapter 2: CA Clarity PPM inUse 25

Project Life Cycle 25
Project Life Cycle Management	25
The Three Keys of Project Success	27

IT Governance in Real Life 28
What Is IT Governance?	28
Why IT Governance Is Necessary	29

Evaluation of Portfolio Management 31
The Origins of Portfolio Management	31
Business Investment Planning	31
The Next Step: IT Governance	32

Road Map and Maturity Assessment 50
Why Do Projects Fail?	50
Assessing Organizational Readiness	53
A Case Study	54
Summary	57

Chapter 3: An Overview of CA Clarity PPM 59

User Interface 59
Main Menu and Navigation Bar	61
Clarity Toolbar	64
Portlets on the Home Page	65

Basic Navigation 65

Application vs. Administration Tool	65
List Pages and Filters	67
Organizer	75
Knowledge Store	84
Personalization	**87**
Account Settings	87
Personalize the Overview Page	92
Reports and Jobs	**94**
Reports	95
Jobs	95
Other Configuration Options in Clarity	**95**
Summary	**98**

Part 2: CA Clarity PPM Modules 99

Chapter 4: CA Clarity PPM Components: Project Management Module 101

Project Management	**102**
Getting Started in the Project Management Module	103
Project Creation	103
Project Properties	106

Chapter 5: CA Clarity PPM Components: Resource Management 125

The Resource Management Module	**126**
Resources	**126**
Roles	127
Create a New Resource	127
Resource Planning	130
Capacity	135
Investments	137
Resource Finder	**137**

Resource Requisitions 138

Chapter 6: CA Clarity PPM Components: Time Management 143

Set Up a Timesheet 144

Time Reporting Period 144

Security Rights 145

Resource Properties 146

Investment Properties 147

Complete Timesheet 147

Tips 148

Approve Timesheets 151

Modify Timesheet Settings 153

Posted Timesheet 154

Clarity Algorithm for Calculating ETC in Timesheets and Posting 156

Posting 156

Timesheet Editing 157

Customer Scenario 1: ETC with Two Timesheets 158

Customer Scenario 2: Pending Actuals and an Adjustment 158

Customer Scenario 3: Pending Actuals and an Adjustment 159

Summary 159

Chapter 7: CA Clarity PPM Components: Financial Management 161

The Clarity PPM Financial Management Module 161

Financial Processing Flow in CA Clarity PPM 162

Financially Enabling Objects 170

Creating Financial Transactions 174

Creating from Timesheets 174

Creating from Transaction Entry (Vouchers) 174

Creating a Voucher (Clarity Administrators Only) 174

Entering Manual Transactions 175

Transaction Processing..177

Work in Process (WIP) and Actual Cost..179

Correcting Transactions (Clarity and Financial Administrators Only).........................181

Clarity Invoices...185

IT Chargeback Recovery 188

Summary 190

Chapter 8: Demand Management 191

Introduction to Idea Management 192

Introduction to Incident Management 199

Chatper 9: Portfolio Management..209

Investments in Clarity 210

Using Portfolios..212

Create a Portfolio 215

Define Portfolio Content 217

Analyze a Portfolio 221

Scenarios 223

Summary 224

Chapter 10: Process Management..225

Flow of CA Clarity PPM Workflow Process 226

Create a Process 227

Execute a Process 235

Summary 236

Part 3: CA Clarity PPM Utilities...237

CA Clarity PPM Organizational Breakdown Structure 239

Organization Structure..239

OBS Definition 240

OBS Properties 243

OBS Object Association	244
OBS and Financial Entities	244
Associating a Resource with the OBS	247
Granting Access Rights via OBS	251
OBS and Datamart	252
Partitions and Views	253
The Partition Model	253
Define Partition Model	255
Partition Configuration	257
Best Practices	264
Organizational Breakdown Structure (OBS)	264
Partitioning	264
Partition Value	265
Partition Caveats	266
Summary	267
CA Clarity PPM Security	**269**
Introduction to Clarity PPM Security	270
Clarity Security Model	271
Financial/Entity-Based Access Rights	286
Object-Level Access Rights	287
Best Practices	289
CA Clarity PPM Security Audit Report Prepackaged Work Product	289
Summary	290
CA Clarity PPM Components: Prepackaged Work Products	**291**
CA Clarity Smart Phone Time Management App Add-on Services Component	291
CA Clarity Business Analytics Add-on Services Component	293
CA Clarity KPI Monitor Add-on Services Component	295
CA Clarity PPM Excel UI for Resource Management Add-on Services Component	297

CA Clarity PPM Excel UI for Risk, Issues and Change Requests Add-on Services Component 298
CA Clarity PPM Grants Management Add-on Services Component 299
CA Clarity PPM CPIC Add-on Services Component 301
CA Clarity Idea Vision Integration Add-on Services Component 302
CA Clarity Integration Accelerator 303
Base Data Extraction for CA Clarity PPM 304
CA Clarity PPM Cost and Rate Matrix Adapter Add-on Services Component 306
CA Clarity PPM Financial Transactions Adapter Add-on Services Component 307
CA Clarity PPM Projects Adapter Add-on Services Component 308
CA Clarity PPM Resources Adapter Add-on Services Components 309
CA Clarity PPM Time Actuals Adapter Add-on Services Component 310
CA Clarity PPM Data Management Accelerator 311
CA Clarity PPM Advanced Project Management Accelerator 312
CA Clarity PPM Earned Value Management Accelerator 313
CA Clarity PPM Advanced Resource Management Accelerator 314
CA Clarity PPM Advanced Financial Management Accelerator 315
CA Clarity PPM Fiscal Focus Actionable Dashboard Add-on Services Component 316

Index **319**

Foreword

No matter where I go in the world today, I find companies that are launching a variety of development efforts to capture and apply knowledge that is unique to their business. Their goal—regardless of their industry or region—is to increase innovation and make better use of limited resources.

These efforts can face several challenges, including the following:
- Helping business managers understand how they contribute to achieving corporate goals
- Launching only the projects the organization can handle effectively
- Setting project priorities based on business objectives
- Analyzing the need and appropriate resources for each project
- Achieving the efficiencies that lead to real cost savings

To address these challenges, organizations need a thorough process for selecting the right product and portfolio management (PPM) solution. But that's just the start. Once the solution is in place, they need highly skilled administrators who understand the business as well as the technical configuration necessary to keep the lights on and delight their end users.

The authors of this book have extensive experience in dealing with the challenges an organization faces in implementing a PPM solution. Rama Velpuri and Arpit Das have amassed a wealth of business and technical knowledge of CA Clarity PPM and how it functions in the most demanding Fortune 500 customers. Rama has a deep background in CA Clarity product development, and Arpit has significant hands-on experience from CA Services. They have supplemented their expertise with the experience and insight of the "best and brightest" from CA Technologies product development and services. This day-to-day knowledge has never before been so thoroughly compiled and documented.

This handbook will be useful for all Clarity administrators and will be a valuable training tool for the end users of CA Clarity PPM. It is also a must for every organization that has the CA Clarity PPM solution implemented and will complement the existing CA Clarity PPM user documentation.

David Dobson
EVP & Group Executive
Customer Solutions Group
CA Technologies

About the Authors

Rama Velpuri With more than 22 years of managerial and technical experience in the IT industry that spans multiple continents, Rama Velpuri is currently a vice president of software engineering at CA Technologies, in the Clarity PPM division.

Before joining CA Technologies, Velpuri was the CTO of Kenexa Technologies, a Pennsylvania-based company, in the HR vertical. As an officer of the company, Velpuri played an important role in taking Kenexa public (KNXA) on NASDAQ in June 2005. Before that, Velpuri was the founder and CEO of Oramasters, Inc.

Velpuri started his career with Oracle Corporation in 1988, and, over the next 11 years, he successfully worked on numerous strategic initiatives across Technical Support, Worldwide Alliances, and Product Development. As an executive director at Oracle Corporation, Velpuri was instrumental in establishing the Oracle India Product Engineering Center in Bangalore and the Oracle Application Development Center in Hyderabad, India. During his tenure at Oracle, Velpuri authored nine successful technology books (Oracle Press) that were translated into several languages including German, Italian, Spanish, Korean, Dutch, Japanese, and Mandarin.

Arpit Das With 15-plus years of experience in leadership, strategic planning, and delivery effectiveness across various business units, Arpit Das is currently a director of services delivery at CA Technologies, in the CA Services Global Delivery organization.

Arpit started his career with Newtech Computers in 1995 before moving to the United States in 1997 to pursue a master's degree in computer and information systems engineering from Tennessee State University in Nashville, Tennessee. Arpit joined CA Technologies in 2000 in product development, and over the next 11 years he worked for product development, CA Services, and Global Delivery. As a services architect for the North America Clarity practice, he was engaged in creating architecture models, creating design solutions, gathering business requirements and translating them into high-level design documents, and managing vendor relationships. During his tenure as a field services architect, Arpit was actively involved in setting up the Clarity Solution Center and mentoring new services consultants and architects.

Arpit assisted in building an elite global delivery organization including recruiting and hiring technology experts in India, Europe, North America, and Latin America. His responsibility was to set up partner and vendor relationships to scale growing international business. This included beginning-to-end management and negotiation. Arpit assisted in developing a Managed Services business unit to deliver remote production operations for CA clients, specifically focused on the Service Management and IT Governance business units.

About the Technical Reviewers

Debroop Dasgupta has five-plus years of experience in the IT industry doing CA Clarity PPM implementations and support and upgrades. Debroop Dasgupta is a senior services consultant at CA Technologies, in the CA Services Global Delivery organization.

With a bachelor's degree in mechanical engineering, Debroop started his career as a software engineer with Infosys Technologies in 2006 in the APAC Unit of the company. He began his association with CA Clarity as a technical consultant for, what was then, one of the largest CA Clarity implementations in the APAC region for a telecom giant. He learned to engage with multiple teams for different areas of IT delivery—testing, design and development, and even the creation of training aids.

He joined Wipro Technologies in 2008 and was a key member in the growth of their Clarity implementation. He honed his skills as a Clarity functional consultant and worked with a diverse range of clients—manufacturing companies, financial services firms, telecom, and so on. He served in a variety of different roles— functional consultant, business analyst, and team lead.

Debroop moved to CA Technologies in 2010 and has since been engaged in delivering solutions and generating business opportunities as a Clarity functional architect. He actively participates in activities of the unit by running the quarterly all-hands meet, delivering Clarity boot camps, and editing the in-house newsletter.

Ponniah Rajagopal is the director of quality assurance for Clarity. He started his career as a developer. Inspired by the tough challenges of test automation, he switched to testing and test automation very early in his career. Throughout the journey, Ponniah has relished the demanding quality needs arising from continuously evolving technology, changing business models, and rapidly changing market conditions. He considers that to be his primary motivation at work. In his career spanning more than 13 years, Ponniah has held different positions, from being an engineer to heading the QA function of a company. Ponniah is married to Bhanu, and the couple has a lovely two-and-a-half-year-old son, Rithvik.

Acknowledgements

Numerous people helped us in many ways to make this book a reality. We would like to thank Brian Bell, GM of Service Assurance; Carl Orthlieb, VP Software Engineering; Kai Wang, SVP Engineering Excellence; Sanket Atal, SVP Software Engineering; Matt Strazza, GM; and Kurt Kilgore, VP Practice Services; for encouraging us to write this book. Thanks to David Dobson for writing the foreword to our book.

We would like to thank our family and friends, Anuradha, Akhil, Manasa, Aruna, Raja, Sudha, Monika, Anika, Aanya, and Anjali, for all the support they have given us while writing this book. Thanks to Bob Peacock, Senior Services Architect, for his valuable advice. Thanks to the reviewers Kurt Steinle, Debroop Dasgupta, and Ponniah Rajagopal for their critical review.

Thanks to the crew at Apress—Jeffrey Pepper, lead editor; Jennifer Blackwell and Rita Fernando, coordinating editors; Kim Wimpsett, copyeditor; Nancy Wright, formatter; Brigid Duffy and Christine Ricketts, the production team; and Kumar Dhaneesh, indexer. Special thanks to Jennifer Blackwell for her support and patience.

Thanks to our colleagues at Clarity Product Development and CA Services in the PPM practice for providing valuable input in the functional and technical forums that were used in the book. Many thanks to Karen Sleeth at CA Press for shepherding the project through to completion.

Thanks to our colleagues, Sridhar Parimi, Manmohan Jain, Subramanian Venkataraman, Jayashree Gururaj, Sakaar Anand, Bipin Pendyala, Bharat Kalyanram, Brian Smith, Craig Yarwood, James Mount, Or Ron, Kunal Shah, and Sam Chandra Sekaran, for all their moral support while writing this book.

The information in this book was culled from a number of sources. Some of the authors include Jerod Buckel, Stephen Forney, Ash Usman, Sydney Zenger, Sean Harp, Michael Richman, Arun Thiagarajan, Paul Maxwell, Carol Tsang, and Ellen Cronin. E-mail messages sent by the CA Services Clarity forum were also used. Clarity user guides on Clarity PPM provided the foundation for Chapters 2 and 3. We would like to thank Bob Peacock, Debroop Dasgupta, Dustin Laun, Brian Smith, Ravi Sawant, and Laureen Heinz for providing their input on Clarity PPM queries. The "Evolving the maturity level of a PMO" white paper by Christopher Craig-Jones and "Best Practice Methodologies for the Project Management Office (PMO)" white paper by Thomas Haydn and Julie Tilke were used as references. Most of the Clarity user documentation set was used.

Rama Velpuri
Arpit Das

Preface

This book will assist Clarity PPM end users who are already familiar with the functionalities of Clarity. This book provides detailed view of each module within CA Clarity, which will help end users to find answers to basic questions/challenges faced in day-to-day Clarity operations.

The idea to write this book was conceived based on the feedback received by Clarity PPM end users and best-practice recommendations made by CA Services field consultants. The book is broken down into 13 chapters.

The initial chapters cover an overview of Clarity PPM, challenges faced by the users/companies that use Clarity, how Clarity is used to manage project life cycle in an organization, quick navigation of Clarity PPM tool, and how it can be personalized in a fingertip. The later chapters dive into Clarity modules: Project Management, Resource Management, Time Management, Financial Management, Demand Management, Portfolio Management, Process Management, Organizational Breakdown Structure and Security. The last chapter covers key prepackaged work products developed by the CA Services Global Delivery team, which is based on best practices and helps expedite Clarity project implementation cycle.

Throughout the book we give tips and techniques that can be used by end users to troubleshoot daily operational problems and also give recommend best practices. We hope that this book will supplement the Clarity user guides and will help end users to find answers to effectively implement world-class PPM solutions using Clarity PPM.

PART 1

CA Clarity PPM Fundamentals

This part gives you an introduction to the basics of project portfolio management and to the CA Clarity PPM product. It describes its basic usefulness, why you should use the product and what you will gain through its use.

CHAPTER 1

Introduction to CA Clarity PPM

Project and portfolio management (PPM) is a set of processes and tools to enable an organization to improve investment decision making, enhance productivity and efficiency, and quickly adapt to dynamic business conditions. CA Clarity PPM is a functionally rich and comprehensive PPM solution that provides the control and flexibility necessary to improve investment decision making and, subsequently, strengthen an organization's ability to deliver on its commitments. CA Clarity PPM can be applied to business challenges across the enterprise. It is the ideal solution when strategic planning must be married to tactical execution—especially when the commitments of specialized resources and the allocation of investment funds are critical success factors.

In this chapter, we examine three fundamental questions:

- *What* are the CA Clarity PPM product and its modules?

We give a brief overview of the Clarity PPM modules. Next, we address this question:

- *Why* do our customers use Clarity, and what benefits do they get?

We discuss the five major developments that happened in the IT universe that changed the way enterprise applications are developed and used in the world today. And finally, we answer this question:

- *Who* uses Clarity PPM in the market today?

We discuss several industry verticals that are currently using Clarity PPM and how they are recognizing the benefits in their business.

What Is CA Clarity PPM?

The CA Clarity PPM application enables organizations to increase agility, visibility, and optimization in the areas of project execution, resource management, and portfolio and financial management. CA Clarity PPM can help organizations do the following:

- Make smart portfolio decisions
- Accelerate delivery on commitments
- Achieve PPM success

CA Clarity PPM gives executives a real-time view into their organization's investments, initiatives, and resources, and it empowers managers to deliver controlled and predictable execution of projects and programs.

Figure 1-1 shows the value proposition of Clarity PPM. CA Clarity PPM provides the visibility, control, automation, and reporting to support today's most critical business processes, including IT governance, new product development, professional services automation, and enterprise program management, as shown in Figure 1-1.

Figure 1-1. CA Clarity PPM: value proposition

The CA Clarity PPM solution is built on a pure Java 2, Enterprise Edition (J2EE) web-based platform and includes PPM functionality, prepackaged content, and ITG-specific modules, as shown in Figure 1-2.

Figure 1-2. CA Clarity PPM modules

The CA Clarity PPM solution is comprised of nine modules that combine to enable an organization to optimize the alignment between IT resources and an organization's business initiatives and strategies. Figure 1-3 shows the nine modules of CA Clarity PPM. The following is a brief description of each module of the Clarity PPM product.

- CA Clarity IT Portfolio Manager
- CA Clarity IT Financial Manager
- CA Clarity BRM
- CA Clarity PPM
- CA Clarity Resource Manager
- CA Clarity Project Manager
- CA Clarity Demand Manager
- CA Clarity Project Financial Manager
- CA Clarity Process Manager

Figure 1-3. The nine modules of CA Clarity

CA Clarity IT Portfolio Manager

CA Clarity IT Portfolio Manager

The following is a brief description of the main features of the IT Portfolio Manager module and its benefits.

Features:

- Portfolio scenarios enabling investment trade-offs
- Scenario comparison analysis
- Efficient frontier analytics for optimizing the mix of investments
- Insight into total cost of providing IT services
- KPI dashboards for portfolio status
- Aggregation of complex investment hierarchies: aggregating assets, applications, people, projects, and support into a complete service
- "Portfolio horizon" controls, allowing stakeholders to exclude financial and resource data outside of the portfolio effective period

Benefits:

- Enables portfolio managers to use "what if" capabilities for optimizing portfolio investments

CA Clarity IT Financial Manager

CA Clarity IT Financial Manager

The following is a brief description of the main features of the IT Financial Manager module and its benefits.

Features:

- Enables unlimited cost plans, benefits plans, and forecasting for resources and projects
- Creates a hierarchy of the investments involved in providing a service, including assets, projects, and applications

Benefits:

- Provides comprehensive financial planning for all IT services
- Provides essential financial information—detailed views of total cost and effort—for bottom-up budgeting and forecasting, as well as top-down analysis and customer invoicing

CA Clarity BRM

CA Clarity BRM

The following is a brief description of the main features of the Business Relationship Manager module and its benefits.

Features:

- Works with CA Clarity Demand Manager to provide a gateway between the business and IT
- Includes portals and dashboards that facilitate the ability to engage with business customers about planning and the quality of the service delivery

Benefits:

- Provides visibility into available and subscribed services, their status, and associated costs

CA Clarity PPM

CA Clarity PPM

The following is a brief description of the main features of the Project and Portfolio Manager module and its benefits.

Features:

- Brings all projects' costs and benefits together in one dashboard to facilitate project management decisions

Benefits:

- Enables an organization to align resources and investments with corporate goals by providing structured environments for deciding which projects, programs, and initiatives to fund, sustain, or terminate
- Facilitates determining how projects and resources support an organization's strategic initiatives

CA Clarity Resource Manager

CA Clarity Resource Manager

The following is a brief description of the main features of the Resource Manager module and its benefits.

Features:

- Provides visibility into skills, assignments, and the capacity of all resources

Benefits:

- Enables an organization to effectively conduct capacity planning—achieving an equitable balance between resource capacity and project demand

- Balances resource capacity against work demand—a required component of a project and resource management strategy

CA Clarity Project Manager

CA Clarity Project Manager

The following is a brief description of the main features of the Project Manager module and its benefits.

Features:

- Comprised of the core components of projects and collaboration
- Powerful project management capabilities for task and work breakdown structure definition, dependencies, tasks assignments, scheduling, risk and issue management, and so on
- Project Manager dashboards for up-to-date visibility into a project's status

Benefits:

- Provides a rich set of functions to help ensure that an organization can follow best practices for projects and produce optimal plans

CA Clarity Demand Manager

CA Clarity Demand Manager

The following is a brief description of the main features of the Demand Manager module and its benefits.

Features:

- Gives a holistic view of all demand points, including new ideas, project requests, service work, and incident-driven requests
- Enables an organization to identify demand throughout the company to approve and prioritize later

Benefits:

- Provides information necessary for determining a balance among all demand points

- Links to Clarity Financial Management and Resource Management to give insight into how staff time is spent on a project and normal service-oriented work to help forecast resource requirements

CA Clarity Project Financial Manager

CA Clarity Project Financial Manager

The following is a brief description of the main features of the Financial Manager module and its benefits.

Features:

- Lets an organization budget and track project financials
- Includes flexibility that helps differentiate capital from expenses and labor from nonlabor expenditures
- Ability to track financial benefits, ROI, NPV, and IRR

Benefits:

- Separates capitalized expenditures from expenses for appropriate financial reporting and compliance
- Through its chargeback functionality, maps and allocates an equitable distribution of project costs across business units and departments

CA Clarity Process Manager

CA Clarity Process Manager

The following is a brief description of the main features of the Process Manager module and its benefits.

Features:

- Creates structure around the business processes of a company to make its processes observable and repeatable
- Manages all of the characteristics inherent in a process

Benefits:

- Makes automating, optimizing, and standardizing business processes across the organization possible
- Helps the organization's business processes become streamlined, adaptable, collaborative, and reusable

Why Use CA Clarity PPM?

PPM systems have entered the mainstream, joining ERP, CRM, HR, and e-mail as part of the standard enterprise application landscape. This development is primarily because of the convergence of five changes in the IT universe. Today IT is run like a business. The following are the five substantive changes in IT:

- The systems that IT provides to the enterprise are now used by end customers, contractors, and stakeholders, not just internal employees, raising the bar for IT's management and governance processes.
- Enterprise applications are now central to virtually every business initiative, leading to an unprecedented need for alignment between IT and line-of-business executives.
- Cost reduction opportunities are now numerous and compelling within IT. Outsourcing and consolidation are the highest profile of these.
- The return on IT must now be demonstrated, as would be expected of any mature and critical business function.
- Today's expensive and mandatory requirements for compliance and transparency fall disproportionately on IT.

The current PPM systems have been developed to address these challenges. This has led to a change in behavior for leading CIOs: their first order of business is now to make certain that their own organization is universally supported prior to systematically improving their customers' organizations.

The Challenges

Today, IT organizations spend a large amount of their time delivering projects. While success rates have improved to approximately 34 percent, 15 percent of all projects still fail, and 51 percent are somehow *challenged*, according to research from the Standish Group. IT projects fail for many reasons—many of which can be attributed to a lack of visibility into long-term project needs. Without proper visibility, organizations are unable to see what is needed six months, three months, or even two months down the road, resulting in poorly constructed project plans that do not capture critical dependencies, including assigning project resources and key milestones.

Information technology organizations and the executives who lead them find themselves in the most challenging of times. IT, so long perceived as a natural engine of progress, emerged from the recent spending bubble caught between a rock and a hard place: its budget has been reduced, often dramatically, while expectations for its contribution remain undiminished.

Moving beyond this paradox requires a fresh approach to IT management and governance—one that facilitates partnership between IT leaders and fellow operating executives and that delivers tactical execution at a level of excellence rarely seen in the past. Specifically, today's world-class IT operations must remain in alignment with the strategic priorities of the enterprise, must deliver promised results with control and predictability, and must transparently report costs, progress, and problems in time to act on them.

Achieving this is a challenge because IT management and governance has always been a uniquely difficult operation to evaluate. Even those who understand its technical minutiae often have trouble objectively judging the quality of results delivered by the CIO.

As it happens, IT is different from other operational departments. This is not because of the technical underpinnings of servers, networks, and applications but because IT provides the infrastructure for every other department—almost all of which is critical, though only some provides differentiation for the enterprise. Whether or not it is organized on a shared services model, IT must accommodate the competing demands of departmental heads, business unit chieftains, board-level strategic priorities, and budgetary constraints. These must be met while rationalizing the typical set of accumulated systems from 20 years of mergers and reorganizations. This web of competing priorities makes for both a strategic planning nightmare and a profusion of programs, initiatives, and projects the likes of which are not seen anywhere else in the enterprise. To top off this 21st-century management challenge, the specialized resources necessary to mobilize modern IT are expensive or scattered, or both.

The CIO's current challenge is somewhat comparable to that faced by manufacturing 20 years ago. The parallel rise of electronics—assembled from thousands of small, expensive, and rapidly obsolescing piece parts—and Japanese JIT production methods forced manufacturing executives to reengineer processes and adopt new classes of operational management systems. IT will do the same. The reengineering will come from the savvy use of outsourcing (more about this later), web services, and utility computing. Of equal importance, new management and governance systems are required.

Now let's take a closer look at the areas within industry domains that use CA Clarity PPM to improve processes.

- IT management and governance
- New product development
- Professional services automation
- Federal government

IT Management and Governance

The demands on IT organizations have never been higher. In addition to fulfilling their traditional responsibilities, IT organizations are faced with the following challenges:

- Running IT like a business by forecasting and delivering results with accuracy and precision
- Aligning IT spending with business priorities and rapidly adjusting as conditions change
- Demonstrating measurable business value from technology investments
- Taking advantage of outsourcing, consolidation, and other cost reduction vehicles
- Communicating effectively with business partners and other stakeholders to create transparency, accountability, and ownership

- Operating in accordance with today's stringent corporate governance requirements

New Product Development

Using CA Clarity PPM in NPD provides the comprehensive and forward-looking view that vice presidents of engineering, marketing, and product development need in order to beat the competition. Using CA Clarity PPM, organizations have benefited in the following ways:

- Shorter time-to-market, often dramatically shorter
- More products introduced through improved "idea to launch" new product development processes
- Improved visibility into the product portfolio, resource utilization, project and program costs, and status
- Better decisions to balance development and mix of new risks and benefits

Professional Services Automation

Professional services organizations, whether stand-alone or captive within product-oriented companies, need to manage resources, opportunities, and billing to world-class standards. Even then, it takes controlled and predictable services delivery, coupled with clear executive visibility, to succeed in today's difficult business climate. CA Clarity PPM, with its world-class enterprise project management, deep resource management, and uniquely strong financial management capabilities, has long been a premier professional services automation solution. With CA Clarity PPM, organizations have benefited in the following ways:

- Better utilization of resources
- Improved visibility
- Reusable best practices
- Faster response to opportunities
- Consistent delivery

Federal Government

The U.S. Congress and the executive branch have recognized how critical IT management is to the business of governing. In addition to fulfilling their traditional responsibilities, IT organizations within federal agencies must do the following:

- Provide assurances that technology expenditures are necessary, are purposeful, and will result in demonstrated improvements in mission effectiveness and customer service
- Make more sophisticated business cases for IT investments that include risk management, flexibility and cost estimations, and performance measurement

- Provide visibility of and accountability for IT spending in a decentralized allocation environment
- Communicate effectively with other government agencies to identify overlap and duplication and to explore ways to jointly invest in projects
- Implement effective IT human capital management that identifies the need for training, skills refreshment, hiring, and other practices
- Operate in accordance with today's stringent federal mandates

Meeting these challenges requires a coordinated approach to IT management and governance (IT-MG) for optimal capital planning and investment control (CPIC) in the federal government. CA Clarity PPM's functionality spans the full IT life cycle, encompassing three continuous integrated processes that help federal IT organizations achieve successful capital planning and investment initiatives.

CA Clarity PPM Provides Visibility for Effective Project Management

Businesses need to stay focused when the economy and business climate is tumultuous. CA Clarity PPM can help bring that focus to IT and provide the visibility and insight needed to keep important projects and initiatives on track. Without effective project management, many efforts start out in good stead but fall inevitably to the wayside when more pressing priorities come along. But a project management program pretty much eliminates excuses as long as the people running the program bring on board all the key stakeholders. Projects get done, efficiencies are created, and innovation plans are put into place. PPM helps IT sharpen its priorities and get the job done.

PPM provides visibility for tracking and managing new and existing projects within an organization. It mitigates heavy demands on staff resources with projects and initiatives that compete for the same budget dollars. The functionality includes projects, schedules, resources allocated, status, and actual vs. project budget allocations. PPM tools provide all of these capabilities and can be a CIO's best friend for keeping IT on track with business objectives.

CA Clarity PPM solutions include decision support capabilities, financial tracking, and linkages to other IT planning and management tools. Many slices of information are available for the CIO. For instance, with evolved solutions, the CIO can get a look at how the IT organization is performing financially, by division, by strategic objective, and by schedule, along with many other criteria. PPM can specifically help with the following decision categories that are so common yet very important for IT executives.

Resource Utilization

Resource utilization provides a view of how any given resource or group of resources are being used in the environment. This information can be compared with changes in company direction to determine whether those resources are being used to the best *value* in the organization in a given timeframe. Resource managers can develop what-if scenarios to analyze the trade-offs of varying project and resource decisions. Various types of utilization snapshots are discussed in the following sections.

Actual Utilization

Actual utilization is the actual and true utilization of a resource or a group of resources. Figure 1-4 gives you a sample snapshot of the actual utilization of resources.

Figure 1-4. Snapshot of actual utilization of resources

Forecasted Utilization

Forecasted utilization, on the other hand, projects an estimate of how much of utilization may be required for a given resource or group of resources. Figure 1-5 gives a sample snapshot of forecasted utilization.

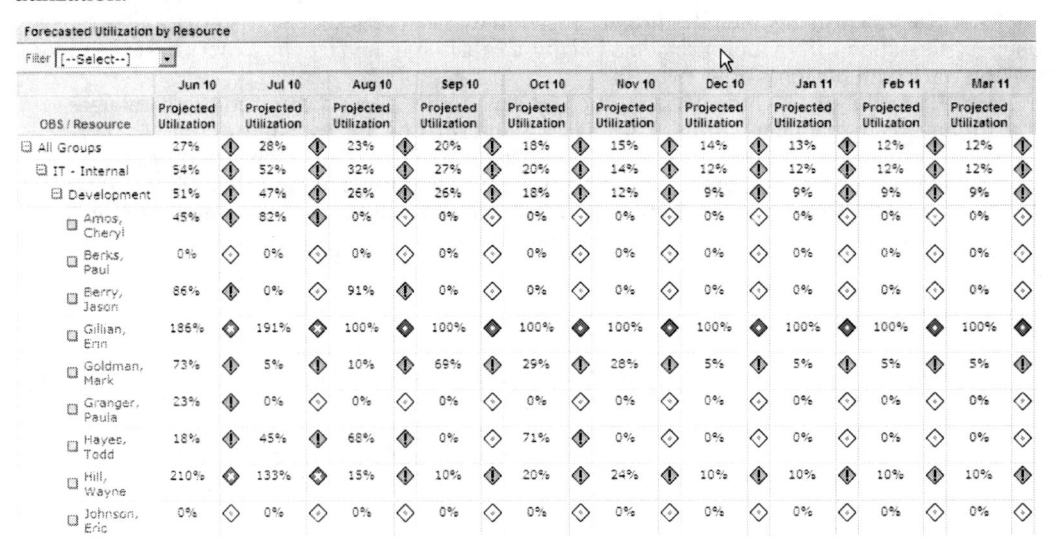

Figure 1-5. Sample snapshot of forecasted utilization

CHAPTER 1 ■ INTRODUCTION TO CA CLARITY PPM

Executive Analytics

Visualization tools within PPM solutions make them particularly useful for sharing status and project performance indicators with business executives. You can capture timelines, resource shortages, and trade-offs in making one decision vs. another when it comes to IT investments. For example, the Project Status and Role Capacity views in Figures 1-6 and 1-7 provide executives with simple and powerful insight into resource availability and project health and status. Figure 1-6 shows a snapshot of the project status, and Figure 1-7 shows a snapshot of the role capacity.

Figure 1-6. A snapshot of project status

Figure 1-7. A snapshot of role capacity

Risk Mitigation

The CA Clarity PPM solution enables decision makers to assess risk factors and determine whether a project can succeed in its own right and what, if any, are the implications of its failure or success on other important projects in the enterprise. The risk management dashboard provides all the data regarding risks for a given project, including the risk description, probability, and possible target resolution date. Figure 1-8 gives a sample snapshot of the risk management dashboard.

15

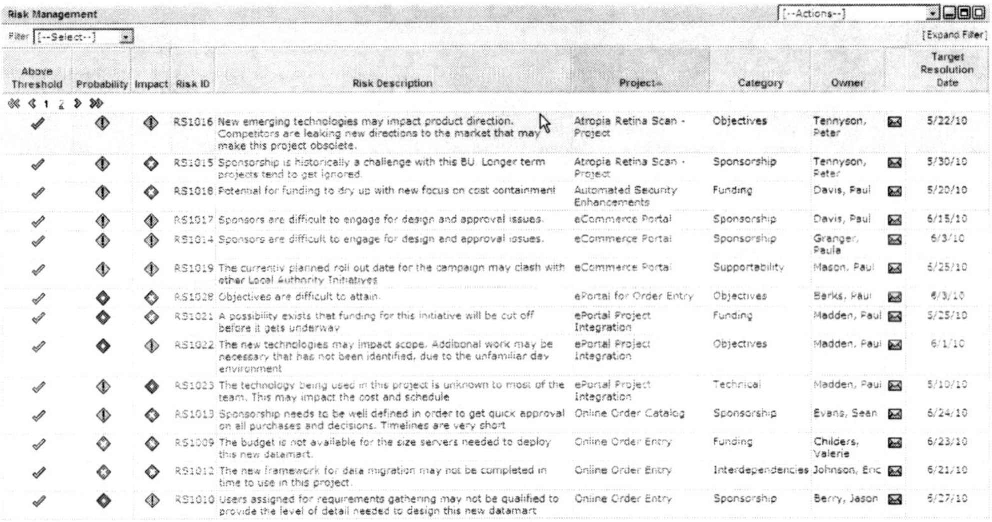

Figure 1-8. Risk management dashboard

Quantifiable Metrics for Performance

Quantifiable metrics are most useful when they are tracked and monitored by a PPM system vs. ad hoc spreadsheet or scheduling tool. Ideally, these metrics will be presented in an automated fashion and demonstrate obvious successes and shortcomings. The key project indicators (KPIs) of each project can be displayed in the project KPIs dashboard. Figure 1-9 shows a sample snapshot of the project KPIs dashboard.

Figure 1-9. A Sample snapshot of the project KPIs dashboard

Benefits of Integrating Clarity PPM with External Systems

CA Clarity PPM integrates with a host of enterprise-class management products like SAP, Oracle Financials, PeopleSoft, Salesforce, and so on. The following is a summary of the features of CA Clarity PPM and the value it provides:

- *A streamlined method of project evaluation*: The project evaluation method needs to be streamlined, systemized, and thus organized in an orderly fashion in order to ensure that project evaluation becomes a smooth and comprehensive process.

- *Resource planning*: Resources of an organization are always finite. It doesn't make sense for any organization to plan a project portfolio that goes beyond the limits of the resources they have.

- *Tracking of costs and benefits*: This ensures that the budgeted and the actual costs and benefits are recorded and compared so as to ensure that the logic used for project portfolio management can be checked and corrected if required. This data can also be used in the future within the organization for creating comprehensive PPM policies.

- *Cost-benefits analysis*: This is a key element in any project management venture. However, within the purview of project portfolio management methods, this analysis can be conducted across all projects held within the organization.

- *Opportunity cost analysis*: This is again an important aspect of project portfolio management. This can help organizations analyze the effectiveness of each and every project when compared to its efficiency and value addition to the entire project portfolio.

- *Reports on the progress of the various projects at different levels of execution*: Again, this is an important PPM tool. All this data and information should be easily translated and collated into various types of reports that can be circulated to all levels of management within the organization.

- *Communication enablement*: These PPM tools should also include a communications module that will ensure that the relevant data gets communicated to the different operational heads so that they can bear the organizational goals in mind while executing their projects.

- *Accessibility*: This is one of the basic and important functions that must be included, especially in today's world. These PPM tools must be both accessible for the relevant people within the organization, and the accessibility must cover all IT-related aspects as well (such as web accessibility, cross-platform accessibility and integration, and so on).

Who Uses CA Clarity PPM?

Some of the largest and most sophisticated customers in the world have deployed CA Clarity PPM throughout their enterprises. Today there are hundreds of thousands of users of CA Clarity PPM products at hundreds of customer locations throughout the world.

In this section, we discuss some of the challenges of each of the industry verticals and some of the benefits they achieved by using CA Clarity PPM.

The Public Sector and Utilities Companies

The first vertical with large organizations is the public sector and the utilities companies. As always, all organizations have a few challenges. Table 1-1 describes the challenges in this vertical and how the businesses benefit by using CA Clarity PPM.

Table 1-1. Challenges of Public Sector and Utilities Companies and CA Clarity PPM Benefits

Challenges	Business Benefits by Using CA Clarity PPM
• Streamline customer project/work requests by implementing project management methodologies that result in better control of project/work requests. Improve customer satisfaction and better manage customer expectations.	• Running IT like a business and transforming to provider-consumer organization. For example, every department providing a service should get credit, and every department consuming the services should be charged back. This gives a CIO full visibility of how resources (labor, equipment, material, expense, and so on) are utilized. • Effectively manage external stakeholders and thus reduce operating cost. • Leverage cross department resources by using blended rates across entities. • Use scenarios-based capabilities to manage multiple portfolios. • Align investments with organizational goals. • Effectively track return on investments (ROI).
• Manage resource demand and capacity to handle spikes in increased project demand and reduce IT service costs.	• Increase customer satisfaction. • Improve project delivery and reporting. • Visibility into resources demand and capacity. • Manage and control project cost and schedule.

The Professional Services Companies

The professional services companies is the second vertical industry that is worth mentioning. Table 1-2 describes some of the challenges in the professional services vertical and how the businesses benefit by using CA Clarity PPM.

Table 1-2. Challenges of Professional Services Companies and How They Resolve Them

Challenges	Business Benefits by Using CA Clarity PPM
• Improve efficiency by implementing standardized tools, processes and methodologies.	• Shorten sales cycle by increasing credibility with customers. • Improved visibility in resources utilization, thus maximizing revenue. • Do it right, and do it the same way every time by consistent project delivery processes, tools, and methodologies. • Reduce average project completion time.
• Capture opportunities and follow up to execution.	• Get insight into incoming opportunities either by capturing them in the tool or by integrating with external tools, thus reducing the sales cycle timeline. • Align resources with captured opportunities, and make sure the organization is ready to execute when the sales cycle closes. • Automation of resource requisitions for approved opportunities reduces ad hoc resource negotiation processes.
• Improve on project delivery timeline and budget overruns.	• Reduce project cost, through capturing and management of the project's actual costs for improved decision making, estimation, and sizing models. • Improve project decision making, defined by the project charter, monitor project performance, define project communication plan details, provide project documentation management, report project performance, and provide project stakeholder management.

The Financial Sector Companies

Table 1-3 describes some of the challenges in the financial sector vertical and the benefits of using CA Clarity PPM.

Table 1-3. Challenges of Financial Sector Companies and Benefits of Using CA Clarity PPM

Challenges	Business Benefits by Using CA Clarity PPM
• Provide high-quality and affordable services despite escalating costs. There is always a need to find ways to operate more cost-effectively and increase productivity.	• More accurately schedule resources and optimize resource competencies, timing, and activities to maximize ROI. • Make IT transparent to management to increase productivity. • Deliver on time and on schedule. • Improve on planning and forecasting IT initiatives. • Track and manage government regulatory challenges.
• Manage IT services and infrastructure like a business to increase productivity.	• Provides a single source of repository for all investments (projects, resources, opportunities, and so on). • Real-time reporting of data. • Improved and efficient executive dashboarding. • Support organization's objectives and goals. • Automate the creation of auditable, FASB/SOP-98-1 compliance. • Certify processes and controls for compliance with reporting for the Sarbanes-Oxley Act.

The Oil and Gas Industry

Table 1-4 describes some of the challenges in the oil and gas industry vertical and the benefits of using CA Clarity PPM.

Table 1-4. Challenges of the Oil and Gas Industry and How They Resolve Them

Challenges	Business Benefits by Using CA Clarity PPM
• Improve the global resource management platform to allocate the right workforce resources over the entire project life cycle. There is a need to plan and track a vast workforce, blended from various sources, including internal employees from various entities and external contractors.	• Translate all of the company's project factors into hourly measurements that help track a project's performance. • Manage all engineering, procurement, installation, and construction tasks for complex plants and associated infrastructure from design through startup. • Provide greater operational flexibility and the ability to react faster to changes in the market. • Perform strategic long-term planning to meet business goals laid down by executive management, providing valuable foresight to help drive most important business initiatives.

The Entertainment Industry

The last vertical in this section is the entertainment industry. CA Clarity PPM helps music and media companies to track customer incidents and align projects to portfolio for business stakeholders.

Let's say ABC Music Corporation is a music record label company that gets requests from the users via the Web for their artist labels. The challenge ABC Music Corporation faces is the lack of visibility into the requests coming in and tying them back to the business groups for reporting. Also, the business group - Consumer Direct gets the request in an ad hoc way and cannot report on the analytics such as how many requests were received and worked on. Figure 1-10 shows the corporate structure of ABC Music Corporation.

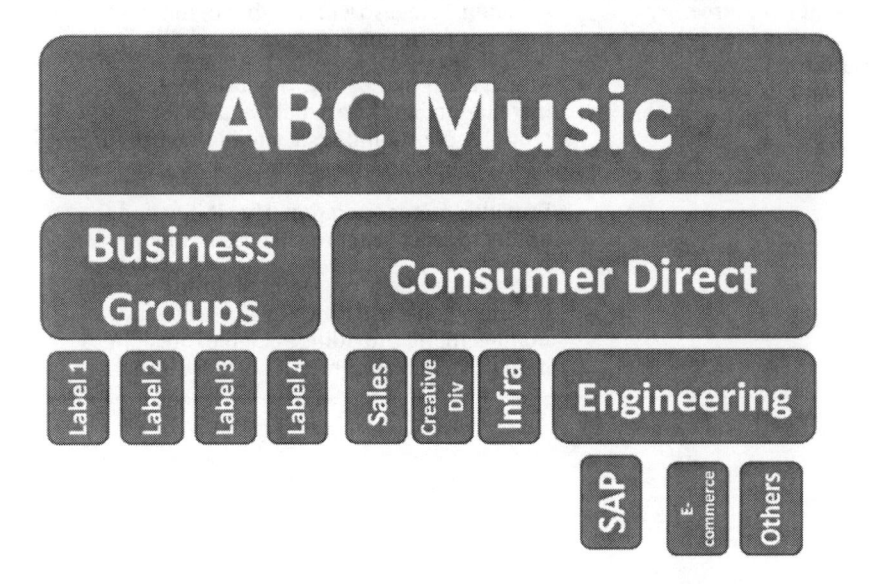

Figure 1-10. The corporate structure of a typical music company

ABC Music Corporation implemented the CA Clarity PPM tool to give them a single yet flexible solution to help their organization manage the increasing demand for user requests and to implement more controls and get visibility into their user request. With CA Clarity PPM, they are capable of doing the following:

- Capture user requests in a single system
- Automate routing of the user request to the appropriate Consumer Direct group based on the data entered
- Categorize their user requests based on the label
- Track efforts spent on the user requests
- Tie the user request back to an existing initiative
- Work on user requests to create a new enhancement/project or work on it as part of an existing initiative

- Roll up the user requests to existing investments and then back to the appropriate Consumer Direct portfolio
- Get clear visibility into the number of user requests opened for a particular label and track total effort spent to analyze resource workload and assignments
- Track financials and evaluate business group portfolio investments

After implementing CA Clarity PPM, ABC Music Corporation was able to streamline its work request process and was able to create an executive-level portfolio for all investments (work requests, applications, ideas, projects, programs). Figure 1-11 shows the layout of ABC Music Corporation that achieved this success using CA Clarity PPM.

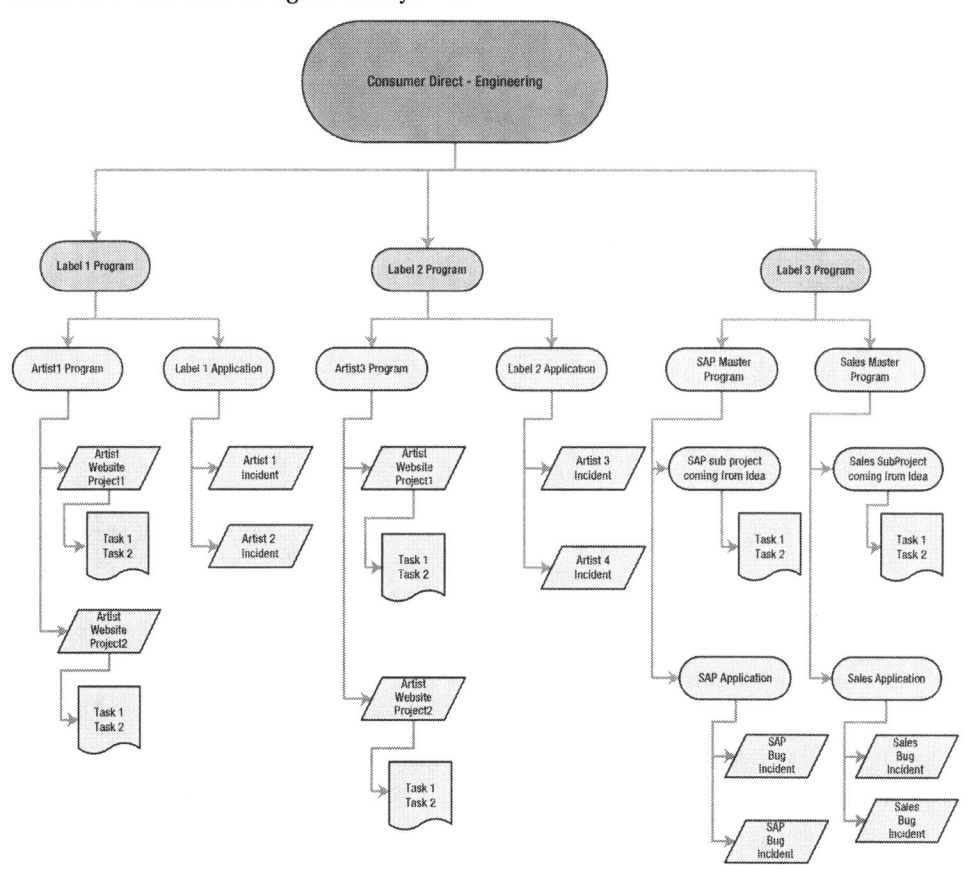

Figure 1-11. Layout of a successful music company that implemented CA Clarity PPM

Each Consumer Direct unit has a portfolio that consists of programs delivered by this group. Each program contains projects and applications either for the record label or for internal enhancements. Each work request is tied to an existing label application (for effort tracking), which is rolled to an artist program and to a label program. Work requests can also be tied to an existing project or can be treated as a new project as they are a new enhancement.

By automating this process, ABC Music Corporation was able to improve the work request process, lower project costs, and improve project delivery. ABC Music Corporation achieved the benefits of cost reduction, improved efficiency, and increased revenue after implementing its CA Clarity PPM solution.

Summary

This chapter briefly describes high level concepts of Project and Portfolio Management (PPM) and how they tie back to CA Clarity PPM. It also talks about pain points which PPM customers face and how the PPM solution is used in various industry verticals.

CHAPTER 2

CA Clarity PPM in Use

Corporate strategy remains just a pipe dream unless projects are initiated to move the company toward its strategic goals. Like players on a team, moving the play toward one goal, these projects must be coordinated with each other and with organizational realities and objectives. This coordination is known as *project portfolio management* (PPM). When used effectively, PPM ensures that projects are aligned with corporate strategies and priorities and that they optimize resource allocation. It is the practice that bridges the gap between the executive decision process and project execution.

In this chapter, we discuss three main areas of project portfolio management. In the first part of the chapter we talk about the amount of preparation that goes into setting up project portfolio management. We discuss the key components of setting up processes. We discuss the various stages of project life cycle management such as initiation, planning, control and execution, and closure. We also discuss how to identify the key success criteria of a project.

In the second part of the chapter, we discuss IT governance of a project in real life. We discuss the key elements of why and how much governance is required. Later, we describe a real-life example and present a case study.

In the final part of this chapter, we discuss the most important aspects of a project such as why projects fail. To avoid failing, we give tips on how to create a proper road map and maturity assessment. This chapter contains years of real-life project implementation experience of the authors and talks more on the don'ts than the do's. Finally, we again give you another case study on road map implementation.

Project Life Cycle

Project Life Cycle Management

The project life cycle refers to a logical sequence of activities to accomplish the project's goals or objectives. Regardless of scope or complexity, any project goes through a series of stages during its life. There is first an *initiation* phase, in which the outputs and critical success factors are defined. Following the initiation phase is a *planning* phase, characterized by breaking down the project into smaller parts/tasks, and an *execution* phase, in which the project plan is executed. Last, a *closure* or *exit* phase marks the completion of the project. Figure 2-1 shows the four stages of a project. The project activities are grouped into phases because by doing so, the project manager and the core team can efficiently plan and organize resources for each phase and also objectively measure the achievement of goals and justify their decisions to move ahead, correct, or terminate. It is of great importance to organize project phases into industry-specific project cycles. Why? It's important not only because each industry sector involves specific requirements, tasks, and procedures when it comes to projects but also because different industry sectors have different needs for their life cycle management methodology. And paying close attention to such details is the difference between doing things well and excelling as project managers.

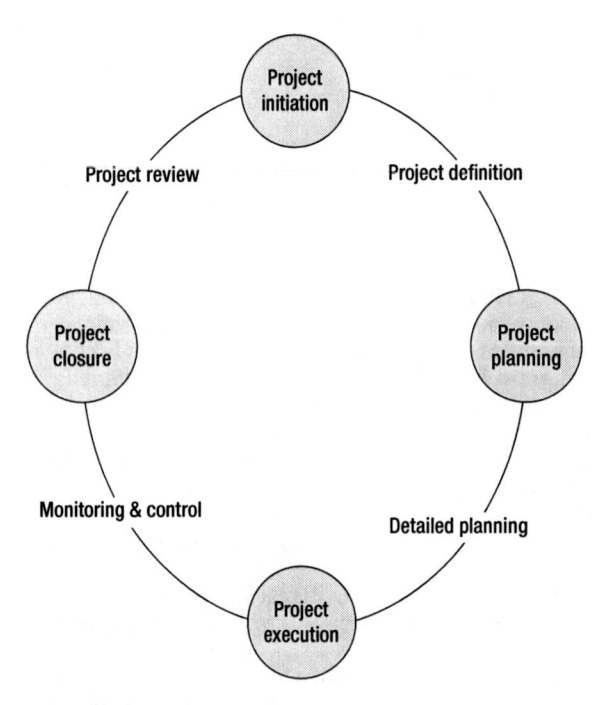

Figure 2-1. Four phases of a project

Diverse project management tools and methodologies prove useful in the different project cycle phases. This section describes what's important in each phase.

Initiation

In this first phase, the scope of the project is defined along with the approach to be taken to deliver the desired outputs. The project manager is appointed, and in turn, he selects the team members based on their skills and experience. The outputs from the initiation stage are *project charter*, *business plan*, *project framework* (or *overview*), *business case justification*, and *milestones reviews*.

Planning

The second phase should include a detailed definition and assignment of each task until the end of the project. It should also include a risk analysis and a definition of criteria for the successful completion of each deliverable. The governance process is defined, the stakeholders are identified, and the reporting frequency and channels are agreed upon. The most common tools or methodologies used in the planning stage are the business plan and milestones reviews.

Execution and Controlling

The most important issue in this phase is to ensure project activities are properly executed and controlled. During the execution phase, the planned solution is implemented to solve the problem specified in the project's requirements. In product and system development, a design resulting in a specific set of product requirements is created. The convergence from original requirements and planned solution is measured by prototypes, testing, and reviews. As the execution phase progresses, groups across the organization become more deeply involved in planning for the final testing, production, and support. The most common tools or methodologies used in the execution phase are an update of risk analysis and score cards, in addition to business plan and milestones reviews.

Closure

In this last phase, the project manager must ensure that the project is brought to its proper completion. The closure phase is characterized by a written formal project review report containing the following components: a formal acceptance of the final solution by the client, weighted critical measurements (matching the initial requirements specified by the client with the final delivered product), rewarding the team, a list of lessons learned, releasing project resources, and a formal project closure notification to higher management.

The Three Keys of Project Success

Unfortunately, many project and portfolio management systems are complicated and cumbersome, and managers and frontline employees quickly become frustrated and eventually give up, further handicapping the process. Evidence suggests that successfully managing projects from concept to completion requires corporations to rethink their approach to the project life cycle. Successful systems should address management, collaboration, and integration—key elements that empower managers and team members to fully participate in the system and deliver projects on time and on budget.

Management

The key stakeholders who decide which projects best fit into the organization's strategic goals need tools that allow them to understand and address project life cycle problems immediately. They need forecasts and visibility in order to avoid being blindsided by unexpected problems.

What are the best practices to meet the management needs for the organization? The executives begin the process with the first two steps of the project life cycle: evaluating requests and planning projects that match up with strategic objectives. Current PPM best practices require demand *management*. Basically, demand management is managing requests that come from within the company or from customers in a way that strategically makes sense for the organization. Managers should create a process that allows them to evaluate project requests based upon what provides the most benefit to the company, rather than making decisions based upon the "squeaky wheel."

In the spirit of making data-driven and not decibel-driven decisions, managers should practice capacity planning. In other words, making decisions based on current demands and available resources is essential because it ensures that projects chosen for execution have all the necessary resources dedicated to guarantee their success. An appropriate evaluation and analysis process will include recognizing potential benefit to the company, cost, alignment with company objectives, and resource requirements. Demand management is a very important factor in building efficient and effective organizations.

Collaboration

Collaboration happens between project managers and teams. Collaboration allows project managers and team members to optimize project plans, gain continuous feedback from projects, and use that feedback for business process improvements.

Project collaboration ensures that team members and management are communicating. Experts suggest that projects are likely headed for trouble unless informed end users are giving meaningful input during every phase of requirements gathering, product design and programming. This is especially important when team members are not in the same office or parts of a project have been outsourced.

Reconciling management's project plans with team schedules is the third step in the project life cycle. The faster decisions cascade from the boardroom to project teams, the faster organizations can react strategically to changes in the marketplace. Consider the advantage of a collaborative system that allows decisions made in the boardroom this morning to begin being implemented this afternoon.

Collaboration is essential to efficiently executing projects and a successful postmortem review. Smooth communication clears many of the roadblocks to productivity.

Integration

Integration refers to how easily a new system can be introduced into an organization. These are the questions you need to ask yourself: Does the new system impose a conflict with processes that are already refined and working well? Will it work with hardware or software already in place? Is it difficult for users to adopt?

Integration is what makes effective management and collaboration possible. If an organization is going to use a PPM tool, it should mold the system to fit into an organization, not the other way around. It should be compatible with the other existing business-critical software applications, allow for custom data, offer custom reports specific to a business, be usable with any platform (such as Mac, PC, or Linux), and work on any browser. That means employees don't have to change the way they work to integrate with a PPM solution; *it* fits them.

With the right technology, business leaders in any industry can use PPM best practices to help them complete projects successfully. Seamlessly blending management, collaboration, and integration are three valuable keys to project success.

IT Governance in Real Life

In this section, we focus on information technology governance (IT governance) and its importance.

What Is IT Governance?

Corporate governance is the set of processes, customs, policies, laws, management practices and institutions affecting the way an entity is controlled and managed. It incorporates all the relationships among the many stakeholders involved and aims to organize them to meet the goals of the organization in the most effective and efficient manner possible. An effective corporate governance strategy allows an organization to manage all aspects of its business in order to meet its objectives.

IT governance, however, is a subset discipline of corporate governance. Although it is sometimes mistaken as a field of study on its own, IT governance is actually part of the overall corporate strategy.

IT governance focuses specifically on information technology systems, their performance, and their risk management. The primary goals of IT governance are to assure that the investments in IT generate business value and to mitigate the risks that are associated with IT. This can be done by implementing an organizational structure with well-defined roles for the responsibility of information, business processes, applications, and infrastructure.

IT governance should be viewed as how IT creates value that fits into the overall corporate governance strategy and should never be seen as a discipline on its own. In taking this approach, all stakeholders would be required to participate in the decision-making process. This creates a shared acceptance of responsibility for critical systems and ensures that IT-related decisions are made and driven by the business, and not vice versa. Hence, in a nutshell, IT governance can be defined as follows:

- IT governance includes the structure, oversight, and management processes that ensure the delivery of the expected benefits of IT in a controlled way to help enhance the long-term sustainable success of the enterprise.

- IT governance is the responsibility of the board of directors and executive management. It is an integral part of enterprise governance and consists of the leadership and organizational structures and processes that ensure that the organization's IT sustains and extends the organization's strategies and objectives.

- It includes a structure of relationships and processes to direct and control the enterprise in order to achieve the enterprise's goals by adding value while balancing risk vs. return over IT and its processes.

- It includes specifying the decision rights and accountability framework to encourage desirable behaviors in the use of IT.

- Governance is not about what decisions get made—that is management—but it is about who makes the decisions and how they are made.

- IT governance is the term used to describe how those persons entrusted with governance of an entity will consider IT in their supervision, monitoring, control, and direction of the entity. How IT is applied will have an immense impact on whether the entity will attain its vision, mission, or strategic goal.

Why IT Governance Is Necessary

Let's see what necessitates IT governance.

Problem Statement

- Many companies fail to leverage their IT resources as a strategic tool.
- The companies' IT spending is out of proportion with resulting benefits.
- The business organizations often have little or no control over IT priorities and preferences.
- IT risks are too often identified and or addressed after a severe breach or significant failure.
- Most companies have little or no way to measure and monitor IT performance and results.

Statistics

- More than 80 percent of IT projects are delivered late and over budget (Standish Group, October 2006).
- Delays of 100 percent are typical for high-tech projects, despite the use of project management tools (University of California – Berkeley).
- Nearly 60 percent of all IT projects are delivered with less functionality that originally promised (Standish Group, March 2007).
- Less than 5 percent of project deliveries fail because of technical reasons. Nearly all obstacles are related to poorly defined requirements, poor sponsorship, weak management controls, or all of the above (Gartner Group, May 2006).

IT governance is needed to ensure that the investments in IT generate value-reward-and mitigate IT-associated risks, avoiding failure. IT is central to organizational success—effective and efficient delivery of services and goods, especially when the IT is designed to bring about change in an organization. This change process, commonly referred to as *business transformation*, is now the prime enabler of new business models both in the private and public sectors. Business transformation offers many rewards, but it also has the potential for many risks, which may disrupt operations and have unintended consequences. The dilemma becomes how to balance risk and rewards when using IT to enable organizational change.

A complete IT governance process includes a suite of five key components that are designed to ensure a sustainable benefit to the IT organization and the company as a whole. The key to a comprehensive IT governance model covers the following areas:

- *Strategic alignment*: Integrated business goals and IT processes that function cooperatively, with heavy emphasis on the planning process that includes full business engagement.
- *Value delivery*: Assisting the IT organization to define and accept projects or investments that deliver the benefits promised. *Value delivery* processes allow you to gain insight into your investments in technology and to help evaluate and approve projects for the IT team.
- *Resource management*: Management of both internal and external resources effectively and efficiently. This serves to ensure that the correct resources are deployed to perform the needed assignments. Additionally, it includes a review of value/benefit for the investment in each resource.
- *Performance measurement*: Putting structure around measuring business and IT performance. The purpose in this area is to measure the performance of the IT services that are delivered to the company. This may be in the form of SLAs or other metrics that are gathered and reviewed internally to IT, with the entire business or both.
- *Risk management*: Institute a formal risk framework that puts some rigor around how IT measures, accepts, and manages risk. Understand how the IT function identifies, quantifies, prioritizes, and responds to risks. The risks may be operational, project based, technology based, or geographic, or they may be generated in other complex areas.

Evaluation of Portfolio Management

IT must adopt a structured, transparent, consistent, and defensible investment planning methodology. Today's business needs and growing IT spends demands that an organization runs IT like a business. IT should have means to get credit back for the service delivered to support an organization's infrastructure as well as its keep the lights on effort.

The Origins of Portfolio Management

In looking for a proven investment planning methodology, one might look to the literal originator of the term. Anyone who has attended even a single retirement planning session has a passing familiarity with portfolio management, the core management structure of financial planning. Portfolio management is based on asset allocation models, where a portfolio is viewed as a pie that can be divided—and analyzed—by any of several attributes. These analytic attributes—goals, risk levels, costs, and forecasted returns—also serve as planning buckets. For instance, if the set of goals within a financial portfolio are growth, income, and capital preservation, then the first decision becomes how much of the overall portfolio to allocate to growth, how much to income, and how much to capital preservation. Only subsequently do decisions come into play as to which financial instruments in each category to sell, retain, or buy. These tactical decisions are much easier to make when constrained by their relatively minor role in the overall asset allocation model. For example, deciding which large capitalization financial services stock to buy is a relatively easy decision to make when such investments as a group comprise only 8 percent of the portfolio.

Business Investment Planning

When the asset allocation model as applied to business investment planning is applied within IT, the set of goals might be revenue growth, cost reduction, regulatory mandate, and business continuation. Simply answering how much of the overall IT capital and operating budget should be allocated to each of these is an executive-level question of considerable depth, requiring evaluation of strategic priorities, planning horizons, capital allocation criteria, and so on. As with financial portfolio planning, the evaluation of specific assets and projects within each category occurs only after determining how much to invest in each category. In addition to analyzing goal alignment, the portfolio must also be analyzed by a variety of other criteria, including risk, strategic alignment, and expected return, among others.

Contrast the asset allocation model with how IT planning is often done; individual projects, systems, and initiatives are approved or rejected in the abstract, with little analysis performed or considered as to their impact on the portfolio as a whole. It is bottom-up, in contrast with classical strategic management, which is top-down. No wonder the results appear—and often are—chaotic.

While an asset allocation model can point the way to the future, it first requires a high-level yet current portfolio inventory, no small matter in a large IT shop. An IT portfolio inventory sufficient for planning purposes need not be exhaustive. Rather, it should characterize at a macro level everything that must be considered when drawing up the IT portfolio plan: applications, physical assets, projects (ideally grouped into programs and/or initiatives), infrastructure assets (such as networks and bandwidth), and resources (internal, contracted and outsourced). These classes of portfolio items are what give rise to various forms of portfolio management, such as application, asset, and project portfolio management, all of which are related.

Initial IT portfolio inventories often reveal copious and expensive redundancies, such as an insurance company with eleven billing systems, a manufacturer with four AP systems, and a financial services provider with seven customer portals. Portfolio management projects often stop at this point, however, because the new visibility of these redundancies triggers a system or asset rationalization program that can be expected to save millions of dollars all by itself.

But the march of progress never stops. New projects are always knocking at the door. Examples include a fast-growing division with a major new business initiative that must be enabled, another division that is being spun off, and yet another that is being acquired. IT will be called upon to respond, because none of these can succeed without IT. No one, least of all the CIO, wants IT to be the roadblock to strategic imperatives. And so implementing portfolio management gets pushed to the following year or maybe the year after that.

A portfolio management system is required to make sure savings are realized, to respond effectively to dynamic circumstances, and to keep IT aligned with the business. Such a system provides for comprehensive IT portfolio modeling and macro inventorying, analysis (by goal, risk, status, budget, expected return, and so forth), and scenario planning. Importantly, the portfolio management system must seamlessly link to the systems that drive controlled delivery of the tactical programs that are derived from the investment planning process. Otherwise, the strategy may become undone by poor execution.

The Next Step: IT Governance

Given this portfolio management framework, IT is in a position to engage with executive stakeholders in an IT governance process. This often takes the form of an IT governance committee (sometimes called the IT steering committee), which functions like a board of directors, first deliberating and ultimately approving budgetary parameters, such as how much portfolio investment to direct toward cost reduction programs.

Every IT governance committee must address which parts of the portfolio to outsource. In some cases, the determination will be that all of IT should be outsourced and in other cases that none should be outsourced. More common is the determination that specific assets should be outsourced: levels of infrastructure, areas of development or support, or specific systems. Determining the right mix, and then crafting transition programs to the proposed portfolio, is a challenge perfectly suited for portfolio management.

Demand management—requests for significant new systems and projects—should also be processed through portfolio impact assessments, with the request sponsors self-assessing how the proposal will score in terms of goal, risk, status, and so forth. This works best if an "idea box" can be deployed as a web-based workflow, allowing for self-assessment right at the source of an idea and then funneling ideas from every corner of the enterprise through a structured review and escalation process.

In short, IT governance is, first and foremost, the structured executive oversight of IT investment to ensure alignment with strategic priorities. The framework provided by the portfolio management module of a PPM system significantly increases the likelihood of the IT organization achieving the defined goals that emerge from the governance process.

Case Study

This case study describes how a public utility company (ABC Corp) uses CA Clarity PPM to enforce IT governance to manage its incoming customer requests and improve on project execution rate.

Executive Summary

ABC Corp, through its wholly owned regulated subsidiaries, is primarily engaged in the generation, transmission, and distribution of electricity in parts of state A and the purchase, transmission, and sale of natural gas in portions of state B and state A. Through a wholly owned nonregulated subsidiary, the company markets natural gas to retail customers in state D and to wholesale customers primarily in the southeast. Other wholly owned nonregulated subsidiaries perform power plant management and maintenance services and provide fiber-optic and other telecommunications services and provide service contracts to homeowners on certain home appliances and heating and air conditioning units.

Business Requirements and Goals

ABC Corp currently has implemented a project and resource management application solution to track employee time against project tasks. The application is reaching its end of life and ABC Corp wants to enhance its project and resource management process to take better advantage of industry best practices and move to the next level of PPM capabilities. There are multiple business divisions at ABC Corp, and each has its own requests or can work as a cross-functional team on a particular request.

Business Drivers

ABC Corp is looking to improve its current project and portfolio management process by meeting the following requirements.

Stability

ABC Corp wants to implement a system that can provide the company with better project, resource, and portfolio management and can provide a more stable environment.

Improved Resource Time Management

To reduce costs and more effectively manage resource time, ABC Corp is looking to ensure that any activity undertaken is correctly recorded against the appropriate project. The current system has no control over its resource time entry and ABC Corp's timekeeper has to undergo the cumbersome process of time locking, time reminders, error checking, and missing time adjustments for employees.

Better Resource Management

ABC Corp wants to better manage the resource pool at its disposal to ensure that the correct resources are allocated to the correct projects at the correct time and to keep the appropriate business managers aware of potential conflicts.

Improve Project Initiation

ABC Corp wants to make use of proper demand management methodology where potential ideas are identified at an early stage and converted to projects. Currently, ABC Corp has to create a project for every idea that is initiated, and it has no control over idea creation.

Better Project Management

ABC Corp wants to make use of its internal framework life cycle for every project and wants to ensure that an investment is following the correct framework and approval processes to more effectively manage the investment decisions. Currently, project managers at ABC Corp may or may not follow a project framework life cycle. ABC Corp also wants to standardize with project management tools such as Open Workbench or Microsoft Project.

Solution Requirements

The following requirements for the proposed solution have been identified. The proposed solution must address all of the following requirements.

Centralize Time Tracking for All IT Employees

CA Clarity PPM will replace the current system as the central time tracking system for all IT and customer service employees.

Centralize Project Management

Clarity will replace the current system as the central repository for all IT and customer service projects and will allow stakeholders to view their project portfolio.

Provide an Interface Between HR System and CA Clarity PPM

An interface between the HR system and CA Clarity PPM will be needed to validate resource data, feed timesheet data, and validate contractors' data.

Provide an Interface Between Current System and CA Clarity PPM

An interface between the current project and time entry system and CA Clarity PPM will be needed to perform a onetime upload of project and resource information onto Clarity.

Provide an Interface Between Contractor System and CA Clarity PPM

An interface between contractor systems and CA Clarity PPM will be needed to feed contractors timesheet data to Clarity.

Provide an Interface Between Chargeback System and Clarity

An interface between the chargeback system and CA Clarity PPM will be needed to feed chargeback data to Clarity.

Resource Management

Provide improved resource management and allocation tools. Allow for resource search based on skill sets and availability to avoid over-allocation of resources. Provide a platform for resource management.

Demand Management

Provide an improved project initiation process using ideas in CA Clarity PPM. Allow creation of ideas and convert approved ideas to IT and customer projects.

CHAPTER 2 ■ CA CLARITY PPM IN USE

Workflow Processes

CA Clarity PPM workflow processes will be used to allow for proper routing and send notifications for approvals for ideas and projects following an appropriate project framework life cycle.

Centralize Document Management

Centralize the document management tool to view current project status and generate project-related reports.

Life Cycle of a Customer Request at ABC Corp

Let's look at a real-life example. Figure 2-2 shows the life cycle at ABC Corp for managing its incoming customer requests and projects.

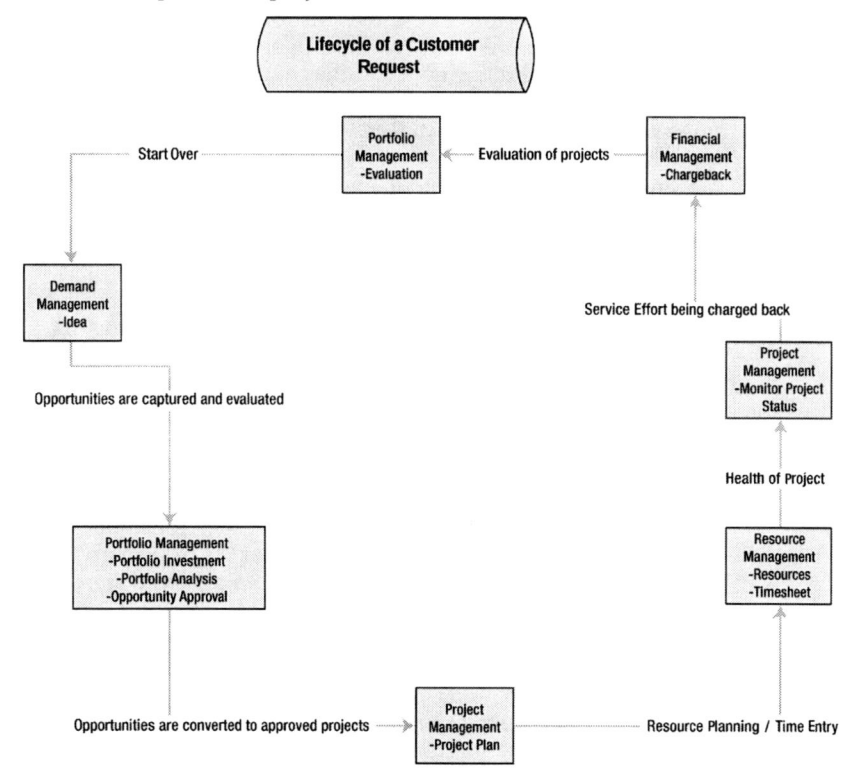

Figure 2-2. Life cycle of a customer request at ABC Corp

> Figure 2-2 has used some of the modules of CA Clarity PPM to fulfill the lifecycle of a customer request. Here is a list of the modules used and a brief one-liner description of those.
>
> - Demand management: for capturing ideas and requests

- Portfolio management: for reviewing and approving opportunities and for performing analyses and evaluating portfolio investments
- Project management: for planning projects and monitoring status
- Resource management: for requisitioning and allocating resources and for managing resource capacity versus demand
- Financial management: for cost accounting and charging back project costs

Table 2-1 describes the roles and their description in this example.

Table 2-1. Roles and Descriptions

Role	Description
Executive committee	Members of the steering committee, including the PMO director, business sponsors, and other PMO managers. The committee is responsible for evaluating opportunities and monitoring investments. The executive role in this example is used to represent various members of the steering committee.
Application development manager	The application development manager is responsible for working with executives of a business line to initiate and develop an investment opportunity and to oversee the project once it is approved.
Customer service manager	The customer service manager is responsible for performing the impact assessment and determining the scope of work for products and services related to incoming customer requests.
Project manager	The project manager is responsible for project planning and resource requisitioning.
Finance group	The financial group is responsible for working with the application development manager to develop a budget for the project or program and to set up chargebacks for services rendered.
Resource manager	The resource manager includes any line manager who is responsible for managing staff of a functional area. Resources managers respond to requisitions, identifying staff members who meet required skills. For example, resource managers include the system operations manager, help desk manager, and application development manager.
Team member	Team members include a business analyst, architect, application developers, QA engineers, system administrator, database engineer, and systems operators.

CHAPTER 2 ■ CA CLARITY PPM IN USE

Demand Management

ABC Corp has identified the following areas that need improvement in the company:

- A central system to capture incoming customer demand from multiple business units
- An approval process to filter incoming ideas
- Identification of resource capacity for executing the approved ideas

Idea Creation

Ideas are the initial stage of creating new opportunities/requests for investment. With proper management of incoming ideas and governance around idea approval, an organization can weed out ideas that are not aligned to organization's strategic goals.

For example, a team member from the application development group captures an incoming idea from a customer to improve the look and feel of the user interface. Once the team member enters all the information to create an idea, the customer service manager reviews the idea, which is then routed for analysis and approval. Figure 2-3 shows a sample idea.

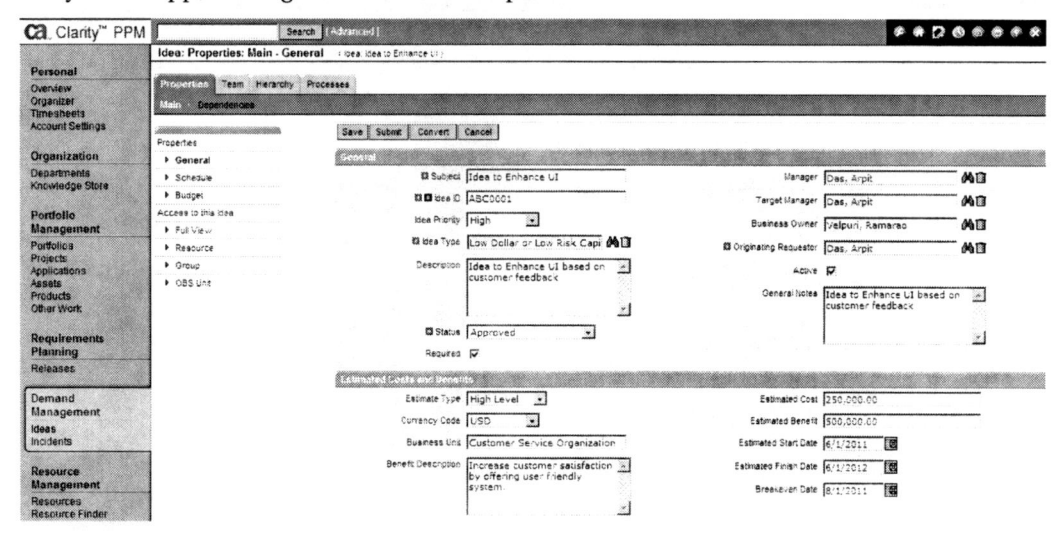

Figure 2-3. Snapshot of an idea

Idea Approval

The customer service manager is responsible for reviewing any new ideas for approval. The manager gets an action item from CA Clarity PPM to review the idea and then takes action and approves or rejects the idea. The customer service manager has an incoming demand portlet as shown in Figure 2-4 that helps analyze the initiated demand and make an approval decision. Figure 2-5 shows a view of the incoming demand where the customer service manager reviews the ideas and then approves them.

37

CHAPTER 2 ■ CA CLARITY PPM IN USE

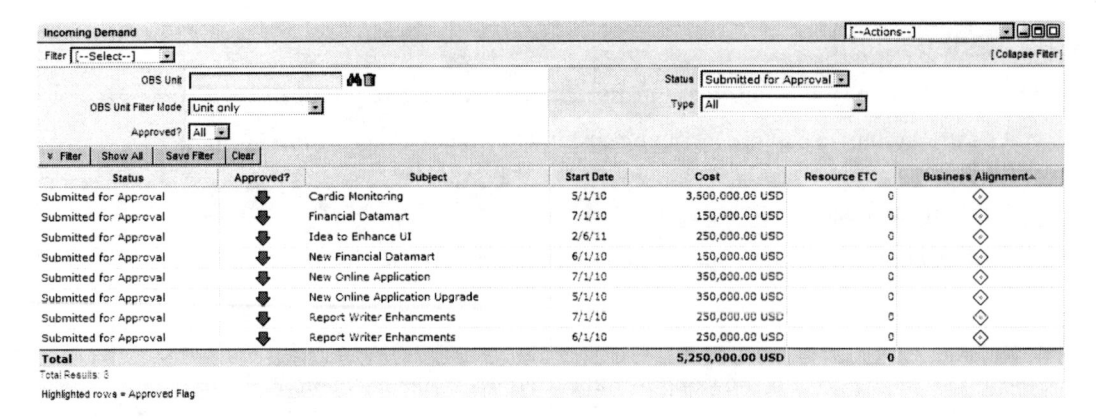

Figure 2-4. Incoming demand of an idea

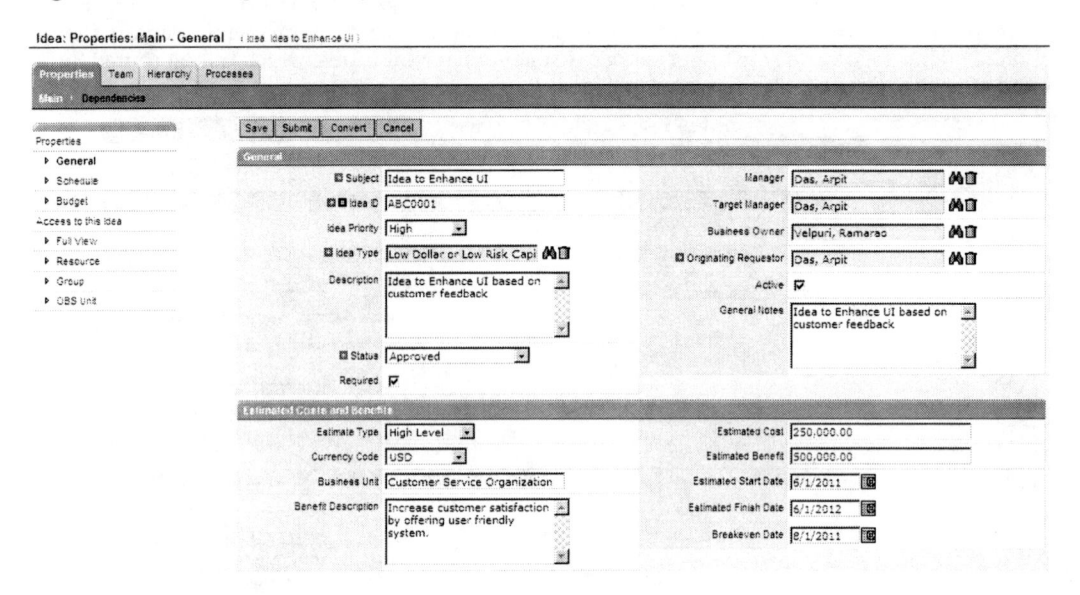

Figure 2-5. Idea approval

Once the idea is approved, the customer service manager converts it to an unapproved project investment type. Figure 2-6 shows how to convert a project to an unapproved investment type.

CHAPTER 2 ■ CA CLARITY PPM IN USE

Figure 2-6. Converting the project to an unapproved investment type

An unapproved project is then created, which is then reviewed by an application development manager, the finance group, and a resource manager. Figure 2-7 shows an unapproved project.

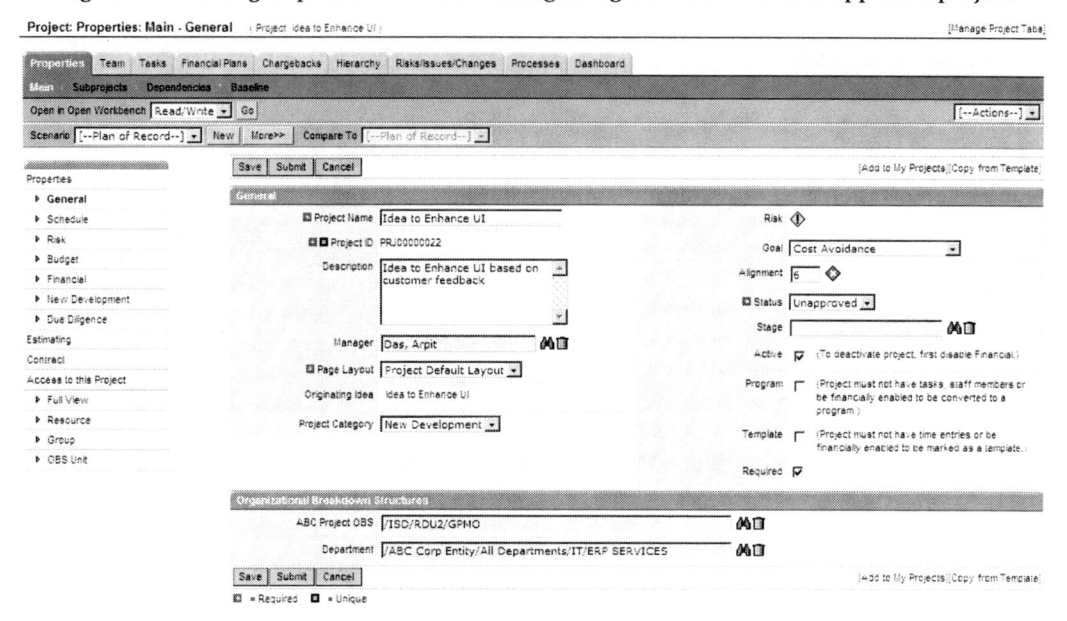

Figure 2-7. Creation of unapproved project

Approval Process

The application development manager conducts an impact assessment of the investment to make sure the scope and estimates are accurate or are in +/- 20 percent rough order of magnitude (ROM) range.

The finance group assesses the investment based on following criteria.

39

Planned Cost and Benefit

The portfolio shows how the investments are positioned based on planned cost and benefit analysis, which allows them to make "go/no-go" decision. Figure 2-8 shows the portfolio view.

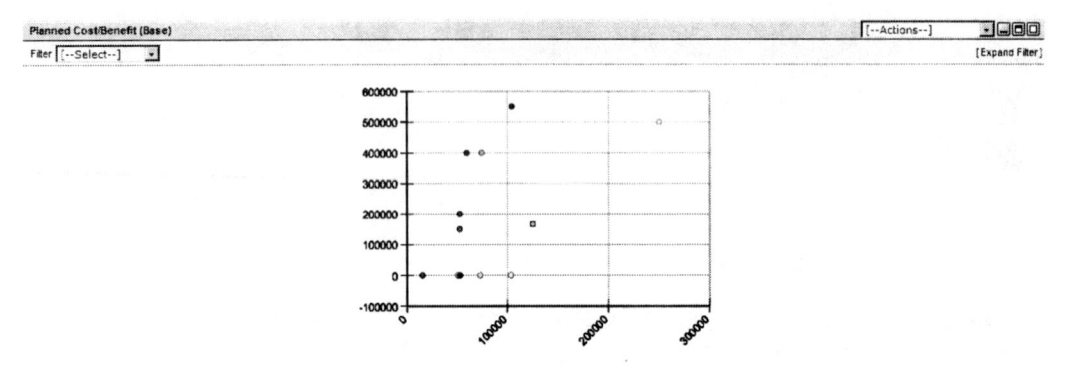

Figure 2-8. Planned cost and benefit

Risk score

This portfolio view shows the risk quadrant and how the investments are placed. This helps a portfolio manager to make a decision after assessing investment risk. Figure 2-9 shows the risk quadrant.

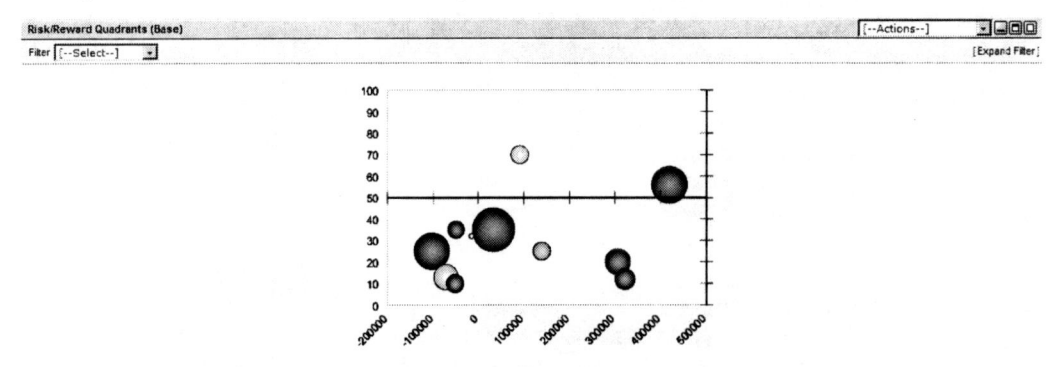

Figure 2-9. Risk quadrant

Budget

This portfolio investment view shows a list of investments that matches the portfolio budget range. The positive variance shows that the portfolio is under budget. Figure 2-10 shows the portfolio investment view.

CHAPTER 2 ■ CA CLARITY PPM IN USE

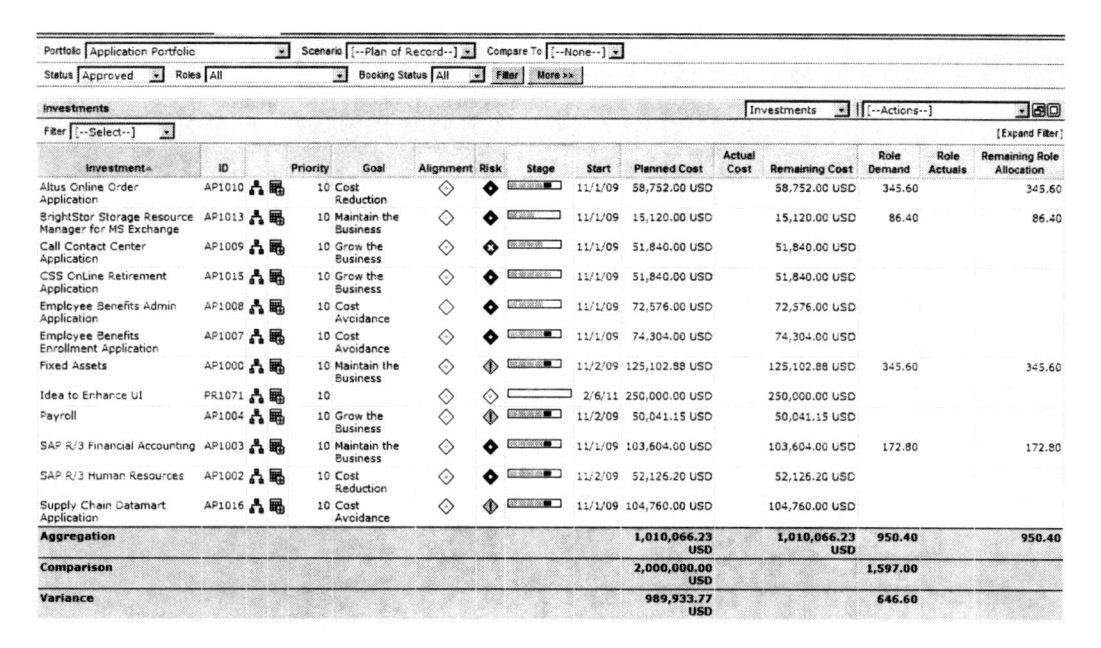

Investment	ID	Priority	Goal	Alignment	Risk	Stage	Start	Planned Cost	Actual Cost	Remaining Cost	Role Demand	Role Actuals	Remaining Role Allocation
Altus Online Order Application	AP1010	10	Cost Reduction	◇	◆		11/1/09	58,752.00 USD		58,752.00 USD	345.60		345.60
BrightStar Storage Resource Manager for MS Exchange	AP1013	10	Maintain the Business	◇	◆		11/1/09	15,120.00 USD		15,120.00 USD	86.40		86.40
Call Contact Center Application	AP1009	10	Grow the Business	◇	◆		11/1/09	51,840.00 USD		51,840.00 USD			
CSS OnLine Retirement Application	AP1015	10	Grow the Business	◇	◆		11/1/09	51,840.00 USD		51,840.00 USD			
Employee Benefits Admin Application	AP1008	10	Cost Avoidance	◇	◆		11/1/09	72,576.00 USD		72,576.00 USD			
Employee Benefits Enrollment Application	AP1007	10	Cost Avoidance	◇	◆		11/1/09	74,304.00 USD		74,304.00 USD			
Fixed Assets	AP1000	10	Maintain the Business	◇	◈		11/2/09	125,102.88 USD		125,102.88 USD	345.60		345.60
Idea to Enhance UI	PR1071	10		◇	◇		2/6/11	250,000.00 USD		250,000.00 USD			
Payroll	AP1004	10	Grow the Business	◇	◈		11/2/09	50,041.15 USD		50,041.15 USD			
SAP R/3 Financial Accounting	AP1003	10	Maintain the Business	◇	◆		11/1/09	103,604.00 USD		103,604.00 USD	172.80		172.80
SAP R/3 Human Resources	AP1002	10	Cost Reduction	◇	◆		11/2/09	52,126.20 USD		52,126.20 USD			
Supply Chain Datamart Application	AP1016	10	Cost Avoidance	◇	◈		11/1/09	104,760.00 USD		104,760.00 USD			
Aggregation								1,010,066.23 USD		1,010,066.23 USD	950.40		950.40
Comparison								2,000,000.00 USD		1,597.00			
Variance								989,933.77 USD		646.60			

Figure 2-10. Portfolio investment view

Return on Investment (ROI)

The next portfolio view shows how the investments are placed based on planned ROI and alignment. Figure 2-11 shows return on investment.

41

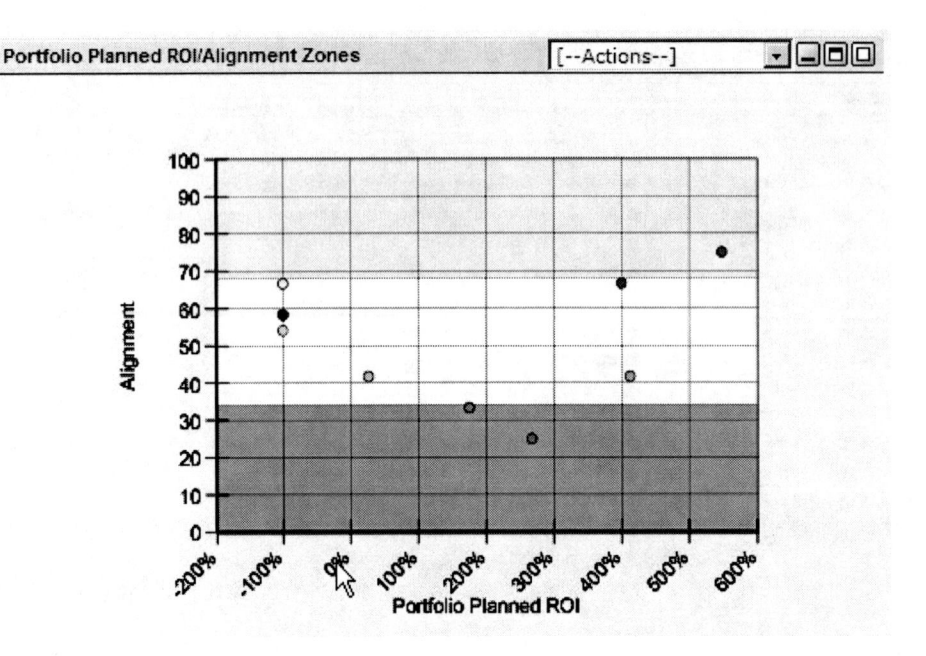

Figure 2-11. Return on investment

Automated Processes

The customer service organization at ABC Corp uses automated processes to standardize their workflow. For example, when an idea or opportunity is created, the automated idea approval process routes the approval request to the appropriate people who then can take action on the request. Application development team members can check the progress of the ideas they initiated by viewing the Processes tab on their personal organizer page. Figure 2-12 shows the view of initiated processes.

CHAPTER 2 ■ CA CLARITY PPM IN USE

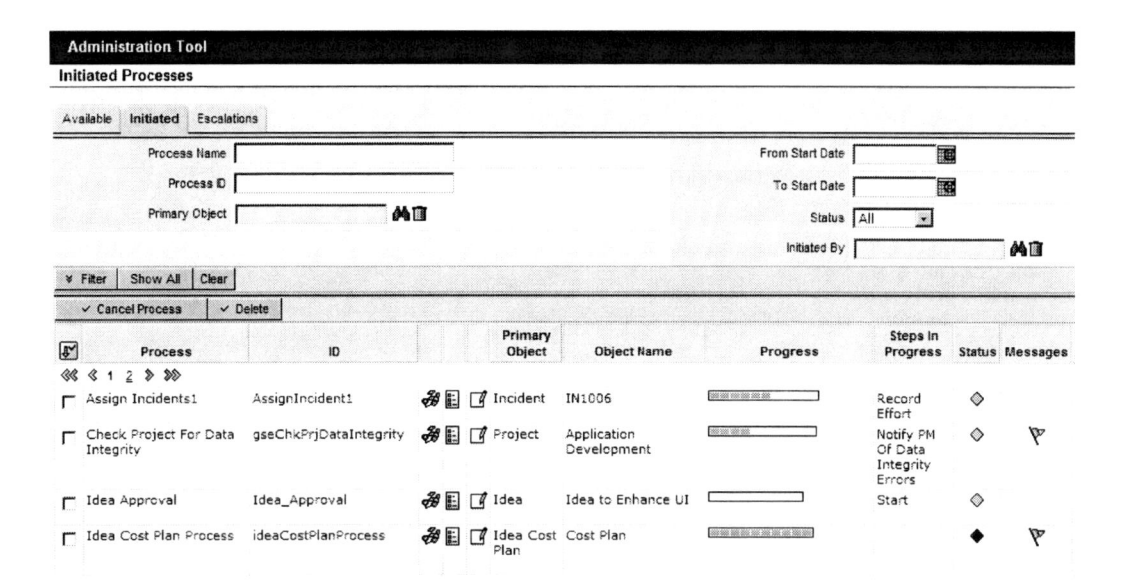

Figure 2-12. View of initiated processes

Once the workflow is triggered, the approver receives an action item to review the investment and take action. Figure 2-13 shows the view of an action item.

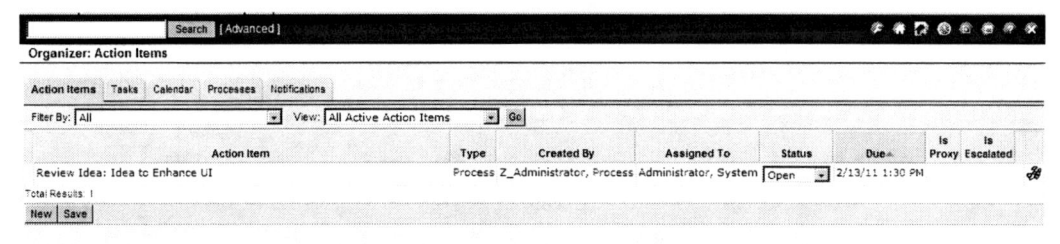

Figure 2-13. Action item to approver

Once the reviewer clicks in the action item, the details are displayed. Figure 2-14 shows the action item details.

43

CHAPTER 2 ■ CA CLARITY PPM IN USE

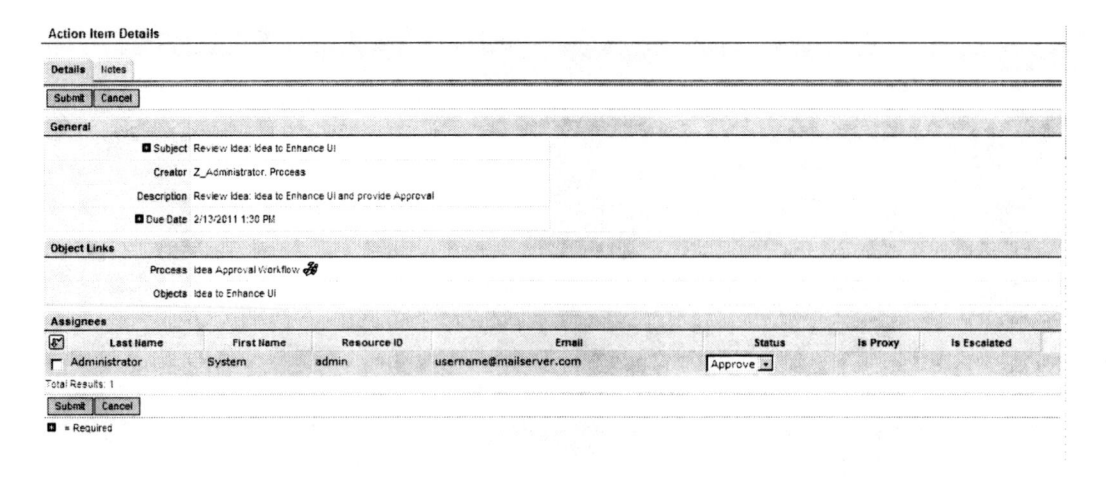

Figure 2-14. Action item details

Once the project is approved, the application development manager works with the project manager to create a project plan. The new program is created using multiple projects. Also, project dependencies are created. Figure 2-15 shows the detailed work breakdown structure (WBS) of the project.

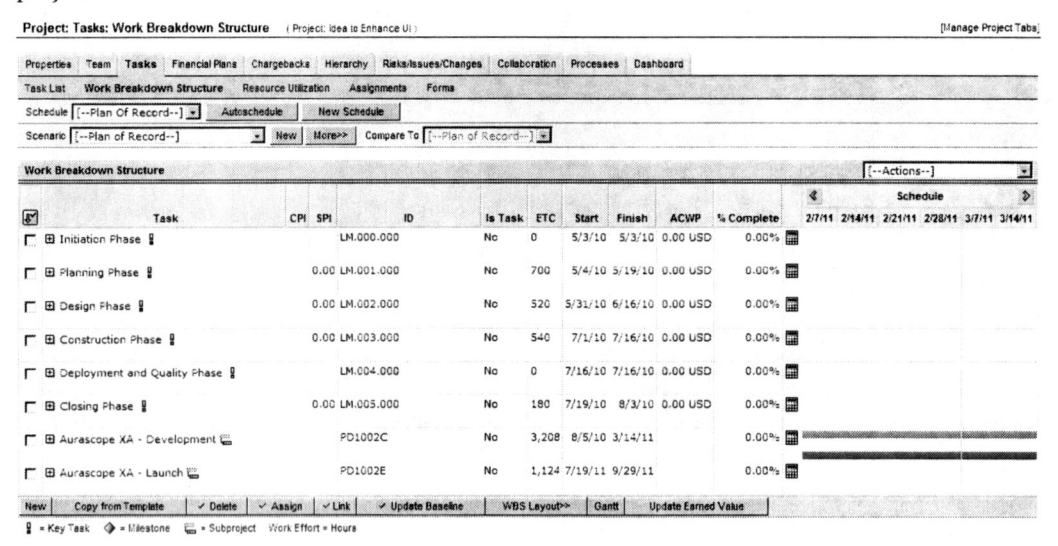

Figure 2-15. Work breakdown structure

The project manager then creates dependencies between master and subprojects. Figure 2-16 gives a view of the subprojects.

CHAPTER 2 CA CLARITY PPM IN USE

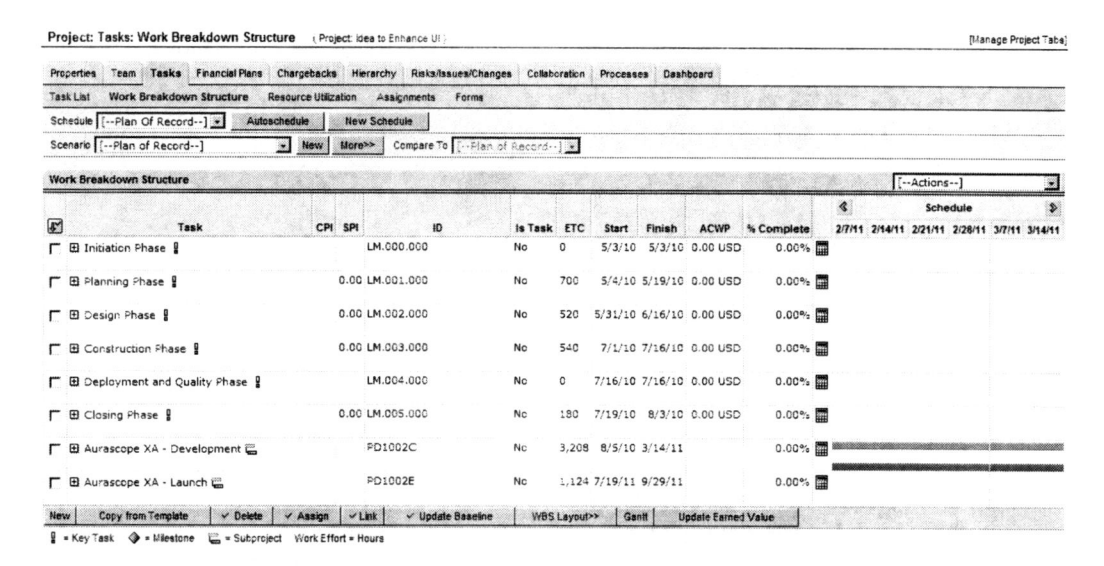

Figure 2-16. View of subprojects

The project is then rolled into the program. Figure 2-17 shows the program properties.

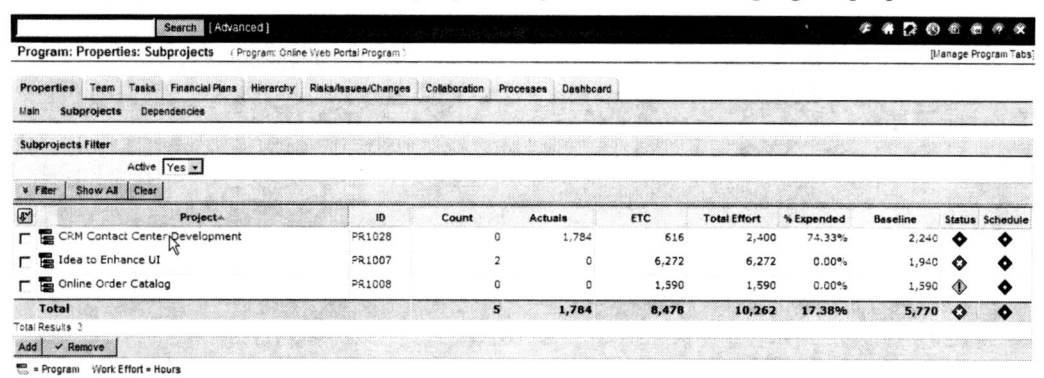

Figure 2-17. Program properties

The project manager then staffs the following roles and named resources on the project:

- Architect
- Developer
- Lead

Figure 2-18 shows the staff of the project team.

45

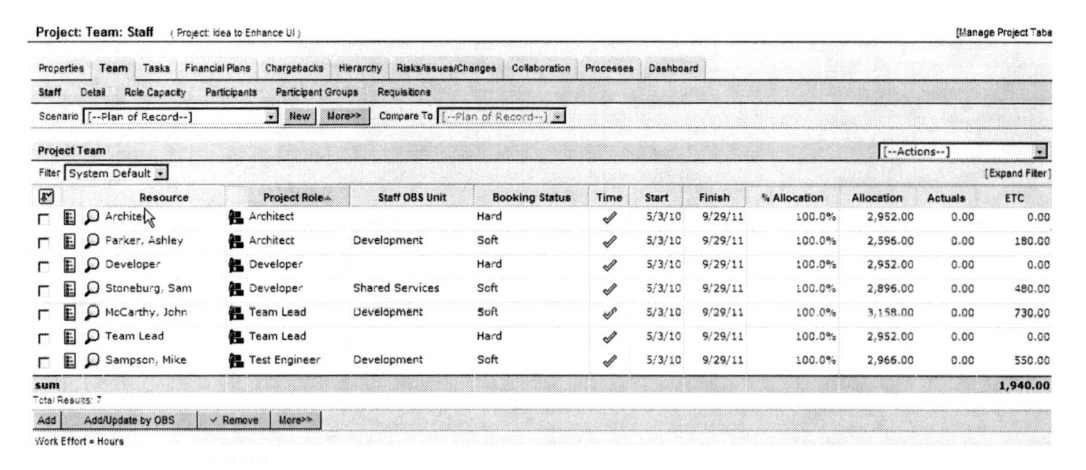

Figure 2-18. View of the staff

Finally, as shown in Figure 2-19, the project manager then creates a resource requisition for the named resource to replace the following roles:

- Architect
- Developer
- Lead

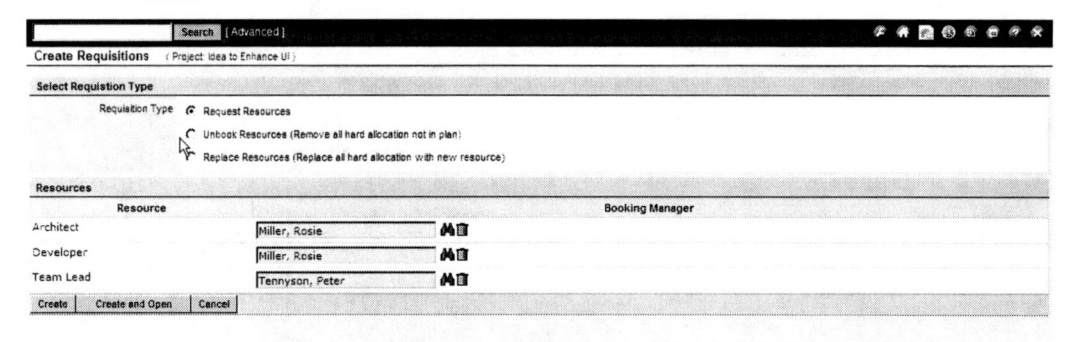

Figure 2-19. Creating named resources

Once the requisition is created, the booking manager (who could also be the resource manager in some cases) receives notification to review the open requisition to fill it. They can go to their Notifications page in their personal organizer to review the requisition. Resource/booking managers respond to the requests by identifying available resources meeting the required skill set. Figure 2-20 shows a resource requisition.

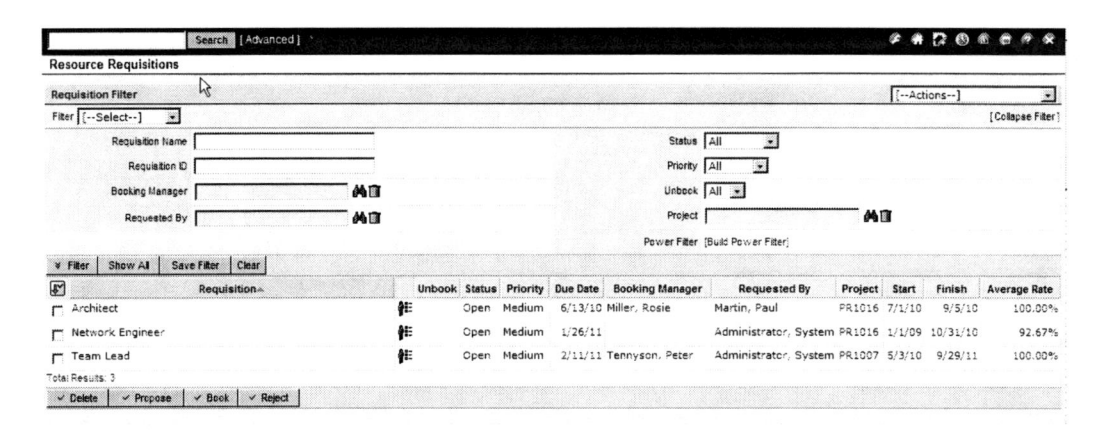

Figure 2-20. Resource requisition

After the resource manager proposes the matching of resources to the roles, the project manager hard-books and allocates team members to the project and assigns them tasks. At this point, the team members are ready to begin their work as scheduled. Figure 2-21 shows the final work schedule for the team.

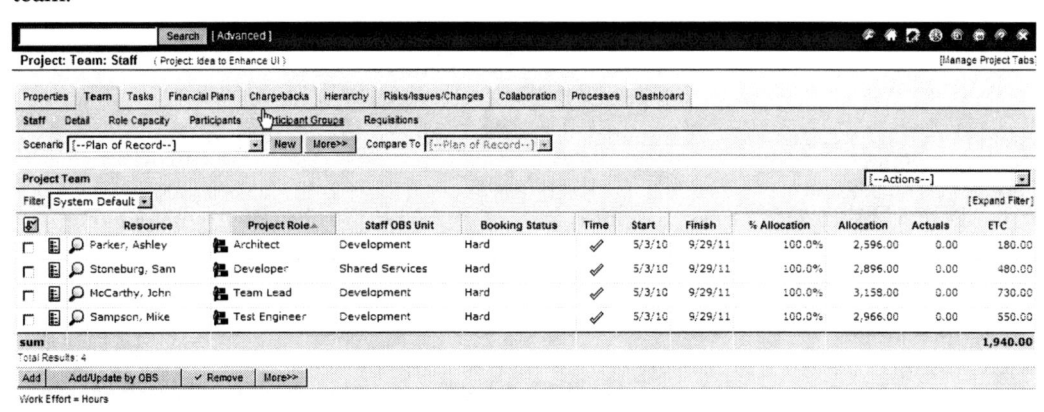

Figure 2-21. Final work schedule

Project Execution

Each week, team members work in their assigned tasks and enter their time against the task. Figure 2-22 shows a typical weekly timesheet.

Figure 2-22. Weekly timesheet

Once the team members fill in their timesheet, they submit the timesheet for approval. The submitted timesheet is routed to the project manager for approval. Once the timesheets are approved, they are ready for posting. The *Post Timesheets* job posts approved timesheets in the system. Once the timesheet is posted, the actual hours are recorded against the task and the estimate to complete (ETC) is reduced.

Project Reporting

The customer services manager and application development manager review the project status on a regular basis and report to executive management. They personalize their views to review the investment details such as project tasks, ROI, and labor estimates. Figure 2-23 shows a project dashboard. Figure 2-24 shows the project baselines, and Figure 2-25 shows the important upcoming milestones of the project.

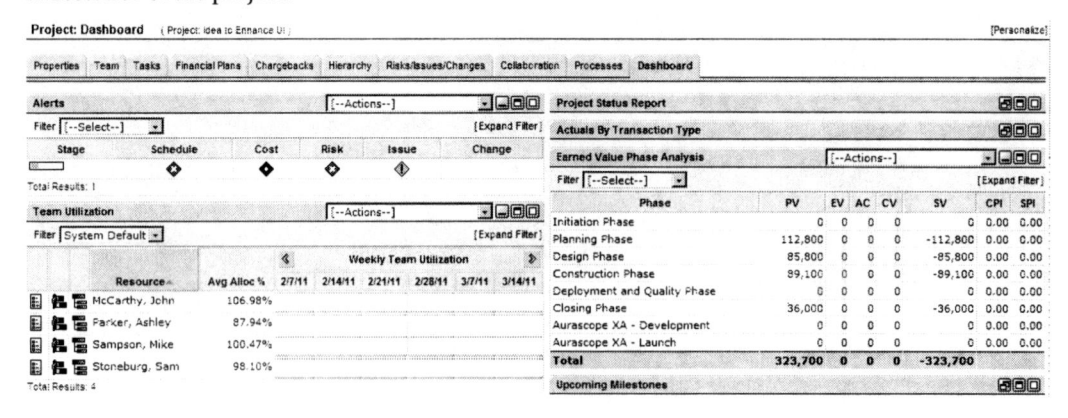

Figure 2-23. Project dashboard

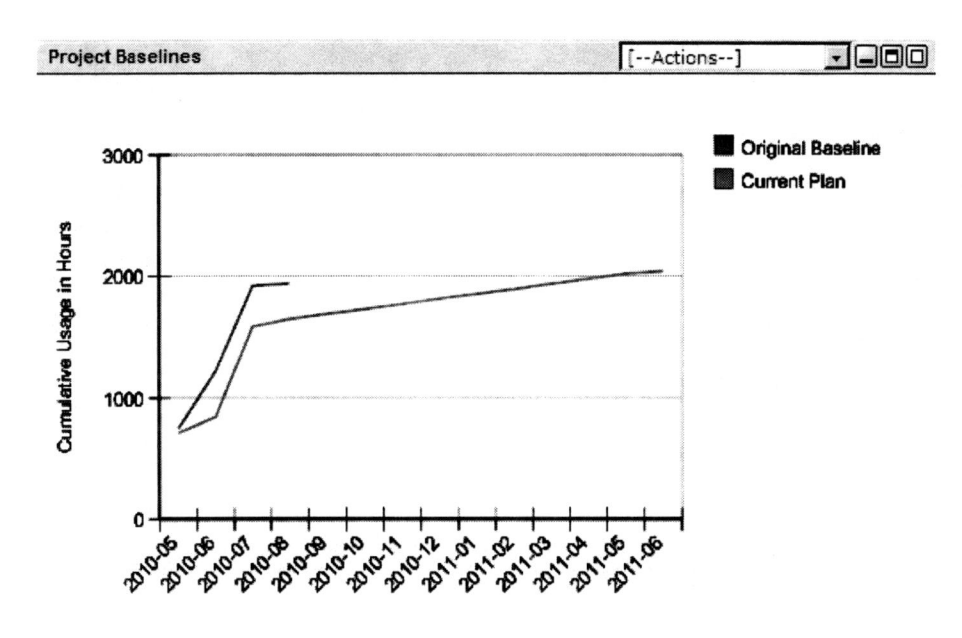

Figure 2-24. Project baselines

Figure 2-25. Upcoming milestones

Chargeback

Once the project is complete, the project cost is charged back to the business unit that requested this IT service. The financial group has set up a demand billing system in CA Clarity PPM to chargeback the labor cost of the entire project to the customer service group. During the next billing cycle, the cost of the project is charged back to the customer service group, which receives the bill with details of the project costs. Figure 2-26 shows a view of the recovery statement.

Investment	Type	Incurred Cost	Recovered Cost	Recovery Variance	Credits	Credits Variance
CRM Enhancements	project	218,400.00 USD	0.00 USD	218,400.00 USD	0.00 USD	0.00 USD
eCommerce Portal	project	71,500.00 USD	0.00 USD	71,500.00 USD	0.00 USD	0.00 USD
Email	service	62,400.00 USD	31,200.00 USD	31,200.00 USD	31,200.00 USD	0.00 USD
Global Expense Service	service	327,600.00 USD	163,800.00 USD	163,800.00 USD	163,800.00 USD	0.00 USD
Online Web Portal Service	service	784,244.75 USD	234,266.50 USD	549,978.25 USD	234,266.50 USD	0.00 USD
Security Compliance	project	49,950.00 USD	0.00 USD	49,950.00 USD	0.00 USD	0.00 USD
Totals		**1,514,094.75 USD**	**429,266.50 USD**	**1,084,828.25 USD**	**429,266.50 USD**	**0.00 USD**

Figure 2-26. Recovery statement

To recap, the project cycle started with an idea that was then approved and converted to a project. The project is reviewed, planned, staffed, executed, and closed. Once the project is closed, the IT department is given credit for the service delivered. This life cyle of a project shows how IT can be run like a business where the department delivering a services is credited and the department consuming the services is debited. Project reporting gives stakeholders insight into project health and lets them analyze the project effort and financials and make sure the project is aligned to an organizational goal.

Road Map and Maturity Assessment

Businesses of all sizes embark on thousands of projects in support of new products and services every year. Unfortunately, most projects are doomed to fail outright, or at launch, because the original success criteria were not met. Some project failures lead to delays in product launches, such as those occurring at major airline manufacturers; others incur huge cost overruns. These examples, as well as the results from survey after survey, show that businesses have not been able to figure out how to consistently get products and services delivered on time, on budget, and with the highest quality.

Why Do Projects Fail?

Businesses invest a great deal each year in people, consultants, processes, and technology to improve project success rates, but without much success. The project success rates have improved over the years, but there has not been the kind of dramatic increase that one would expect given the size of the investments businesses have made.

The reality is that the businesses have made plans, but the majority are not ready or willing to make the *true* investments needed to achieve meaningful change—the type of change that will be delivered on time, on budget, and with high quality near 100 percent of the time. There are eight steps that, if followed as a single unit and truly embraced by the entire organization, provide the road map to project management perfection. Let's examine these eight steps.

Definition

It is critical to start with a solid foundation. The foundation must be built at the organizational level and not with individuals. It is imperative that, from the CIO down, there is understanding and buy-in when it comes to defining or redefining the following items:

- *Roles and responsibilities*: This can be painstaking, but the effort will pay off when it's time to execute. The exercise may outline the need to develop new organizational structures to better support efficiency and communication within the delivery teams.
- *Standards*: The creation of a project management methodology will allow for consistency in delivery and terminology. An added benefit can be bringing new employees on board who rapidly move up the learning curve and thereby provide immediate value.
- *Policies*: Having a set standard and a consistent methodology provides the platform to document and enforce policies. It's difficult to document when things are moving quickly and always changing, but taking the time to do so will provide benefits such as improved control measures. Performing audits allows an organization to proactively identify risks and gives them the ability to mitigate them before they turn into a true problem.

Evaluation

It's important to know where and when to make investments to achieve the goals of the business. Unfortunately, there are always more ideas than there are resources to execute them. Therefore, organizations need to formalize a process for evaluating which new projects should be approved. The process must define the decision-making criteria that will be used during the evaluation and also take into consideration the firm's capacity and capabilities to successfully deliver the projects.

Resources

For a business to succeed without people—or more importantly, the right person—is near impossible. An organization's resources are hired for specific reasons, such as unique skill sets or deep industry experience. Creating an environment for success is crucial to an organization's business and to employees' careers. It is critical for an organization to take time to match the staffing needs for a new project with the skills.

Goals and Objectives

It happens way too often that team members don't understand why they are doing what they are doing. They don't know how important their project or task is to the success of the business. It is critical that goals are clearly defined for every project, from corporate initiatives down to one-off departmental projects. It is also important that they all tie together. Even the smallest project should support corporate goals in some way.

Control

One of the true single points of failure to the success of any project is the lack of control, specifically around scope and budget. Most people realize that for every action there is a reaction, but for some reason that logic goes out the window when it comes to a project. Some of the common signs of scope creep are when you hear the following: "My request is easy" or "This is just a small change." Project stakeholders say these things without realizing the impact of their "small change" on the project plan or budget. In order to succeed, project stakeholders must understand that a change to the scope, timeline, or budget for a project will produce a failed project if those variables aren't subsequently adjusted to accommodate the change. As well, project managers need to define a strong change control process that is embraced from the highest levels down. It is easier said than done, but if accomplished, it will allow an organization to deliver its product and services on time and on budget.

Monitor

It's a hard reality that many businesses do not formally and concisely track the status of projects. It is critical that project managers and the project team fully know and document a project's progress, stakeholders' commitments, results achieved, and the leading indicators of success as well as potential failure. The knowledge from the information gathered from project monitoring will determine the decisions that are made, the course of corrections that may be needed, and the comfort that the projects are being tracked. There needs to be transparency into and accountability to the plan, goals, budget, and scope in order to achieve confidence that the information is accurate and actionable.

Measure

When a project is planned and started, certain goals are set, plans are created, and commitments are made. The biggest failure of a project would be that after all that work there is no insight or information on whether project objectives were quantifiably met. Being able to define, capture, and track the metrics surrounding each project and the entire portfolio of projects is a must for any executive and management team. There are many methodologies, such as Six Sigma, that place a great deal of importance on the ability to capture and quantify success or failure. There is a lot of power in black-and-white data. The data and the history that is captured will pay benefits when making initial decisions during the evaluation step. Project managers can baseline the proposed project against those in the past and determine what changes may be needed in order to give a new proposal the best chance to succeed and not repeat past problems. One can learn from the past only if the past has been documented for reference.

Improve

Even in the most successful projects there is always something that could have been done better. Being able to capture those lessons will enable an organization to improve its project delivery capability and deliver more complex and challenging projects in less time, for less cost.

There are three main areas for improvement:

- *Invest in people:* Improve the skill sets of people with training and by giving them challenging project assignments.

- *Continual improvement*: Formalize a process to capture the lessons learned for each project. That process should also outline how recommendations for change are prioritized, approved, and implemented. As with other items, measure the progress of each step and each approved recommendation to determine whether its goals were met.

- *Project technology*: Be on the lookout for how technology can help increase the efficiency and quality of project delivery.

Assessing Organizational Readiness

For an organization to be mature enough to practice portfolio management, it has to have certain basic organizational attributes and infrastructure in place. Let's examine some of these attributes.

The Organization Should Have a Coherent Strategy

Portfolio management uses project activities to move the organization forward toward a goal. Groups and individuals that conduct strategic planning are consistently more successful at achieving goals than those who don't utilize it. Research also indicates that maintaining a constant focus on the goal of the group has a high correlation with goal attainment.

The Organization Should Know How to Manage a Project

"Crawl, walk, and then run" is perfect advice while you manage a project. Trying to implement portfolio management before mastering the basics of managing individual projects is putting the cart before the horse. Without project management methodology and practices in place, an organization will not have the most basic data to work with. Bad project management means cost and schedule estimates that are exercises in fantasy.

The Organization Should Know What Projects It Has

The biggest challenge in an organization is lack of visibility in a portfolio or definition of what portfolio means. A complete list of all the initiatives competing for resources is a baseline requirement to even begin portfolio management. Many companies set criteria for what counts as a project to be listed (for example, only projects that surpass a predetermined threshold number: a schedule of 60+ days or 80+ hours; or a budget of at least $250,000). Visibility into projects is a first step toward deriving value from portfolio management, because certain realities are quickly revealed. For example, if an organization over-allocates its resources on a project by say 120 percent, then lots of things will slip and productivity of resources will go down.

The good news is that even this most basic step surfaces redundancies and dead issues, allowing a portfolio management initiative to create value for the company almost immediately. The inventory of projects has to include all projects that meet the criteria, since resources are working on all these projects—not just on the high-profile ones. The inventory should also include projects that are being carried out by outsource providers and consultants, as well, since even those projects have at least someone within the company as a liaison, contract manager, and/or project manager. These hours often get "lost" in the decision-making process, only to show up later as a cost or schedule overrun.

The Organization's Projects Should Be Defined Consistently

Once the parameters of the list are decided upon, each project on it must be described. Details such as technologies required; estimates of time, cost, and personnel required; and a basic risk/reward calculation give portfolio managers the data they need to compare and contrast projects. Companies skilled at opportunity identification on one hand, and at tracking existing projects on the other, have a significant advantage at this stage. Their lists will be more complete, and their estimates will be more meaningful.

The Organization's Project Data Should Be Reliable

An organization cannot make good decisions based on bad information. This is where the enterprise-level project management tools with portfolio management capabilities really earn their keep. Gathering data in such a way that it can be put into context—becoming information—is where software reigns supreme. How long will each project take? How much will it cost? What's the expected ROI? What's the status on the projects already underway? Being able to view the most salient information on each and every project in thumbnail-sketch form allows executives to compare apples to apples and weigh the relative benefits of apples vs. oranges. What is less certain is the organizational willingness to use these features of the software and train appropriately for them.

The Organization Should Know Who Is Available to Work on Projects, and When

A second part of the inventory process should be insight into the project team including the project managers and where they sit in an organization's structure or chart. The biggest challenge for an organization is getting a project manager who can manage a project to success. The following are some of the basic questions that come up when creating an inventory list:

- Number of project managers
- Availability of project team members
- Current allocation of project team members
- Skill sets of project team members

All of these questions cannot be answered without a central system, which creates a challenge in managing a portfolio.

A Case Study

ABC Pharmaceutical Company Inc. is using the CA Clarity PPM tool to achieve the following:

- Predict resourcing needs
- Replace functionalities of the existing tools
- Link to external systems for work plans
- Get insight into actual work effort
- Track budget released for projects in phases

- Estimate cost based on resource plans
- Use CA Clarity PPM, which becomes a "single point of truth" for all project portfolio management needs
- Use CA Clarity PPM for standardization of processes
- Plan for CA Clarity PPM implementation for easy user adoption

ABC Pharmaceutical Company Inc. already has base functionalities of the CA Clarity PPM tool implemented, and it wants to define a clear road map to address the previous needs and to overcome the following pain points:

- Define the big picture for the CA Clarity PPM implementation
- Define a clear implementation road map to avoid rollout delays
- Differentiate between CA Clarity PPM and the system of record for finance
- Utilize the *out-of-the-box* flavor of the CA Clarity PPM tool and fix the internal business processes

The CA Services Clarity architect had a brainstorming meeting with ABC Pharmaceutical Company Inc. stakeholders and created a clear implementation road map to roll out Clarity in a phased manner over the period of 18 months and raise the project execution maturity of ABC Pharmaceutical Company Inc. Figure 2-27 shows the implementation road map suggested to the company.

CHAPTER 2 ■ CA CLARITY PPM IN USE

Implementation Road Map

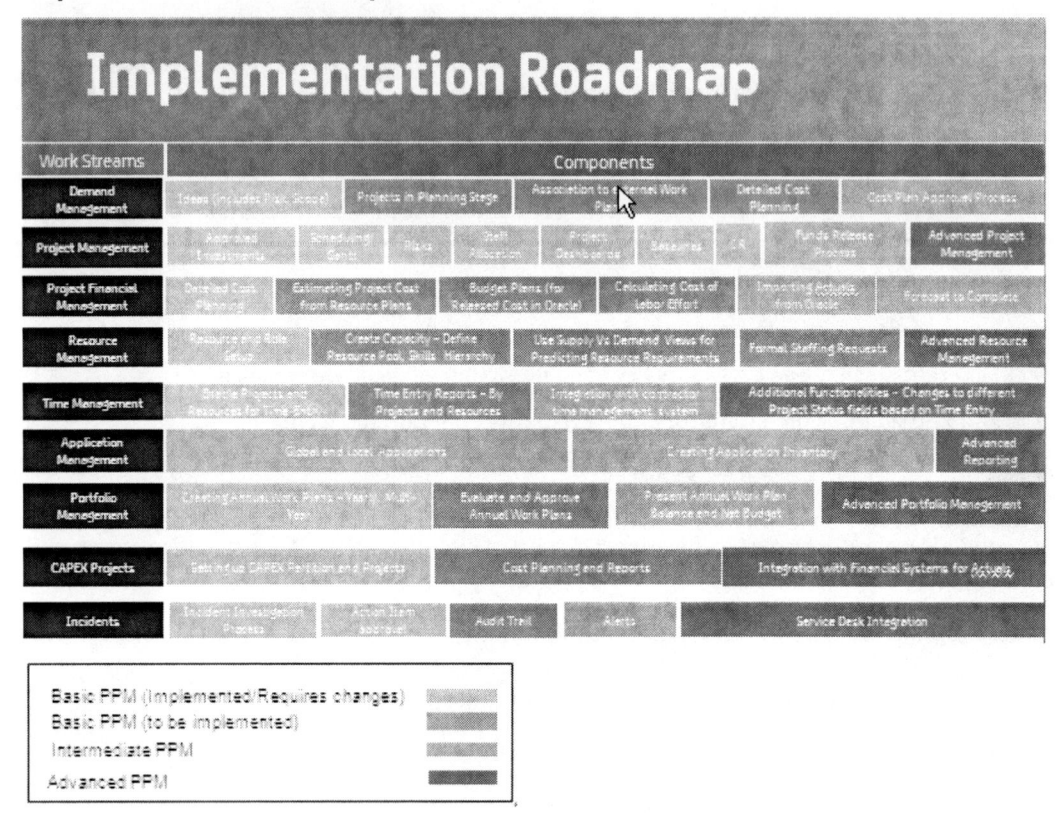

Figure 2-27. Implementation road map

Based on the road map shown in Figure 2-27, the CA Services Clarity architect laid out a timeline to achieve the maturity, as shown in Figure 2-28.

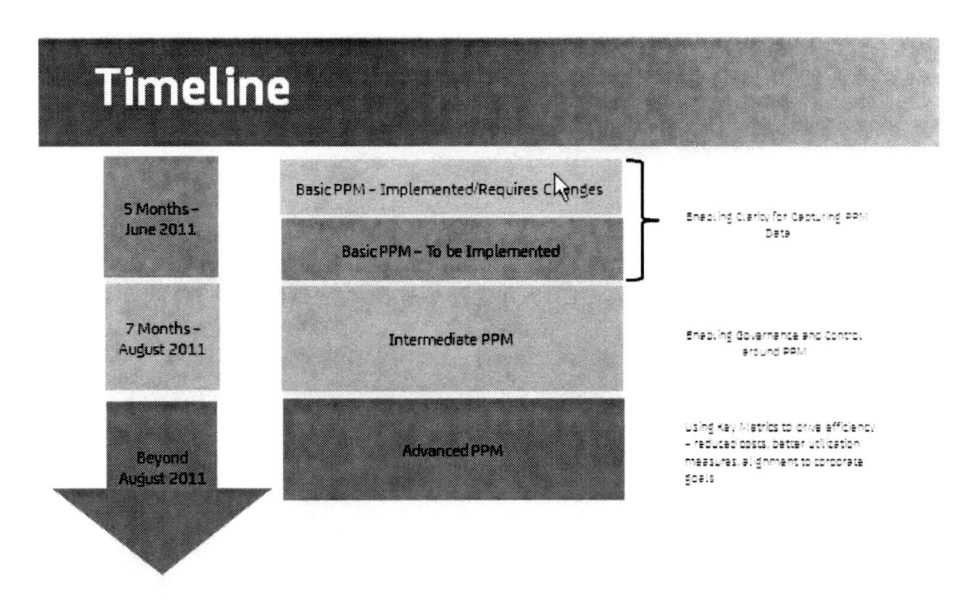

Figure 2-28. Maturity timeline

Summary

This chapter described what a typical project life cycle looks like in the real world. It also described what factors led customers to an evaluation of project and portfolio management. Then it described how IT governance is used in real life. Then the chapter described the implementation road map and timeline (as an example) to reach a high level of maturity for project and portfolio management. Finally, it described how an organization can make commitments for PPM to reap its long-term benefits.

CHAPTER 3

■ ■ ■

An Overview of CA Clarity PPM

This chapter gives an overview of the CA Clarity PPM tool and how the tool can be easily configured for end users. We also give some tips that are helpful for users and system administrators.

We have divided the chapter into four major parts: "User Interface," "Basic Navigation," "Personalization," and finally "Reports and Jobs." We will showcase the tool through the eyes of a real life company: Acme Data Systems Inc.

Acme Data Systems Inc. (ADS) is the world's largest merchant processing company. ADS wants to replace its current project management system, which is reaching its end of life. ADS is analyzing an enterprise-level tool that can offer the following:

- The same functionality that their current tool offers

- Ease of use so that risk of user dissatisfaction is low

- A solution that can be implemented by configuring the tool and not customizing it

The CA Clarity PPM tool provides a solution that is configured and not customized. It offers out-of-the-box options to configure the user interface (UI) on the fly to suit end user requirements.

This chapter will describe how CA Clarity PPM can be configured to overcome user acceptance challenges at ADS.

User Interface

Users at Acme Data Systems Inc. want a platform-independent tool that can be accessed via a web browser. John, the project manager at ADS, opens the Internet Explorer browser and types in the URL for CA Clarity PPM. He is taken to a user login screen where it prompts him for his username and password, as shown in Figure 3-1. We will watch John take a look at the projects area in the user interface so that you get a feel for how easy CA Clarity is to use.

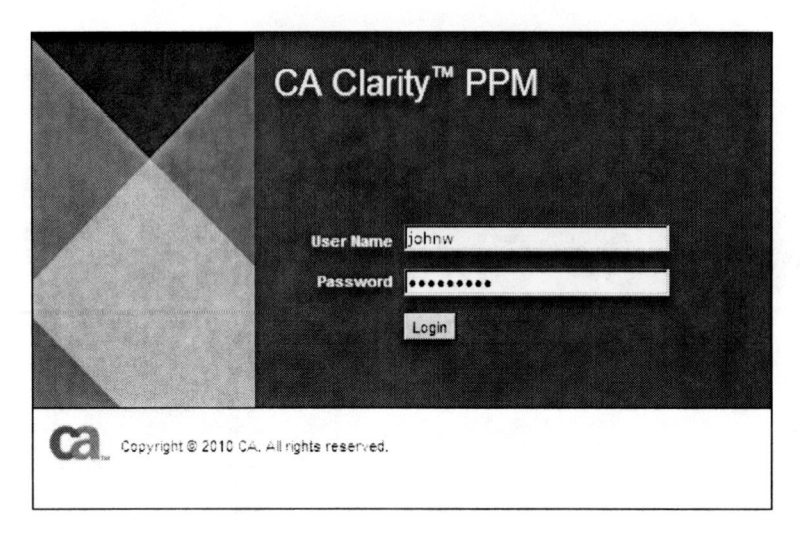

Figure 3-1. *Login screen*

John enters his username and password and is directed to the Clarity application home page. If ADS is using ADS user authentication, then the username and password will be John's network username and password. Figure 3-2 shows the personal overview home page that John sees. It has three main areas:

- The main menu and navigation bar on the left side
- The Clarity toolbar at the top
- The portlets on the home page

CHAPTER 3 ■ A QUICK GLANCE AT CA CLARITY PPM

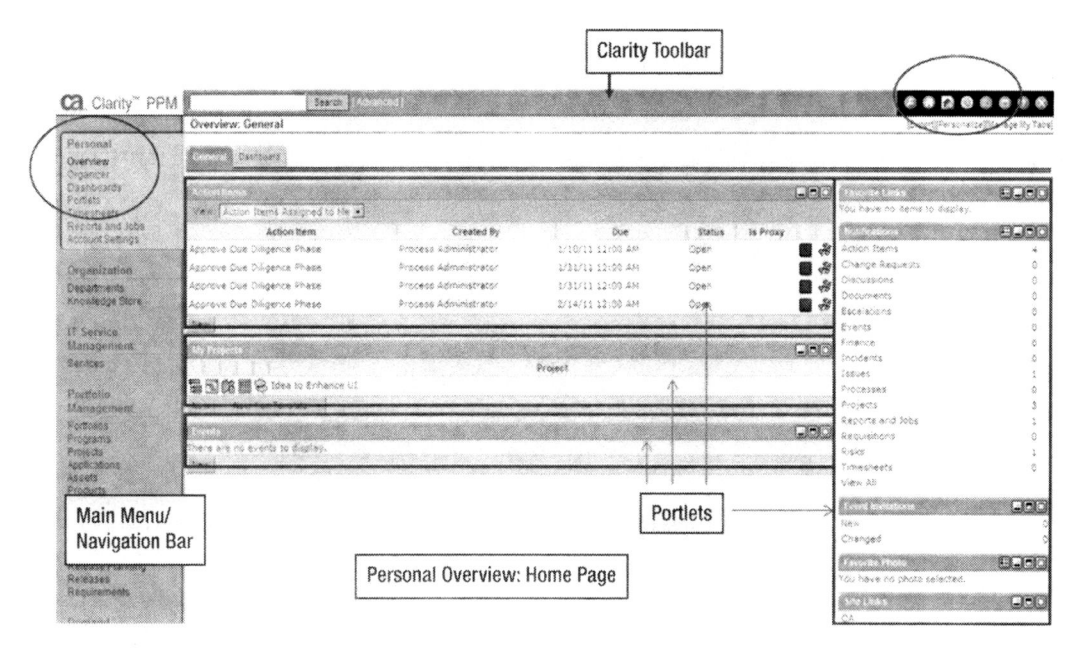

Figure 3-2. Personal overview home page

Main Menu and Navigation Bar

Let's look at the main menu and navigation bar and the options there. Figure 3-3 gives a snapshot of a typical main menu and navigation bar.

61

CA Clarity™ PPM

Personal
Overview
Organizer
Dashboards
Portlets
Timesheets
Reports and Jobs
Account Settings

Organization
Departments
Knowledge Store

IT Service Management
Services

Portfolio Management
Portfolios
Programs
Projects
Applications
Assets
Products
Other Work

Figure 3-3. Main menu and navigation bar

The users view the content on the Menu Manager based on their security rights. Each item in the Menu Manager provides a link to the main content page. For example, if John clicks the Projects link in the Menu Manager, it takes him to the project list page, as shown in Figure 3-4. Note that the project list page has a filter section at the top and a place to create a filter expression. The filter details will be listed at the bottom part of the page, as shown in Figure 3-4. (We will discuss filters in the next section.)

CHAPTER 3 ■ A QUICK GLANCE AT CA CLARITY PPM

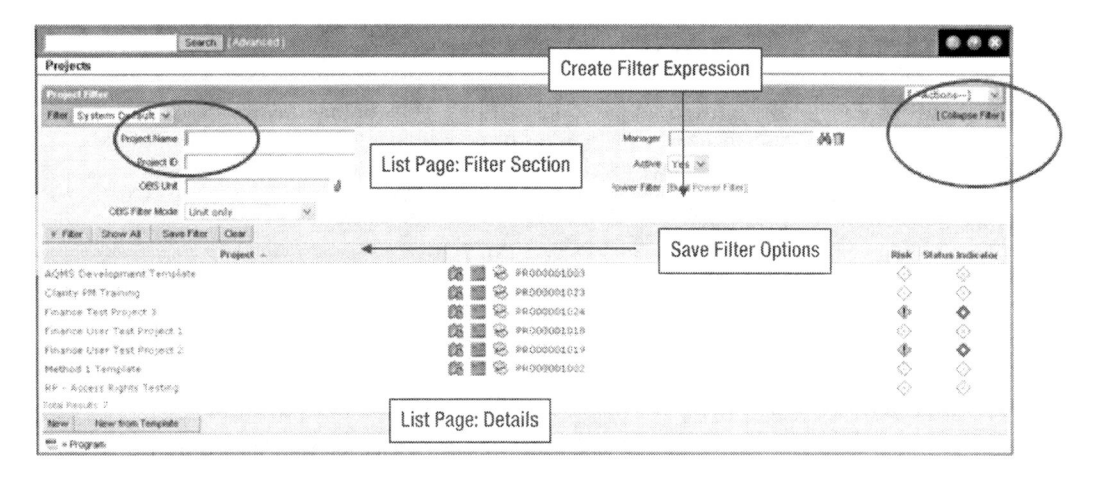

Figure 3-4. Project list page

Now John scrolls down and clicks the project called HR System Migration, which takes him to its content page, as shown in Figure 3-5.

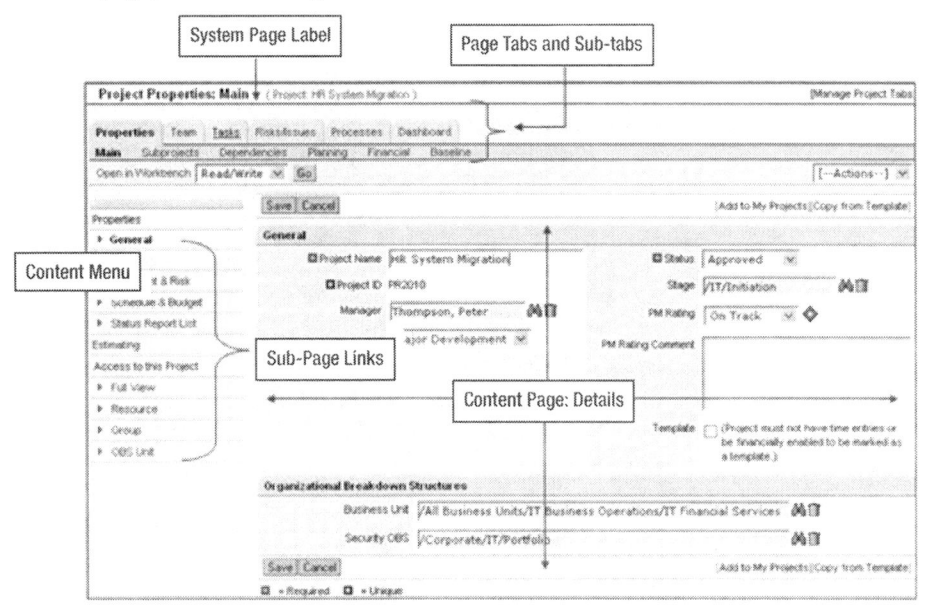

Figure 3-5. Content page

63

Clarity Toolbar

A user-friendly Clarity toolbar allows John to set personal settings. This toolbar always appears on top, no matter which section John is navigating in Clarity. A number of icon options are available to John. Table 3-1 summarizes them and shows their icons.

Table 3-1. Icon Options in the Clarity Toolbar

Icon	Description
[search box: actor Search [Advanced]]	This allows users to perform a global search of documents stored anywhere in CA Clarity PPM. It also provides options for advanced search.
[key icon]	The user will see this icon if they have administrator access rights. Clicking this icon allows the user to access the Administration Tool.
[home icon]	Takes the user to the home page set in CA Clarity PPM. Every user has an option to set any navigation page as their home page.
[home+ icon]	This allows the user to set the home page in CA Clarity PPM. Users can set any navigation page as their home page, and they can set any frequently visited page as their home page. Every time they log in to Clarity, they are directed to the home page. This reduces the number of clicks in the tool.
[clock icon]	This allows the user to navigate to the current timesheet. This reduces the number of clicks, especially for timesheet users who log in to the system just to enter the time.
[calendar icon]	This allows the user to access a personal calendar in the Organizer to view their events, notifications, tasks, and more.
[hide icon]	This allows the user to hide the side navigation bar.
[help icon]	This allows the user to access online help.
[logout icon]	This allows the user to log out of CA Clarity PPM.

Portlets on the Home Page

John can configure his home page by adding and removing tabs and portlets that are applicable to him for everyday activities. Figure 3-6 shows John's home page:

- John has all his active projects added in his My Projects portlet.

- John can also add more portlets to his home page via the Personalize option (we will discuss this in detail later in this chapter).

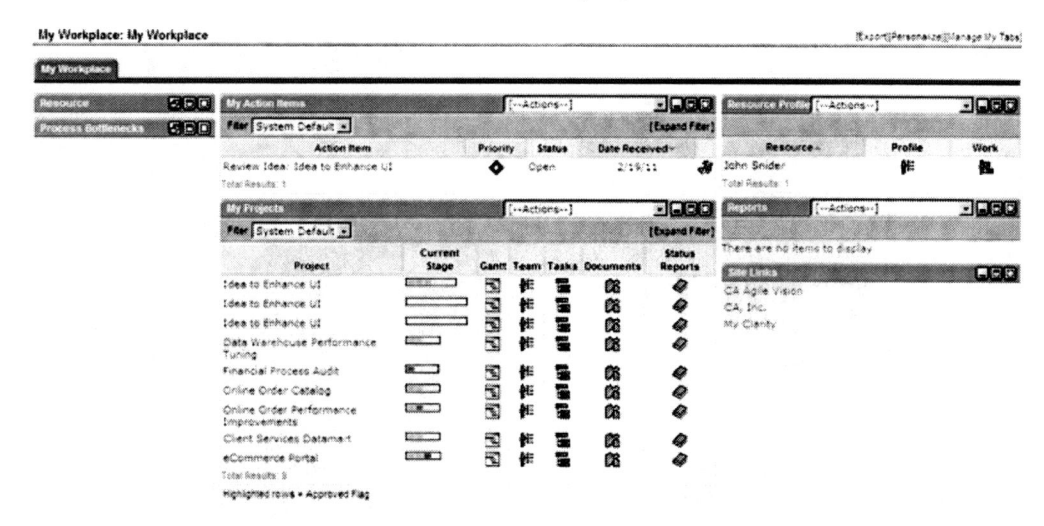

Figure 3-6. John's home page

Basic Navigation

This section describes how John can navigate CA Clarity PPM and make his own views for effective use of the tool.

We will look at two sides of the PPM navigation (the application vs. the Administration Tool), review the list pages and filters, review the features of the Organizer, and finally explore the Knowledge Store.

Application vs. Administration Tool

CA Clarity PPM has two navigation sides:

- Application

- Administration Tool

John has administrator access on Clarity, so when he logs in, he can see the Administration Tool icon, which allows him to navigate to the Administration Tool.

Once again, John logs in to CA Clarity PPM by entering the application URL and is directed to his home page on Clarity, as shown in Figure 3-7.

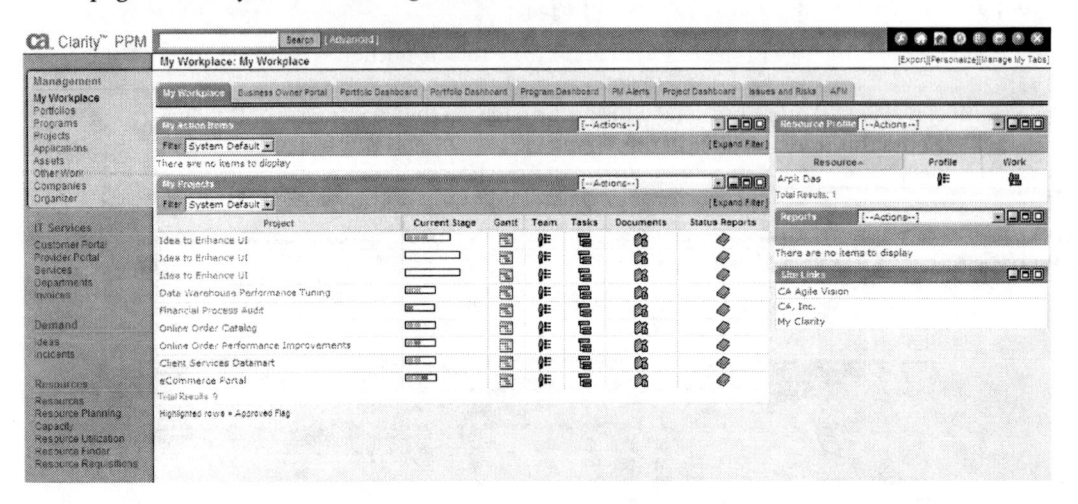

Figure 3-7. Application home page

Now John clicks the admin icon in the upper-right corner. This directs him to the Administration Tool where, based on his access rights, he can do the following:

- Create users

- Set the organization breakdown structure (OBS)

- Create and manage security rights

- Perform Clarity studio activities

- Manage data administration settings

- Configure the financial setup

- Configure project management settings

- Set up chargeback rules

- Set up general settings

List Pages and Filters

John clicks Projects in the left Menu Manager so he can view the list of the projects he has access to (as shown in Figure 3-8). The list page consists of two sections. At the top of the page, the filter section contains search fields that allow John to specify search criteria. Below the filter section is the list section. This section displays an itemized list of projects based on the filtering criteria entered by John. If no filtering criteria is entered, all items will be displayed in the list for which John has view rights.

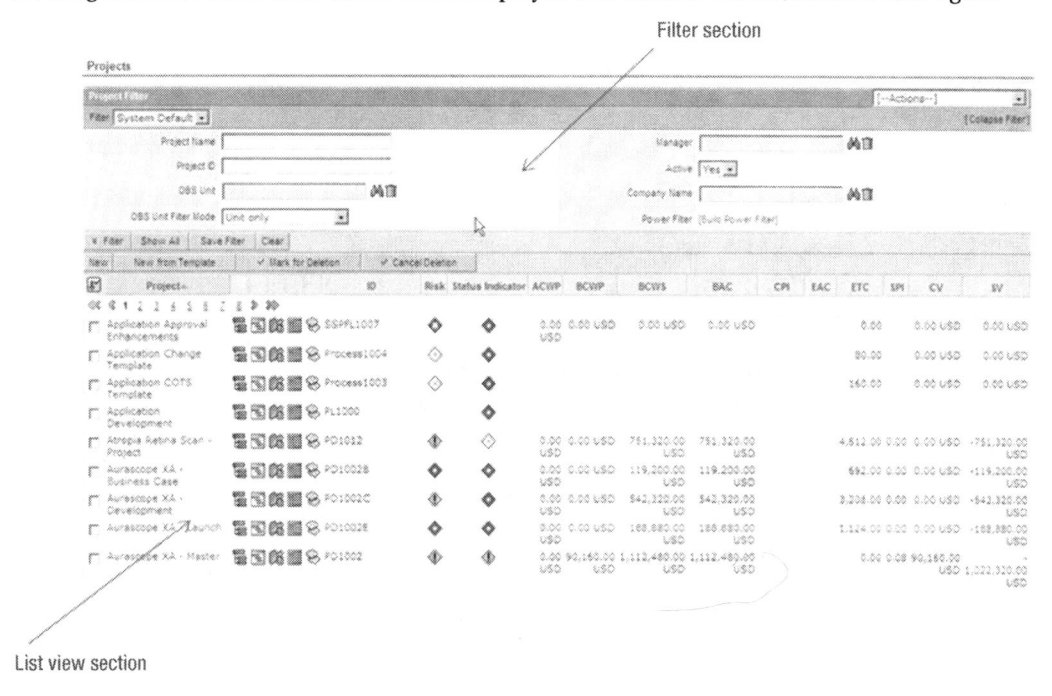

Figure 3-8. List of projects John has

Expand and Collapse Filter

The filter section is expanded or collapsed by default based on the settings set on the administration side or personalized by John. John can use the Collapse Filter or Expand Filter link on the filter section's toolbar to change the section's state.

The following are the two places where the expand or collapse filter can be set:

- The portlet definition properties on the Administration Tool where the filter section properties are defined. This setting is global and affects views for all users. Figure 3-9 shows a snapshot of the Administration Tool.

CHAPTER 3 ■ A QUICK GLANCE AT CA CLARITY PPM

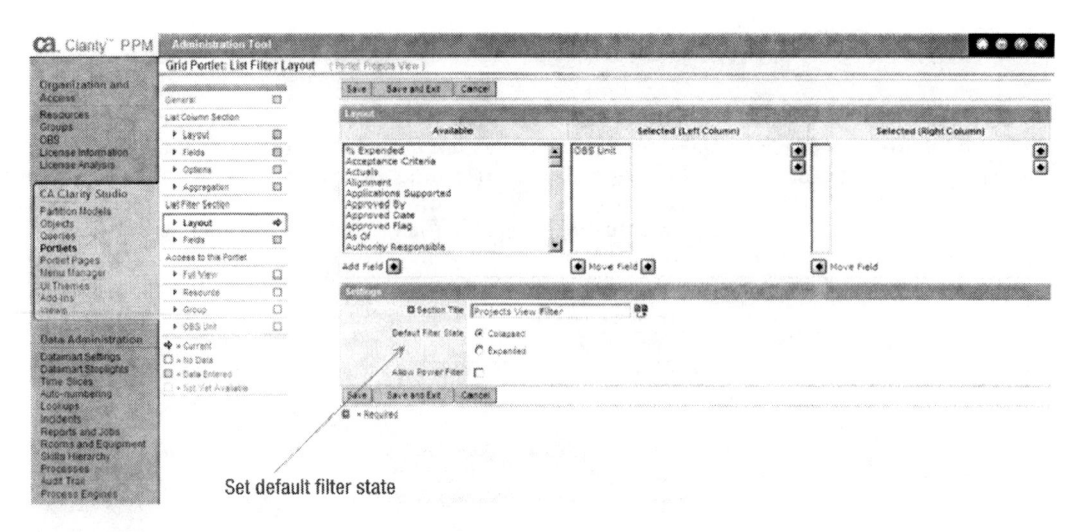

Figure 3-9. Expand/collapse filter in the Administration Tool

- A user can change the default filter state by using the Configure option under Actions on the toolbar for the list page, as shown in Figure 3-10.

Figure 3-10. Configure option under Actions on the toolbar

Then change the default filter state on the List Filter Layout page. This change affects only John's (or the logged-in user's) filter layout, as shown in Figure 3-11.

CHAPTER 3 ■ A QUICK GLANCE AT CA CLARITY PPM

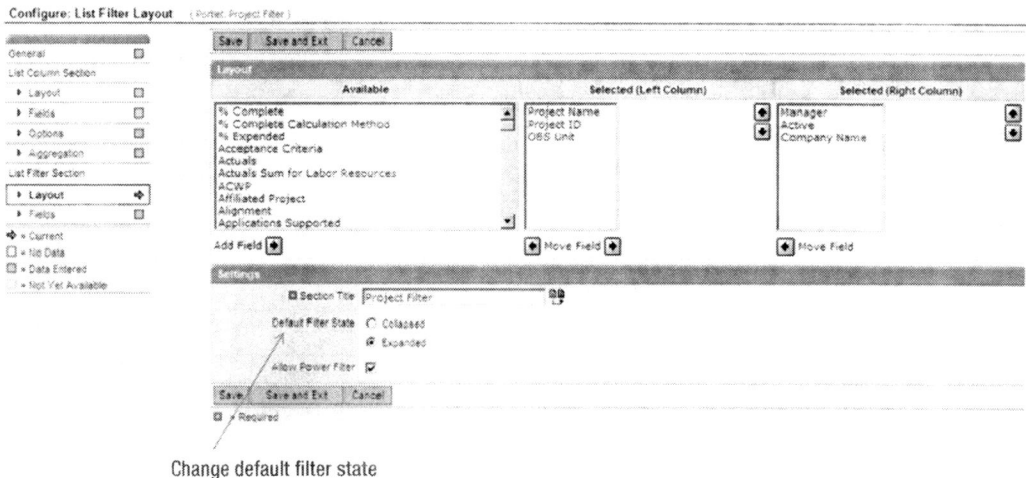

Figure 3-11. Changed default filter state

Figure 3-12 shows the filter section with a collapsed filter.

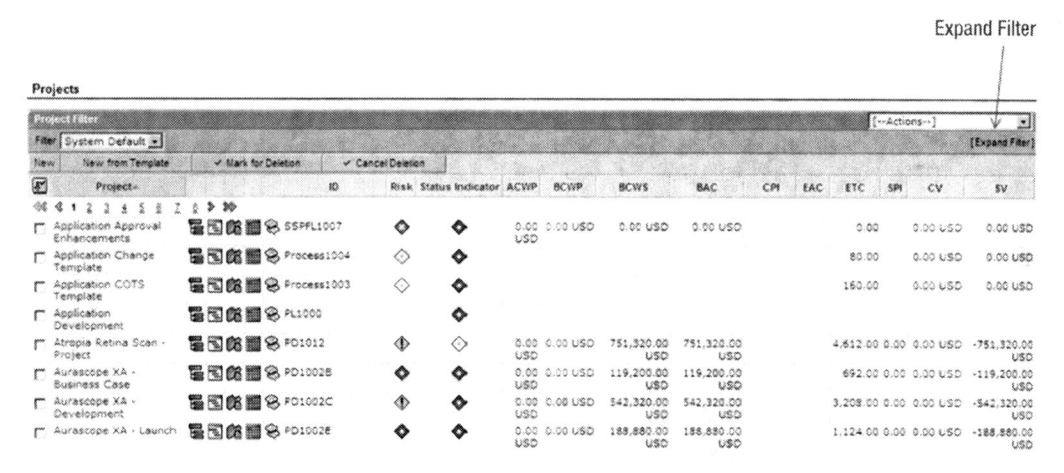

Figure 3-12. Collapsed filter

Now John wants to expand the filter, so he clicks the Expand Filter link. Figure 3-13 shows the filter section view with the expanded filter.

CHAPTER 3 ■ A QUICK GLANCE AT CA CLARITY PPM

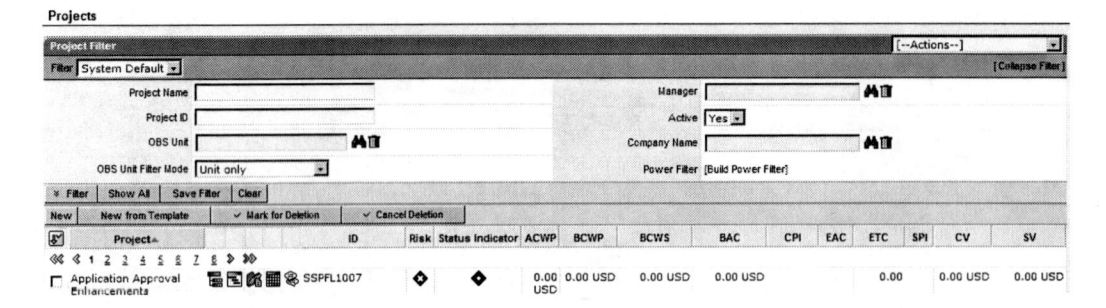

Figure 3-13. Expanded filter

Initiate Search

John can now initiate a search by entering filtering criteria into the fields in the filter section of the page. Now, John wants to see all of his projects under the Product Development department. He selects the Product Development OBS unit under the Corporate Department OBS, as shown in Figure 3-14.

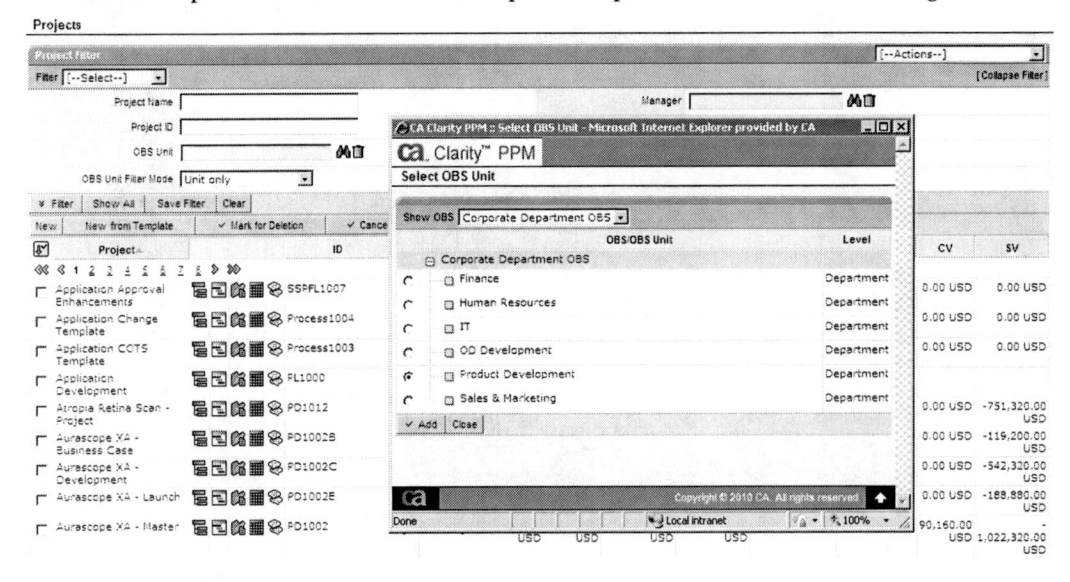

Figure 3-14. Projects under the Product Development department

Now he hits Filter and sees all his projects under the Product Development department, as shown in Figure 3-15.

CHAPTER 3 ■ A QUICK GLANCE AT CA CLARITY PPM

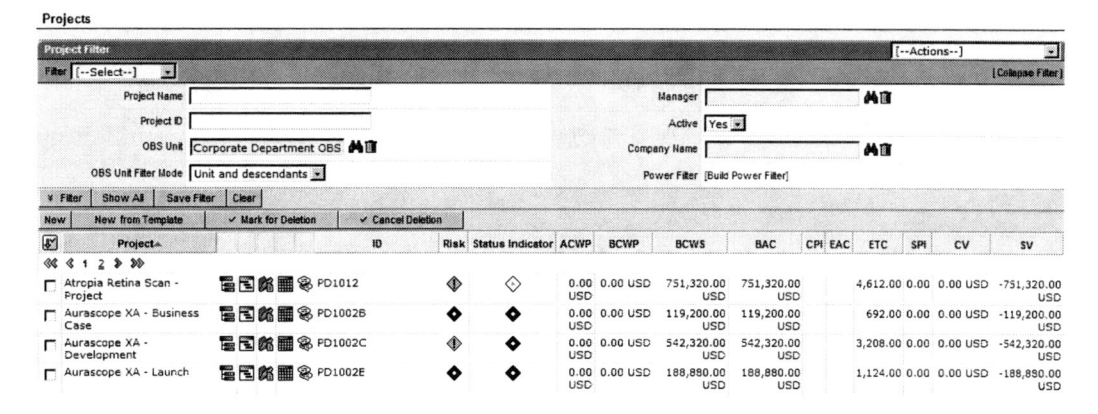

Figure 3-15. All projects under the Product Development department after filtering

Tip Filter search strings and words are not case sensitive. Therefore, the user can use wildcard characters (*) and needs them only at the start of a phrase. So, for example, if John wants to search for a project named Idea to Enhance UI, he can just put *enhance* in the search criteria.

Power Filter

John wants to create his own search criteria by combining multiple conditions. He discovered the option of using a power filter in the filter section. This link may or may not be available based on the Allow Power Filter check box selection. This selection can be set globally from the List Filter layout properties for a portlet from the Administration Tool or can be set or overridden by an individual user from the Configure option's list filter properties setting on the list page toolbar on the application side.

Figure 3-16 shows the option for allowing a power filter from the Administration Tool. This setting is global and affects views for all users.

71

CHAPTER 3 ■ A QUICK GLANCE AT CA CLARITY PPM

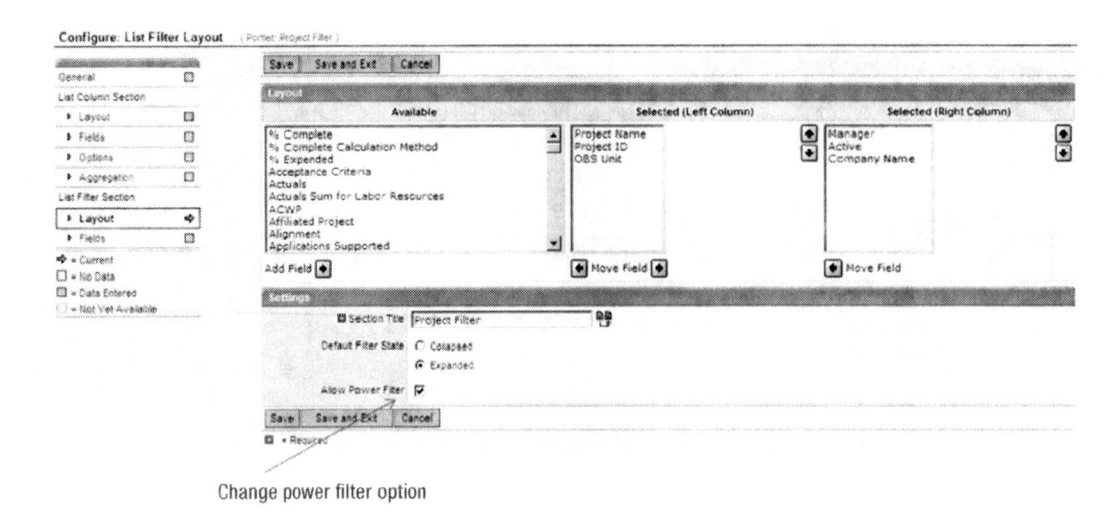

Figure 3-16. Changing the power filter in the Administration Tool

Figure 3-17 shows the option for allowing a power filter from the list page toolbar from the application side. These changes affect only John's (or the logged-in user's) filter list section, as shown in Figure 3-18.

Figure 3-17. Changing the power filter from the application side

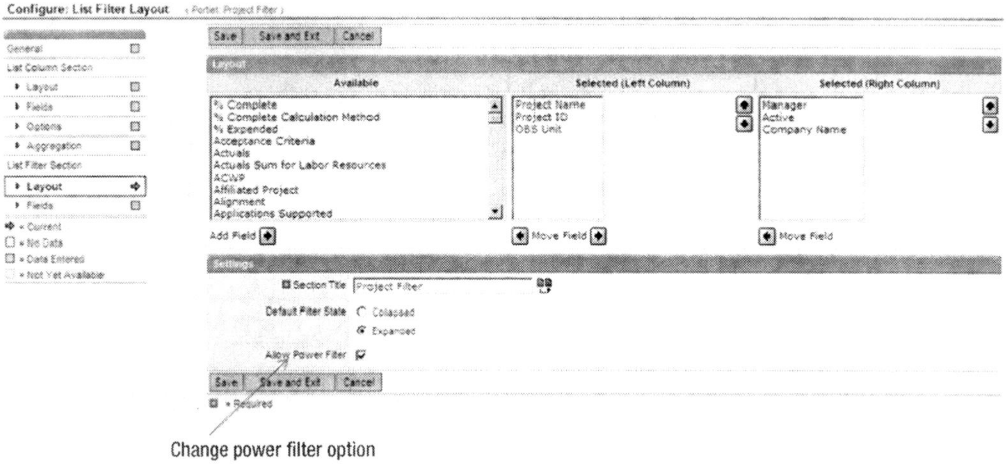

CHAPTER 3 ■ A QUICK GLANCE AT CA CLARITY PPM

Figure 3-18. John's filter list

Next, John wants to search for the projects with the following criteria:

- Projects with approved status, *and*
- Projects that are part of product development or the IT department

He clicks the Build Power Filter link to build the filter criteria with a few simple clicks, as shown in Figure 3-19.

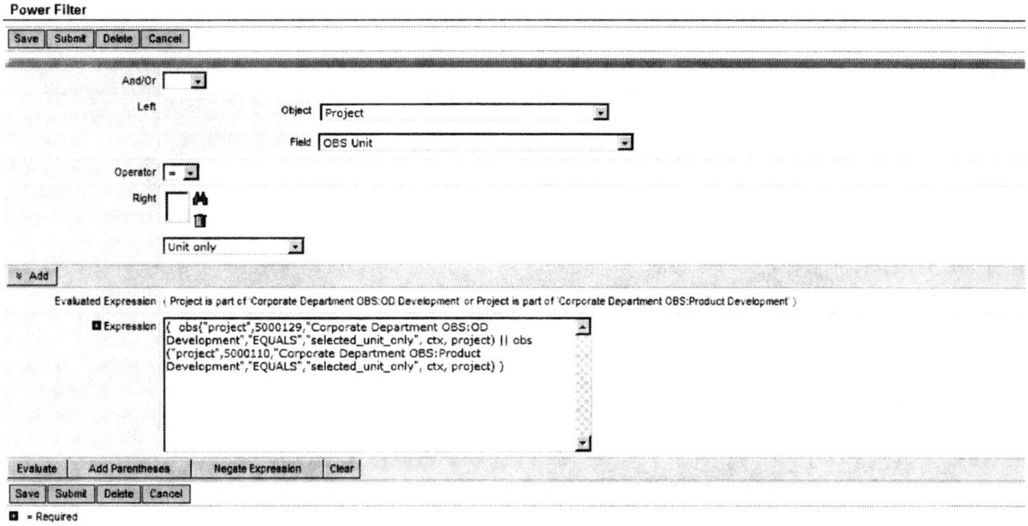

Figure 3-19. Building a power filter

73

CHAPTER 3 ■ A QUICK GLANCE AT CA CLARITY PPM

Manage and Save Filters

Now that John has created the filter criteria, he would like to save the filter options, as shown in Figure 3-20, so that he can reuse them every time he clicks the project list page because these are the projects he wants to view. CA Clarity PPM provides options to manage and save filters with a few simple clicks. These features align to ADS's requirements for a tool that is configured and not customized.

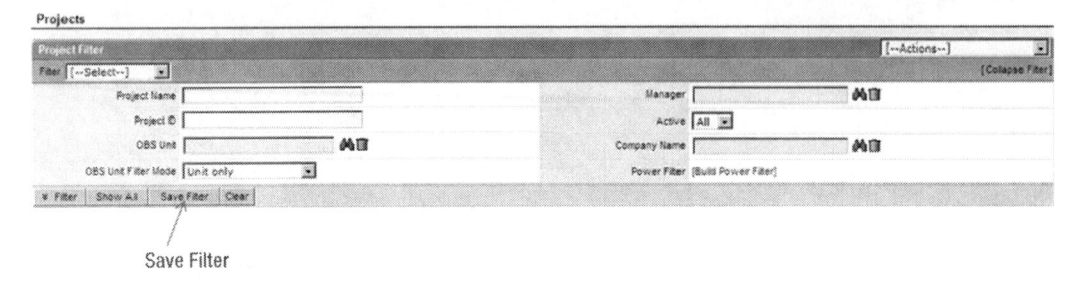

Figure 3-20. Saving a filter

John names the filter and checks the default box to make this filter the default for his project list page, as shown in Figure 3-21.

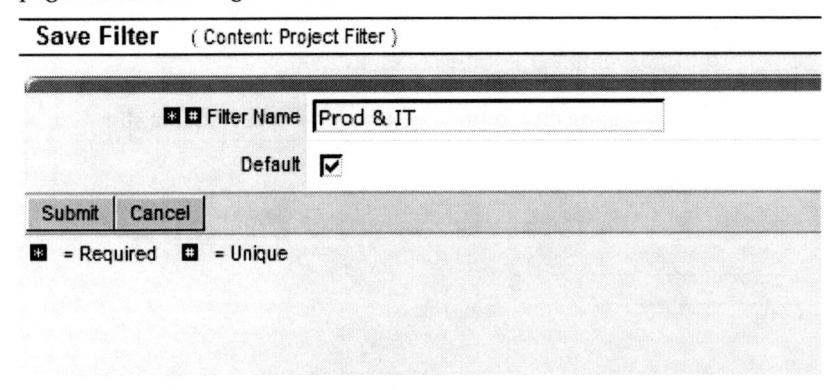

Figure 3-21. Making the filter the default

The Manage Filters option allows John to manage his list of filters, set a default filter, or delete an existing filter. Figures 3-22 and 3-23 show various options of the Manage Filters pages.

Figure 3-22. Manage Filters page

Figure 3-23. Manage Filters page details, continued

Organizer

The Organizer provides John with a central access point for all of the action items, tasks, calendar events, processes, and alert notifications to which he has been assigned or invited. Figure 3-24 shows a snapshot of the Organizer. John can use the Organizer to perform his daily project work by accessing the following different functional tabs:

- *Action Items*: Access, view, and manage all of his action items.

- *Tasks*: View and track the progress of the tasks to which he has been assigned.

- *Calendar*: Manage calendar events that John has created and those to which he has been invited.

- *Processes*: View, run, filter, and delete the processes to which John has access.

- *Notifications*: John can view notification alerts he receives in CA Clarity PPM tool.

Figure 3-24. Organizer

Action Items

Action items are assigned to a user, and the user can be asked to act upon them. Action items can be generated from a workflow process in CA Clarity PPM. They also can be items like "FYI" and may not require any action from the user. Figure 3-25 shows a snapshot of the Action Items tab.

John can review all of his assigned action items on the Action Items tab in the Organizer. In the figure, he has received an action item to review an idea and provide his approval.

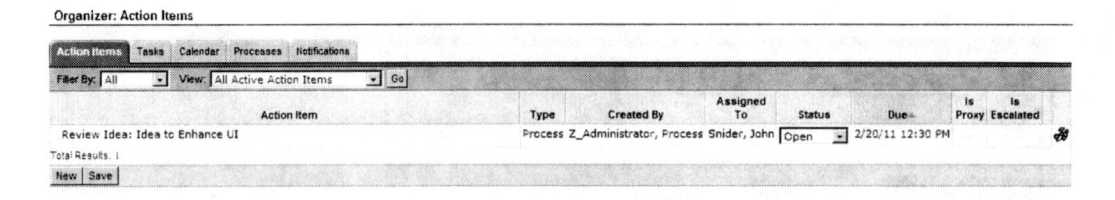

Figure 3-25. Action Items tab

John clicks the action item to review the details and can click the Idea link to go to the properties of the idea, as shown in Figure 3-26.

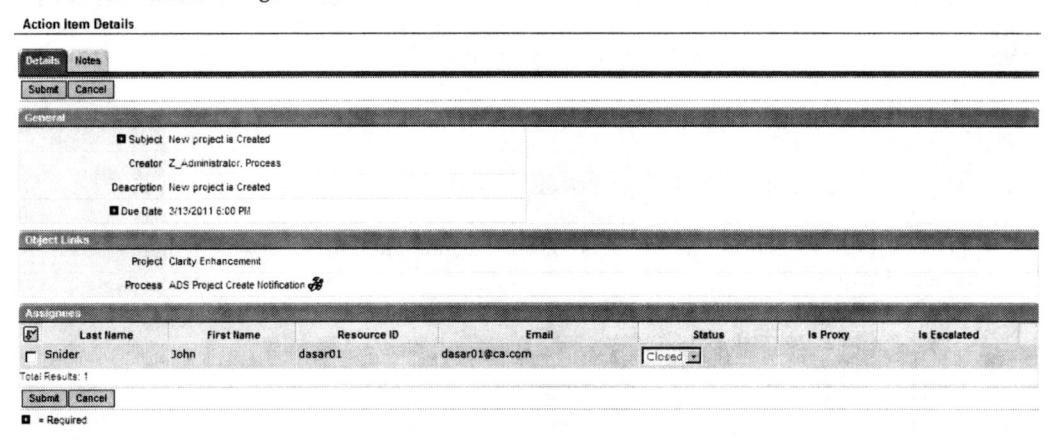

Figure 3-26. Action Item details

John can also create a new action item and assign assignees. A check mark in the Is Proxy column indicates whether the user assigned to the item was assigned by proxy. A check mark in the Is Escalated column indicates that the action item has been escalated to John from someone else.

Tasks

The Tasks tab in the Organizer lists all the tasks a user has created or is assigned to work on by others. Figure 3-27 shows a snapshot of the Tasks tab. This tab is very useful for managing your day-to-day tasks, especially when there are a large number of tasks assigned. You can set the task status for effective management of your daily load.

Tip Changing the task status in the Organizer does not change the task status on the project.

CHAPTER 3 ■ A QUICK GLANCE AT CA CLARITY PPM

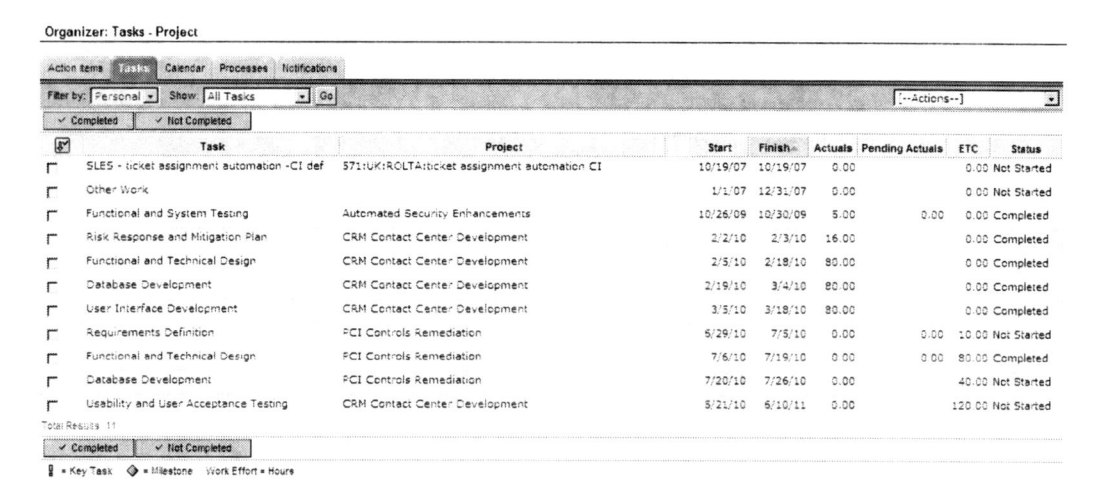

	Task	Project	Start	Finish	Actuals	Pending Actuals	ETC	Status
☐	SLES - ticket assignment automation -CI def	571:UK:ROLTA:ticket assignment automation CI	10/19/07	10/19/07	0.00		0.00	Not Started
☐	Other Work		1/1/07	12/31/07	0.00		0.00	Not Started
☐	Functional and System Testing	Automated Security Enhancements	10/26/09	10/30/09	5.00	0.00	0.00	Completed
☐	Risk Response and Mitigation Plan	CRM Contact Center Development	2/2/10	2/3/10	16.00		0.00	Completed
☐	Functional and Technical Design	CRM Contact Center Development	2/5/10	2/18/10	80.00		0.00	Completed
☐	Database Development	CRM Contact Center Development	2/19/10	3/4/10	80.00		0.00	Completed
☐	User Interface Development	CRM Contact Center Development	3/5/10	3/18/10	80.00		0.00	Completed
☐	Requirements Definition	PCI Controls Remediation	6/29/10	7/5/10	0.00	0.00	10.00	Not Started
☐	Functional and Technical Design	PCI Controls Remediation	7/6/10	7/19/10	0.00	0.00	80.00	Completed
☐	Database Development	PCI Controls Remediation	7/20/10	7/26/10	0.00		40.00	Not Started
☐	Usability and User Acceptance Testing	CRM Contact Center Development	5/21/10	6/10/11	0.00		120.00	Not Started

Figure 3-27. Organizer: Tasks tab

Calendar

Calendar events are milestones such as meetings or appointments that are scheduled for a specific time and location. A calendar event can include one or more participants.

The Organizer: Calendar page lists the entire calendar of events to which a resource has been invited or has created. There are three types of calendars in CA Clarity PPM.

Event Calendar

This is the calendar that the user can access via the Organizer: Calendar page. This calendar is used to create and view events and has daily, weekly, and monthly views. Figure 3-28 shows the Day view of the calendar.

77

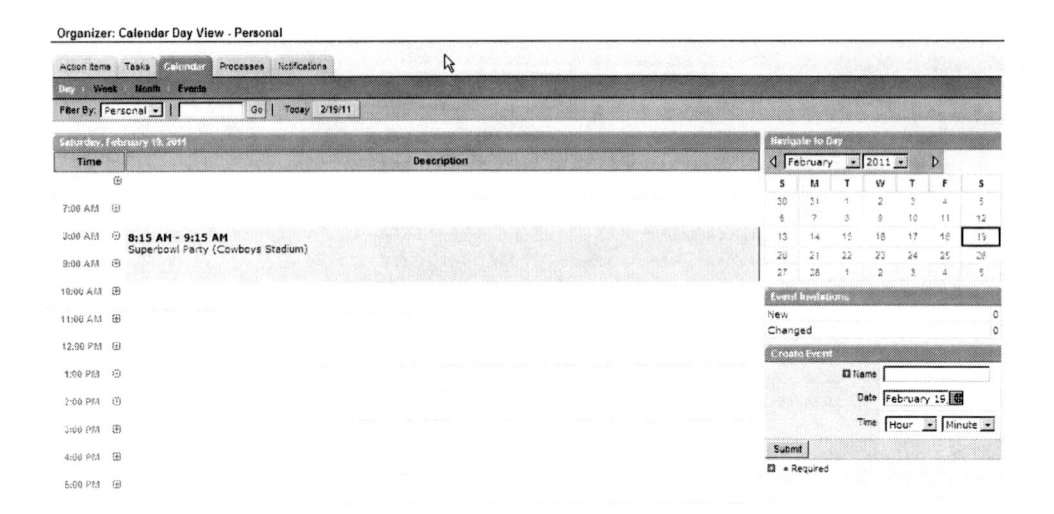

Figure 3-28. Calendar: Day view

Resource Calendar

The resource calendar shows resource availability for various assignments.

A resource can use the calendar to view or add working days, nonworking days, and changes to the resource's calendar. To access a resource's calendar, click the resource or role whose calendar needs to be viewed and then select the Calendar tab. Figure 3-29 shows a typical resource's calendar.

Figure 3-29. A resource calendar

CHAPTER 3 ■ A QUICK GLANCE AT CA CLARITY PPM

To mark a nonworking day, check the box next to the date and click Make Non-Workday. This blocks the resource availability for that date so that they are not considered for project staffing.

The CA Clarity PPM resource calendar provides the ability to modify a shift for a particular day, week, or month. For example, let's say John is working only four hours for the week of February 20. He can select all working days in that week and click the Set Shifts button, as shown in Figure 3-30.

Figure 3-30. Modifying a shift

Now John can set shifts for the week of February 20. Once the shift is set, his availability for that week is set to four hours, as shown in Figure 3-31.

Figure 3-31. Changing availability for the week

The Project Calendar

A project calendar is tied to each instance of a project and is available as a collaboration feature on a project. The project team member has to be a participant on a project to access the calendar. The Project calendar can be used by the project manager to schedule events, invite project participants, and view scheduled events. This calendar provides a daily, weekly, and monthly view, as shown in Figure 3-32.

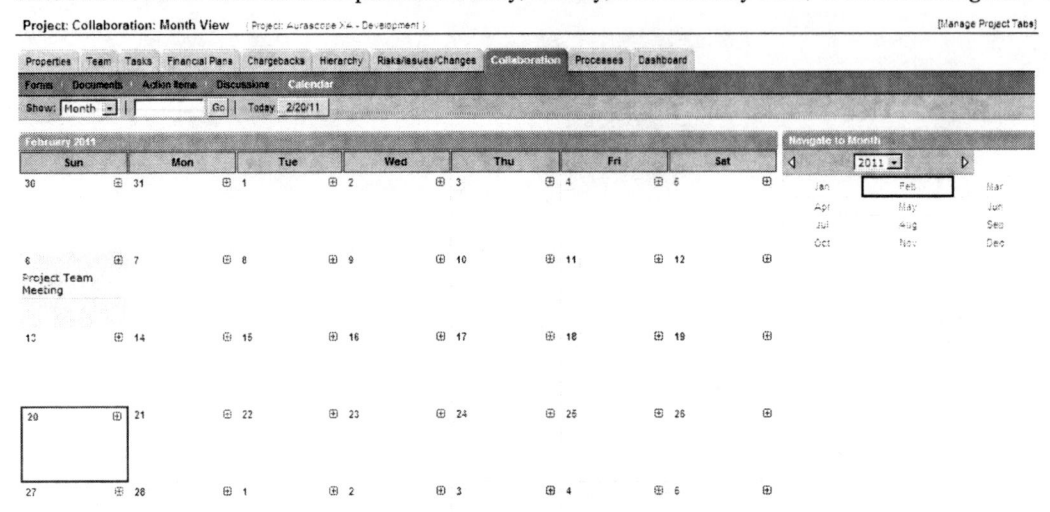

Figure 3-32. A project calendar

Processes

The Processes tab in the Organizer allows a user to view the following processes:

- *Initiated*: Process instances that a user had started or to which a user has a view access

- *Available*: A list of processes available for a user to initiate and/or to edit their process definitions based on access rights

Figure 3-33 shows the initiated processes.

CHAPTER 3 ■ A QUICK GLANCE AT CA CLARITY PPM

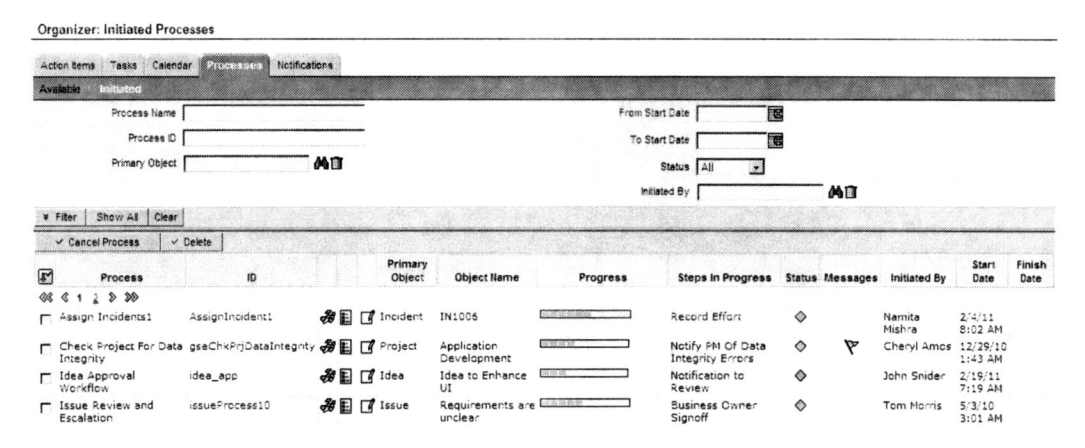

Figure 3-33. Initiated processes

Notifications

The Notifications tab in the Organizer shows a list of all notifications. It notifies a user of all new activities or changes in CA Clarity PPM. The method in which a user receives notifications depends on the notification method specified on the Account Settings: Notifications page.

The Organizer: Notifications page lists all of the alert notifications according to the notification's functional area, message content, data sent, sender's last name, or sender's first name, as shown in Figure 3-34. A user can receive notifications for the following objects/functional areas:

- Action items
- Change requests
- Discussions
- Documents
- Escalations
- Events
- Finance
- Incidents
- Issues
- Processes

81

- Projects
- Reports and jobs
- Requisitions
- Risks
- Timesheets

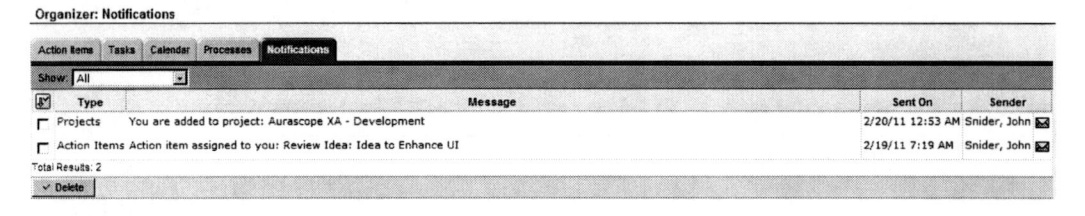

Figure 3-34. Notifications

Table 3-2 shows a comprehensive list of CA Clarity PPM tool notification criteria. This table shows whether notifications should be sent and, if so, to whom they should go.

Table 3-2. CA Clarity PPM Notifications

Notification Category	Trigger	Users Notified
Action Items	Workflow reaching a step with an action item configured.	Recipient(s) of the action item.
Change Requests	A change request is assigned/reassigned.	The resource selected in the field Raised By, as well as the owner of the change request, if changed.
Discussions	New messages are created, and the Notify option is enabled upon creating the message.	All or selected participants, depending on topic definition.
Documents	Check-in of a document and use of the Notify option.	Document owner.
Escalation	Escalation either succeeds or fails.	Only resources/groups identified as part of the escalation rules.
Events	Creating an event and reminder of an event, if notifying participants.	Selected participants.

Notification Category	Trigger	Users Notified
Incidents	Changing the Assigned To setting on an incident. Add a project manager and set Flagged for the Conversion field to True.	Resource that is identified in Assigned To. New project manager.
Issues	Creating an issue. Updating the ownership.	The resource selected in the field Created By, as well as owner of the issue, if changed.
Processes	Steps with notification options selected in the definition. Depending on the options: Step Started, Step Error, Step Completed.	Notification goes to selected roles, groups, resource, or resource field based information. Can also select to notify the owner.
Projects	A resource is added to a team as a participant (in other words, at the creation of a project; the default participants from the template), adding a team member to a project, replacing a resource.	The identified team member or participant. (Based on project settings, adding a team member can automatically make them a participant.) Note: If a resource is added to team on a project but is not a participant, then no notification is generated.
Reports & Jobs	Failure or completion of running a scheduled job or report based on the settings selected when submitting.	Resources or groups identified as part of the submission of the report or job.
Requisitions	Requisition status changes.	User in the Requested By field; users in the Booked By field (may be empty unless default).
Risks	Creating a risk. Updating the ownership.	The resource selected in the field Created By, as well as the owner of the risk, if changed.

Notification Category	Trigger	Users Notified
Timesheets	Timesheet is submitted. Timesheet is returned. Approver sends reminders via the Notify option.	Resources with approval rights for that timesheet submitted. Resource who submitted the timesheet. Identified resources for selected timesheets. Note: By default the resource manager does not get notification to approve a timesheet when the user submits a timesheet. The resource manager needs a timesheet approval right for the resource in order to receive notification.

Knowledge Store

While evaluating the CA Clarity PPM tool, Acme Data Systems had a requirement to store all project-related documents, business process guidelines, templates, resource resumes, and application forms in one central repository.

Users can access and manage their documents via the following:

- Knowledge Store

- Document Manager

Knowledge Store

The Knowledge Store is the central source of document repositories that ADS wants to publish to all or selected Clarity users. They can publish documents such as guidelines, project methodologies, forms, and so on. The folders and documents are protected by user security access rights. Figure 3-35 shows a snapshot of the Knowledge Store page.

Figure 3-35. Knowledge Store

The features available via the Knowledge Store are described next.

Create new folder structure

The create new folder structure feature shows the folder properties for the new folder to be created. Figure 3-36 shows a snapshot of the create new folder structure properties.

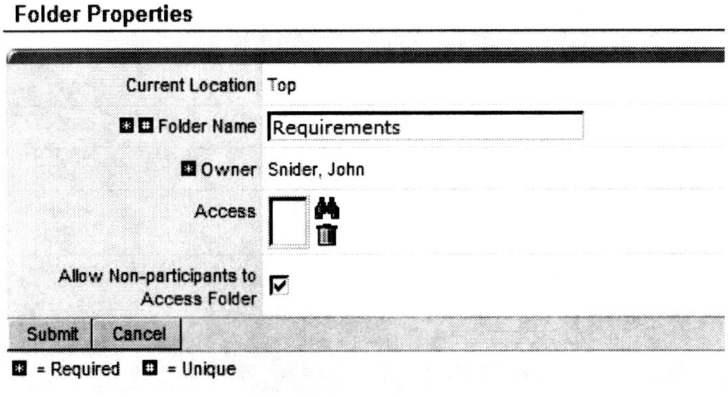

Figure 3-36. Folder Properties section

Add Documents

The Add Documents feature allows you to browse the file system and add documents. Figure 3-37 shows a snapshot of the Add Documents feature.

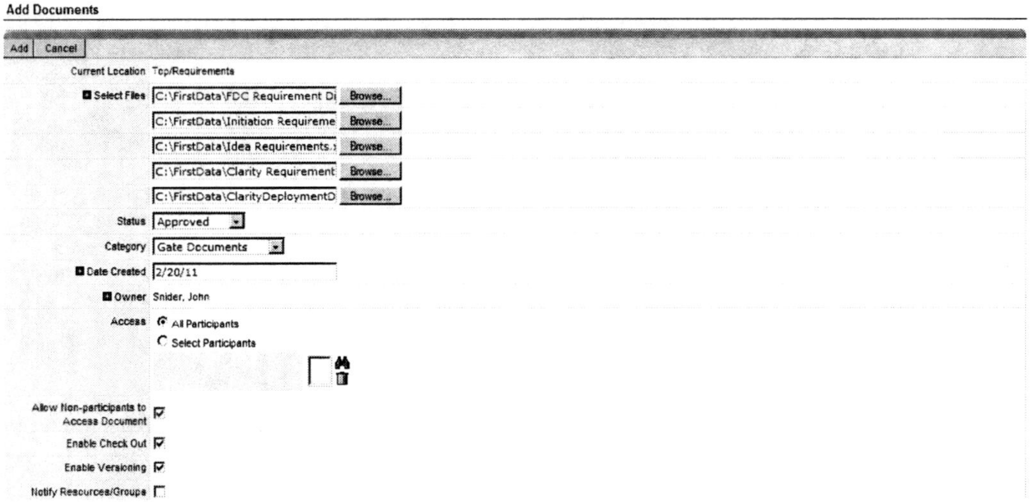

Figure 3-37. Add Documents feature

Set Document Permissions

The Set Document Permissions feature allows you to set permissions for documents. Figure 3-38 shows a snapshot of setting permissions on a document.

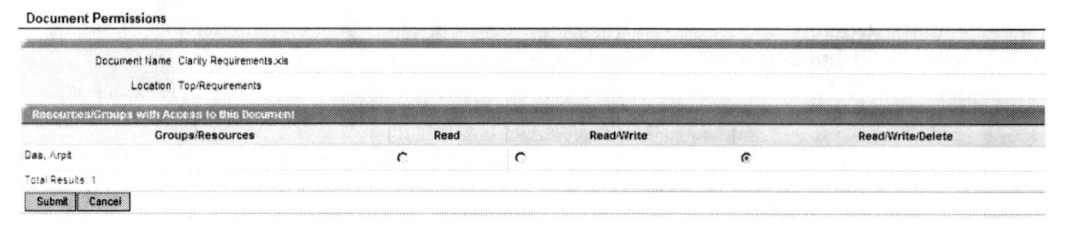

Figure 3-38. Set Document Permissions feature

Document Check-In and Checkout with Versioning

Figure 3-39 shows a snapshot of the document version details. The date, time, file size, person who checked in, and other details for each version of the document can be displayed.

Figure 3-39. Document versions

Document Manager

There are two places in the CA Clarity PPM tool where users can access Document Manager.

The first is through the Documents link on the Collaboration tab for any instance of a project, as shown in Figure 3-40. A user has to be added as a participant on a project to access the collaboration feature. The Document Manager can be used by the project manager and project team members to store project-related documents.

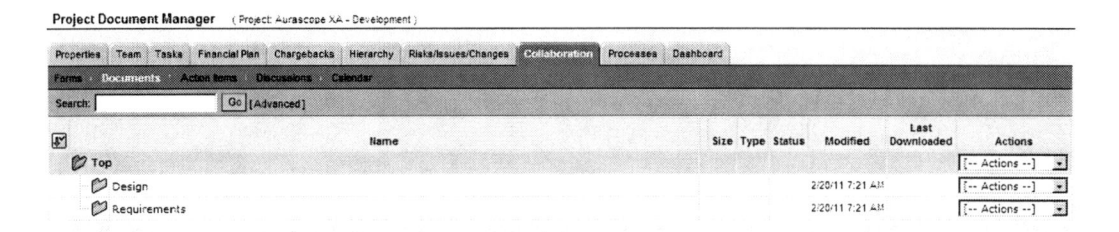

Figure 3-40. Accessing the Document Manager through the Collaboration tab

The other place is through the Document Manager tab on the Resource Properties page, as shown in Figure 3-41. This document repository can be used to store resource-related documents such as a skill sets spreadsheets, resumes, and so on. The access to these documents under Document Manager is controlled by the user's security access rights.

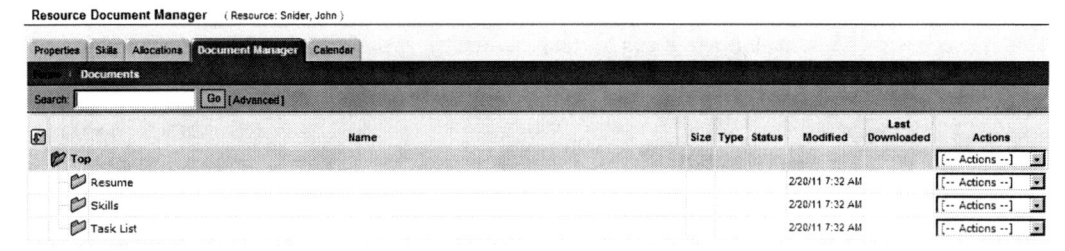

Figure 3-41. Accessing the Document Manager through the Resource Properties page

A document approval process can be created and initiated for uploaded documents.

Personalization

As mentioned in the "User Interface" section, Acme Data Systems wants to implement a tool that is easy to configure by the end users. Using CA Clarity PPM ADS, users can easily configure their views and change their personal settings such as the time zone, their contact information, their passwords, and so on.

Account Settings

The Account Settings link in the Personal section allows a user to change their personal settings and set a proxy, font settings, notifications, and software downloads. Figure 3-42 shows a snapshot of the Personal section.

Figure 3-42. Personal section

Personal Settings

Figure 3-43 shows the settings available to users in the Personal Information subpage under Account Settings.

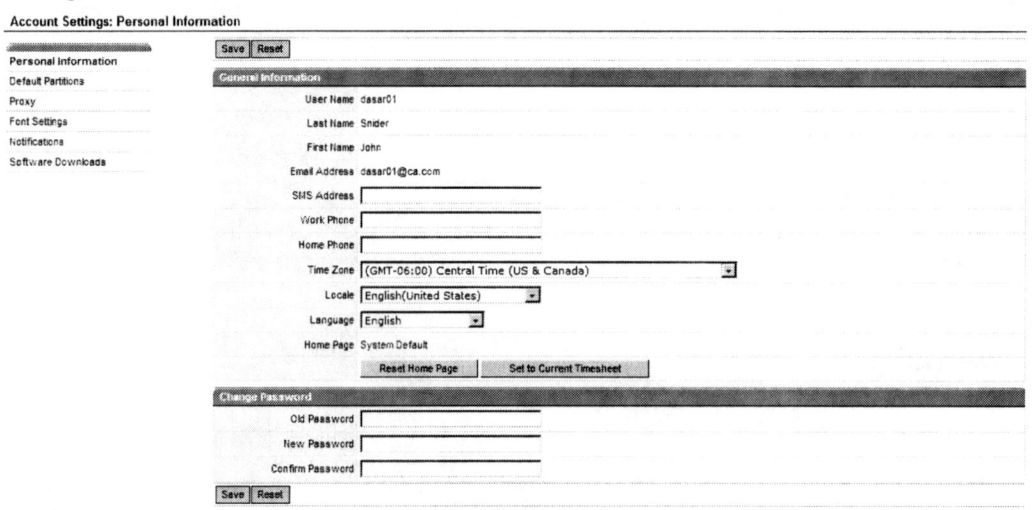

Figure 3-43. Personal Information subpage under Account Settings

Default Partitions

With partitions, organizational units can implement and see CA Clarity PPM (pages, processes, user interface themes) in different ways. Partitions allow an organization to deploy and support different fields, forms, processes, methodologies, and branding as well as control content access rights within an organization. The Default Partitions link is available only when partitions are defined in CA Clarity PPM and the user is associated with the partitions. A user has options to change the partition association and to configure their object views and the UI theme. Figure 3-44 shows a sample Default Partitions page.

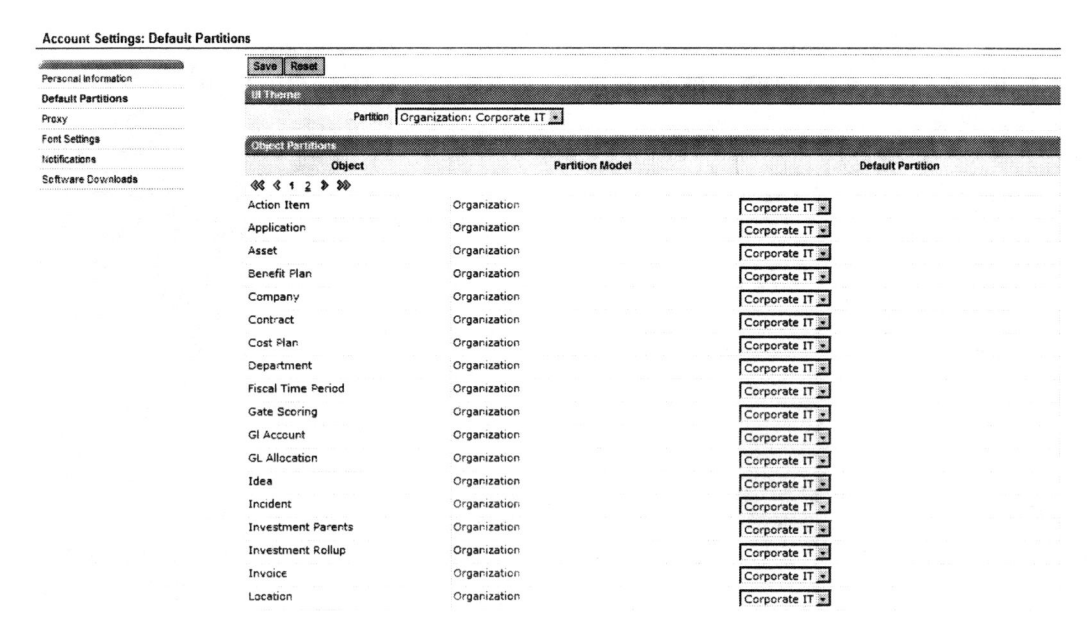

Figure 3-44. Default Partitions page under Account Settings

Proxy

A proxy allows a user to temporarily delegate Clarity action items to the user designated in the resource field. The designated proxy user will receive action items for the users they are acting as proxy for. These action items will appear on the Action Items tab in the Organizer and also on the Action Items view on the Overview page. The Proxy field has a check mark if they are receiving action items as a proxy user. Also, a user can view the list of resources for which they are acting as a designated proxy user, as shown in Figure 3-45.

Figure 3-45. Proxy user

> **Tip** Setting a user as a proxy only delegates action items to the proxy user. It *does not* transfer any security rights of the user for whom they are acting as the designated proxy. For example, if John is acting as a proxy for Beth while she is on vacation, John receives action items to approve time for direct reports of Beth. John has not been granted view/edit timesheet rights for Beth's direct reports, so he will not be able to open and review timesheets for the resources. Beth needs to provide with John instance rights to view/edit her direct reports if she wants John to view their timesheets.

> **Tip** Please contact CA Services Global Delivery if there is a need for a solution where security rights need to be granted or revoked based on proxy start and end date.

Font Settings

The Font Settings feature allows users to set font settings for the Clarity UI. Figure 3-46 shows a snapshot of the Font Settings page.

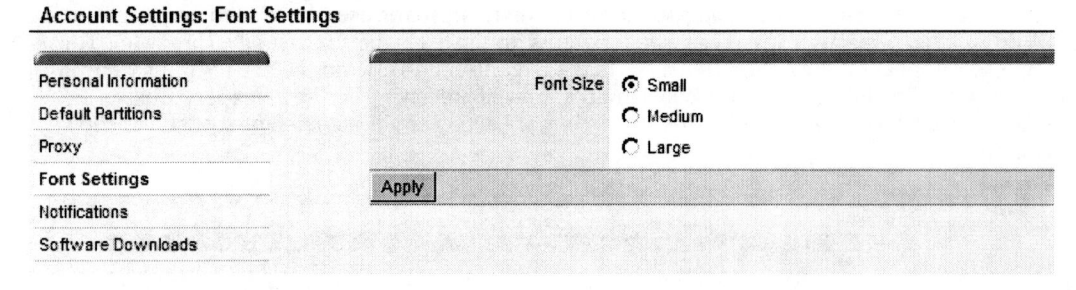

Figure 3-46. Font Settings page

Notifications

The Notifications subpage allows a user to control the notifications and mode of notifications coming out of CA Clarity PPM, as shown in Figure 3-47. These settings are controlled at a user level and cannot be pushed by the system administrator.

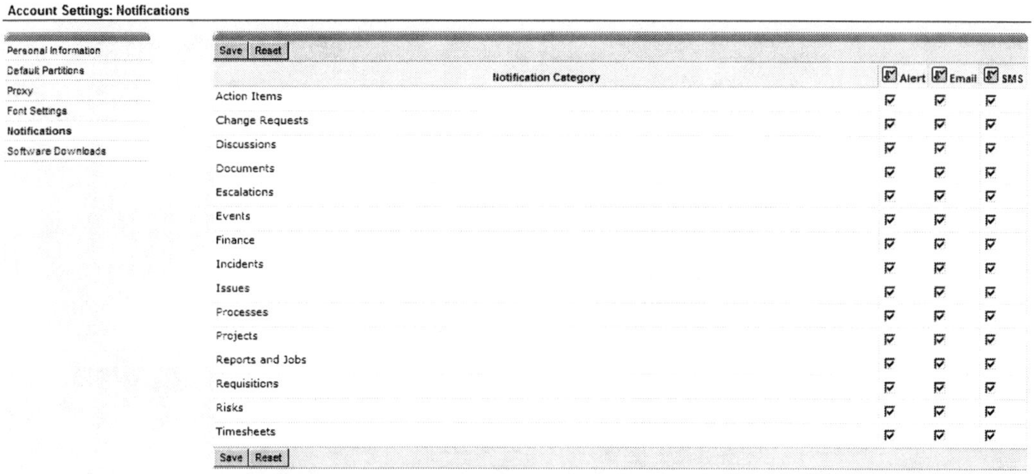

Figure 3-47. Notifications page

> **Tip** CA Services Global Delivery has created an add-on services component called CA Clarity PPM User Notification Manager.

The CA Clarity PPM User Notification Manager provides the following two flavors:

Initially set notification preferences: This option allows an organization's system administrator to initially set the notification preferences of all of their end users in each of the 15 notification categories, and it can be implemented without the next option. Even if an organization wants to allow their end users to later manage their own notification preferences, per native CA Clarity functionality, this option is useful to set the desired defaults for each end user so that they need not do these themselves.

Subsequently enforce notification preferences: This option allows an organization to prevent their end users from changing their notification preferences from those specified in the Notification Administration custom object. A prerequisite to utilize this option is to first implement the previous option.

Software Downloads

The Software Downloads link allows a user (if security access is provided) to download third-party software required to use additional functionalities of the CA Clarity PPM tool. Figure 3-48 shows a snapshot of the Software Downloads page.

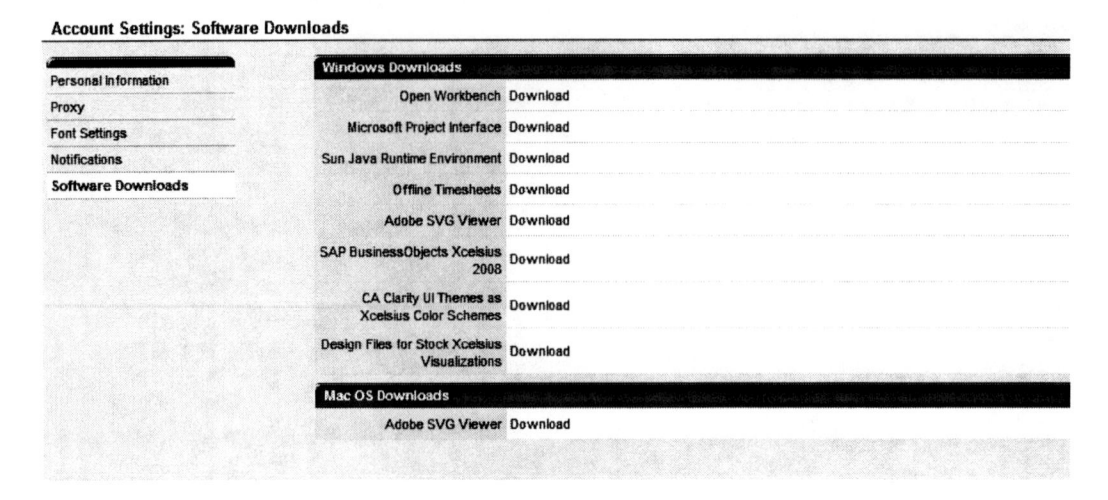

Figure 3-48. Software Downloads page

Personalize the Overview Page

Acme Data Systems users can create their own custom workspace by personalizing the contents of the Overview: General page. They can use the Personalize and Manage My Tabs links to change the appearance of their Overview: General page. Figure 3-49 shows a snapshot of the Overview: General page.

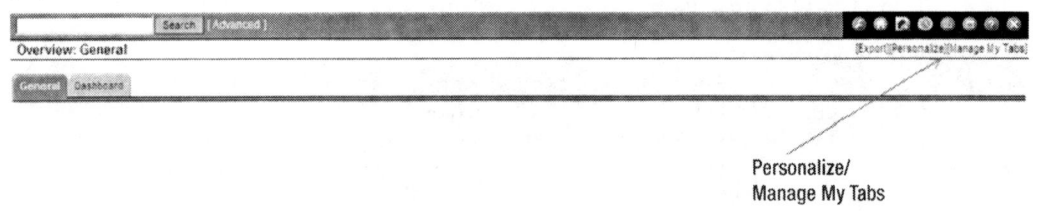

Figure 3-49. Overview: General page

Personalize Link

The Personalize link gives the users the option of adding or removing portlets from the Overview: General page. Adding a new portlet is dependent on the user's access rights. Figure 3-50 shows the Personalize: Page Content page.

Figure 3-50. Personalize: Page Content page

You can change the title of the portlet page by clicking the title of the portlet, as shown in Figure 3-51.

Figure 3-51. Changing the title

You can also add filter portlets that coordinate filtering operations between portlets to any tab that appears on the Overview: General page, as shown in Figure 3-52.

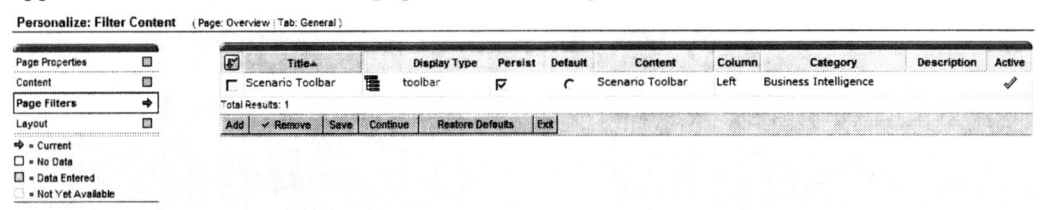

Figure 3-52. Personalize: Filter Content page

In addition, you can change the Overview: General page layout and rearrange the page content, as shown in Figure 3-53.

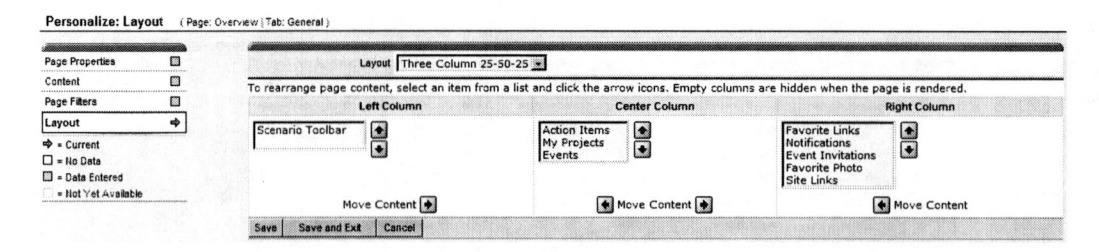

Figure 3-53. Rearranging page content

Manage My Tabs

The Manage My Tabs link allows users to add new tabs on their Overview: General page and add/modify contents of the tab, as shown in Figure 3-54.

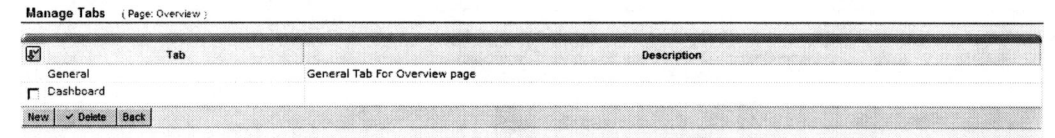

Figure 3-54. Manage Tabs page

Reports and Jobs

Acme Data Systems wants its users to access and run reports from the CA Clarity PPM tool. The company wants to restrict access to confidential reports. In addition, the company wants certain users to schedule and run jobs in CA Clarity PPM. The users having access enabling them to run reports and jobs can click the Reports and Jobs link in the Personal section of the Menu Manager, as shown in Figure 3-55.

Link for Reports and Jobs

Figure 3-55. Reports and Jobs link

Reports

The Reports tab shows all the reports to which the user has access. Once the user clicks the Reports tab under Reports and Jobs link, they will be provided with all of the user parameters required to run the report. Reports can be run immediately or can be scheduled. Once the report is run, it can be saved in PDF, DOC, RTF, and Excel formats.

Jobs

The Jobs tab shows all the jobs to which the user has access. Once the user clicks the Jobs tab under Reports and Jobs link, they will be provided with all the user parameters required to run the job. Jobs can be run immediately or can be scheduled. Available jobs are all the available jobs to which a user has access. Scheduled jobs are all jobs that are scheduled, based on the access rights. The log shows the completion status of the jobs that either the user has executed or the user is set as the assignee in the Sharing section.

Other Configuration Options in Clarity

So, what is *configurable* in Clarity? The following is a description of *customization* vs. *configuration*.

Any configuration performed within the Clarity interface itself is fully supportable by CA. CA tends to call this type of customization *configuration* rather than *customization*.

In general, the following can be configured within Clarity by an administrator:

- Replace Clarity bitmaps

- Add custom attributes to objects (such as projects and resources)

- Modify the left navigation menu

- Add tabbed portlet pages

- Configure object subpages, properties subsections, and so on

- Configure list views

- Configure filter views

- Assign color themes

- Create processes

The Clarity logos in the upper left of each screen can be replaced, as shown in Figure 3-56.

CHAPTER 3 ■ A QUICK GLANCE AT CA CLARITY PPM

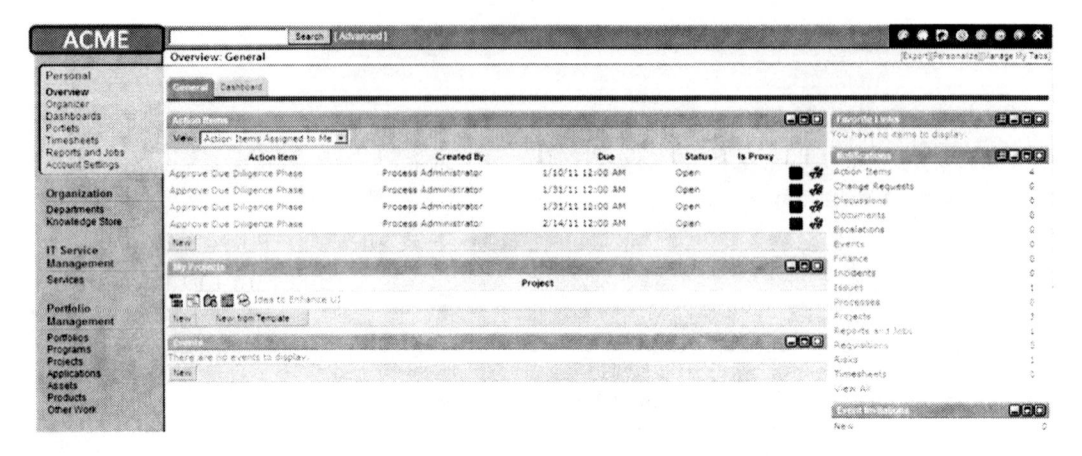

Figure 3-56. Customized logos

In the navigation bar, the link names and sequencing are customizable, as shown in Figure 3-57.

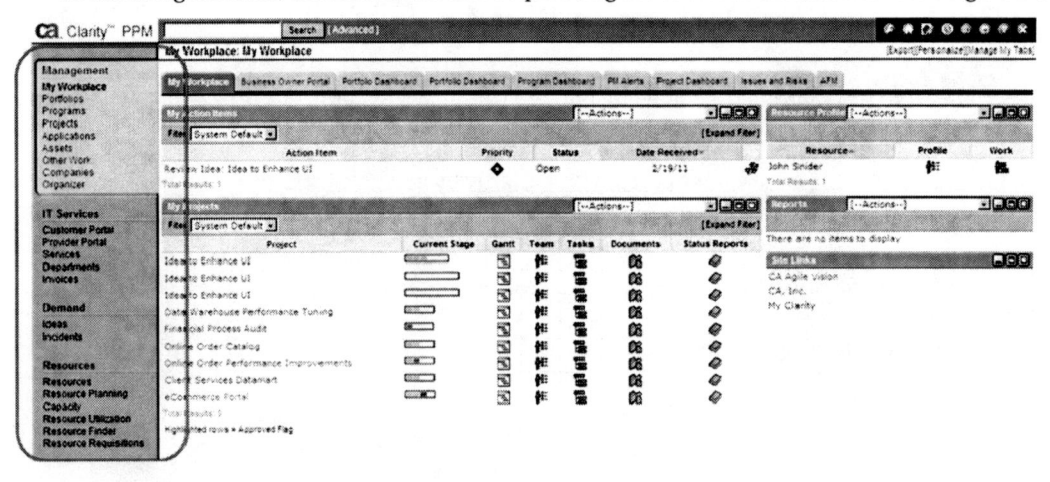

Figure 3-57. The navigation bar is customizable.

List pages (projects, resources, and programs) display multiple instances of an object in a view. These pages tend to be customizable, as shown in Figure 3-58.

CHAPTER 3 ■ A QUICK GLANCE AT CA CLARITY PPM

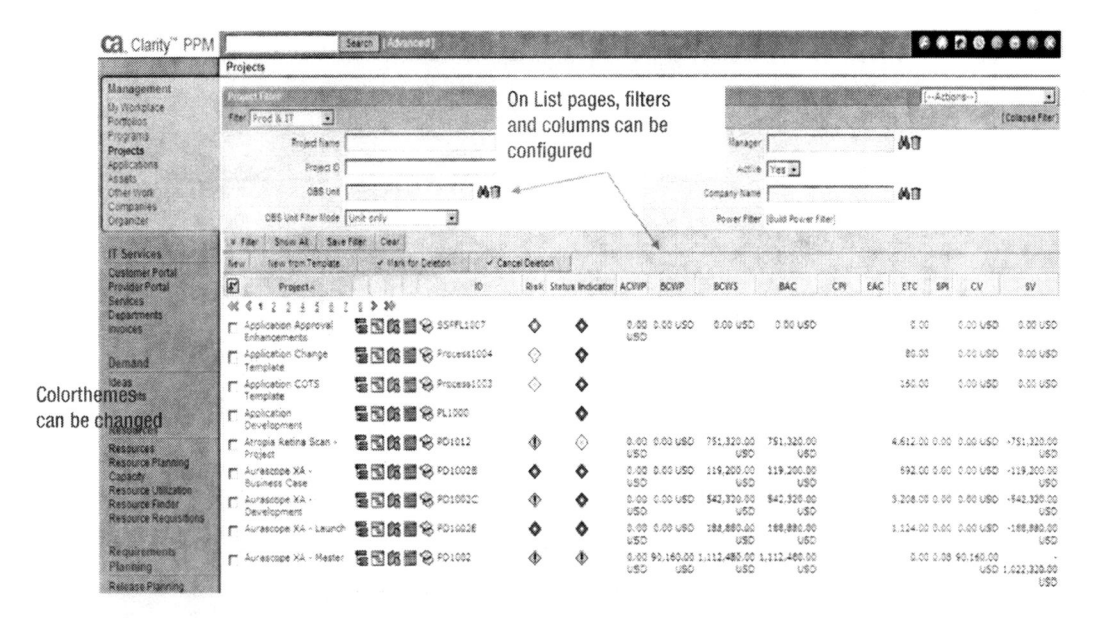

Figure 3-58. List pages are customizable.

Object properties provide users with the details for a single object (i.e., projects and resources) and usually have multiple tabs, sublinks, subpages, and field attributes, as shown in Figure 3-59. Many of these items can be configured, as shown in Figure 3-59. They are as follows:

- Addition of personalized tabs

- Subpage section names

- Field attributes

- Drop-down values

- Subpages: addition/deletion/rename

- Subobjects: addition/deletion/rename

However, the following items cannot be modified, as shown in Figure 3-59:

- Button labels

- Labels for tabs

- Labels for sublinks that display under tabs

97

- Labels for links that display in brackets
- Labels for items listed in "action" menus
- Labels for system pages

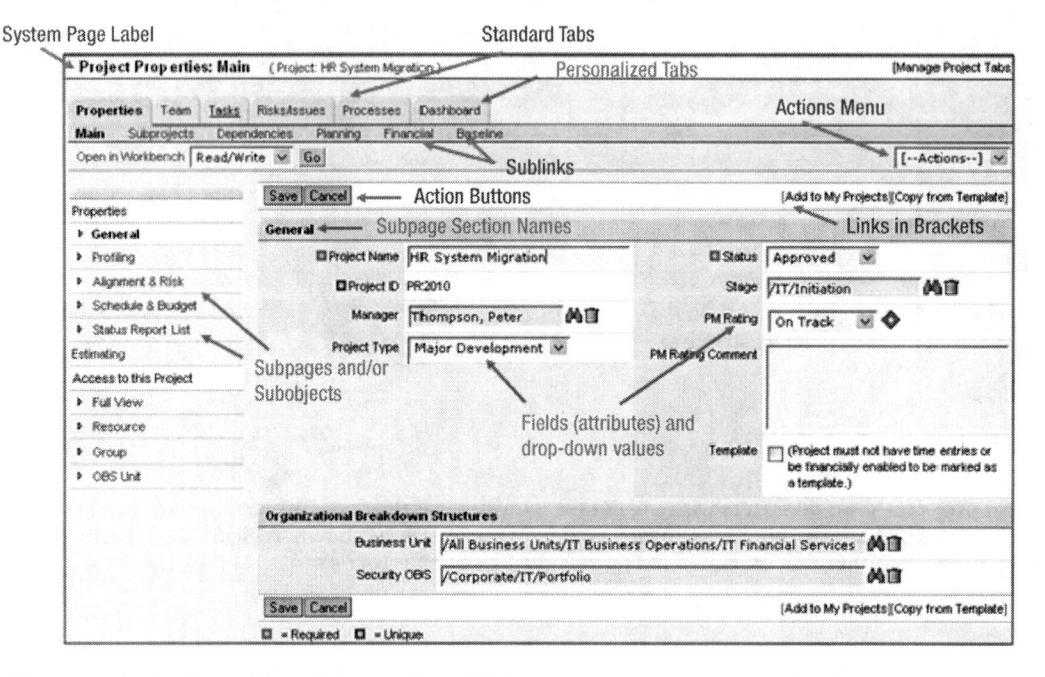

Figure 3-59. Configurable and nonconfigurable items

Summary

In this chapter, we gave a quick overview of the CA Clarity PPM tool and how the tool can be easily configured for end users. We described tips that are helpful for users and system administrators. Please contact CA Services or CA Services Global Delivery for any customization needs you may have.

PART 2

CA Clarity PPM Modules

In this part, each chapter gives an overview of one of the PPM modules and walks you through some of the most common tasks so that you can get a sense of how they work.

The different modules (and therefore chapters in this part) in PPM are:

- Project Management
- Resource Management
- Time Management
- Financial Management
- Demand Management
- Portfolio Management
- Process Management

CHAPTER 4

CA Clarity PPM Components: Project Management Module

The Project Management Body of Knowledge (PMBOK) defines projects as "a temporary endeavor undertaken to create a unique product, service, or result." A project could be about building a bridge, constructing a building, or developing a railway reservation system. In each of these cases, the effort will have a finite start and an end date and will create something unique—the bridge, the building, or the railway reservation.

Projects help organizations meet their strategic goals. They may need to be undertaken because of the following factors:

- A market demand for a new product

- A legal or regulatory requirement

- An organizational need

- Technology obsolescence

Projects will have scope, time, and cost constraints. Project management deals with the challenge of effectively delivering results (achieving all the project goals while managing these constraints).

Project management today is a sophisticated discipline that requires the constant monitoring of key project parameters to increase the predictability of results. It includes, but is not limited to, the following:

- Defining the scope of the endeavor

- Identifying and requesting the right resources for working on the project

- Identifying and managing risks

- Drawing up the schedule (the sequence of activities to be performed, the dates, and the resources who will perform the activities)

- Determining the budget

- Tracking and managing changes in scope

- Monitoring and controlling the progress of the project

Successful project management increases the likelihood of good results, which means great products and services and happy customers.

CA Clarity PPM is based on a web services architecture and supports a flexible, phased approach to implementation. CA Clarity PPM offers customers like ADS pick-and-choose solutions that suit their organization's needs. In addition, it offers a flexible solution for implementations as small as 50 users to as large as 100,000 users, taking advantage of different modules offered within the tool. The chapters in this part of the book are dedicated to describing the modules of CA Clarity PPM.

The different modules in PPM are as follows:

- Project Management (the subject of this chapter)

- Resource Management

- Time Management

- Financial Management

- Demand Management

- Portfolio Management

- Process Management

To understand these modules in detail, an organization has to go through a maturity curve. We have ordered these modules according to the maturity curve and will discuss them in that order. In this chapter, we discuss the Project Management module. In the following chapters, we discuss the Resource Management and Time Management modules, which are also fundamental to master before moving up the maturity curve. Then we discuss the Financial Management module in Chapter 8. Finally, Chapters 9, 10, and 11 focus on the Demand Management, Portfolio Management, and Process Management modules, respectively.

Project Management

The Project Management module in Clarity PPM provides best-practice tools for estimating, budgeting, planning projects, allocating resources, and doing other project-related activities for your projects as defined earlier in this chapter. The module allows you to pick the level of detail you want to use for the project; it provides collaboration and scheduling tools, resource and costing resources, tracking tools, and predefined methodologies and templates to ease your project management processes.

Getting Started in the Project Management Module

A project is a set of activities designed to achieve a specific objective. A project has a definitive start and end date and consists of following key elements:

- Tasks
- Resources

Projects are guided by time, scope, and budget constraints that estimate the following:

- Task duration
- Project duration
- Project cost

Project Creation

In CA Clarity PPM, projects can be created in following four ways.

Clicking New on the Projects List Page

The Projects link appears in the Menu Manager within the left navigation of CA Clarity PPM. The New option in this page lets a user create a project from scratch, as shown in Figure 4-1, and the user has to enter all the required information. Users should be granted the Project - Create right to see the New button.

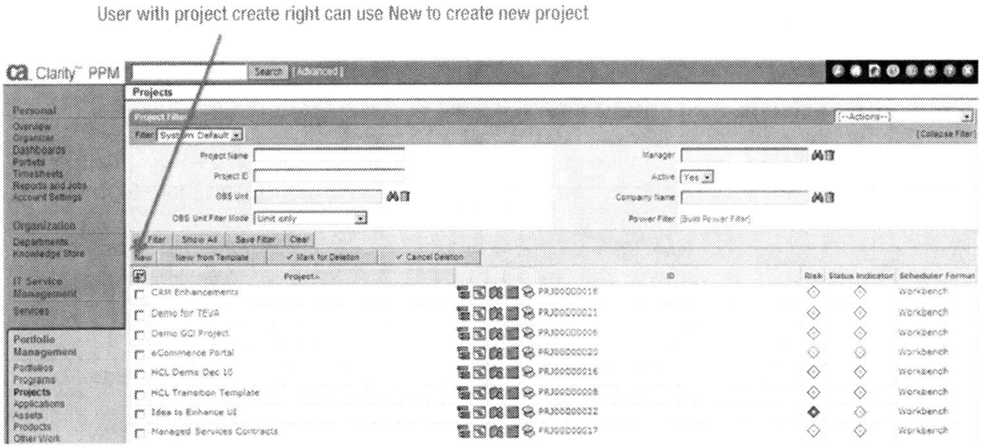

Figure 4-1. Creating a new project using the New option on the Projects list page

Clicking New from Template on the Projects List Page

The second way of creating a new project is to click the New from Template option on the Projects list page, as shown in Figure 4-2. This option allows the user to create a new project using a preexisting project template in CA Clarity PPM. The following data is copied from the template into the new project:

- Standard project attributes
- Organizational breakdown structure (OBS) unit associations
- Financial plan
- Document and folder structure
- Processes
- Staffing
- Tasks

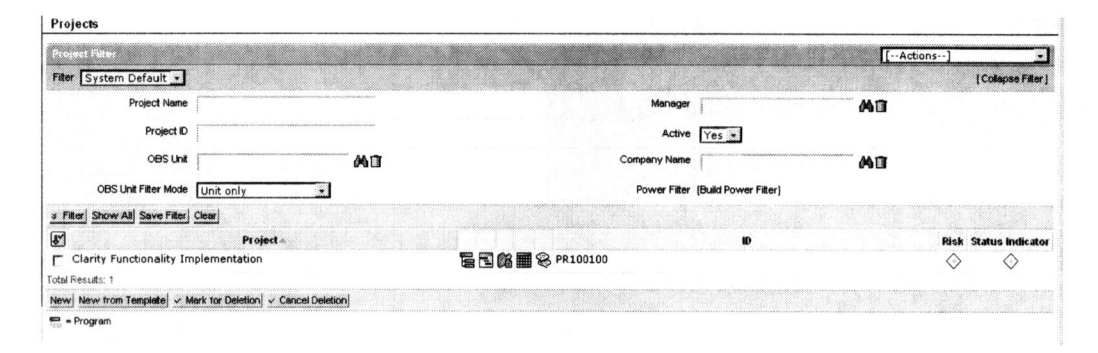

Figure 4-2. Creating a project using a preexisting project template

Once the user clicks the New from Template option, a list of project templates to which the user has View rights appears. By selecting a particular template, it copies the data from the template to the newly created project, as shown in Figure 4-3.

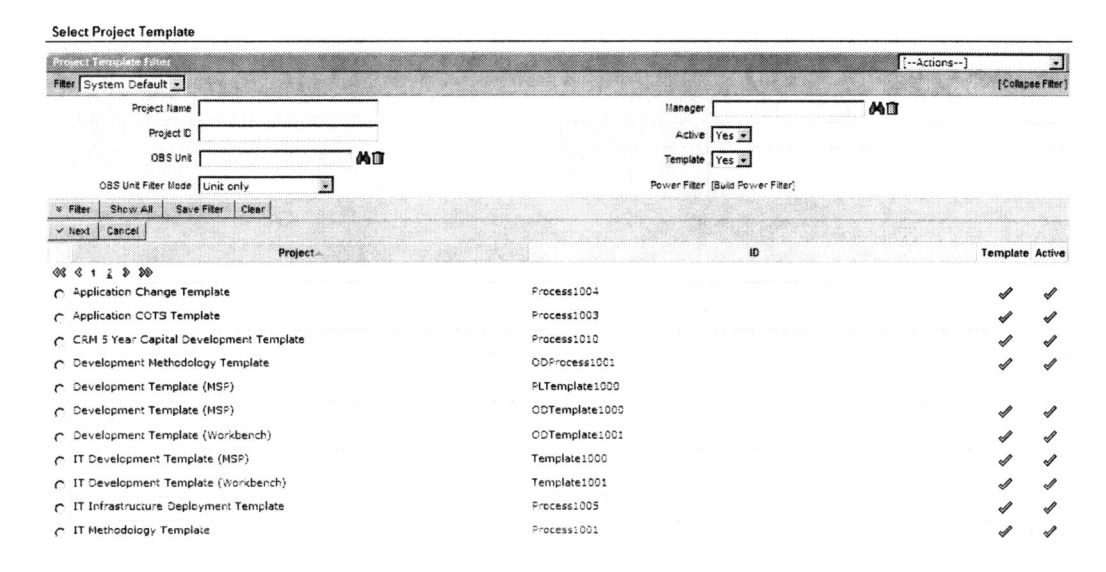

Figure 4-3. Selecting a project template

Convert an Idea to a Project

The third way of creating a project is to convert an approved idea into a project. The following data elements are copied from the idea to the new project:

- Standard idea attributes

- Custom idea attributes

Custom idea attributes are copied if the following conditions are met:

- If they are created within the investment object and are used in the idea and project views

- If idea and project attributes have the same ID

- If they are mapped via a mapping XML script and the process is used to convert the idea to a project

- If custom scripts are used to update attributes from an idea to a project

XOG in from an External System

The last way of creating a project is to import an external system via the XML Open Gateway (XOG) API in CA Clarity PPM.

Project Properties

This section briefly describes various project details (properties) that are part of the Project Management module in CA Clarity PPM, namely, general properties, the schedule, risk, and the budget.

General

The data elements in the General section capture basic project properties such as the goal, stage, alignment, and so on, as shown in Figure 4-4. The following is an overview of some of the key fields on the General page.

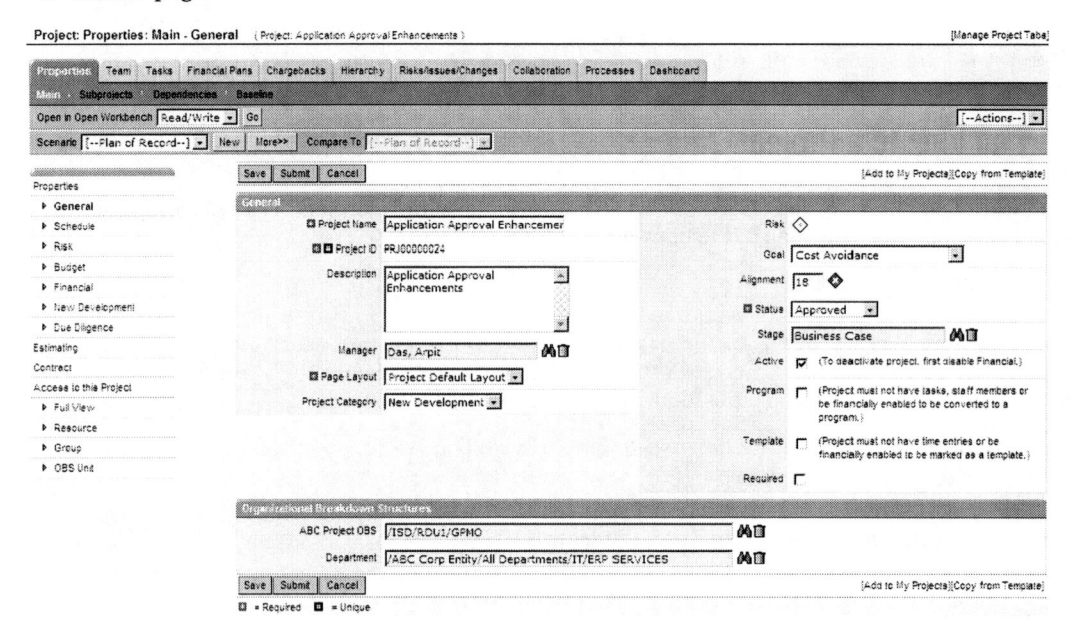

Figure 4-4. General project properties

Active

The Active field specifies whether the project is active. The project needs to be active for billing and to let users view projects in portfolios and in capacity planning portlets. Uncheck this box to deactivate the project. The project needs to be deactivated before it can be deleted. The project cannot be deactivated if there are open financial transactions and the financial status is not closed.

Program

This field allows the conversion of the project to a program. For projects to be used as a program, they cannot contain tasks, cannot contain staff member assignments, and cannot be financially enabled.

Template

This field specifies whether a user wants to use the project as a template for other projects.

Note For projects to be used as templates, they cannot have time entries against them or be financially enabled.

Required

This field is used during scenario generation, and it specifies whether this project should be pinned (included in the portfolio scenario)

Organizational Breakdown Structures

The organizational breakdown structure (OBS) section in a project allows OBS security enablement, with filtering based on organization and for reporting purposes. The department OBS is used to associate the project with a department that then associates the project with an *entity* and financially enables the project. If a project is associated with multiple OBSs, then the department OBS is last in order.

Schedule

This section captures a project's start and end dates, time tracking mode, and earned-value (EV) calculation options, as shown in Figure 4-5.

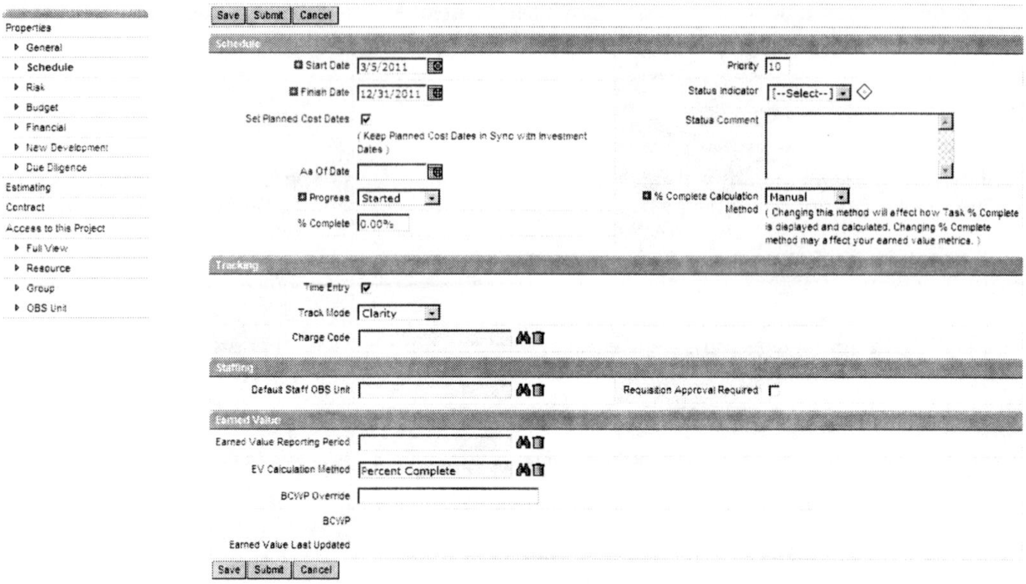

Figure 4-5. *Schedule properties of a project*

The following are a few important data elements on the Schedule subpage.

Time Entry

As shown in Figure 4-5, this field is under the Tracking section. The check box in this field opens the project for time entry. In addition, the team member should be enabled for time entry. This check box controls time entry only at the project level. In addition to this, time entry should be enabled at the resource, team member, and task levels for time entry to happen.

Track Mode

After Time Entry is the Track Mode field. The selection in Track Mode indicates the tracking method used to enter time for an investment. There are several options to choose from, as follows.

Clarity

This option of time entry allows for the assigned staffed members to use Clarity timesheets.

None

This option indicates that time entry using Clarity timesheets is not applicable. Nonlabor resources, such as expenses, materials, and equipment, track actuals through transaction vouchers or through a scheduler, such as CA's Open Workbench or Microsoft Project.

Other

This option also indicates that time entry using Clarity timesheets is not applicable. The actuals are imported from a third-party program.

As Of Date

This field defines the date by which the information is to be included in time and budget estimates. This date is used in earned-value analysis (EVA) calculations, such as budgeted cost of work scheduled (BCWS).

% Complete Calculation Method

This field specifies the method for calculating the percent complete value for the project and tasks. There are several methods to choose from, as follows.

Manual

This method is used to manually enter the percent complete for the project, summary task, and detailed task levels. The % Complete field is on the task properties page.

Duration

This method is used to track the percent complete based on duration. The duration is a measure of the total span of active working time for a task, based from the start date to the finish date of a task. With this method, you enter the percent complete for the detail tasks. The percent complete for summary tasks is automatically calculated based on the following formula:

`Summary Task % Complete = Total Detail Task Duration Complete / Total Detail Task Duration`

Effort

This method is used to calculate the percent complete for summary and detail tasks automatically based on the work units completed by resource assignments. The calculations are based on the following formulas:

`Summary Task % Complete = Sum of Detail Task resource assignment Actuals / Sum of Detail Task resource assignment Effort`

`Detail Task % Complete = Sum of resource assignment Actuals / Sum of resource assignment Effort`

Tip If you are using CA Clarity PPM with Microsoft Project or if you are using an external job to calculate the percent complete, select manual as the percent complete calculation method.

> **Tip** If assigning a resource other than labor to a task and the % Complete Calculation Method field on the scheduling properties page is set to Effort, the effort and actuals for that resource are ignored in the calculation.

Risk

CA Clarity PPM allows you to capture project risks (based on an organization's maturity), as shown in Figure 4-6. CA Clarity PPM gives you a risk score matrix (defined on the administration side) to determine the degree of risk (low, medium, or high) based on the risk's impact and probability factors. The risk probability values are plotted against the risk impact values. The intersection of every probability and impact value is the risk score. The probability and impact values are set for those projects that have detailed risks.

Risk capturing is done in two forms:

- You can do basic risk capturing based on certain categories. CA Clarity PPM offers standard out-of-the-box risk categories based on industry best practices. Each category has values of low, medium, and high, and then a weighted score is rolled up to the risk score attribute. Based on the score, the risk indicator shows red (68 to 100), yellow (34 to 68), or green (0 to 34). The lower the score, the lower the risk on the project. New categories can be added based on an organization's business requirements.

Figure 4-6. Risk properties of a project

CHAPTER 4 ■ CA CLARITY PPM COMPONENTS: PROJECT MANAGEMENT MODULE

- CA Clarity PPM offers a way to capture detailed risk based on predefined categories. Detailed risk can be created from the Risks/Issues/Changes tab on the project's properties page, as shown in Figure 4-7. Once the detailed risk is created for a particular category, that category becomes read-only on a basic Risk subpage. Figure 4-8 shows the basic and detailed risk capturing page for the risk Hardware Delayed.

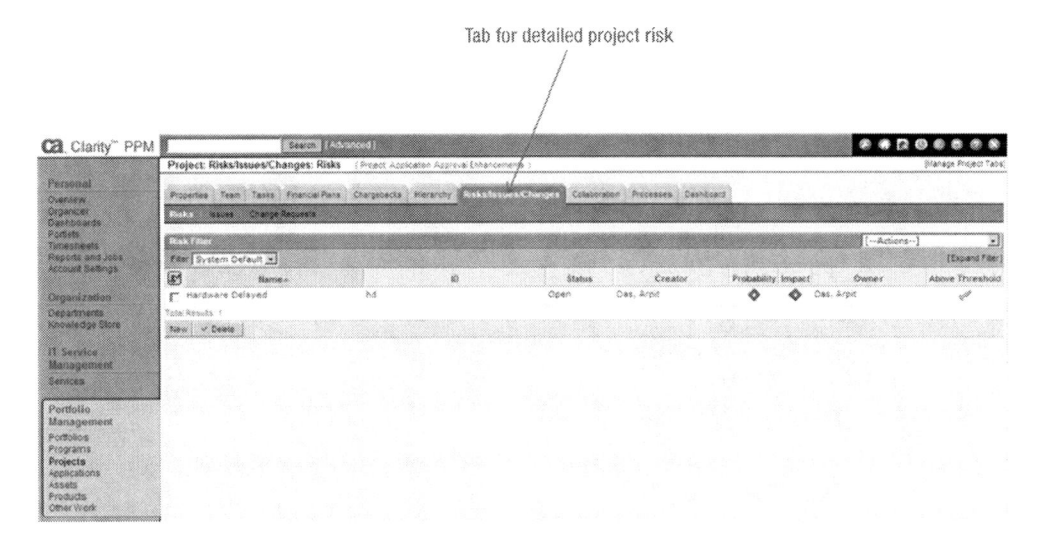

Figure 4-7. Risks/Issues/Changes tab

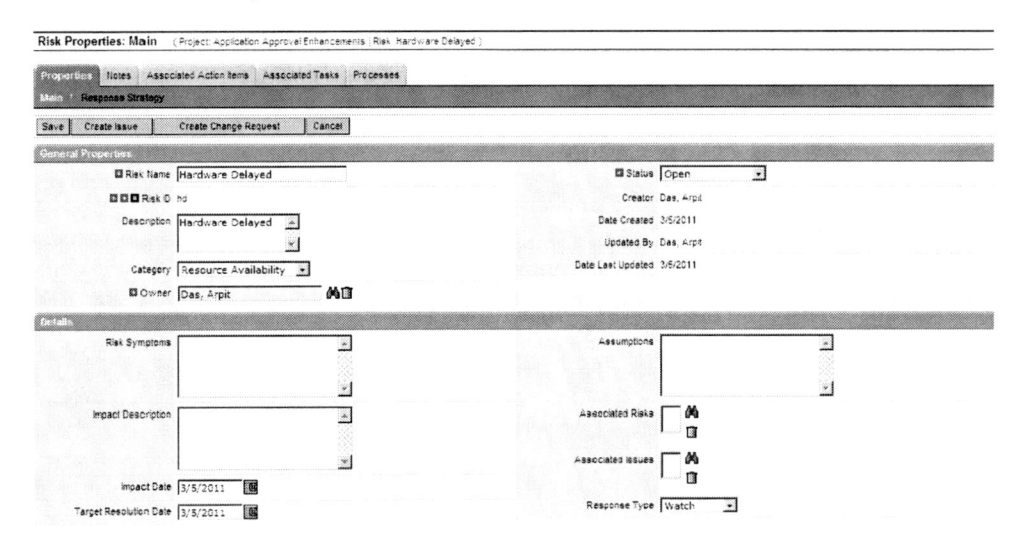

Figure 4-8. Adding basic and detailed risks

111

Since the risk in Figure 4-8 belongs to the Resource Availability category, this category becomes a read-only risk on the Risk subpage, as shown in Figure 4-9.

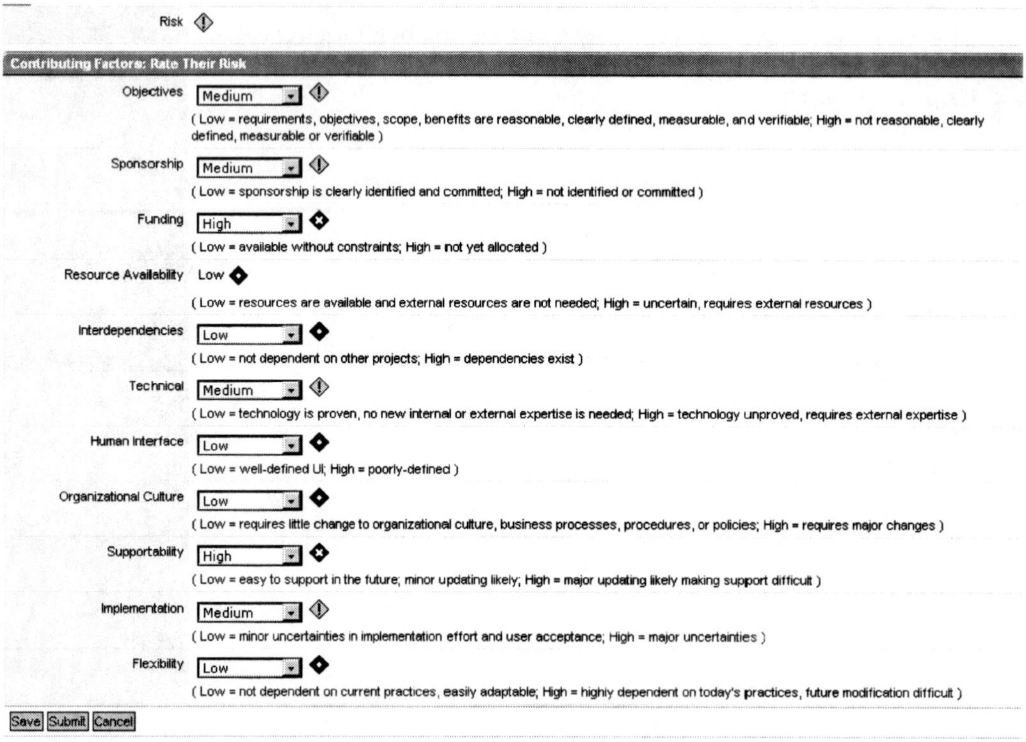

Figure 4-9. Resource availability is a read-only category.

Budget

CA Clarity PPM provides the ability to capture basic as well as detailed budget information. The Basic budget page provides the ability to capture planned cost, planned benefit, planned ROI, and planned NPV. The user has an option to enter planned NPV and ROI or let Clarity calculate it, as shown in Figure 4-10.

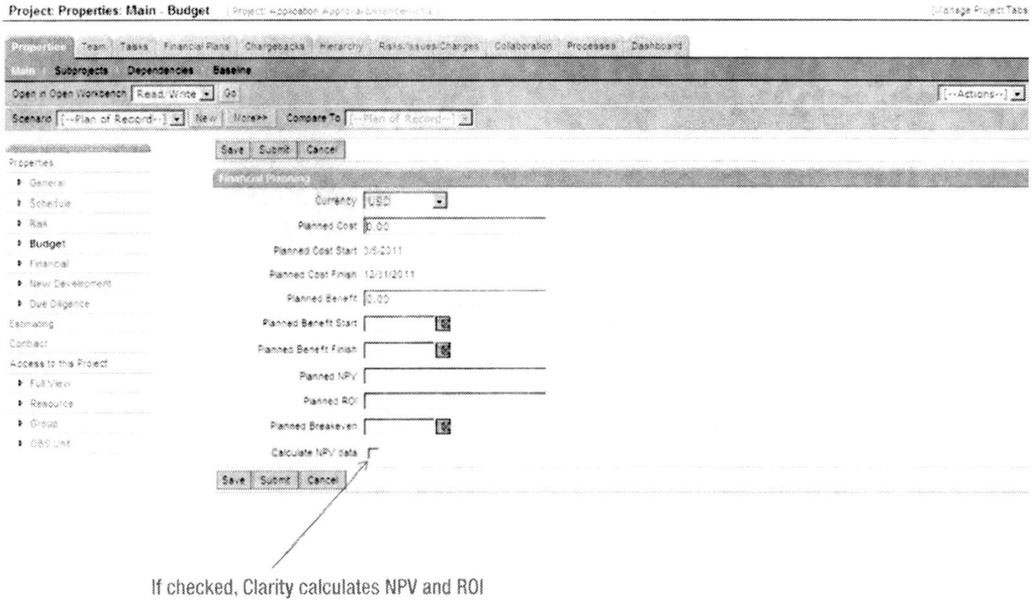

CHAPTER 4 ■ CA CLARITY PPM COMPONENTS: PROJECT MANAGEMENT MODULE

Figure 4-10. Budget properties of a project

CA Clarity PPM provides the ability to capture detailed budget data via these financial plans:

- Cost plan

- Benefit plan

- Budget plan

You can create a cost plan manually or by basing it on resource allocation or an assignment. The benefit plan is tied to the cost plan. The cost plan (plan of record), once approved, becomes the budget plan. You can see these plans on the Financial Plans tab, as shown in Figure 4-11.

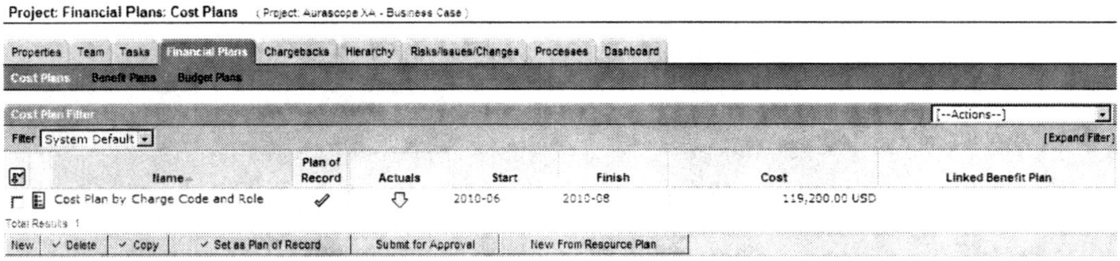

Figure 4-11. Financial plans

How Does Clarity Calculate Net Present Value?

The general formula for net present value (NPV) in a certain period is as follows:

`NPV(period) = PV(benefits, period) - PV(costs, period)`

where

`PV(value, period) = value/((1+ interest rate)^period)`

The *interest rate* corresponds to the period (for example, 12 percent annually implies a 1 percent interest rate if the periods are months). The *period* should be zero for the current period, and this assumes that the value is at the beginning of the period. The formula for NPV of a stream of benefits and costs is simply the previous formula applied to all time periods. The formula for ROI of a stream of benefits and costs is similar, where

`ROI = NPV / PV(costs, period)`

Note The calculations cannot be modified.

The data elements and terms used in the above formula are described below:

- *Actual cost*: Time is recorded by using timesheets or by entering transactions in CA Clarity PPM. Then these transactions are posted in WIP tables via a Post to WIP process. If the rates and costs are set in a matrix, the actual cost is calculated and populated.

- *Budgeted NPV*: This is the present value of the Budgeted Benefit distribution less the present value of the Budgeted Cost distribution; it can be directly entered or system-calculated.

- *Forecasted NPV*: This is the present value of the Forecasted Benefit distribution less the present value of the Forecasted Cost distribution; it can be directly entered or system-calculated.

- *Budgeted ROI*: This is the Budgeted NPV divided by the present value of the Budgeted Cost distribution; this can be directly entered or system-calculated

- *Forecasted ROI*: This is the Forecasted NPV divided by the present value of the Forecasted Cost distribution; it can be directly entered or system-calculated.

- *Budgeted Break-Even*: This is the end of the day on which the accumulated present value-adjusted budgeted benefits equal the accumulated present value-adjusted budgeted costs; it can be directly entered or system-calculated.

- *Forecasted Break-Even*: This is the end of the day on which the accumulated present value-adjusted forecasted benefits equal the accumulated present value-adjusted forecasted costs; it can be directly entered or system-calculated.

Note The code makes an explicit check that both revenue and cost are greater than 0.001; if either fails the test, then NPV, ROI, and Breakeven are explicitly set to NULL.

Automate "New From Resource Plan" Functionality

A cost plan is created from resource staffing on a project by using New From Resource Plan functionality. It allows the user to create a cost plan based on resource allocation on a project or a resource assignment on a task. CA Services Global Delivery has a prebuilt add-on script to automate this functionality by Clarity job. The component updates the Plan of Record cost plan based on the parameter specified as either Allocation or Assignment.

Team Tab

The project team is comprised of two types.

Project Staff

Project staff resources can be divided into two general categories:

- Labor resources are resources who work on investments and

  - Can be classified as roles or specific people
  - Can be allocated to investments
  - Can be assigned only to project tasks
  - Can submit timesheets

- Nonlabor resources are the equipment and materials and other necessary expenses required to complete the project. Figure 4-12 shows the project staff on the Team tab.

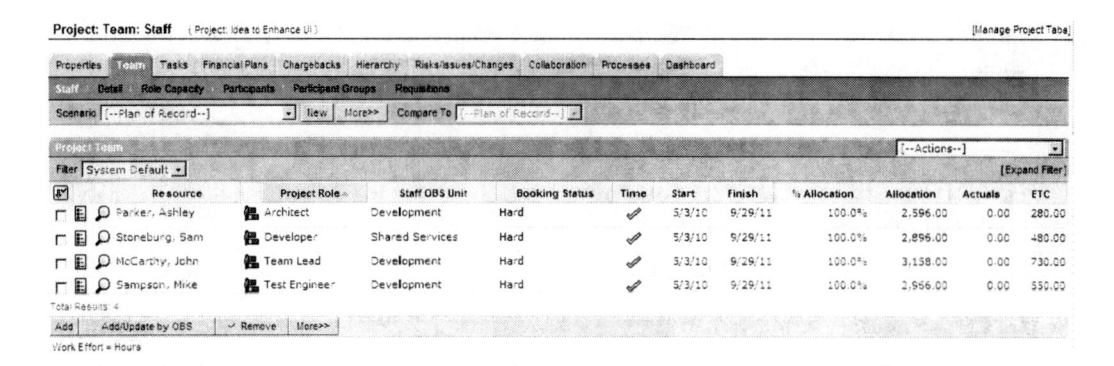

Figure 4-12. Project staff on Team tab

Participants

Participant resources are individuals who use a project's collaboration features and

- Are labor resources only

- Can include collaboration managers, who possess editing rights to all project collaboration areas

Collaboration features include the creation, storage, and sharing of project documents, action items, events, and discussions.

Figure 4-13 shows the participant resources on the Team tab.

Figure 4-13. Participants on the Team tab

There can be situations where a collaboration manager wants to add multiple resources who are part of a system group as participants. This can be done by selecting System Groups in the drop-down and then clicking Add to add a group. All the resources in that group become participants on that particular project. Figure 4-14 shows adding a group of participants for a given project.

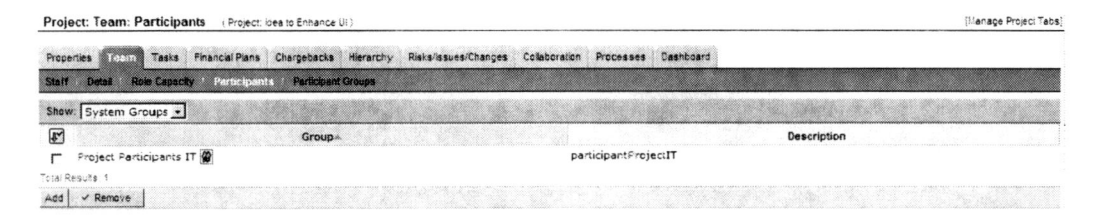

Figure 4-14. Adding a group of participants

Tip When a participant is added to a project, a notification is sent to that user about being added to the project.

Tip By default, the project creator becomes the collaboration manager.

Tip Only the collaboration manager can add new or remove existing participants.

Tip Only the collaboration manager can make other participants the collaboration manager.

Tip The collaboration manager has an actor icon in front of their name.

Tip The collaboration manager can create or delete discussion topics.

Tip The project manager is not a participant or the collaboration manager by default. The CA Services Global Delivery team has provided an add-on script that makes a project manager the collaboration manager.

Tip CA Services Global Delivery has an Outlook integration add-on component that sends calendar invites to project staff members when they are added to a project or removes entries from the calendar when the member is removed from the project.

Participant Group

Collaborators are not direct workers, so participants on a project can become quite numerous and can contribute in many different ways. Participant groups are created by the collaboration manager to help manage these resources. The collaboration manager can apply changes to a predefined participant group and so can impact large numbers of resources at once. Figure 4-15 shows the group properties of a participant group.

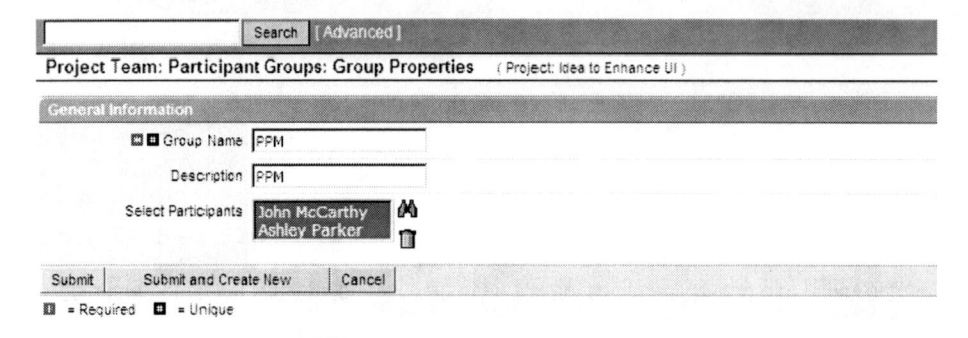

Figure 4-15. Participant group properties

Staffing Options

There are two staffing options.

Formal

In the formal staffing process, project managers relay any specific requirements for a resource or role to the resource manager through the resource requisition process. The resource manager can then search to find appropriate resources to fill these requirements and forward proposed resources to the project manager. Staffing using requisitions will be covered in the "CA Clarity PPM Resource Management" chapter

Informal

While specific procedures for informal staffing will vary depending on how the organization handles resource and role assignments, its primary feature is that managers themselves assemble their teams from those resources in the system to which they have access rights, rather than going through the resource manager. When a labor resource is added to the staff, the system can be configured to automatically make a participant list as well.

Booking

There are three staff booking options on a project: soft booking, hard booking, and mixed booking. They are discussed next.

Soft

Soft booking can be configured by a manager in a formal management environment. When resources are soft booked:

- Resources are usually allocated by the investment manager.

- The resource manager might need to confirm allocations.

- Resource availability will generally be decreased by the number of soft-booked allocations of the resource used for that investment.

- Resources can book their own time to the investment timesheets. Some portlets (such as Resource Planning) and searches do not treat soft booking as firm and so do not incorporate it into the remaining availability calculations.

Hard

In a formal resource management environment, the hard booking status indicates that the resource manager has approved the investment allocation. In an informal resource management environment, the hard booking status indicates that the investment manager owns the resource and has chosen to indicate a firm booking. A manager with hard booking rights can also create soft bookings.

Mixed

The mixed booking option can be set only by the CA Clarity PPM system. It identifies where the values in the Planned Allocation segments do not match the Hard Allocation segments. When there is a mixed booking, allocation segments can be aligned using the Accept Hard allocation option or the Commit Planned Allocation option.

Collaboration

A participant of a project has access to the Collaboration tab in a project, as shown in Figure 4-16. The collaboration feature includes the following:

- Forms

- Documents

- Action items

- Discussions

- Calendar

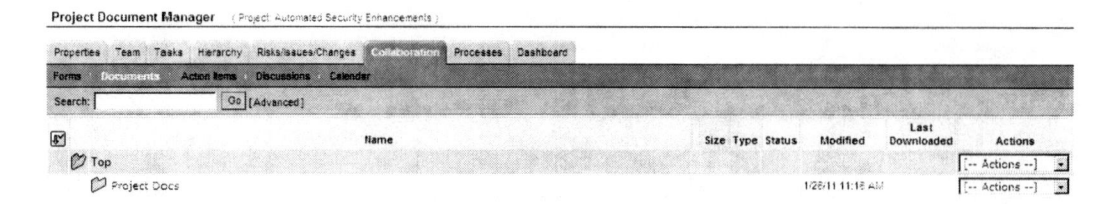

Figure 4-16. Collaboration tab

> **Tip** If a user is unable to see the Collaboration tab, it's possible that the user is not a participant on a project.

> **Tip** By default, the project manager is not a participant and so will not be able to see the Collaboration tab. The project manager needs to be added as a participant to see the Collaboration tab.

> **Tip** Forms are not used and cannot be created on CA Clarity PPM version 8.*x* onward but are available for backward compatibility.

Task Tab

Tasks within the project determine what needs to be done to complete the project, who will do the work, and how long it will take. A work breakdown structure (WBS) enables you to organize tasks and create a project schedule from those tasks. Each task has its own set of properties, which drives how tasks react to other tasks within your project plan. Putting in logical links, or *dependencies*, between tasks and milestones creates the project plan. Figure 4-17 shows the tasks of a typical project.

The Task tab allows a project manager to do the following:

- Create tasks
- Define a WBS
- Define task properties
- Create dependencies
- Create assignments

The logical steps from project creation to staffing to baseline are the following:

1. A new project is created.
2. Staff members are allocated on a project.

3. The WBS structure and task dependencies are created.

4. Staff members are assigned to a task.

5. Effort allocation (estimates) is set on a task for staff members.

6. Project is baselined.

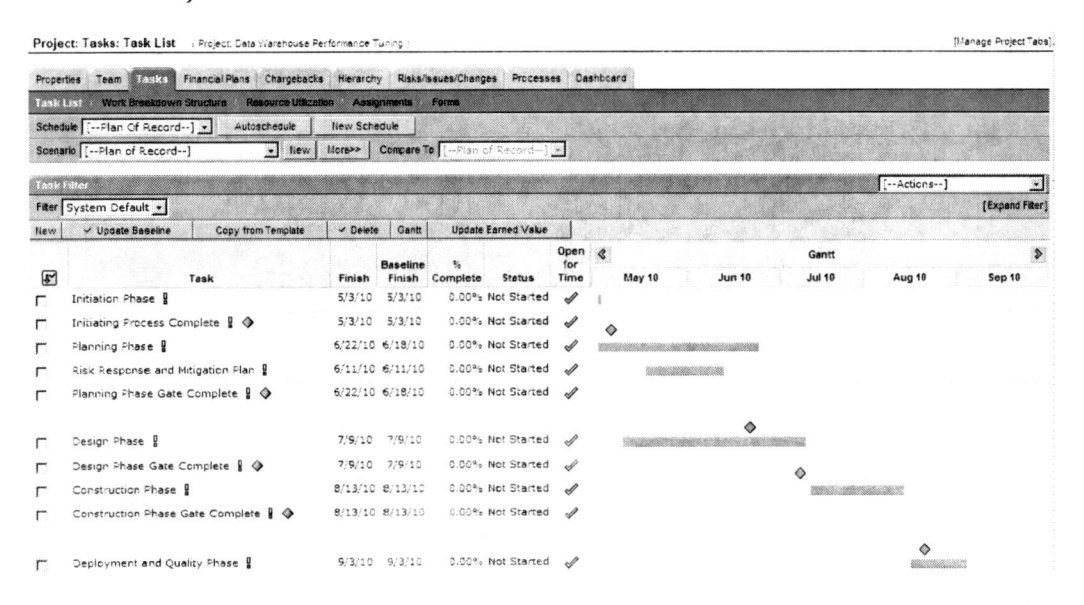

Figure 4-17. Task list of a project

Risk/Issues/Changes Tab

This tab contains links to risks, issues, and change requests, as shown in Figure 4-18, where a project manager can create detailed risks, issues, and change requests for a project. A risk can be converted to an issue or change request, an issue can be converted to a risk or change request, and a change request can be converted to an issue or risk.

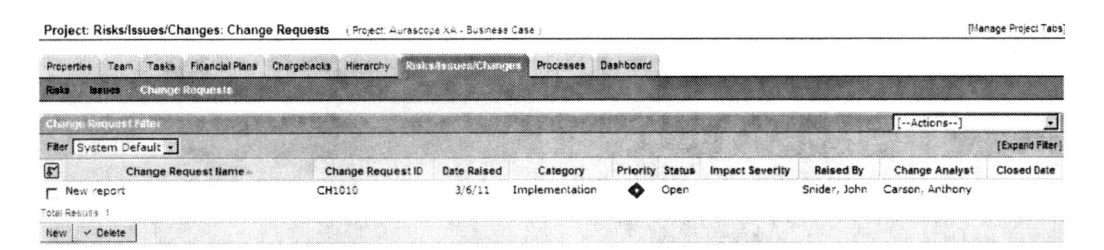

Figure 4-18. Risks/Issues/Changes tab

■ **Tip** By default a project manager or staff member does not have access to the Risk/Issues/Changes tab. They need to have access to view or edit risks, issues, and change requests to access this tab.

Dashboard

Dashboards are used to provide easy access to a series of portlets that provide valuable investment data. Dashboards enable CA Clarity PPM to display real-time data for fact-based decision making, providing better alignment between the IT organization and the lines of business it supports. Figure 4-19 shows the Dashboard tab of a project.

The dashboard provides access to a series of portlets showing investment data. The administrator can customize the layout of the dashboard by using CA Clarity Studio. Only projects have a standard Dashboard tab.

The dashboard displays summary views of project labor and team utilization data in the following portlets:

- General

- Alerts

- Earned Value Phase Analysis

- Project Baselines

- Team Utilization

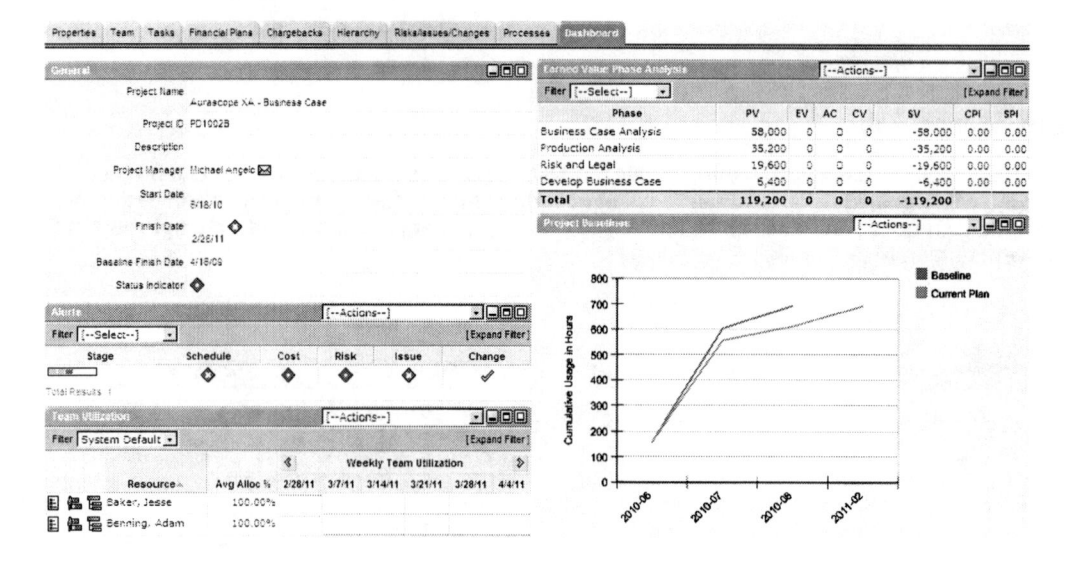

Figure 4-19. Dashboard tab

Program

Programs are top-level projects that serve as the parent or umbrella project to one or more child projects. Unlike master projects, which also serve as parent projects to child projects, you can use programs to view combined actuals and effort for all of the projects contained within them. In this way, programs provide an important top-down summary view of an organization's goals and the plan to meet them.

Though a program is a project and shares some of the same functionality as a project or master projects, it also differs in a few significant ways. For example, you cannot create nonmilestone tasks at the program level, and you cannot staff a program. Programs cannot be financially enabled, but you can create a financial plan for it and view plan data in a graph format. In addition, you can view the combined actuals and other totals for all of the projects in a program.

Table 4-1 summarizes the differences and similarities between programs, master projects, projects, and subprojects.

Table 4-1. Differences and Similarities Between Programs, Master Projects, Projects, and Subprojects

Attribute or Ability	Program	Master Project	Project	Comments
Displays sum of values from subprojects	Yes	No	N/A	You can view the combined actuals and effort for all the projects in a program. You cannot do this from master projects.
Assign staff members	No	Yes	Yes	You cannot assign staff at the program level. The roles that display on the Program: Team: Staff page are read-only and are aggregated from the program's subprojects. The project role assigned to a team member is displayed. If a resource does not have an assigned team member role, then their name appears individually in the list. You cannot edit this list.
Add participants	Yes	Yes	Yes	You can add participants to programs, master projects, and subprojects.
Create and apply a work breakdown structure (WBS)	No	Yes	Yes	Because you cannot staff or add nonmilestone tasks to programs, you cannot create and apply a WBS to programs.
Use tasks	Milestones only	Yes	Yes	You can add milestones to programs, but you cannot add key tasks or task estimates.
Use planning features	Yes	Yes	Yes	You can create budgets and forecasts for programs and projects.
Connect to scheduler	Read-only	Read/write	Read/write	Because it does not contain actuals of its own, a program can be viewed only as read-only in a desktop scheduler, such as Open Workbench and Microsoft Project.

CHAPTER 5

CA Clarity PPM Components: Resource Management

Resource management involves the efficient and effective deployment of an organization's resources when they are needed. Resources may include human capital, financial capital, or material inventory. Managing human labor is the most critical aspect of resource management. In IT organizations, deploying skilled professionals to the right projects is a key factor for success.

Resource management enables visibility into an organization's ability to do work, in other words, capacity. What does this ability to do work signify? For starters, it could answer certain questions such as "Do we have resources available to enhance the SAP Finance module?" or "Could your team provide me with a project manager on the development of this iPad application?" or "Do we need to hire Java developers for the new ERP application?" Enhancing the SAP Finance module, developing an iPad application, and using a new ERP application are all examples of work. The work indicates the "demand" on the resources. This demand emanates from any new initiative an organization may undertake, existing initiatives that need to be supported, or just routine operational activities.

A resource manager is a person who is responsible for supervising a resource's time. The resource manager constantly monitors and manages the capacity that is available to him or her to meet the current and future work demand. To effectively address resource management needs, an organization must be able to do the following effectively:

- Maintain a repository of resources with the appropriate level of detail for each resource such as skills, job description, experience, and employee type
- Staff or allocate resources to current and future work demand
- Monitor workloads and allocations
- Request resources within or outside the organization
- Monitor capacity and demand

In PPM terms, resource management (capacity) is tied intrinsically to project management (work demand).

The Resource Management Module

The CA Clarity PPM Resource Management module provides a centralized location for creating, editing, and viewing investments in resources and roles. It includes deploying skilled resources to the right project teams and roles, as well as monitoring the actual workload and availability of all resources.

Resource Management provides the ability to do the following:

- Create resources and roles
- Identify the skills, primary role, and characteristics of each resource or role
- View and monitor resource workload and availability from a central location
- Monitor capacity and demand of roles across all projects
- Provide resources to investments using the formal requisition feature
- Refine searches to find the best resource for a position

The four main components of Resource Management are the following:

- Resources
- Resource requisitions
- Resource Planning
- The Resource Finder

Resources

CA Clarity PPM allows for extensive flexibility when defining and managing the people and resources in and around the organization. CA Clarity PPM Resource Management also includes the input of resource types other than strictly labor or people. Resources can also include any material, equipment, or expense items that need to be assigned to projects, tracked, and possibly billed. These are called *nonlabor resources*.

A resource is a person or object (such as a piece of equipment or material) that is used to fill a role or perform a task. A role is a generic description of a function or an object.

Four types of resources and roles can be created in CA Clarity PPM:

- *Labor*: This type designates work performed by an individual or role.
- *Equipment*: This type refers to machinery, such as computers, printers, and overhead projectors, that are used to perform a job.
- *Material*: This is material used to perform a job, such as paper or fuel.
- *Expense*: This identifies the costs associated with a resource or a role. Though roles can be assigned to projects to help identify tasks and timelines, in most cases resources replace roles in order to perform the work and complete the tasks.

Roles

Roles and subroles can be defined as follows in CA Clarity PPM:

- Roles are defined as the *part* or *job* a resource is performing.
- Roles include positions such as project manager, resource manager, or database administrator, among others.
- Roles hold cost information, can be used for initial staffing, and can be used within capacity planning.
- Every resource in the system can be associated with a primary role and may change roles for a particular project or task if necessary.

The importance of roles can be described as follows in CA Clarity PPM:

- Roles can act as placeholders in project templates.
- Roles are used to create cost plans.
- Resources are assigned a primary role to designate their main area of expertise.
- Roles can be used in rate and cost matrices.
- Roles can be used when creating requisitions.

Roles play an integral part of the CA Clarity PPM application. A role setup is treated exactly as resources are in the application; they can be assigned to an OBS, can be assigned to tasks, can have skills associated with them, and can be used for capacity planning.

A set of roles is created in a role hierarchy that enables parent-child relationships. To streamline data entry, the role hierarchy should be established before resources are entered into the system to allow for role assignment to resources.

Create a New Resource

The tasks of creating a resource and maintaining it in CA Clarity PPM are done from two locations.

Administration Tool: Users

Users created from the Administration Tool can log into CA Clarity PPM to do the work, as shown in Figure 5-1.

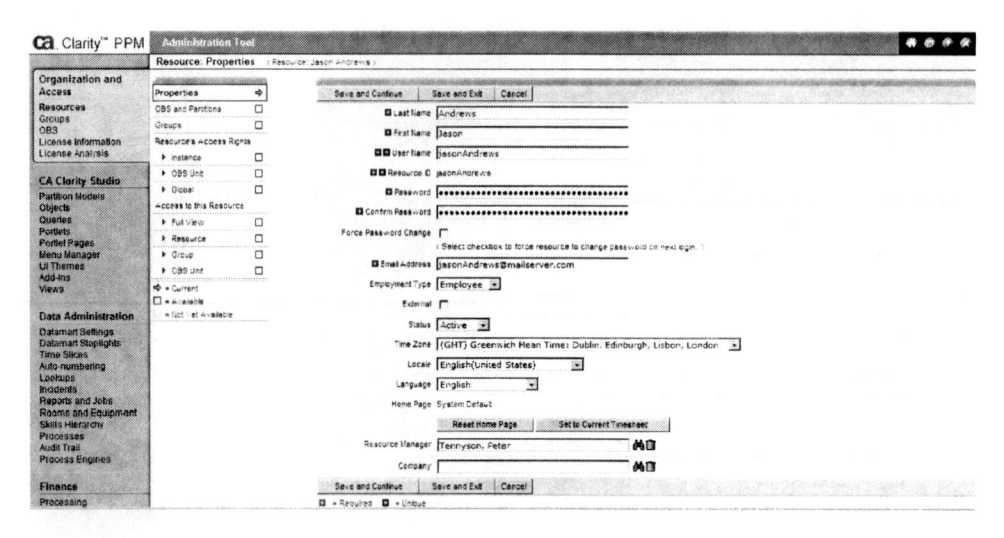

Figure 5-1. Resource properties from the Administration Tool

Application Administration: Resource

Resources created from application administration are "locked" when viewed from the Administration Tool resource menu, as shown in Figure 5-2.

Resources can include the following:

- People
- Equipment
- Material
- Expenses
- Nonlabor resources

Clarity creates an entry on both sides, regardless of where the original entry was made, as shown in Figure 5-3.

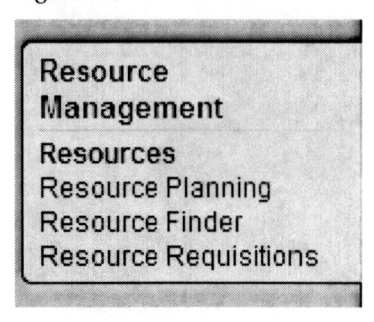

Figure 5-2. Resource Management menu

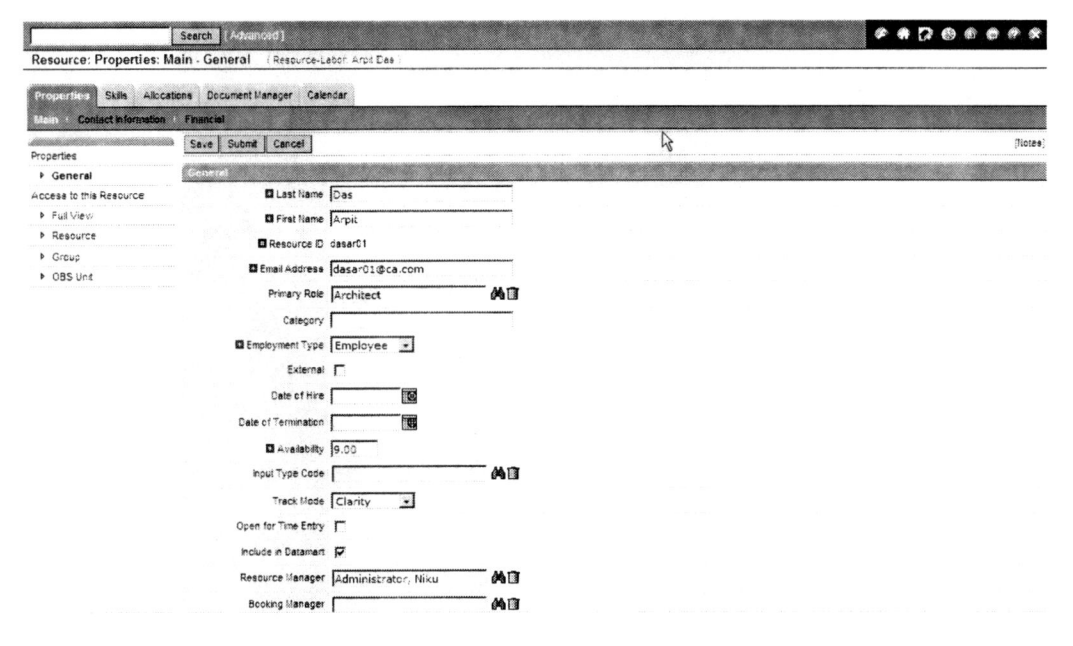

Figure 5-3. Resource properties

▌ **Tip** The resource manager gets edit rights to resource properties including OBS and financial information via inherited rights.

The resource manager does not automatically get timesheet edit/approval rights.

CA Clarity PPM Resources Adapter Add-on Services Component

CA Services Global Delivery has a prebuilt add-on service component that is a connector that imports resource information from various HR and ERP systems into the CA Clarity Resource and User modules to do the following:

- Facilitate keeping your resource relationship structures current
- Help with appropriate resource capacity management processes
- Handle cascading updates to resource information

Resource Planning

The Resource Planning feature provides views of the following:

- Resource allocation
- Resource availability
- Comparison of resource and role allocations with resource and role availability
- Aggregate allocation and availability for all roles/resources across all investments
- Individual resource and role allocations
- Individual resource and role availability
- Views by investment or by service week
- Views by investment start and finish dates
- Graphic histogram formats contrasting allocation vs. availability
- Table format contrasts
- Demand on resources by OBS unit

The out-of-the-box view for Resource Planning contains four tabs, as shown in Figure 5-4:

- Workloads
- Allocations
- Capacity
- Investments

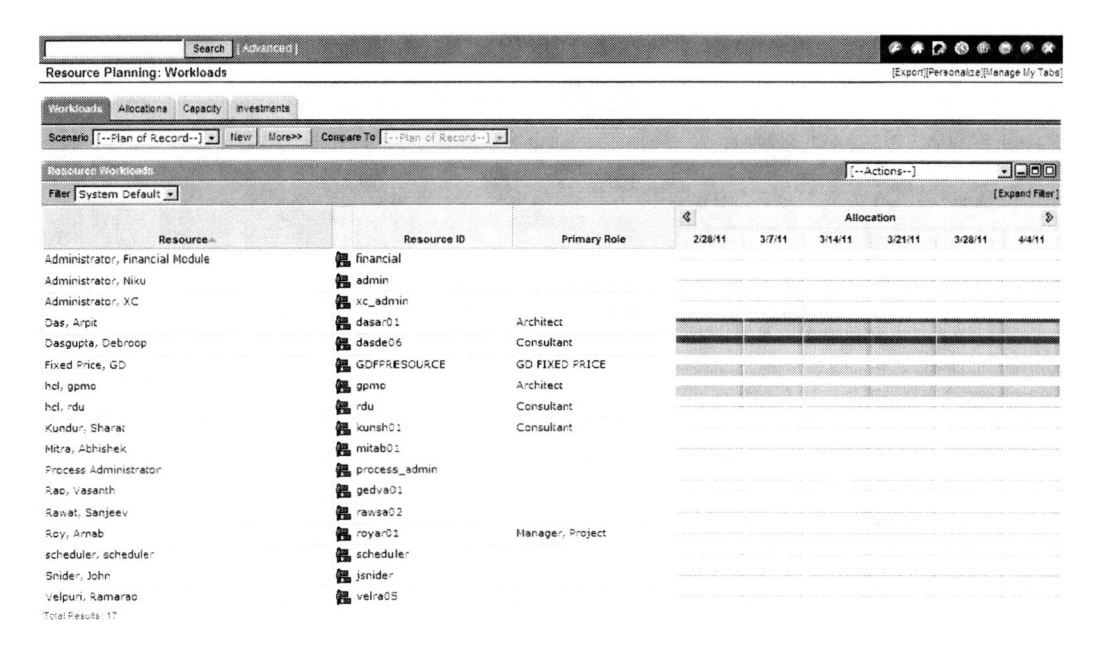

Figure 5-4. Resource Planning view

Workloads

Workload reflects combined allocations for all investments to which a resource is assigned. The primary role is the role assigned to the profile of the resource, not necessarily the role the resource is assigned to on a project. The Workload portlet displays each resource's allocations on all investments combined by week. Figure 5-5 shows resource workloads.

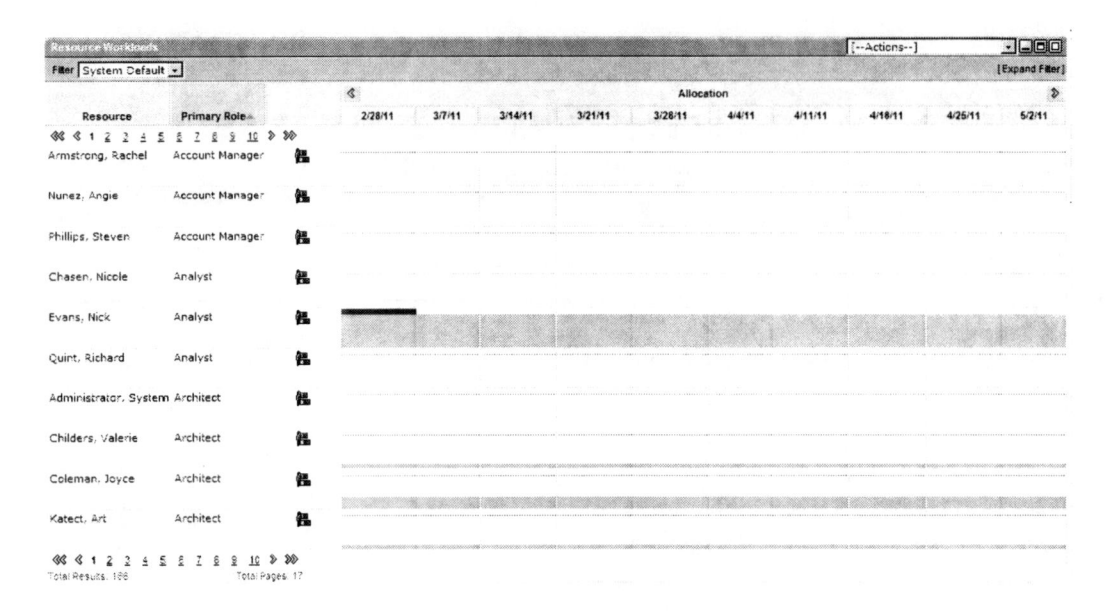

Figure 5-5. Resource workloads

One row is visible for every resource, based on security rights. By default, the grid provides a weekly view that is today plus six periods. Allocations are visible in yellow and available in red. The Configure and Time Scaled Value options in the Actions drop-down can be used to change the time periods as well as the look and feel of the portlet. Clicking in the histogram will allow the user to access the Allocations and Details link for the specific resource. The accessible data is not just resource-specific information but also data elements from other data providers that will reduce/increase the numbers shown rather than the line items shown.

Allocations

Resource Allocation provides a tool to view, edit, compare, and manage resource demand and availability. Resource Planning provides resource managers with a tool to compare individual resources and role allocation with the current and upcoming demand. Graphical portlets help resource managers compare resource availability with the demand across all the company's investments and set up "what if" scenarios to better distribute the workforce.

The Allocation tab contains four portlets.

Weekly Detail

The Weekly Detail portlet displays a line-by-line view of the information displayed on the Workloads portlet. On the Workloads portlet, investment information is rolled up into one row, while on the Weekly Detail page each investment is represented by its own row. On the Weekly Detail page, when a resource is assigned to multiple investments, we will see multiple rows bearing the resource's name—a different row for each of the resource's investments. Figure 5-6 shows the Weekly Detail page.

Access to the resource's properties, the Resource Finder, and resource staffing information is available directly from the page via links. The filter allows you to filter data using both the Resource and Investment attributes. This portlet is configurable using the options in the Actions drop-down.

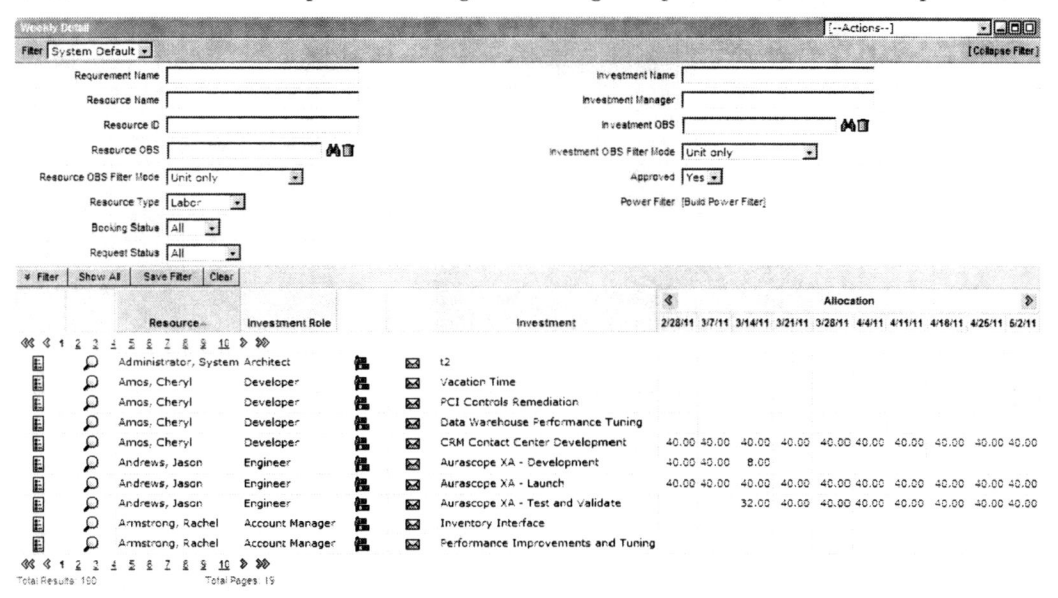

Figure 5-6. Allocations, Weekly Detail

Unfilled Requirements

This portlet will show those roles that have not been replaced by a resource on an investment. These are considered unfilled allocations because the role will need to be populated at some point before the actual work begins. This will allow the resource manager to view all the needed staffing requirements in one place rather than accessing each investment. The investment manager can also use this portlet to view the outstanding allocation needs using the filter capabilities that provide role and investment fields. Access to the resource's properties, the Resource Finder, and resource staffing information is available directly from the page via links. The Actions drop-down allows for the configuration of the view, as well as the opportunity to change the grid to edit mode and to make updates directly. See Figure 5-7 for details on unfilled requirements.

Figure 5-7. Allocations, Unfilled Requirements view

Booking Status

The Booking Status portlet is based on the team data provider and will show every resource on every investment. Unlike the main Workloads portlet, data on all of the Allocations pages is broken out by individual investment as well as by individual resource. Access to the resource's properties, the Resource Finder, and resource staffing information is available directly from the page via links. The filter can be expanded to allow for a resource manager or investment manager to view only their resource or investment-related information. Figure 5-8 gives you details on the Booking Status portlet.

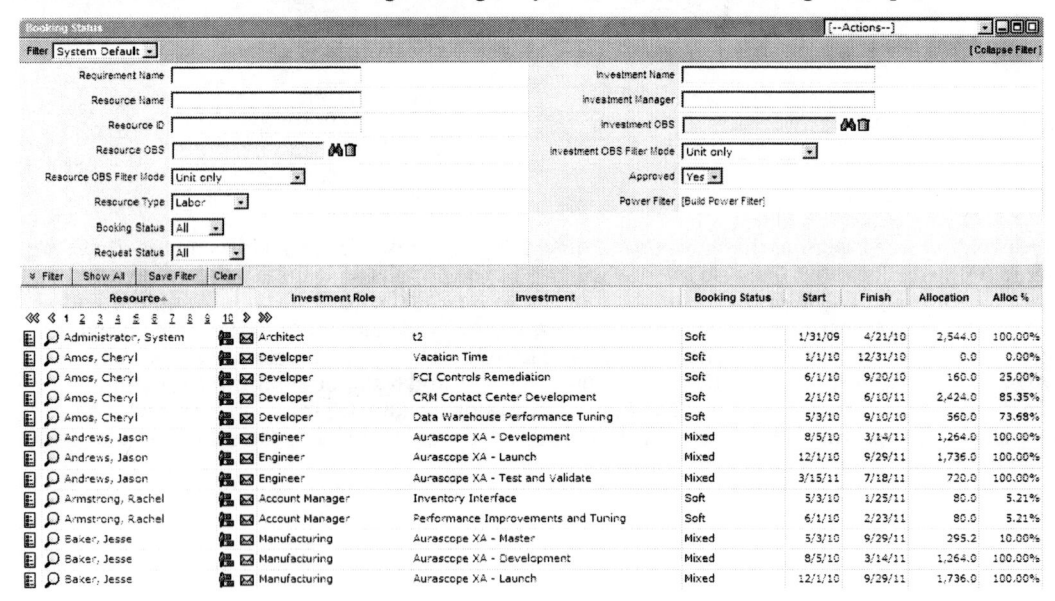

Figure 5-8. Booking Status portlet

CHAPTER 5 ■ CA CLARITY PPM COMPONENTS: RESOURCE MANAGEMENT

■ **Tip** The Booking Status portlet can be used to filter on mixed booking status of resources. This becomes very useful when you try to disable the mixed booking setting on project management setting on the admin side.

Allocation Discrepancy

Allocation Discrepancy lists team members whose intended allocations deviate from the default percentage, which is 20 percent, as shown in Figure 5-9.

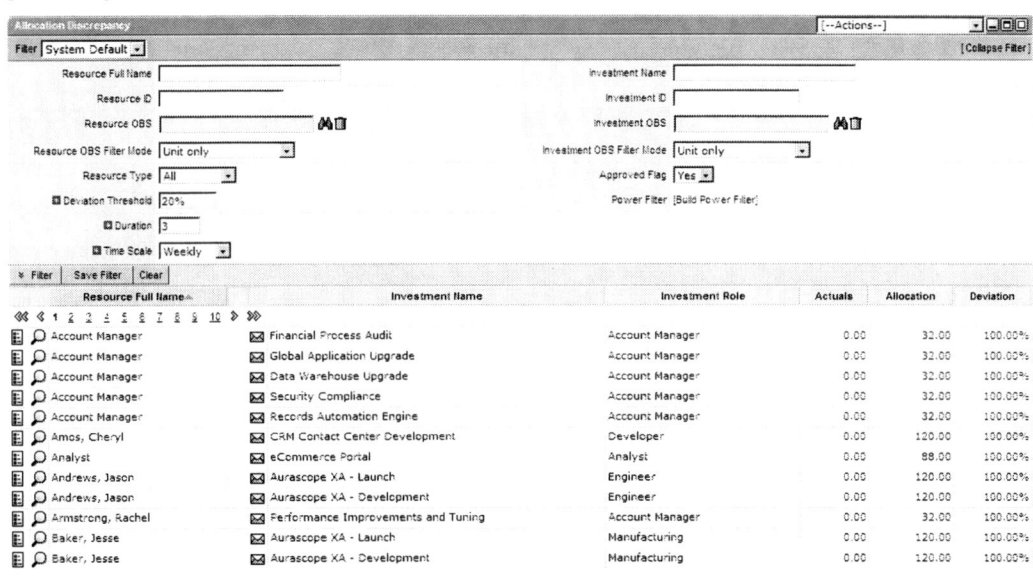

Figure 5-9. Allocation Discrepancy view

Capacity

There are two portlets on this tab that show an organization's resource demand vs. capacity.

Role Capacity

This portlet shows overall demand vs. capacity for resources across all investments aggregated by role. The data is displayed for each month grouped under quarters. Data regarding how total demand varies from total capacity for each role is visible. A filter can be used for *to-be-hired* resources to include or exclude resources that are yet to be hired. Figure 5-10 shows the Role Capacity portlet.

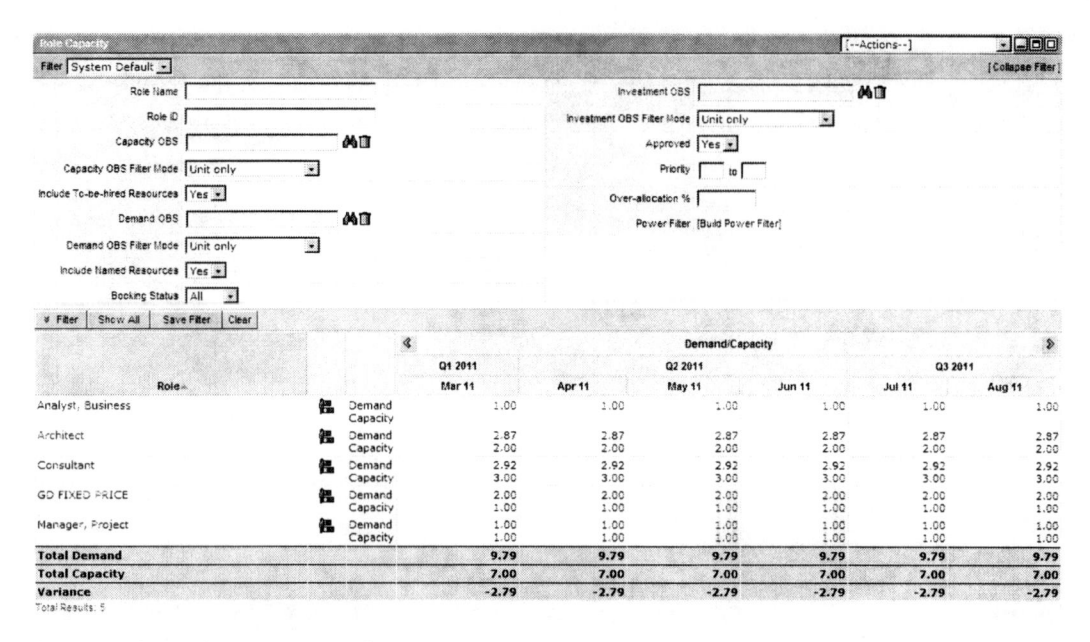

Figure 5-10. Role Capacity portlet

OBS Resource Aggregation

This portlet shows overall demand vs. capacity for resources across all investments aggregated by OBS units. This portlet allows you to drill down through the OBS hierarchy into an individual OBS to see the list of investments and the aggregated demand in a time-sliced view, as shown in Figure 5-11.

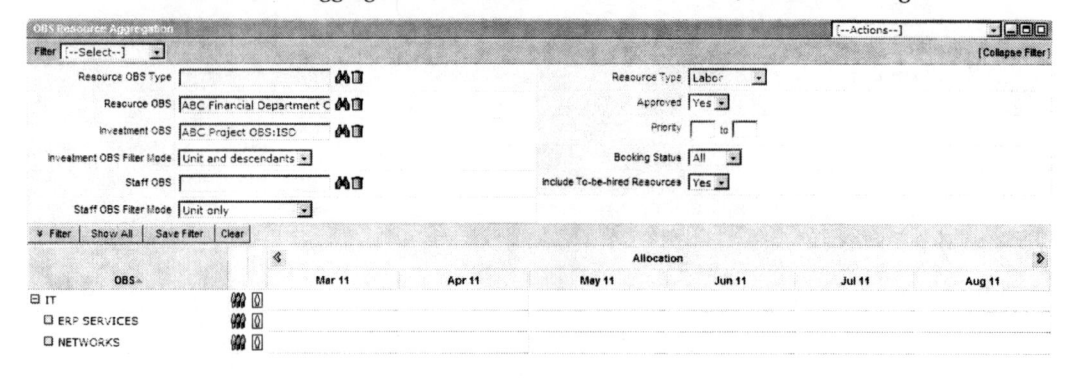

Figure 5-11. OBS Resource Aggregation portlet

Investments

The OBS Investment Aggregation portlet is the only portlet on the Resource Planning: Investments page. The portlet shows aggregated demand for investments by OBS units, as shown in Figure 5-12.

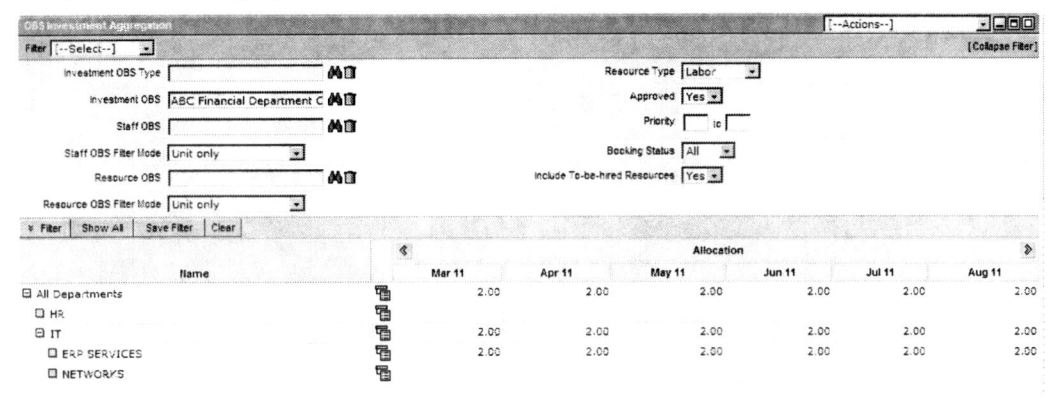

Figure 5-12. OBS Investment Aggregation portlet

> **Tip**
> - CA Services recommends not changing a resource or role's investment, service, or idea allocations from resource management pages unless it's changed by the manager of the investment.
> - CA Services recommends changing allocations from within the investment, from the investment's Team: Staff page.
> - Modify resources' allocations from the resource planning pages; communicate changes to the investment's manager.
> - The Data Mart must be run once before the time-sliced data can be seen on the Resource Management screens, which includes capacity planning.
> - Use the admin tool's Setting option to enable resource requisitions.
> - Resource managers may need to be assigned to OBS units at higher levels for broader views and planning.

Resource Finder

Organizations need to fill various roles with appropriate resources that can do the job, either internally or externally. The Resource Finder provides a comprehensive yet flexible method to perform the search based on the required dates, roles, skills, and so on.

The Resource Finder can be used to search for labor resources and roles but cannot be used to locate material, equipment, or expense resources. The Resource Finder consists of a filter that allows you to specify search criteria. The Resource Finder filter contains a number of standard search parameters such as name, role, ID number, employment type, skills, and availability. Figure 5-13 shows the Resource Finder.

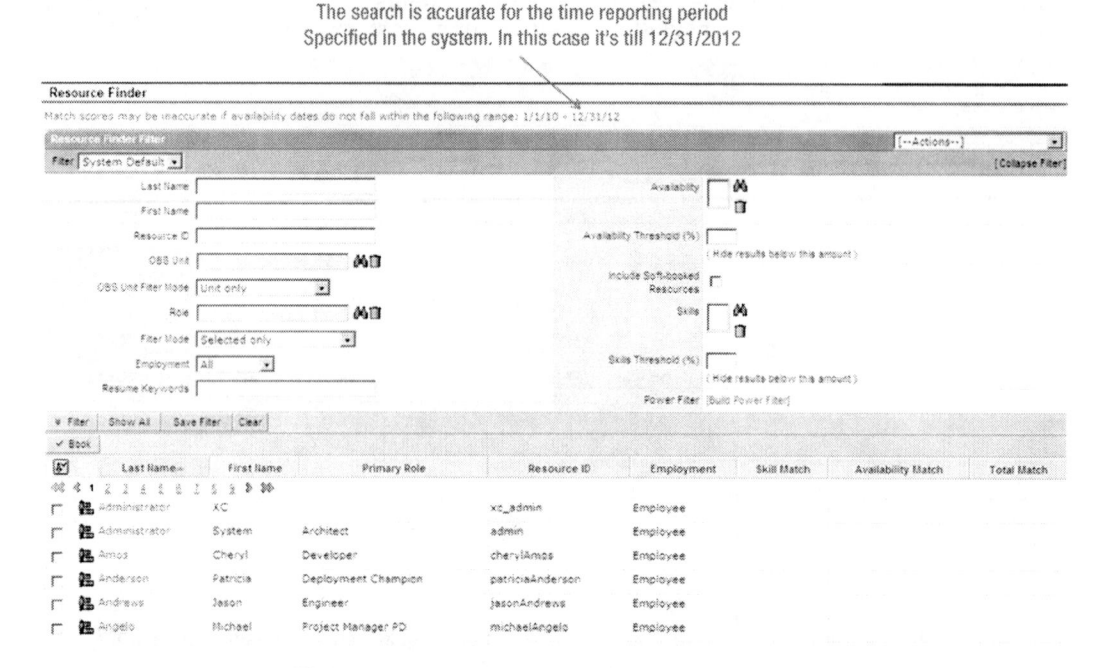

Figure 5-13. Resource Finder

Resource Requisitions

Requisitions can be used to formalize the staffing process. Project managers can formally request resources via a resource requisition. Resource managers can then find the appropriate resources to fill the need.

Formal requisitions set criteria for the resources required for a project. The criteria can be specific skills, an OBS unit, or a certain employee type. In some organizations, resource managers manage the allocation and booking of resources to distribute the workloads, project for upcoming projects, and make the most effective use of resources.

For example, clients or sponsors may request particular resources, based on past projects. Resource managers can also review resource availability from a higher level of an OBS structure and shift resources as needed. Figure 5-14 shows a view of the Resource Requisitions page.

CHAPTER 5 ■ CA CLARITY PPM COMPONENTS: RESOURCE MANAGEMENT

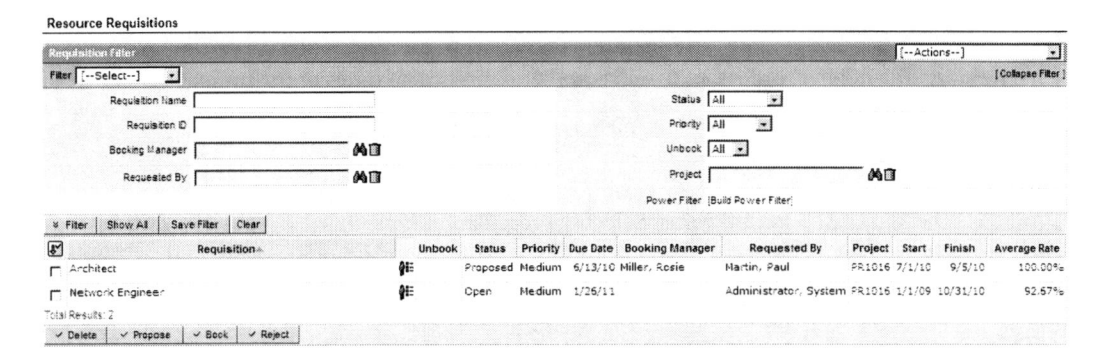

Figure 5-14. Resource Requisitions filter

■ **Tip** *Allow Override Requisition Approval* allows the default setting of Requisition Approval Required to be changed by project managers on the individual projects. When the Requisition Approval Required option is turned on, a project manager or a resource manager requires Project Edit rights to book a requisition.

Requisitions are available only with projects.

CA Services Best Practice for Staffing Resources to Projects

There are two best practice recommendations for staffing resources to projects within CA Clarity PPM. These separate processes are dependent upon the users who are initiating them and their role within the organization. Both processes are described next.

Process 1: Resource Requisitioning

The best practice for resource requisitioning involves two separate user roles:

- *Requisition Creator (RC)*: This user is typically the project manager; however, it could be anyone whose role it is to create a resource requisition but not staff it.

- *Booking Manager (BK)*: This user is typically the resource manager; however, it is whomever is responsible for working the requisition and proposing staff for it. This person is not the same as the requisition creator.

Scenario

The RC adds desired roles to a project via the Team: Staff page. If a role is needed for more than one FTE (Full Time Employee) on the project, that role is added multiple times. At this time, the following applies to each role:

- The booking status is Soft.

- The request status is New.
- The start/finish dates, unless adjusted, equal the start/finish dates of the project.
- The allocation percentage, unless adjusted, equals the default allocation percentage set in Clarity.

You create a new requisition by placing a check next to each role that needs to be filled, selecting the More button, and clicking Create Requisitions. Select the requisition type on the Create Requisitions page and identify the appropriate booking manager. If the booking manager is specified on the resource properties page, then this can be left blank, and the requisition will pick the value set on the resource properties. At this time, the RC can choose either *Create* or *Create and Open*.

- *Create*: Choosing Create opens a requisition with a status of New. Requisitions can be edited by the RC only when in a New status. Typically, RCs do not have edit rights for open requisitions. If the requisition is not complete, use the Create option. No notifications are sent when a requisition has a status of New. If this option is chosen, the RC must access the Resource Requisitions list within their project to change the requisition status to Open when it is ready to be staffed.
- *Create and Open*: When the requisition contains the correct staffing requirements, choose Create and Open. When the status of the requisition is changed to Open, the RC can no longer edit the requisition, and a notification is sent to the booking manager that a requisition requires staffing.

Each role selected will be given a separate requisition ID, allowing independent processing of each requisition. There can be only one open requisition (with a status of New, Open, or Proposed) for each staffing requirement at any given time. The requisition name defaults to the name of the role/resource being requisitioned.

Upon notification of an open requisition, the booking manager accesses it via the Resource Requisitions list or through the Notifications tab on their overview screen. The Requisition Properties screen is displayed; the booking manager reviews the specifics and then must find the appropriate resources. The booking manager can do this by selecting the Resources tab and then clicking the Add button to search for staff. Using the Resource Finder, the booking manager can search for resources, based upon skills, availability, and so on. The booking manager then selects resources and clicks Add. The Resource Requisitions list now shows all the chosen resources. The booking manager proposes the resources to the RC by placing a check next to the resource name and clicking Propose. A notification is sent to the RC stating that a resource proposal has been made.

The RC accesses the requisition via their Notifications tab on the overview screen or through the Resource Requisitions list in the project. The requisition should now show the following:

- *Status*: Proposed.
- *Priority*: The default is Medium.
- *Due Date*: The default is Proposed Date.
- *Booking Status*: Soft.

The RC reviews the proposed resources and then either books or rejects the proposal. If the RC chooses to book the resource, the following should be true and is viewable via the Team: Staff page:

- *Role Request Status*: Booked.
- *Role Booking Status*: Soft.

- *Role Allocation Percent*: Remains the same as on the requisition.
- *Role Allocation Hours*: Zero.
- *Resource Request Status*: Booked.
- *Resource Booking Status*: Hard.
- *Resource Allocation Percent*: Displays the agreed-upon percent.
- *Resource Allocation Hours*: The calculated hours are based upon the allocation percent and start/finish dates.

When the requisition status changes to Booked, the requisition can no longer be edited. When all work on the requisition is complete, the RC should change the requisition status to Closed via the Team: Staff page.

If the RC chooses to reject the proposal, the following is true:

- The booking manager is notified about the reopened requisition.
- The status of the requisition changes from Proposed to Open.

Process 2: Direct Staffing

The best practice for direct staffing involves one user role whose responsibility it is to both assign the roles to the project and staff the resources to the project. For purposes of this chapter, this resource will be referred to as the booking manager.

Scenario

The booking manager adds the desired roles to a project via the Team: Staff page. If a role is needed for more than one FTE on the project, that role is added multiple times. At this time, the following applies to each role:

- The booking status is Soft.
- The request status is New.
- The start/finish dates, unless adjusted, equal the start/finish dates of the project.
- The allocation percentage, unless adjusted, equals the default allocation percentage set in Clarity.

When the booking manager is ready to staff the project and replace the roles with resources, they select the icon to go directly to the Resource Finder. Filter for a resource, select one, and click Replace. The role assigned to the project is replaced with the selected resource, and the resource inherits all allocations, and so on.

In this process, there is no requisition created because the role of the user is a combination of both user roles from the first scenario. The creation of a formal requisition in this scenario would only create extra steps for the same user.

Out-of-the-Box Requisition Notifications

Table 5-1 shows the out-of-the-box notifications that are generated by Clarity during the requisition process.

Table 5-1. Out-of-the-Box Notifications

Requisition Status Changes	Requested By	Booking Manager
Created		
From New to Open		Notified.
From Open to New		Notified.
From Open to Propose	Notified	
From Proposed to Booked		Notified.
From Open to Booked (if requisition approval is not required)	Notified	
Booking Manager Changes	Notified	New and old booking managers are notified.
Requested By Changes		
Closed		
Deleted		

Note Say a project manager sends a resource requisition to the resource manager for 1/1/2009 to 1/31/2009 for a 100 percent allocation and the resource manager approves 50 percent allocation. So when the booking is approved (Booked), we will see a planned and hard allocation segment for the team members of a project. If rights are set up correctly, the project manager will not be able to overwrite the Hard Allocation with Planned Allocation. The project manager should be able to overwrite only Planned Allocation with Hard Allocation. This will ensure that PMs don't overwrite approved segments.

CHAPTER 6

■ ■ ■

CA Clarity PPM Components: Time Management

Have you ever faced customers who complained of overbilling? Have you managed projects and constantly worried about schedule slippages? Does your organization differentiate between "billable" (chargeable to customer) and "nonbillable" hours (nonchargeable to customer)? Do you usually have the right data available to determine estimates for the completion of work? Does your company define mandatory training hours in a year? Does your business require actual resource utilization to be calculated? Time management helps address all of these concerns.

The following are some of the key aspects of time management:

- Making projects and resources available for time entry
- Capturing actual effort of resources on tasks, such as project work, training, or even vacations
- Defining approval processes
- Assessing the impact of actual time entries on tasks and the project schedule
- Attaching cost and rates to the resource effort for financial planning and billing purposes

Effective time management helps managers assess the productivity of resources and take appropriate corrective measures wherever necessary. Giving customers/managers the ability to approve time entries serves as a mechanism for ensuring consent. By keeping track of actual effort, project managers will know whether resources are going over the assigned effort. This is a key input for updating the project schedule. Actual effort logged on tasks also forms the basis for determining future estimates for similar tasks. Tracking actual utilization of resources is much easier when organizations have time entry data for all resources. Additional attributes could be defined for time entries to help companies qualify time entries. For example, you can differentiate project time from vacation time or billable time from nonbillable time.

Therefore, time management is of paramount importance to any business, and effective tools for time management are essential for driving efficiency.

CA Clarity PPM enables users to enter time against the tasks they have been assigned to on various projects and investments; it also enabled them to record their nonplanned time in timesheets. CA Clarity PPM automates timesheet population by creating timesheets directly from project plans, which increases efficiency and productivity.

The following are the basic steps in time management:

1. Set up a timesheet.
2. Complete the timesheet.
3. Approve the timesheet.
4. Modify the timesheet settings.

Set Up a Timesheet

In CA Clarity PPM, you can access timesheets in two ways:

- Click the Current Timesheet icon in global tools, as shown in Figure 6-1.
- Click the Timesheets link on the main menu to navigate to the timesheet list page.

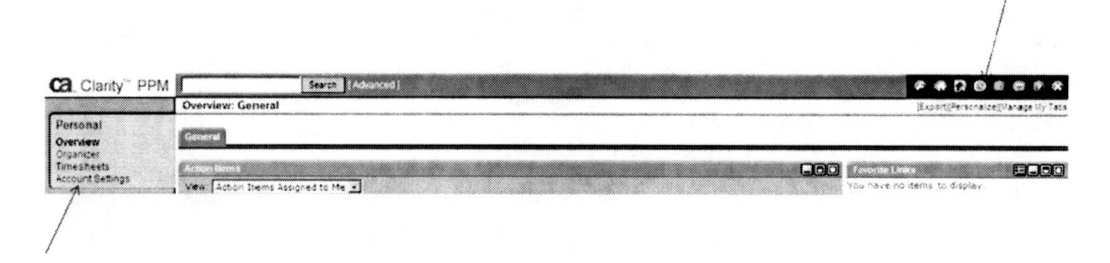

Figure 6-1. Accessing timesheets through the icon

The following should be set up for the user to access and use the timesheet in CA Clarity PPM.

Time Reporting Period

You set up time reporting periods in the Administration Tool under the Project Management settings, and they are in the Open state, as shown in Figures 6-2 and Figure 6-3. Time reporting periods can be weekly, monthly, and so on, and they are an organizationwide setting.

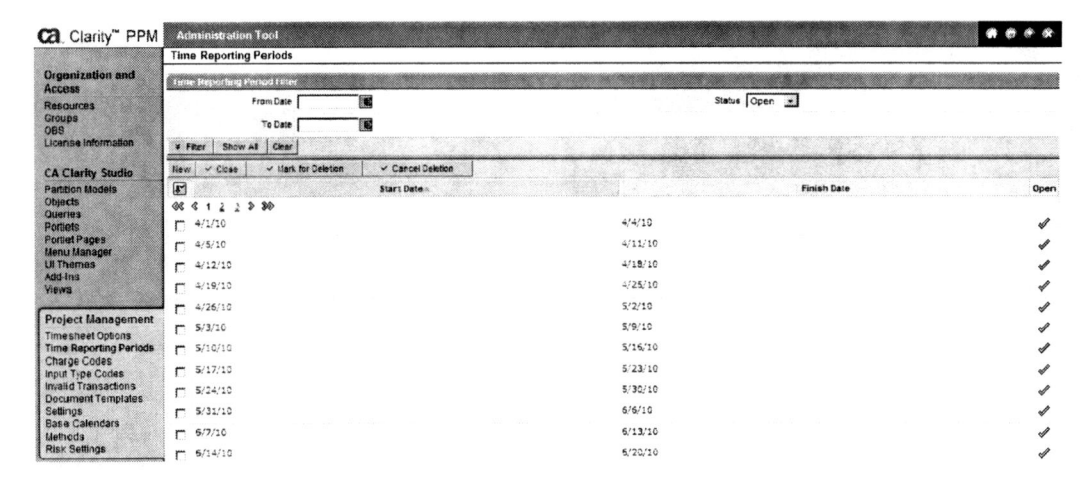

CHAPTER 6 ■ CA CLARITY PPM COMPONENTS: TIME MANAGEMENT

Figure 6-2. Setting up time reporting periods

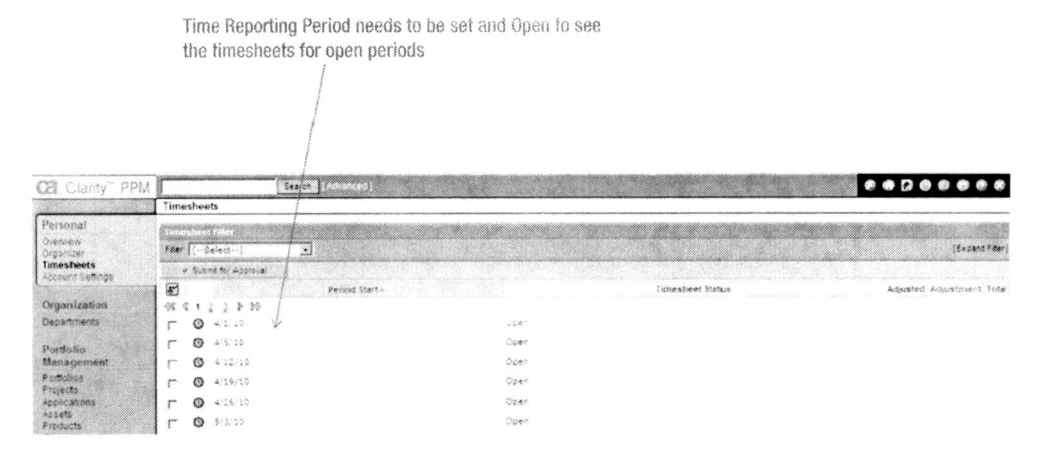

Figure 6-3. The timesheet status is open.

Security Rights

User should have the global Timesheets – Navigate right, as shown in Figure 6-4 to see the Timesheets link in the main menu.

Figure 6-4. The Timesheets – Navigate right is needed.

145

CHAPTER 6 ■ CA CLARITY PPM COMPONENTS: TIME MANAGEMENT

Figure 6-5. The Timesheets link in the main menu

Resource Properties

The resource should be open for time entry, and the track mode should be set to Clarity, as shown in Figure 6-6.

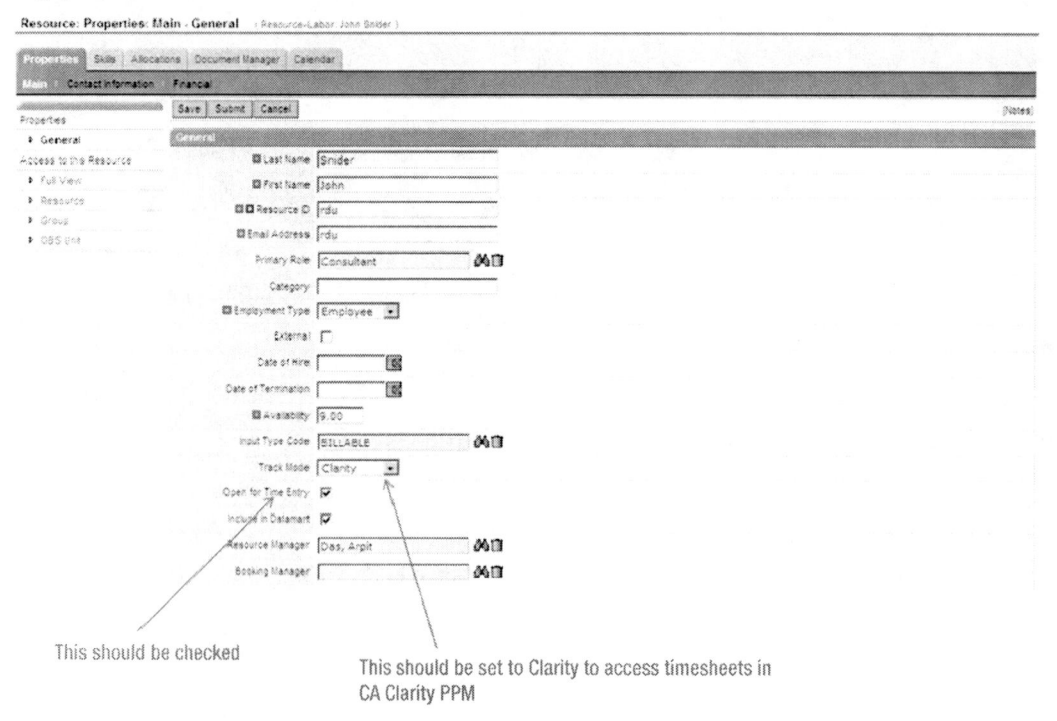

Figure 6-6. Resource properties

CHAPTER 6 ■ CA CLARITY PPM COMPONENTS: TIME MANAGEMENT

Investment Properties

The investment should be open for time entry, and the track mode should be set to Clarity, as shown in Figure 6-7.

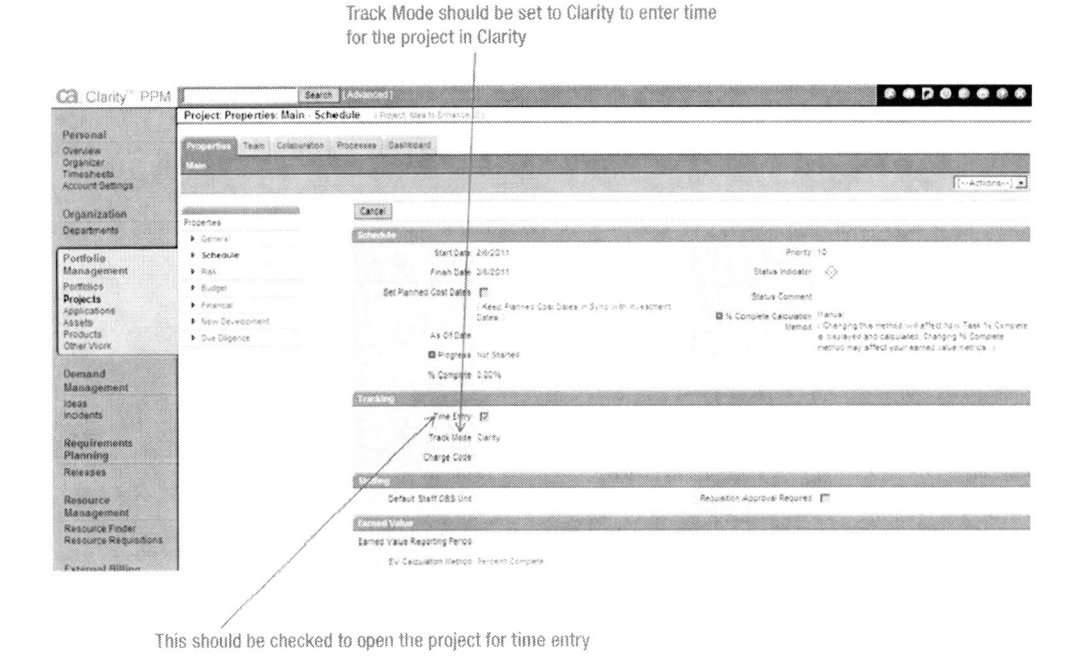

Figure 6-7. Project properties for time entry

Complete Timesheet

Once you access the timesheet via the Timesheets link, you can click the icon to open the timesheet, as shown in Figure 6-8.

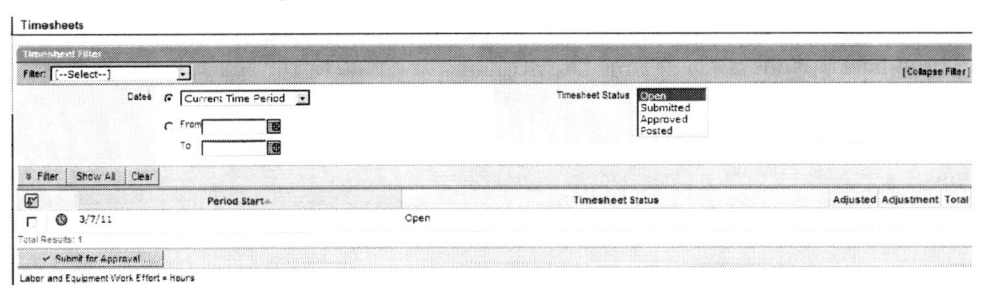

Figure 6-8. Timesheet filter

147

Once the timesheet is opened, the user can populate the timesheet and submit it for approval, as shown in Figure 6-9.

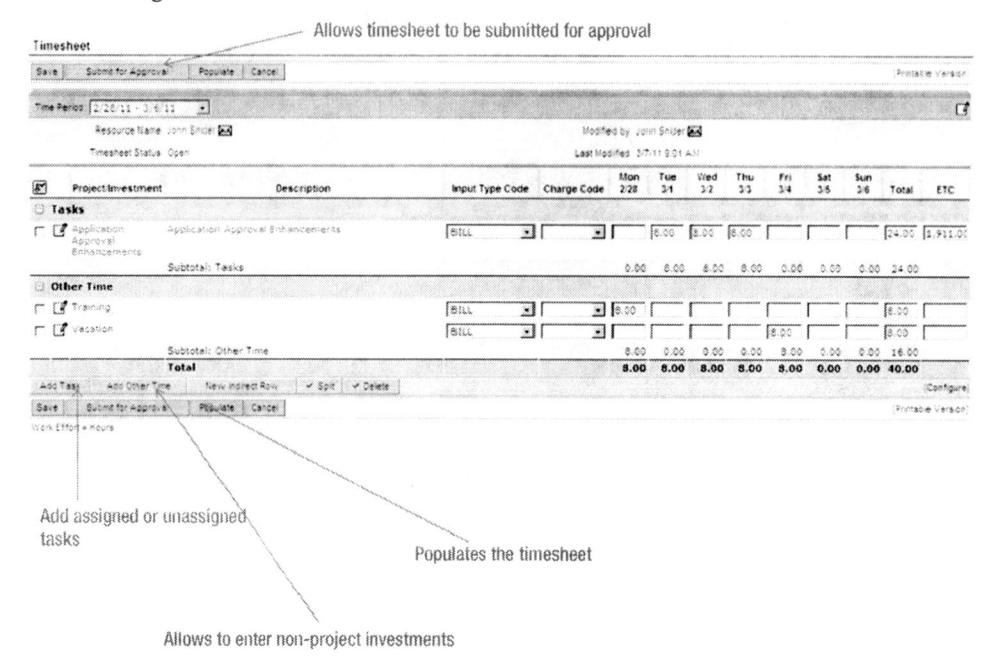

Figure 6-9. Populating a timesheet

Tips

The following are some tips for populating timesheets.

How Populating Timesheet Works

The timesheet's Populate button populates the timesheet with the assignments that the resource is currently working on for a certain range of dates around the time period.

The range is determined by the system admin in the Administration Tool. Go to Project Management   Timesheet Options   Default Time Entry Options, and then set the field called Populate Time Range. The default values are seven days before and seven days after.

The following rules explain the logic used to determine whether an assignment (a task as it is seen by the user) will be populated onto a timesheet.

An assignment is populated onto a timesheet if:

- Its start and end date range falls within the open time periods range.

or

- It has a proposed estimate that has been specified *and* its finish date is before the oldest open time period.

and

- It is not a milestone. Milestones never populate to a timesheet and cannot take assignments anyway.

and

- Its assignment status is not complete.

So, if the assignment is marked as completed (with estimated time of completion [ETC] = 0 and Task Status = Completed and Assignment % complete = 100%), then that task will never automatically be populated to the timesheet; it would have to be manually added.

Figure 6-10 shows the example of a user with a time reporting period set up for weekly timesheets from 7/15/2007 to 7/21/2007.

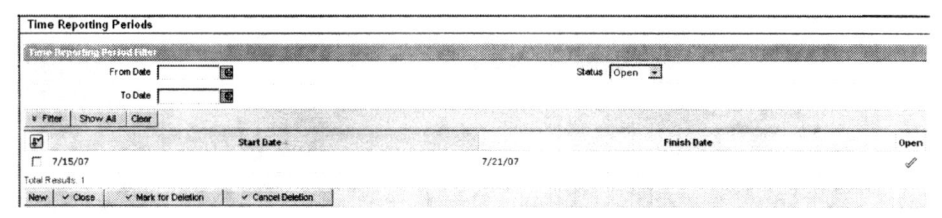

Figure 6-10. Time reporting period example

In this example, the user is using the default Populate Time Range setting of seven days before and seven days after, as shown in Figure 6-11. So, for this time reporting period, the date range is 7/8/2007 to 7/28/2007.

Figure 6-11. Using the default Populate Time Range setting

CHAPTER 6 ■ CA CLARITY PPM COMPONENTS: TIME MANAGEMENT

The user also has a project set up with a series of tasks, to which he assigned himself as a resource to each of the tasks, as shown in Figure 6-12. The user's assignment dates align to the task start and finish dates.

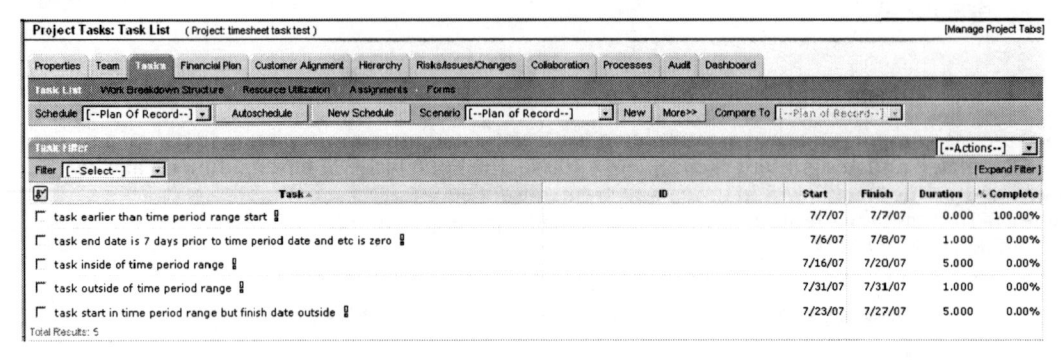

Figure 6-12. Setting up tasks

One task has the start and finish dates prior to the time period date range, and the ETC is zero. The user expects that this will not autopopulate.

The second task has a start date outside of the time period start date range, but the end date falls on the time period start date range. The user expects that this will autopopulate.

The third task has the start and finish dates within the time period date range. The user expects that this will autopopulate.

The fourth task is outside of the time period end date range. The user expects that this will not autopopulate.

The fifth task has a start date within the time period date range but a finish date outside of the time period end date range. The user expects that this task will autopopulate.

Remember, any task that is marked as completed will not autopopulate, and any task that has the remaining ETC (no matter how much earlier the finish date is outside of the time period start date) will populate.

So, the user expects the second, third, and fifth tasks to populate in the timesheet when the user clicks Populate.

All of the tasks the user is expected to autopopulate did populate in the timesheet, as shown in Figure 6-13. Remember that the date range settings are used only to support the algorithm for which assignments populate to the timesheet.

Figure 6-13. Autopopulated timesheets

Approve Timesheets

Once the timesheet is submitted for approval, the approver gets notification to approve the timesheet, as shown in Figure 6-14. There could be multiple approvers, but once the timesheet is approved by the first approver, the timesheet status changes to Approved.

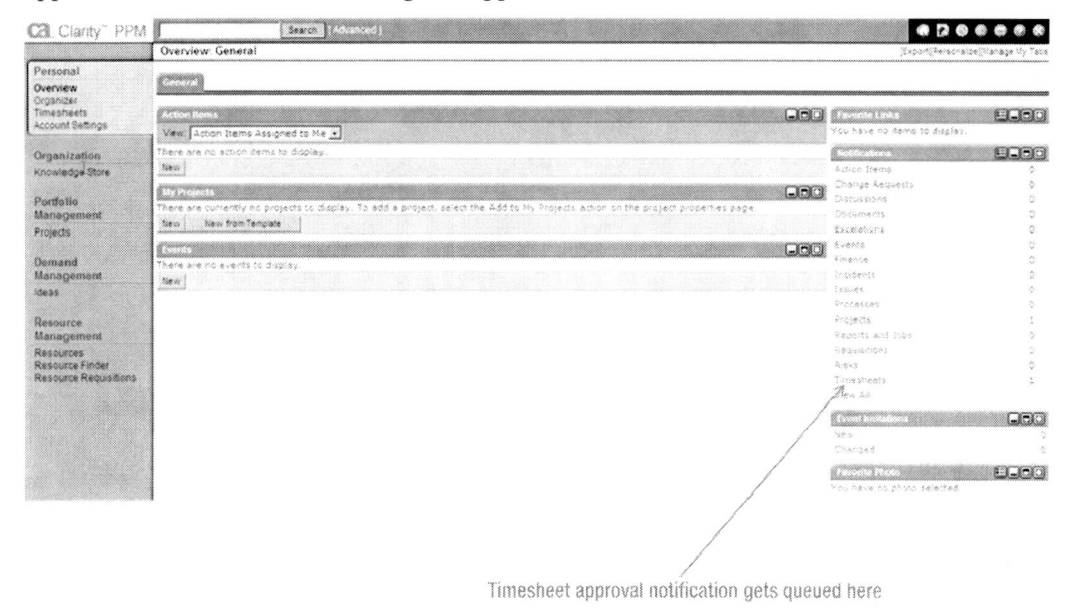

Figure 6-14. Timesheet approval notification

The user can open the notification and click the link to go to the timesheet instance, as shown in Figures 6-15 and 6-16.

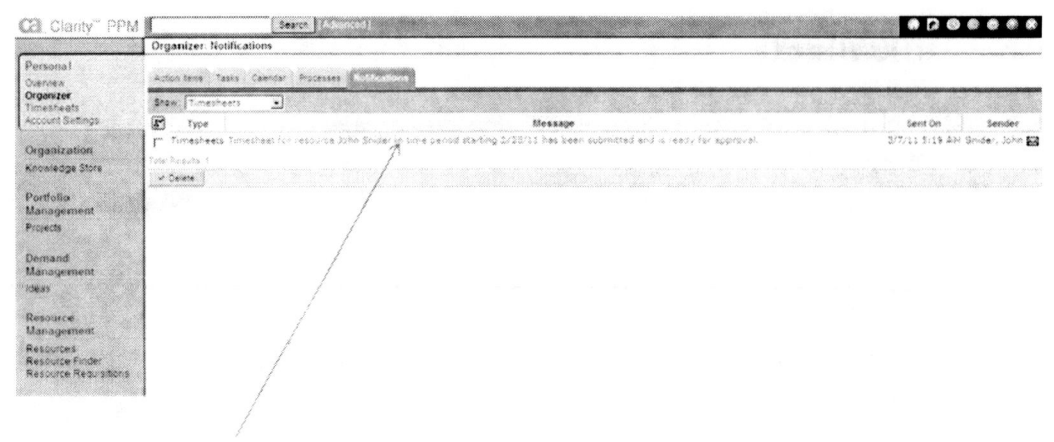

CHAPTER 6 ■ CA CLARITY PPM COMPONENTS: TIME MANAGEMENT

Click on the notification link to access the timesheet

Figure 6-15. Accessing timesheets through notifications

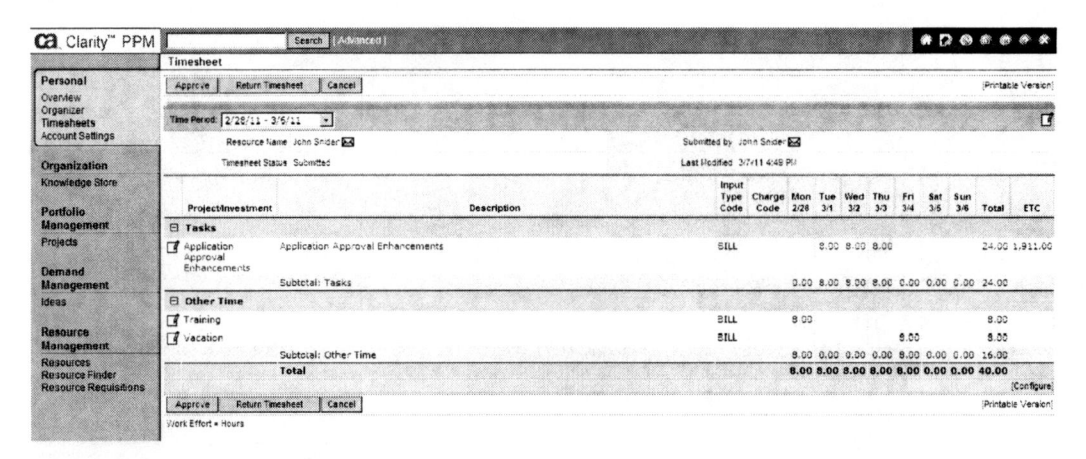

Figure 6-16. Timesheet approval

The approver can approve or return the timesheet after reviewing it by clicking the appropriate button, as shown in Figure 6-17. After the timesheet is approved, it can be posted by executing the Post Timesheets job.

CHAPTER 6 ■ CA CLARITY PPM COMPONENTS: TIME MANAGEMENT

Tip
- Once the timesheet is approved, wait for five minutes before running a Post Timesheets job.
- If a Post Timesheets job does not post the timesheet, check whether the timesheet is getting posted for a future date, and make sure "Allow posting of future timesheets" (in the Administration Tool under Project Management Settings) is checked.
- When the user enters the time and the timesheet is approved, the entered effort shows as Pending Actuals on a task. After the timesheet is posted, the effort shows as Actuals.
- If using an action item via the workflow process for timesheet approval, then the project manager needs to have Timesheet-Edit rights to view the timesheet. There is no right like the Timesheet-View right in CA Clarity PPM.

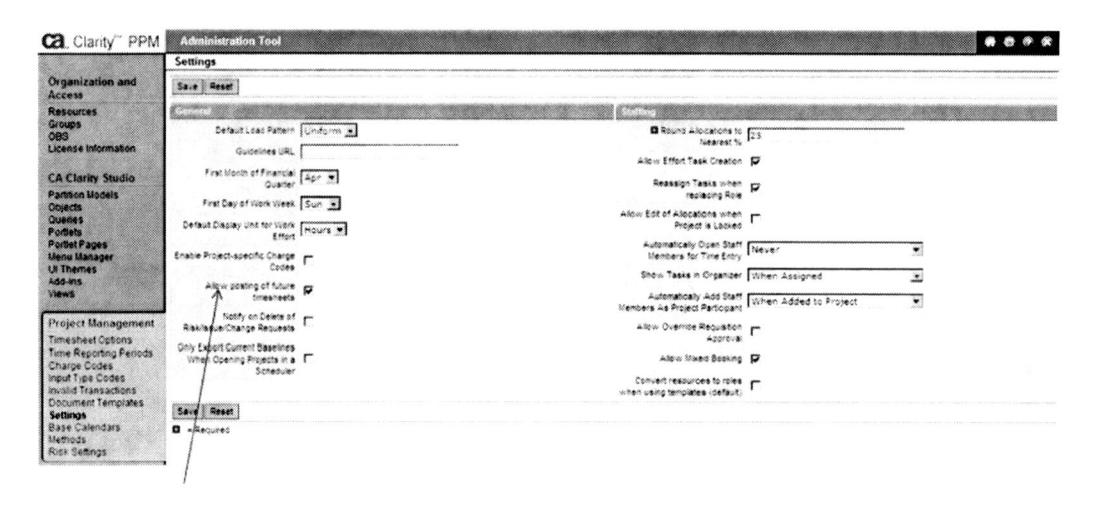

Figure 6-17. Posting of timesheets

Modify Timesheet Settings

Once the timesheet is submitted for approval, it is in read-only state. A timesheet has to be returned if any changes are necessary. A timesheet with a Returned status can be edited.

Tip
When a user returns his own timesheet, the system does not open a Note window to give a reason for the return. It is also possible to change timesheet entries after the timesheet has been approved. To change entries in an approved timesheet, the timesheet needs to be returned by the approver.

Posted Timesheet

To modify the posted timesheet, you use the Adjust button, as shown in Figure 6-18. This button appears only for posted timesheets.

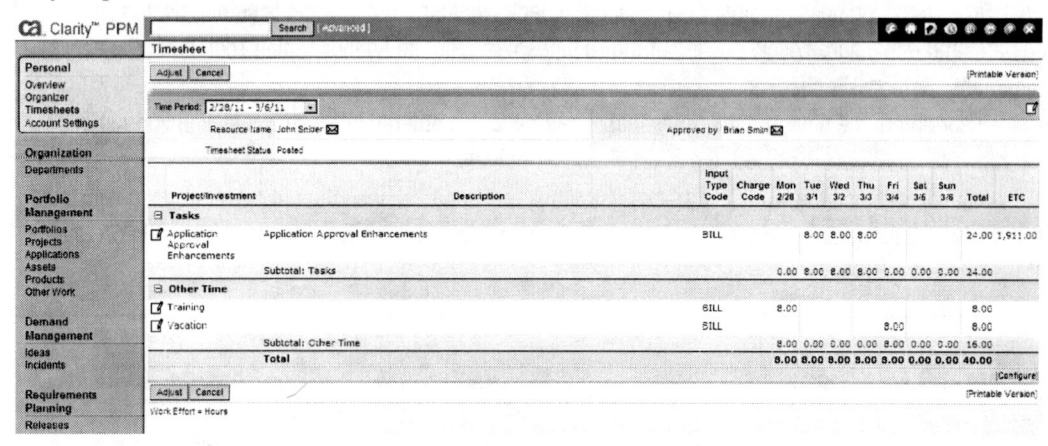

Figure 6-18. Posted timesheet and Adjust button

Clicking Adjust will create a duplicate timesheet, in which the user can make changes, as shown in Figure 6-19.

Figure 6-19. Creating a duplicate timesheet by adjusting it

Adjust puts the timesheet in the Open state. The user modifies the timesheet and submits it for approval. The approver approves the timesheet, and then the timesheet is posted via a Post Timesheets job.

At this point, two entries of the timesheets are created.

Adjusted

This view is the original posted timesheet.

Adjustment

This view is the modified view of the timesheet. See Figure 6-20 for the two entries of the timesheets.

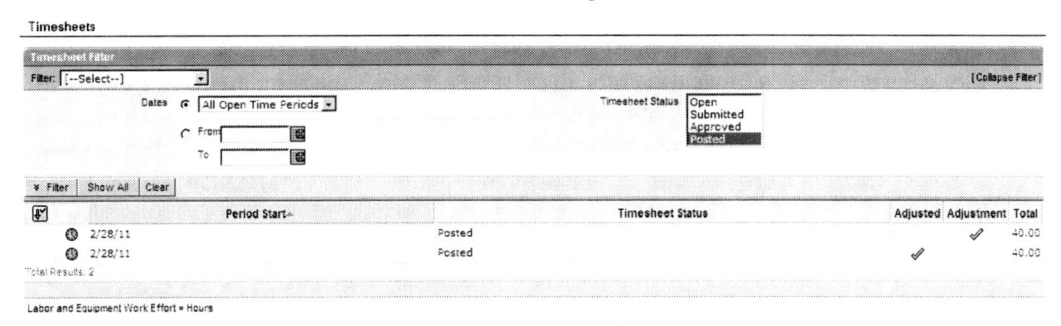

Figure 6-20. Two entries of a timesheet after adjustment

Also, the adjusted timesheet has a *delta* view where the user can see the differences between the two posted timesheets, as shown in Figure 6-21.

Figure 6-21. Adjustment timesheet

Clarity Algorithm for Calculating ETC in Timesheets and Posting

This section explains the logic CA Clarity PPM uses to calculate estimated time of completion (ETC) in timesheets.

Posting

1. During the posting of a timesheet entry, the system examines the assignment and determines what the current estimate is.

2. The system then determines what the remaining estimate is by subtracting the timesheet's actuals from the estimate it had already gathered (as described in step 1).

3. The system then updates the estimate curve based on the following logic. (Note: The estimate curve is a distribution of the estimates over time.)

    a. If the assignment's load pattern is fixed, then the estimate curve is cleared for the time period of the timesheet being posted (the estimates are essentially consumed for this time period). The remaining estimate for the following time periods would remain unchanged.

Note If the estimate was 40 hours for this week and another 80 hours for the next 2 weeks and this week the resource logged only 17 hours of time, after posting there will be 80 hours of estimate, even though 40 – 17 = 23 hours. The 40 hours of estimates are consumed for this week.

    b. If the assignment's load pattern is *not* fixed, then the estimate curve is recalculated according to i, ii, or iii below.

        i. If the work for this time period equals the estimate for the time period being posted, then the estimate curve is cleared for the posted time period. The remaining segments of the estimate curve remain unchanged.

        ii. If there is no remaining estimate, then the entire estimate curve is cleared.

        iii. If there is still some estimate remaining, then

            a) If the actuals through date is beyond the end of the estimate, then we extend the estimate curve's finish date to one day after the actuals through date.

b) The remaining estimate is distributed into the curve starting from the assignment start or actuals through date, whichever is later.

Note If the estimate was 40 hours for this week and another 80 hours for the next 2 weeks and this week the resource logged only 17 hours of time, after posting there will be 103 hours of estimate redistributed after the act through or assignment start date.

---

4. If there is no work done for an assignment but the resource had a timesheet posted for the period, the rules in step 3 would apply, except that the amount of work would be 0. Estimates would be moved forward and recalculated for *nonfixed* and for *fixed*, and the estimate for that period would be cleared.
5. The estimate sum field (ETC) is updated based on any estimate curve updates in the previous steps.

Timesheet Editing

This section explains how ETC works when a timesheet is edited and saved.
For ETC and saving a timesheet:

1. If the value in the ETC field on the timesheet was overwritten, then
    a. If the value was changed to null (the field was cleared), then the system will set the pending estimate to null.
    b. Otherwise, we store the value entered into the pending estimate field in the assignment.
2. If the ETC field was not changed, then
    a. If values were entered into the time entry, then the system will subtract the sum of the time entry actuals from the pending estimate.
    b. If the pending estimate equals (estimate – all pending actuals), then set the pending estimate to null.

Note If the pending estimate is changed and actuals are applied to the time entry, upon save the pending estimate that was entered will remain (no subtraction of the actuals takes place; see 1b in the previous steps).

ETC field shows 32 hours. A user enters 7 hours of actuals and 49 hours into the ETC field. Upon save and refresh, the system displays the 7 hours of actuals and 49 hours of ETC highlighted (which indicates the displayed value is now a pending estimate).

Loading a timesheet and ETC:

1. If there is a pending estimate from the assignment, then we display the pending estimate into the ETC field.
2. Otherwise:
   a. If the load pattern is fixed, then we get the sum of the estimate curve from the end of the current period.
   b. Otherwise, we subtract the pending actuals from the estimate and use that for the ETC field.

Customer Scenario 1: ETC with Two Timesheets

I have two unposted timesheets for May 28 and June 4. Each timesheet will have two tasks, a fixed-load pattern task called *fixed task* and a front-loaded task called *front task*. I entered 40 hours of ETC on each of the assignments. I also entered an end date of June 27 for the assignment on the fixed task. (The assignment started on May 28, so there were 22 workdays with an ETC of 1.81818… hours per day.) I then clicked the Populate button.

The fixed task shows an ETC of 30.91, the amount of estimate per week subtracted from 40 hours. The front-loaded task has 40 hours of ETC. I then enter 10 hours of actuals for each task. The ETC on the fixed task stays the same. The front-loaded task now shows 30 hours.

Then I access the next timesheet (June 4) and populate it. I see that the fixed task shows 21.82 hours of ETC, and the front-loaded task still shows 30 hours. After entering 10 hours on each task, the ETC is reduced to 20 hours on the front-loaded task. The fixed task's ETC remains the same.

If I view the May 28 timesheet, I will see an ETC of 20 hours on the front-loaded task, and I will see 30.91 hours for the fixed task. (Note here the difference in how the ETC of the fixed and front-loaded tasks shows between subsequent time periods.)

Customer Scenario 2: Pending Actuals and an Adjustment

I have an unposted timesheet for May 28. The timesheet has two tasks, a fixed-load pattern task called *fixed task* and a front-loaded task called *front task*. I entered 40 hours of ETC on each of the assignments. I also entered an end date of June 27 for the assignment on the fixed task.

Then I clicked the Populate button and entered 10 hours to each task. The fixed task shows an ETC of 30.91, the amount of ETC per week subtracted from 40 hours. The front-loaded task has 40 hours of ETC. I then enter 10 hours of actuals for each task. The ETC on the fixed task stays the same. The front-loaded task is now showing 30 hours. The pending actuals (prPendActSum) field on the assignment shows 10 hours on each assignment.

I then submit, approve, and post the timesheet. Upon observing the posted timesheet, I see no differences in ETC from the preposted timesheets. The assignment shows 0 hours of pending actuals for each assignment.

If I create an adjustment at this point and replace the 10 hours with 4 hours of actuals on each task, the fixed-task ETC will stay the same, but the ETC on the front-loaded task will change to 36 hours. The pending actuals on both assignments will show as having 4 hours.

Customer Scenario 3: Pending Actuals and an Adjustment

I have an unposted timesheet for the May 28. The timesheet has two tasks, a fixed-load pattern task called *fixed task* and a nonfixed task called *front task*. I entered 40 hours of ETC on each of the assignments.

I also entered an end date of June 27 for the assignment on the fixed task. I then clicked the Populate button and entered 10 hours to each task. The fixed task shows an ETC of 30.91, the amount of ETC per week subtracted from 40 hours. The front-loaded task has 40 hours of ETC. I then entered 10 hours of actuals for each task. The ETC on the fixed task stayed the same. The front-loaded task is now showing 30 hours. A check of the pending actuals on the assignment table shows 10 hours on each assignment.

Then I submit, approve, and post the timesheet. Upon observing the posted timesheet, I see no differences in ETC from the preposted timesheets. The pending actuals (prPendActSum) field on the assignment shows 0 hours of pending actuals for each assignment.

If I create an adjustment at this point, override the ETC to 17 hours, enter actuals of 2.2 per entry, and hit Save, the ETC value I entered will remain as 17 hours. However, if I enter another hour of actuals on the task, then the ETC will decrement to 16 on both fixed or front-loaded tasks. The pending actuals on both assignments will show as 3.2 hours.

Summary

In this chapter, we briefly described the Time Management module. The chapter described the timesheet functionality and various elements associated with timesheets in CA Clarity PPM.

CHAPTER 7

CA Clarity PPM Components: Financial Management

In today's environment, businesses face multiple challenges, such as competition, regulatory and compliance requirements, economic recession, political uncertainty, and the introduction of new technologies at a rapid pace. IT forms a key element for most businesses to deal with these challenges. This makes IT governance an imperative in most modern-day organizations.

IT is increasingly being run as a business. Financial management, like other PPM disciplines, helps ensure the alignment of IT goals to organizational goals, provides greater visibility for decision making at multiple levels, and lends the requisite control required to steer the organization in the right direction.

IT financial management enables some critical business processes in the IT organization:

- Planning and estimating costs of investments
- Aggregating the planned spends across the organization to enable yearly budget planning
- Tracking spends for investments in progress
- Analyzing project profitability
- Making informed decisions on continuing, closing, or starting new projects
- Communicating actual costs to service consumers (say business) and recovered costs to service providers (IT)

Financial management in IT allows for better allocation of funding based on predefined parameters. There is greater transparency because executives have a view of where the money is being spent. The balance between discretionary and nondiscretionary spends is likely to be healthier if sound processes are adopted. The importance of financial management can never be overstated from a regulatory and compliance standpoint. It also provides the ability to identify loss-making projects for corrective measures to be taken. Therefore, understanding and adopting IT financial management practices ensures greater predictability in business.

The Clarity PPM Financial Management Module

The Financial Management module is a versatile tool that gives organizations a wide array of tools to manage, control, and report on costs and revenues associated with its projects. It includes the accounting tools you need to monitor costs, invoicing and invoice consolidation, billing, XOG integration with accounting and billing systems, rate matrices, chargebacks, multiple currency support, auditing, revenue projections, WIP summaries, and other powerful reporting functionality.

One of the primary goals of IT governance is to ensure alignment between the business units and IT. IT investments need to be aligned with strategic business objectives in order to be funded and approved. IT needs to run like a business where IT is held accountable for its return on the investments. There should be visibility into what services IT provides and how they are consumed. IT's financial information and control are increasingly scrutinized for internal chargeback requirements and compliance reasons.

To satisfy these goals, IT organizations, especially ones with large numbers of IT investments and resources, demand strong structures and process automation to produce effective and accurate results. The spreadsheet approach simply cannot scale, and it cannot provide timely reporting to support IT management's daily decision-making needs.

With CA Clarity PPM Financial Manager, organizations can utilize its financial planning and chargeback capabilities to successfully conduct the following:

- Planning and managing costs and benefits of individual investments
- Making decisions at the investment portfolio level based on aggregated cost and benefit data
- Charging back costs of shared services to the business units that consume them
- Communicating actual costs to service consumers and recovered costs to service providers

Financial Processing Flow in CA Clarity PPM

The flowchart in Figure 7-1 details the financial process utilized in the CA Clarity PPM system. The following are several key elements of the Financial Management module:

- Financial framework
- Financial attributes
- Budgets and forecasts
- Investments or services
- Portfolios, portals, or dashboards

CHAPTER 7 ■ CA CLARITY PPM COMPONENTS: FINANCIAL MANAGEMENT

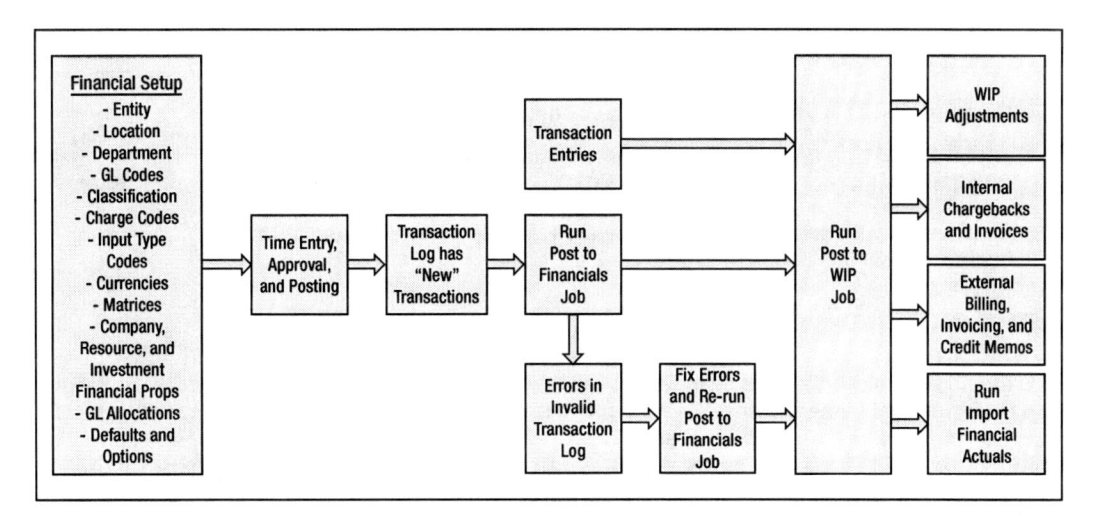

Figure 7-1. Financial process in CA Clarity PPM

Financial Setup in CA Clarity PPM

The first task in enabling financial management is to take care of the financial data setup required to enable financial data to be processed in CA Clarity PPM. We define a 12-step process for the financial data setup. Complete the following steps to set up financial data:

1. Define the location OBS.
2. Define the department OBS.
3. Create an entity (including the location/department OBS).
4. Define fiscal time periods.
5. Define GL codes.
6. Define classifications.
7. Create charge codes and input type codes.
8. Define currency.
9. Create cost and rate matrices.
10. Financially enable companies, resources, and investments.
11. Create GL allocations.
12. Define resource credits.

The entity, location, and department describe the internal financial framework of an organization. Additional financial attributes, described later in this chapter, enable detail-level views and reporting of transactions. They help ensure that investments or services are proceeding as expected. Investments and services can be monitored for the following:

- Comparisons of actual costs to plans and budgets
- Adherence to margin guidelines by analyzing project profitability, which is calculated from revenue and actual cost
- Return on investment and other financial measures that will enable effective business decisions

Entity

An *entity* is the highest organizational level within the CA Clarity financial structure. An entity can be defined as a distinct legal company or set of accounts within the financial system of a company. Multiple entities can be defined as required. Entity-based security is available to help ensure users have access only to information within their own entity. An entity can be used to determine rates and costs in the matrix and allow rollup reporting. The fiscal time period type defined for an entity impacts the availability of the periods for defining the GL allocations for chargebacks.

An entity may be created to represent each unit of an organization that uses a different currency. If you are using multicurrency, you can have a different local currency in each entity, but you must have at least one entity for each distinct currency. You cannot have a single entity using multiple currencies.

While you can define the home currency (the currency used at the project level once it's tied to an entity) once for an entity, it is possible to later edit the reporting and billing currency. For example, if the RBC world headquarters is in the United States and wants the reporting currency to be USD but wants the home currency to be the local currency of the entity, then you can define different currencies for the entity.

You must make sure the currencies are active before completing the currency definition for the entity. To create plan defaults, click the Plan Defaults tab. This tab provides defaults for Financial Planning in CA Clarity. Defaults are core aspects of forecasting and budgeting that automatically populate the Setup and Data Entry screens for all financial plans associated with this entity. These defaults apply when creating manual cost plans, not when copying from the staff plan.

The prerequisites for creating an entity component are as follows:

- The location OBS type
- The department OBS type
- Currencies must be active

Tip The single or multicurrency setting is identified during installation. Changing it from single to multicurrency can be done once through technical assistance, but CA Clarity cannot be modified from multi- to single currency. The system currency is set one time only.

Location

Each location can belong to only one entity. The following are some points to note:

- A single entity can contain multiple locations.
- Locations can exist within other locations as sublocations.
- Locations can be a physical office, an area, a region, or any other logical grouping.
- You must create an entity and a location OBS before the location can be added.
- When new locations are added through the creation screens, they are automatically added as units in the location OBS.
- You can use locations to determine rates and costs in the cost and rate matrices.
- You can use locations to allow for rollup reporting.
- Locations are objects within CA Clarity Studio and can be configured to include additional data or views.

The sublocations page enables the creation of relationships between sublocations and locations.

- Sublocations must be in the same entity as their parent location.
- These relationships are managed to support rollup reporting for locations. For example, the location hierarchy can consist of many levels to accurately describe a physical location; these levels could include Region, Country, State, and City. Because locations are stored in an OBS, the hierarchy can be configured only to a depth of ten levels.

Department

Departments are assigned to a location or set of locations. Departments can have parent-child relationships. During department creation, three processes are completed:

- Departments are linked to entities.
- Department units are automatically added to the department OBS.
- A department portfolio is automatically created.

At least one entity and the department OBS must be created before departments can be created. A department is an element of a company, a resource, and investments. The department for these objects is captured in the financial transactions for successful transaction processing.

Table 7-1 describes the elements of the Department tab.

Table 7-1. Elements of the Department Tab

Department Tab	Description
Properties	General information about the department
Resources	Aggregate staff detail for the department
Investments	Investments linked to this department
Subscriptions	Subscribed services
Audit Trail	Fields that have been changed
Invoices	Invoices that have been created
Provider dashboard	Portlets regarding services provided to other departments
Customer dashboard	Portlets regarding services consumed

Departments have a close association with portfolio management. Every department is also a portfolio, and full portfolio management functionality is readily available to department managers. The department object describes the following:

- Labor capacity, which is the capacity of the resources belonging to the department and all departments within it
- Labor demand, which is the demand of the resources belonging to the department and all departments within it
- The Resources tab on the Departments page that shows capacity as compared to demand for department resources
- Resources that are not staffed in departments in the same way they are staffed in investments
- Resources that are assigned to a department through their resource profile

Departments can subscribe to services. Departments can be consumers. Departments can also be providers of services. A department can be a consumer or provider for the same or different services. The Business Relationship Manager add-in provides views for providers and consumers to see their data through dashboards and portals. Whether the department is a provider or a consumer of services determines the views for cost recovery or invoices. Providers have a view of cost recovery, and consumers have a view of invoices.

GL Accounts

The GL accounts that are set up in CA Clarity enable a detailed allocation of debits and credits for the investment costs of your department. A GL account setup is necessary for each entity that will be using chargeback and recovery statement functionality. The GL account structure can be unique for each entity. A GL account's structure enables CA Clarity to be synchronized with the finance and accounting system. GL accounts must be set up if you will be using internal chargebacks and recovery statements. GL accounts are also objects that can be configured with new attributes and views through CA Clarity Studio.

This section describes how a GL account is created in CA Clarity PPM. The user navigates to the GL account page and adds the main account ID and the subaccount ID. This combination will make up the natural account. If required by your configuration, enter the entity and the account description (a brief description of the GL account properties). Select the appropriate account class (Balance Sheet, P&L) and account type (Asset, Liability, Income, Expense) and any other applicable fields. Based on the account being created, define the account by the asset class and asset type. A balance sheet class must be either the Asset or Liability Expense type; a P&L class must either be an Income or Expense type.

Resource Class

Resource classes enable the logical categorization of resources within an organization. Resource classes are created in the Administration Tool but are assigned in individual resource profiles. Any given resource can belong to only one resource class at a specific time. This designation can be used in the application of rates and costs for an organization. The resource class is a mandatory field for financial processing. A default field must be set up if resource classes are not being used. It is important to understand the client requirements, consider how they may need to differentiate resources for reporting, and figure out how they may need to define costs and rates for resources. The following are examples of resource classes:

- *Organizational*: Executive, management, staff
- *Geographical category*: Local, offshore, EMEA
- *Skill level*: Principal, senior, associate
- *Equipment*: Computer hardware, software, office equipment
- *Materials*: Specifications, presentations, user guides

Resource classes enable specific descriptions of resources that can be associated with resource types of Labor, Material, Equipment, or Expense. If it is unclear how to define resource classes, it is recommended that you create at least one resource class to match each of the resource types.

Company Class

Company classes enable the logical categorization of clients and companies within an organization. For example, company classes are used to indicate vertical markets or lines of business. Company classes are created in the Administration Tool but are assigned in the individual company profiles. A given company can belong to only one company class at a specific time. This designation can be used in the application of rates and costs for an organization. A company class is a mandatory field for financial processing. Set up a default field if a company class is not being actively used in CA Clarity. The company class is unique because it enables a user to create specific descriptions of clients and companies. The company classifications may be as simple as internal customer, external customer, or vendor. Consider how the organization will need to report on companies, investments, and transactions by the company class.

WIP Class

WIP classes enable an additional method of categorizing companies and investments and are used to group projects for reporting purposes. WIP classes are defined in the Administration Tool but are assigned at the company and investment levels. A company or an investment can belong to only one WIP class at any given time. WIP classes can be used in the application of rates and costs for the organization or the calculation of recognized revenue. A WIP class is mandatory for financially enabling company. When determining WIP class values, consider whether there is information that must be known about a company or an investment that will support the determination of costs or rates or that needs to be an element of the financial transactions.

Investment Class

Investment classes enable logical categorization of work within an organization. Investment classes can indicate the types of services provided by an organization to its clients. An investment can belong only to one investment class at any given time. Investment classes are defined in the Administration Tool but assigned at the company and investment levels. An investment class can be used to apply rates and costs for an organization. The investment class is a mandatory field for financial processing. A default field must be set up if you are not actively using this field in CA Clarity. Examples of investment classes are Maintenance Work, Administrative Work, Development Work, and so on.

Transaction Class

A transaction class is a data element used to specify resources that perform work. It is recommended to create at least one transaction class for each of the four transaction types: Labor, Equipment, Expense, and Material. Consider how the organization will need to further classify the four different types of resources or transactions. The system-defined transaction types have predefined transaction classes. They cannot be altered or removed and are identical to their transaction type. Every transaction is associated with a transaction class through the associated resource and can be used to apply rates and costs for an organization. The transaction class is a user-defined field that enables a user to create specific descriptions of transaction classes. It is also a data element that can be used to differentiate costs and rates in the cost and rate matrices and can be used in the cost plan and budget structure. A transaction class should be well planned before configuration because organizations can create cost plans for investments based on the transaction class, which then impacts their forecasting view.

For example, the transaction type of Labor may be too generic for practical financial reporting and analysis. Therefore, a transaction type may be broken down to reflect the various types of labor within the organization (that is, Consulting, Development, and Sales) or the recoverable nature of the work (that is, Billable, Non-Billable).

Exchange Rates

The Foreign Exchange Rate link is used only in conjunction with a multicurrency environment. Exchange rates must be established and maintained within CA Clarity. To perform the currency conversion, conversion rates must be set up.

Exchange rates must be established from and to each currency to avoid errors. For example, if conversions from U.S. to Canadian currency and from Canadian to U.S. currency are required, both exchange rates must be configured. Define the conversion method that will be used to calculate the exchange, either multiplication or division. Exchange rates can have a type of Average, Spot, or Fixed. It is recommended that you establish an integration if managing frequent fluctuations in currency exchange rates.

- The average exchange rate type is a blended rate derived over a period of time, usually weekly or monthly.
- The spot exchange rate type is a rate that typically changes over the course of a day.
- The fixed exchange rate type is a rate that does not change over a defined period of time.

WIP Settings

The Financial Management WIP Settings page enables you to specify source fields. These fields enable you to specify how an entity, location, or department acts as a source. Table 7-2 describes three types of source departments.

Table 7-2. Three Types of Source Departments

Project department	Use if the entity, location, or department is acting as an investment.
Client department	Use if the entity, location, or department is acting as a company.
Employee department	Use if the entity, location, or department is acting as a resource.

The Financial Management WIP Settings page enables you to set WIP aging levels. You must indicate the number of days for each WIP level. The selections made on the WIP Settings page are the values that will be written to the database for each transaction.

Charge Codes

Charge codes enable an additional method of representing any breakdown of work. Charge codes are assigned to investments and become the default for each task within that investment. The charge code value can be overridden at the task level or at the timesheet entry level. Every transaction line must be associated with a charge code before financial posting will process.

Charge codes will typically be used to support capital and expense reporting. Charge codes should also be used to classify work in support of being able to do the following:

- Differentiate costs and rates based on the type of work being performed.
- Define budget line items by the type of work being performed. This is applicable when we are creating manual cost plans or creating plans based on assignments.

Input Type Codes

The input type code is a resource attribute that can also be modified for a time transaction. It differentiates the resource performing the work. The value of the input type code is populated from the resource that is doing the work. The input type code value can be overridden at the timesheet entry level.

Every transaction line must be associated with an input type code before financial posting will process. Input type codes are used primarily to classify resources for reporting or to differentiate costs and rates based on the resource. For example, a resource can work on a task and can associate a transaction line as either regular or overtime, which can then be tied to financial processing. Input type codes also control whether a transaction will be chargeable.

A typical use of input type codes is to identify the type of work being done for the purposes of rates/costs. Examples would include billable/nonbillable or specific types of work such as investment management, functional consulting, technical consulting, or training.

Cost and Rate Matrices

The rate matrix is a user-configurable engine used to determine the costs and rates of external billings and internal chargebacks. The rate matrix can also generate or populate investment budgets (cost plans) based on roles and resources assigned to the investment. Different matrices can be assigned for driving the cost or rates of different resources. For example, an investment can have one matrix assigned to determine the cost for labor, while a different matrix can be assigned to determine the rate charged for labor. This is also the case for materials, equipment, and expenses. Different matrix assignments can be made at the investment, entity, and system default levels. Costs and rates can be captured in one matrix or in separate matrices if needed. Take into consideration the size and manageability of a combined matrix compared to two separate matrices. You can use multiple matrices if you need one matrix for each resource type or one for each project or multiple matrices to support specific needs, such as one for external billing projects and one for internal projects. Complete the general information for the matrix. Then click Manage Matrix in the Finance menu in the Administration Tool. If the Private check box is selected, it indicates that this matrix is restricted to a particular user or set of users.

Financially Enabling Objects

To begin processing transactions and assigning rates to transactions, all impacted objects need to be financially enabled. The following is a list of all objects that are being used by <Company X> followed by a description of how to enable each one:

- Resource
- Project

Resources

Resources need to have financials enabled in order to assign a cost to the units of measure. Please note that financially enabling a resource is different from enabling one for time entry. A resource can be enabled for time entry and generate actual hours via timesheets. However, these transactions will never become financial transactions and assigned a cost unless the resource is financially enabled. A resource must be financially enabled to be selectable both in the rate matrix (provided Resource is a selected column) and in the transaction entry.

To financially enable a resource, navigate to the Resource Information screen and click the Financials link. The Resource Properties screen appears, as shown in Figure 7-2.

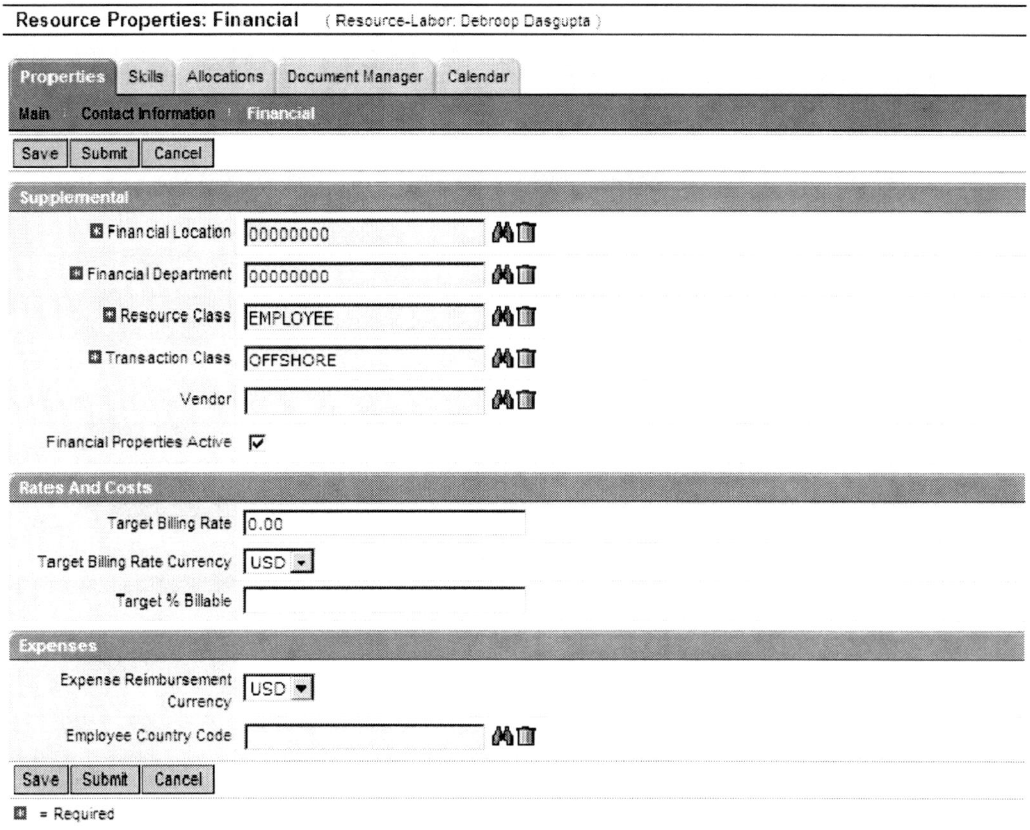

Figure 7-2. Resource Properties screen

There are four different resource types in Clarity: Labor, Equipment, Material, and Expense. These resource types can be broken down further using the resource and transaction classes.

Enter the following data into the financial section. If you are not using Billing and Invoicing, you do not need to fill out the Rates and Costs and Expenses sections.

Note The financial department field is used for identifying the IT department assigned to resources and used on projects to identify customer/department association.

To ensure that all resource transactions are processed correctly, please verify that a default input type code has been selected (on the Resource Properties screen). The default value for some companies is Regular.

Projects

To financially enable a project, navigate to the Project Properties page and click the Financial subpage. You will see the page shown in Figure 7-3.

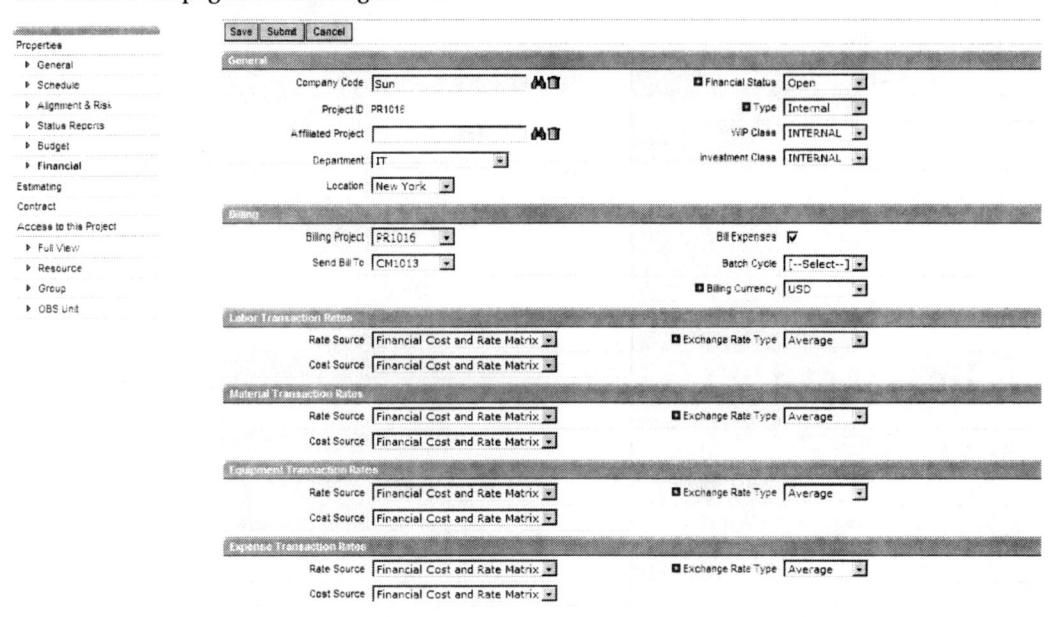

Figure 7-3. Financial subpage

This page is editable only by financial and data administrators (based on user rights). To change the charge code, navigate to the schedule subpage and select the appropriate value. For Department, navigate to the General subpage and select the department from the department OBS at the bottom of the page.

A user can also create a project specific charge code if the Enable Project-specific Charge Codes option is selected under Administration > Project Management > Settings.

It is always a good idea to prepopulate the Charge Code field at the project level to enable population of the Tasks and Timesheet Charge Code field for transaction processing. Charge Code can be also selected at the task level, which will then supersede a project-level selection.

Setting Up Projects for Chargebacks

Chargebacks are the transfer of costs between departments. Chargebacks charge departments for their share of the costs for investments or services that were delivered during a specified period of time. A chargeback represents the debit side of an accounting system. A corresponding credit is issued to departments that provided the investment or service—giving them financial credit for the work they completed.

Charge codes can represent any kind of breakdown of work associated with investments, such as the following:

- Capital vs. expense
- Billable vs. nonbillable

You must set up the following before you can work with chargebacks:

- An entity, including departments and locations
- Transactions classes if you plan to use transactions to match investments with transactions
- General Ledger (GL) accounts to define time-based GL allocations
- Financially enabled team members of projects that are referenced in transactions, including any labor, equipment, material, and expense resources
- Financially enabling the project
- Charge codes and input type codes defined

Debit rules are a set of investment-specific rules that determine how to debit departments for the cost of investments or services that were delivered to them during a specified period of time. A debit rule is composed of a header and time-based GL allocations.

To create a debit rule header, follow these steps:

1. Click the Chargeback tab.
2. Click the Debit Rules link. The Chargebacks page appears.
3. Click New. The Create GL Allocation page appears.
4. Enter the required information.
5. Save changes and continue adding the GL account and department combinations that will be charged for costs. The department will represent the customer (as selected in the project properties), and the GL account will represent the line of business.

Once the rule GL account and department have been created, use the Actions drop-down to change the details screen to Edit mode and enter the percentages based on the allocation code selected on the project's properties screen.

Setting Chargeback Options

Chargeback options determine how and when charges are generated during invoicing. The chargeback type determines whether an investment-defined rule or a standard debit rule is matched to transactions during financial processing. Bill Expense identifies how costs are booked. Bill Expense is also used to match with transactions to determine whether investment costs are invoiced.

Creating Financial Transactions

Financial transactions are created from three main sources:

- Timesheets
- Transaction entry (Voucher Other or Voucher Expense)
- XOG imports/interfaces with external systems

Creating from Timesheets

Transactions that are created from timesheets are created automatically via the Post Timesheets job. When a user enters their time into a timesheet and it has been submitted and approved, the Post Timesheets job is run to parse out the timesheet and create individual transactions. The actual hours are moved from Pending Actuals to Actuals when this job completes. The timesheets can move to the next stage of financial processing using the Post to Financials job. The system validates that all the required financial elements are in place for successful transaction processing. This job moves transactions from projects and resources that are financially enabled to the next stage of processing. Any transaction that does not meet all of the financial processing criteria will show up in the Invalid Transactions log and should be corrected prior to creating monthly invoices. See the "Correcting Transactions" section of this chapter for more information on Invalid Transactions.

Creating from Transaction Entry (Vouchers)

Prior to entering a manual transaction, you must create a voucher. There are two types of vouchers, Expense and Other, and each accepts specific types of transactions. Table 7-3 gives the types of transactions accepted for each type of voucher.

Table 7-3. Transactions Accepted by Each Type of Voucher

Voucher Type	Transaction Type
Voucher Expense	Expense.
	This can include fixed-fee consultant labor being added as an expense.
	These transactions will need to be associated with an expense resource type.
Voucher Other	This voucher type is used for manually entered labor, material, and equipment entries.

Creating a Voucher (Clarity Administrators Only)

Voucher creation will be done on a weekly basis by a Clarity administrator.

To create a voucher, navigate to the Transaction Entry screen and complete the following steps:

1. Click the New button.
2. Select the entry type based on the type of voucher you want to create. Use Voucher Other for labor transactions, and use Voucher Expense for nonlabor transactions including labor being entered as an expense, such as fixed-fee consultants.
3. Enter the entry number. A suggested naming convention is <YYYYMMDD><EXP/OTH>, where <YYYYMMDD> is the day at the end of the week that the voucher was created and <EXP or OTH> is the three-letter code for the type of voucher. For example, when naming the expense voucher for the week ending July 21, 2007, the entry number would be 20070721EXP.
4. Click Save or Submit.

Entering Manual Transactions

Manual transaction entry functionality is used to facilitate the following:

- Fixed-fee consultant costs
- Manual transaction adjustments (completed by financial admins only)

To enter a transaction, do the following:

1. Navigate to the Transaction Entry screen.
2. Select the appropriate voucher based on the type of transaction you will be entering.
3. Under the Transactions section, click New.
4. The Transaction Detail screen displays, as shown in Figure 7-4.
5. Complete the fields.

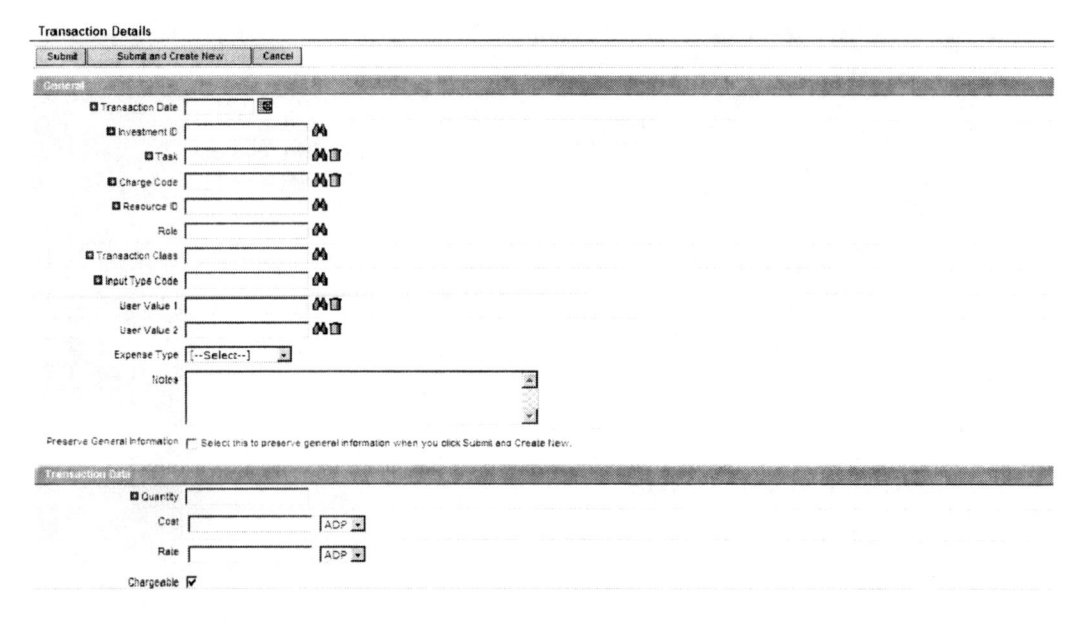

CHAPTER 7 ■ CA CLARITY PPM COMPONENTS: FINANCIAL MANAGEMENT

Figure 7-4. Transaction Details screen

Table 7-4 gives the field names found in Figure 7-4 and a brief description of the fields.

Table 7-4. Fields and Their Descriptions in the Transaction Details Screen Shown in Figure 7-4

Field	Description
Transaction Date	Effective date of the transaction.
Investment ID	ID of the project. NOTE: Only projects that have been financially enabled will appear when browsing.
Task	ID of the task. NOTE: This displays only the tasks for the selected project. Each project should contain at least one task designed to capture expenses.
Charge Code	Charge code ID. NOTE: This will autofill with the charge code of the task if available.
Resource ID	ID of the resource. NOTE: Only resources that have been financially enabled will appear when browsing.

Role	Project role. NOTE: Autofills with the resource primary role.
Transaction Class	Classification of transaction. NOTE: Autofills with the transaction class of the resource. Do not change this.
Input Type	Input type of transaction. Autofills with the input type of the resource (<Company X> default = Regular).
Utility Code 1	Not used.
Utility Code 2	Not used.
Expense Type	Not used.
Notes	Notes entered describing the transaction.
Preserve General Information	Select this indicator if you plan on making multiple entries for the same project/task/resource.
Quantity	The total number of units for the transaction (hours for labor).
Cost	Cost per unit. Leave blank to run through the rate matrix.
Rate	Rate per unit. Leave blank to run through the rate matrix.
Chargeable	Indicator if transaction is chargeable. Not used.

Click Submit to save and exit to the voucher entry screen or click Submit and Create New to save and open a new Transaction Details screen. If we select the Preserve General Information indicator and click Submit and Create New, it creates a new transaction prefilled with the basic data.

Click Cancel to exit the voucher and return to the Transaction Entry screen.

Transaction Processing

Figure 7-5 shows a diagram of the general flow of transactions through Clarity. Note that the boxes highlighted are entry points into the process and reflect the three methods for creating transactions mentioned previously.

This is just a simple flow of data through the system and does not entirely reflect all the tables and data impacted during the processing of financial transactions.

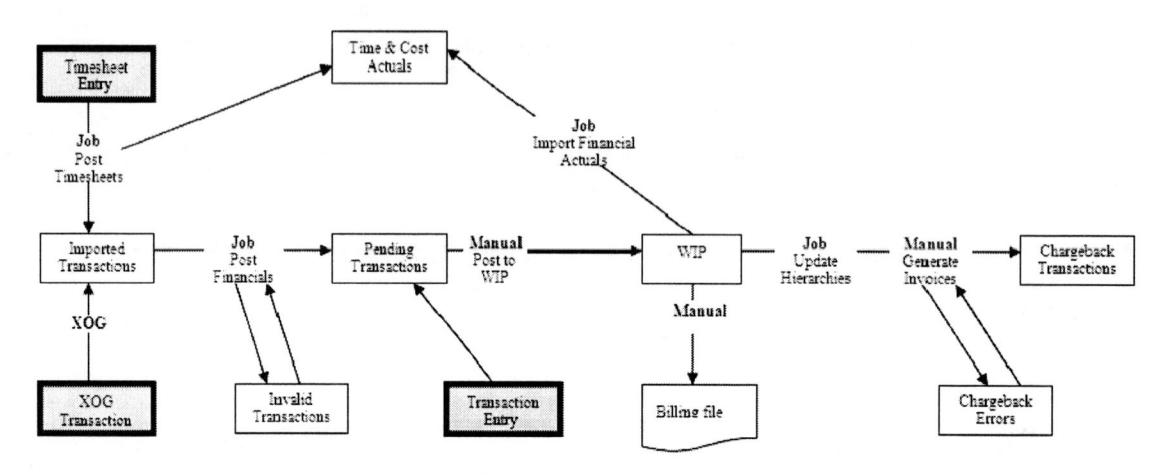

Figure 7-5. General flow of transactions through Clarity

Transaction Movement

Transactions move through the various tables in Clarity by jobs and manual actions. Jobs are usually scheduled to occur at predefined intervals, while manual actions need to be started through the UI by specified individuals. Table 7-5 summarizes each job or manual action that needs to occur to move the transactions through the process. Table 7-5 shows the action and describes the transactions.

Table 7-5. Transaction Actions and Descriptions

Action	Description
Post Timesheets Job	This job runs against only those timesheets with a status of Approved. It takes the timesheet and parses each of the entries into individual transactions for financial processing and for posts to the Time Actuals to the Time & Cost Actuals tables.
Post Financial Job	This job takes the transactions that were created by the Post Timesheets job or XOG and runs them through the rate matrix to assign rates and cost. If the transactions process without errors, the job posts the transactions to Pending Transactions in preparation for posting to WIP. Transactions with errors are sent to Invalid Transactions for review and correction/deletion.
Post to WIP	The Post to WIP process is kicked off manually and moves all transactions in the Pending Transactions table to WIP. In addition, it closes all vouchers (if selected).
Import Financial Actuals	The Import Financial Actuals job moves those transactions in WIP that have not been posted to the Time/Cost Actuals tables. This includes WIP

	adjustments and manual transaction entry.
Update Hierarchies	Updates cost and allocation data for investments hierarchies. Run this job when there have been multiple changes in the investment hierarchy.
Generate Invoices	Generates chargeback invoices within Clarity. This should *not* be confused with the company's IT monthly invoice report, which will still need to be run separately.

Work in Process (WIP) and Actual Cost

WIP is the end of the initial transaction process. When a transaction gets to WIP, it has passed all internal validation and is considered to be an actual cost of projects or other investments. While actual hours entered get posted to projects when the Post Timesheets job occurs, the actual costs of the time entered do not show on the project until after the transactions have been posted to WIP. This includes those project expenses entered directly into the system through the Transaction Entry screens. In essence, something is not considered an actual cost on the project until it has made it to WIP and the Import Financial Actuals job has been run. WIP is where all costs on a project are captured and capitalized.

The set of tables that make up WIP contain the entered transactions that can be subsequently posted to an accounting system. Post to WIP recognizes negative values when transactions are posted. Once a transaction has been posted to WIP, it has passed all validation criteria and is available for billing, invoicing, and posting to the general ledger (GL). From this point on, a detailed record of modifications, adjustments, and billings is logged. You cannot delete posted WIP transactions but can change them through the WIP adjustment process.

Transactions available for posting to WIP are not automatically displayed. You must first search for the transactions you want to post to WIP. Two methods of WIP posting are available:

- *Full Post* lets you select all accumulated transactions within a specified date range. Perform a full post only when the total number of transactions is small. During a full post, you can preview all transactions and decide to continue posting all the transactions.

- *Selective Post* lets you filter transactions. During a selective post, you can limit the selection of transactions based on location, client, project, resource, and transaction type. Selective posts are useful when you want to post a selected batch of transactions or one that was not entered in time for a regularly scheduled post to WIP.

To Post Transactions to WIP

The following is a step-by-step process to post transactions to WIP. Refer to the fields in Figure 7-6.

Step 1: Select Post to WIP from the Financial Management menu. See Figure 7-6.

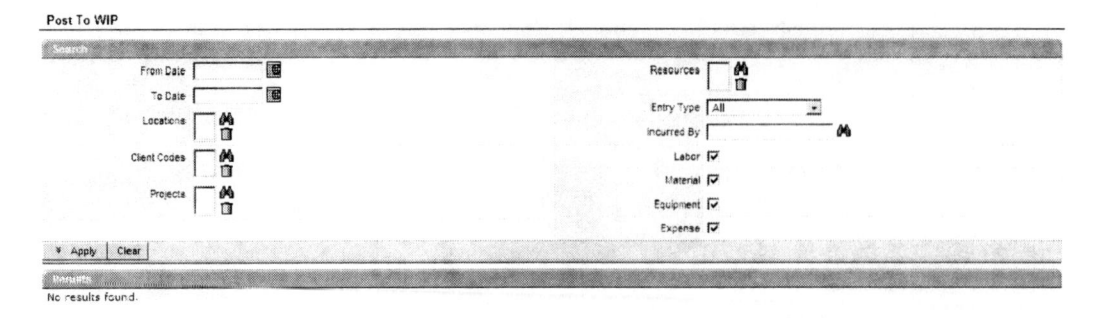

Figure 7-6. Posting transactions to WIP

Step 2: Search for the transactions you want to post. Use the following criteria:

- *From Date and To Date*: Use the date picker to post transactions within the specified date range.
- *Locations*: Use this field to post transactions associated with selected financial locations. Only locations with pending transactions will appear in the browse list. Certain companies don't use this since there is only one default location.
- *Client Codes*: Use this field to select transactions associated with specified client codes.
- *Investments*: Use this to post transactions associated with selected projects.
- *Resources*: Use this to post transactions associated with selected resources.
- *Entry Type*: Post transactions based on the transaction entry. The following are the options:
    - *All*: Post transactions regardless of entry type.
    - *Imported*: Post transactions imported from an external accounting system.
    - *Clarity*: Post transactions generated from timesheets.
    - *Voucher-Expense*: Post transactions entered as Voucher-Expense.
    - *Voucher-Other*: Post transactions entered as Voucher-Other.

Step 3: Click Apply to filter transactions based on the entered criteria. All transactions that match the criteria grouped into a transaction account, such as All for a full post or Location for a selected post based on location, are displayed. By default, the check box next to this account is selected.

Step 4: Click Post to stage the transactions for posting to WIP.

Correcting Transactions (Clarity and Financial Administrators Only)

A transaction may need correction for several reasons. These range from processing errors to user mistakes. Clarity will check all transactions against internal rules prior to moving through the process, but it does not catch external business rules.

Invalid Transactions

Transactions will appear on the Invalid Transactions screen (on the admin side of Clarity) when they do not meet the internal validation rules for Clarity when the Post Transactions to Financials job is run. To view the invalid transactions, navigate to the Administration Tool and click the Invalid Transactions link in the Project Management section of the menu bar. Figure 7-7 shows an Invalid Transactions screen.

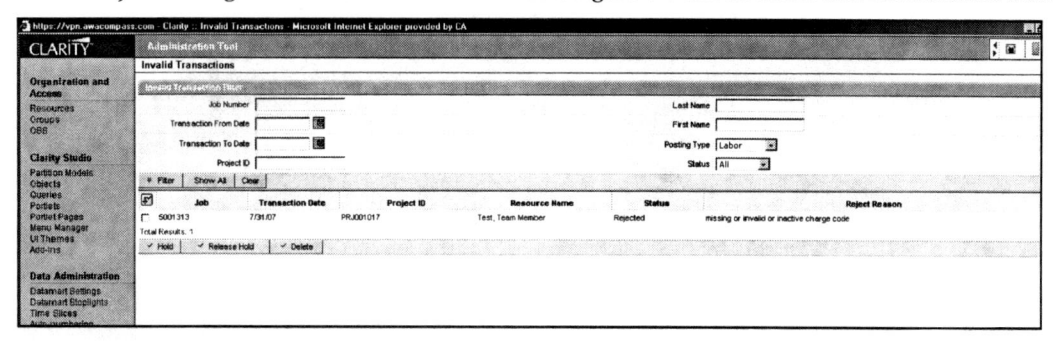

Figure 7-7. Invalid Transactions screen

Invalid transactions will have a description of why each transaction was rejected. Once the issue has been resolved, you can run the Post Transactions to Financial job again, and it should finish processing the transactions. In some cases, you may have to delete the transactions to clear them. These transactions are lost and cannot be recovered. Table 7-6 shows some guidelines for correcting transactions.

Table 7-6. Guidelines for Error Correcting Transactions

Error	Actions
Project Not Financially Active	Verify the Project Financial status is Active. Run the Post Trans to Financials job.
Resource Not Financially Active	Verify the resource's Financial Active Indicator is True. Run the Post Trans to Financials Job.
Missing or Invalid or Inactive Input Type	Verify that the resource's default input type code is set to Regular. Open the timesheet.

	Select Adjust Timesheet.
	Select the input type Code.
	Send the timesheet through the process of posting timesheets and posting transactions to financials.
	NOTE: The system will create negative transactions for the ones that failed. Once processed successfully, you will need to delete both sets of transactions from the Invalid Transactions screen.
Missing or Invalid or Inactive Charge Code	Verify that the task's default charge code has been selected.
	Open the timesheet.
	Select Adjust Timesheet.
	Add the charge code to the Timesheet columns.
	Select the charge code.
	Send the timesheet through the process again.
	NOTE: The system will create negative transactions for the ones that failed. Once processed successfully, you will need to delete both sets of transactions from the Invalid Transactions screen.
Unable to Get Exchange Rate	Verify that the department and location have been selected for the project.
	Verify that the exchange rate has been defined and the types match.
	Run the Post Transactions to Financial job.

Note The system does not catch resources or projects that are not financially enabled or on hold. The assumption for these is that all if a resource is not financially enabled, Clarity should not be attempting to run them through the financial process. Some businesses have created custom reports to list all projects and resources that do not have the required financial fields completed.

Placing a transaction on hold will keep the transaction from being included the next time the Post Transactions to Financials job is run.

WIP Adjustments

Adjustments can be made directly to WIP transactions that are posted via the Post to WIP job. Whenever this is done, a reversing entry is created, and Clarity creates a new entry with the adjusted information.

Any adjustments done will be reflected in the project once the Import Financial Actuals job is run. You can also simply reverse a transaction by selecting the appropriate transaction(s) and clicking the Reverse button.

To create a WIP adjustment, follow these steps:

1. Navigate to the Create WIP Adjustment screen.
2. Enter any filter criteria and click the Filter button.
3. Select the transaction to open it.
4. Make the necessary changes (this is a similar screen to Transaction Entry).
5. Click Submit.

A reversal cancels the original posted transaction before it is billed to a client or charged to an internal department. When a reversal occurs, a new transaction is created for a complete audit trail.

A transfer occurs when a transaction (or set of transactions) is moved from one entity, client, cost code, or employee to another at the same level of grouping. The transfer generates an automatic reversal entry and a new replacement entry.

Once all WIP adjustments have been made, navigate to the Approve WIP Adjustment screen and approve all WIP adjustments. Adjustments cannot be billed and are not visible against cost plans or in the transaction reports until they are approved. Based on the security rights, access to the list of adjusted transactions can be found through the Approve WIP Adjustment link in the Financial Management menu of the home page on the application side of CA Clarity PPM.

Guidelines on Using Transaction Entry, WIP Adjustments, and Adjusted Timesheets

Table 7-7 gives guidelines on the method that should be used to correct the transactions in WIP and the person responsible for the action.

Table 7-7. Method to Correct WIP Transactions

Issue	Recommended Method	Person Responsible
Incorrect project or task	WIP adjustment.	
Incorrect input type code	Adjust timesheet (several transactions on one) or WIP adjustment (single).	User admin
Incorrect charge code	Adjust timesheet (several transactions on one) or WIP adjustment (single).	Project admin
Incorrect rate	Adjust timesheet (several transactions on one) or WIP adjustment (single).	User admin
Incorrect invoice	WIP adjustment.	IT finance

	amount/quantity		
	Missing time (bulk)	Transaction entry.	System admin
	Incorrect resource (nonlabor and fixed fee)	WIP adjustment.	IT finance
	Wrong transaction date	WIP adjustment (use transfer).	
	Transaction was marked as billable and should be nonbillable (or vice versa)		
	Delete a WIP transaction	WIP adjustment (use reverse).	
Chargeback Errors			
	No chargeback type set on investment.	Set the chargeback options for the investment.	Automated
	No credit rule allocation details in range of transaction date.	Define a GL allocation in the credit rule for the transaction date.	Automated
	No debit rule allocation details in the range of the transaction date.	Define a GL allocation in the debit rule for the transaction date.	Automated
	No matching credit rule found.	If no credit rule exists, create a new credit rule. If a credit rule exists, compare its criteria with the transaction and adjust or create a new rule to match the transaction, or adjust the transaction to match the rule.	Automated

You can view all transactions posted to ensure they were posted correctly. If there are errors, you can reverse the charges.

Review Transactions and Reverse Charges:

To review transactions and reverse charges, follow these steps:

1. Select Transactions from the Financial Management menu. A list of transactions appears. By default, transactions are filtered by the current fiscal time period.
2. Filter or browse for the transactions you want to review. Review the transactions.
3. If transactions are incorrect and require adjustments, do one of the following:
   - Select each transaction whose charges you want to reverse and then click Reverse Selected Charges.
   - Click Reverse Filtered Charges to reverse charges of all transactions listed.
4. The selected transactions indicate that charges were reversed, as shown in Figure 7-8.

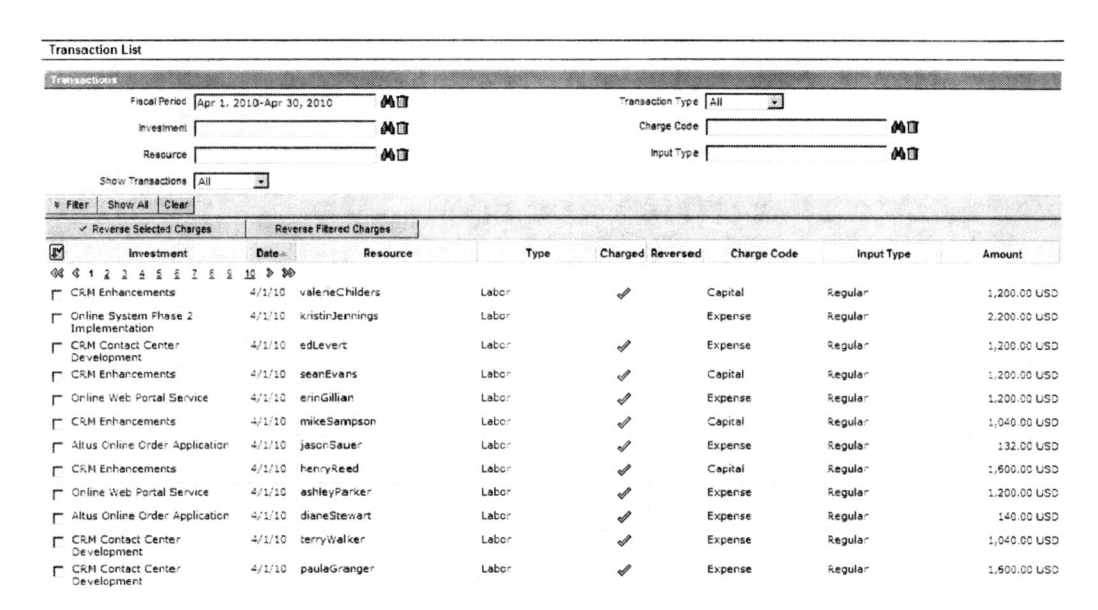

Figure 7-8. Transactions selected for reverse charge

Clarity Invoices

Each department (customer) will receive an invoice for each time period. You can view invoices periodically to monitor charges, make corrections, approve or reject invoices, and manually regenerate invoices. You can view invoices, and you can also drill down and view details and transaction information.

- The invoice is generated by running the Generate Invoice job. The invoice now has a status of Pro-forma. At this point, it is still open to receive additional transactions. The financial administrator can manually regenerate invoices to capture any additional transactions or adjustments.

- Submit the invoice for approval. The status changes to Submitted, the invoice becomes locked, and no further transactions can be added. If additional transactions are processed for that time period, they are added to the next time period's invoice.

- Once the status is changed to Approved, the invoice is complete.

- At this point, the IT monthly invoice report can be generated for each customer.

Financial administrators can view all chargeback-related invoices from the financial management invoice pages. Click Invoices from the Financial Management menu. A list of invoices appears. You can view invoice status and amount, as shown in Figure 7-9. Table 7-8 shows the messages and possible resolutions by the financial administrators while reviewing invoices.

Invoice Number	Department	Period	Invoice Date	Status	Amount
INV1021	fi_it	Jan 1, 2009-Jan 31, 2009	1/30/11	Pro-forma	6,920.00 USD
INV1000	Finance	2009-11	11/30/09	Approved	64,713.60 USD
INV1003	Finance	2009-12	12/31/09	Approved	70,876.80 USD
INV1006	Finance	2010-01	1/31/10	Approved	64,713.60 USD
INV1009	Finance	2010-02	2/28/10	Pro-forma	64,128.00 USD
INV1013	Finance	2010-03	3/31/10	Pro-forma	99,188.80 USD
INV1017	Finance	2010-04	4/30/10	Pro-forma	81,623.20 USD
INV1001	Human Resources	2009-11	11/30/09	Approved	61,622.40 USD
INV1004	Human Resources	2009-12	12/31/09	Approved	67,491.20 USD
INV1007	Human Resources	2010-01	1/31/10	Approved	61,622.40 USD
INV1010	Human Resources	2010-02	2/28/10	Pro-forma	63,680.00 USD
INV1014	Human Resources	2010-03	3/31/10	Pro-forma	124,115.20 USD
INV1018	Human Resources	2010-04	4/30/10	Pro-forma	92,212.80 USD
INV1022	IT	2009-10	2/7/11	Approved	562.50 USD
INV1011	IT	2010-02	2/28/10	Pro-forma	99,840.75 USD
INV1015	IT	2010-03	3/31/10	Pro-forma	98,880.00 USD
INV1019	IT	2010-04	4/30/10	Pro-forma	148,320.00 USD
INV1002	Sales & Marketing	2009-11	11/30/09	Approved	17,976.00 USD
INV1005	Sales & Marketing	2009-12	12/31/09	Approved	19,688.00 USD
INV1008	Sales & Marketing	2010-01	1/31/10	Pro-forma	17,976.00 USD

Figure 7-9. Invoice report

Table 7-8. Messages and Resolutions During Invoice Review

Type	Message	Possible Resolution
Warning	No chargeback type is set on the investment.	Set the chargeback options for the investment.
Error	No credit rule allocation details in range of the transaction date.	Define a GL allocation in the credit rule for the transaction date.
Error	No debit rule allocation details in the range of transaction date.	Define a GL allocation in the debit rule for the transaction date.
Error	No matching credit rule found.	If no credit rule exists, create a new credit rule. If a credit rule exists, compare its criteria with the transaction and adjust it or create a new rule to match the transaction, or adjust the transaction to match the rule.

Reviewing Invoice Details

You can view invoice details, prior period adjustments, and the invoice amount. You can also take various actions on invoices, such as approving or rejecting them.

To view invoice details, follow these steps:

1. Open the invoice.
2. Click the Invoice Number link to view invoice details.

    - *Investment*: The investment (project) from which the charges originated.
    - *Amount*: The amount of the charge for the specified time period. Click this link to drill down and view transaction details.
    - *Prior Period Adjustment*: The amount of an adjustment that occurred during a previous time period. If zero, then no prior period adjustments were made. Click this link to drill down and view adjustment details.
    - *Total Amount*: The total amount of the charges less adjustments for the specified time period. Click this link to drill down and view transaction details.
    - *Subscription*: A check mark appears if you have subscribed to a service.

3. Drill down to view a transaction and prior period adjustment details as needed. Key information includes the following:

    - *Type*: Indicates whether the transaction is a work-in-progress (WIP) or an adjustment
    - *Amount*: The amount of the transaction

- *Percentage:* The percentage charged to the service
- *Scaled Amount:* The scaled dollar amount based on the percentage charged to the service

4. If the invoice is not yet approved, you can do the following (depending on granted access rights):

   - Submit the invoice
   - Lock or unlock the invoice
   - Approve or reject the invoice
   - Regenerate the invoice

IT Chargeback Recovery

A recovery statement shows departments how much of their incurred costs can be recovered from the departments that benefited from services provided. Incurred costs are charged to the departments that receive services. Only departments that provide services can view department recovery statements. Only one department, IT Chargeback Recovery, has been set up as a service provider, so that will be the only recovery statement created. The recovery statement is created when the Generate Invoices job runs. Use the links on the individual costs to drill down to the transaction details. Figure 7-10 shows a recovery statement.

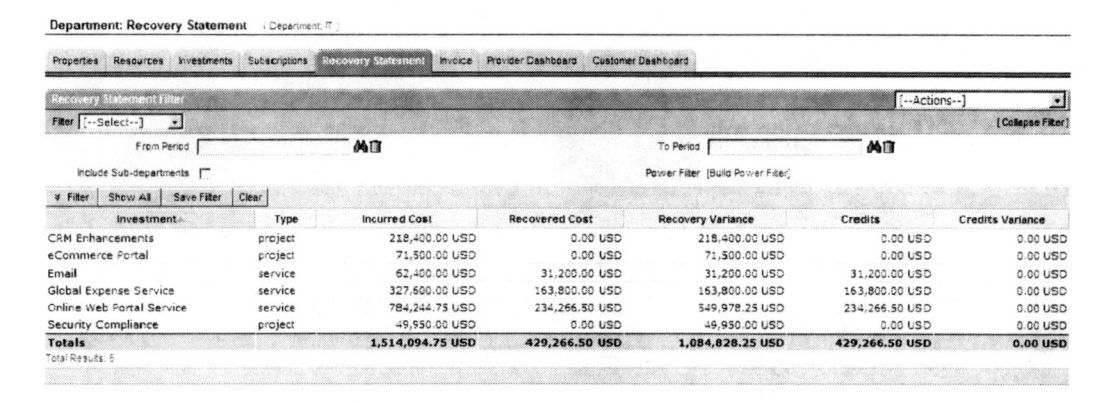

Investment	Type	Incurred Cost	Recovered Cost	Recovery Variance	Credits	Credits Variance
CRM Enhancements	project	218,400.00 USD	0.00 USD	218,400.00 USD	0.00 USD	0.00 USD
eCommerce Portal	project	71,500.00 USD	0.00 USD	71,500.00 USD	0.00 USD	0.00 USD
Email	service	62,400.00 USD	31,200.00 USD	31,200.00 USD	31,200.00 USD	0.00 USD
Global Expense Service	service	327,600.00 USD	163,800.00 USD	163,800.00 USD	163,800.00 USD	0.00 USD
Online Web Portal Service	service	784,244.75 USD	234,266.50 USD	549,978.25 USD	234,266.50 USD	0.00 USD
Security Compliance	project	49,950.00 USD	0.00 USD	49,950.00 USD	0.00 USD	0.00 USD
Totals		**1,514,094.75 USD**	**429,266.50 USD**	**1,084,828.25 USD**	**429,266.50 USD**	**0.00 USD**

Figure 7-10. A sample recovery statement

View a Recovery Statement Summary

To view a recovery statement summary, follow these steps:

1. Select Departments from the Portfolio Management menu, and click the Department link to open the department.
2. Click the Recovery Statement tab.

3. Browse or filter recovery information as needed. A list of investments owned by the department appears with the following information:

- *Investment*: The name of the investment owned by this department and offered as a service to other departments.

- *Type*: Indicates whether the investment is a service or some other type of investment.

- *Incurred Cost*: The total cost incurred to date by this investment that was *charged* to other departments. Click this value to drill down to view transaction details.

- *Recovered Cost*: The total charges *approved* to date by departments charged for this investment. It is the total costs recovered to date by this department. Click this value to drill down to view transaction details.

- *Recovery Variance*: The difference to date between incurred costs and recovered costs. It is the total amount this department is expecting to recover.

- *Credits*: The total possible credit this department can receive. Click this value to drill down to view transaction details.

- *Credits Variance*: The difference to date between incurred costs and credit.

To View Recovery Statement Details

To view recovery statement details, follow these steps:

1. Select Departments from the Organization menu, and click the Department link to open the department.
2. Click the Recovery Statement tab. A list of investments appears.
3. Click any of the following links to view transaction details:

    - *Incurred Costs* (shows a breakdown by resource and resource department)

    - *Recovered Costs* (shows a breakdown by line of business)

    - *Credits* (since 100 percent of costs are recovered for <Company X>, this will be the same as recovered cost)

4. Select the Include Sub-departments check box to view transactions from subdepartments. This check box is inactive if subdepartments do not exist.
5. View the following information:

    - *Investment*: The name of the investment from which costs were incurred

    - *Department*: The name of the department who charged for costs

    - *GL Account*: The general ledger account to which credits are posted

    - *Transaction Date*: The date of the transaction

- *Amount:* The total incurred costs
- *Percentage:* The GL allocation defined in the credit rule by the finance manager

Summary

This chapter briefly described the Financial Management component in CA Clarity PPM and how it can be configured to add business value to an organization.

CHAPTER 8

■ ■ ■

Demand Management

Walt is a proud owner of a play park called HappyLand that he opened about two months ago. Right from the start, the park has been a very big hit, especially with families with kids. It has things for all—be it toddlers, teenagers, or families. Walt, like any other entrepreneur, had expected his business to grow well and had given himself a period of one year for this. Within a span of just two months, things started to look up in Walt's business. While the business was growing rapidly, Walt started seeing long queues at the ticket counters and longer waits to get on the rides. This started affecting customer satisfaction. How does Walt take care of things well in time so that he can improve customer satisfaction? How does he handle this *demand*?

Kathy runs a huge departmental store. Her store acts as a one-stop shop for all requirements of a customer. She provides a good ambience in her store, and it carries quality products. Lately she's been observing long queues at the billing counters over the weekends. What should Kathy do to handle the *demand* over the weekends and especially the long queues?

Claire started an online bookstore about three months ago. She currently has about 40 employees working for her firm. She knows that with the kind of response she has been getting and the way her business is increasing, it won't be long before her employee strength could reach 400. In next few months, how does she handle the *demand* in her growing business?

Demand has a natural tendency of always outperforming supply. If supply is more and demand is less, it incurs a loss to the business. However, if demand is more and supply is less, it impacts customer satisfaction, and eventually you will lose customers. This will lead to losses in business.

You cannot fully and accurately manage the demand in your business, but with proper planning and forecasting, you can mitigate the risk. Therefore, the key to demand management is to capture the right metrics and use the data proactively and effectively, at the right time.

Walt would need to figure out ways to cater to an increasing number of customers. It might be as simple as increasing the number of ticket counters or making tickets available online via a web site. As for the rides, the traffic can be effectively distributed. For example, there could be a sequence of events that could be planned differently so that the waiting time of customers could be greatly reduced.

Kathy will need to think along the lines of opening an express counter, providing additional staff to alleviate the demand bottlenecks.

Claire would need to figure out a proper structure for her business. For example, she can add a set of activity-specific business units such as sales, finance, HR, and administration.

Demand management can be used as a centralized approach or an execution of a set of steps that include automation.

The Demand Management module in the CA Clarity PPM system is a means to capture, classify, evaluate, and dispose of all sources of demand. Demand on an IT organization can take many forms. Demand can be a project request, service request, incident, idea for a new product or service, strategic initiative, or support request.

Clarity's Demand Management module supports the management of unplanned work, specifically the following:

- Ideas
- Incidents

Managing unplanned work is an important part of the overall governance model because it allows Acme Data Systems (ADS) to capture, forecast, and make decisions about the total demand of its resources. ADS can also use Demand Management to assess costs incurred due to unplanned work and to view resource utilization. Demand Management provides visibility into incoming demands from all sources such as:

- Project request
- Service request
- Idea for a new product or service
- Strategic initiative
- Support request

Introduction to Idea Management

Ideas are the initial stage of creating new opportunities for investment such as projects, assets, applications, products, services, and other work. Ideas lay the foundation for a specific type of investment by serving as a container for pertinent information. For example, you may have an idea that you think is valuable enough to be evaluated and converted into a project, service, or investment.

Ideas are where future investment opportunities are nurtured into projects, assets, applications, products, and other work. An idea will foster expedient analysis prior to a full-scale investment launch, minimizing the expenditure of valuable resources and funds. In CA Clarity PPM, users have the ability to submit ideas for approval using two methods: by using an approval process for detailed prognosis by committee or by submitting directly to an assigned decision maker for approval.

Life Cycle of an Idea

Figure 8-1 shows the life cycle of an idea and the corresponding status at every stage of the life cycle.

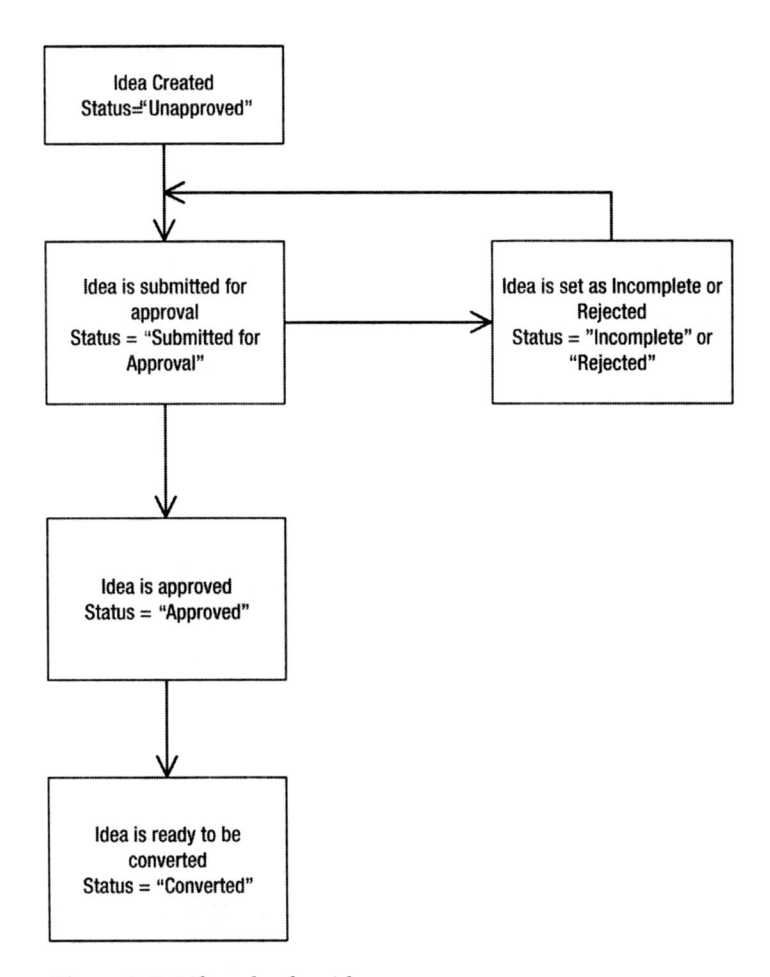

Figure 8-1. Life cycle of an idea

When an idea is created, its status is set to Unapproved. When the idea is finalized, it can be submitted for approval with a status of Submitted for Approval. At this point, the approver may update the status by selecting Approved, Incomplete, or Rejected. Only when the idea is approved will the Convert to Investment option appear.

Idea Creation

A user with an idea can right-click the *Ideas* in the Menu Manager and create a new idea by clicking the New button. A new idea will have a status of Unapproved. Figure 8-2 shows the idea creation screen.

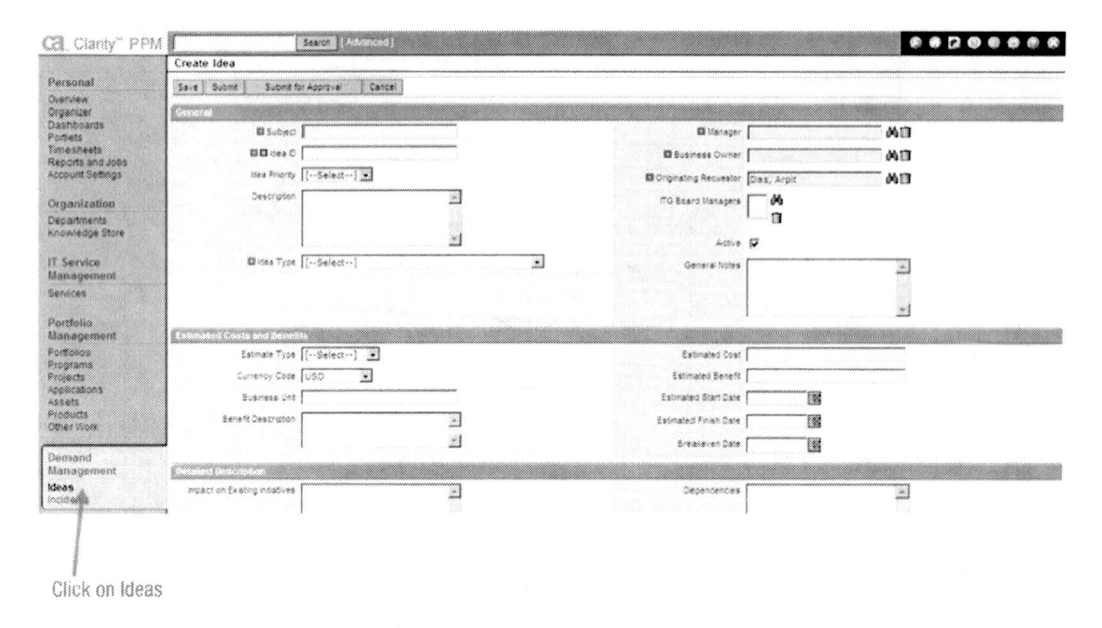

Figure 8-2. Creating an idea

Once the idea creator fills in all the information and clicks Save, a properties page appears, and the idea will be in the Unapproved state. At this stage, the creator can fill in all the information and submit the idea for approval. In certain cases, the idea creator can be different from the originating requestor. For example, if an administrator is delegated to create an idea for a business manager, then the idea creator will be the administrator and the originating requestor will be the business manager. Here's what the important fields and buttons on this page do:

- *Save*: This will save the information on the properties page and stay on the same page.

- *Submit*: This will save and close the properties page and bring you back to the idea list page. This *will not* submit an idea for approval.

- *Submit for Approval*: This button will save and close the properties page and submit the idea for approval. (Figure 8-3 in the next section shows the Submit for Approval button.)

- *Manager*: The user in the Manager field inherits idea edit rights if the idea instance user is selected.

- *Originating Requestor*: By default, the currently logged in user is selected in this field.

- *Target Manager*: The user selected in this field becomes the investment manager when an idea is converted.

Idea Approval

Figure 8-3 shows the screen when the user fills in all the required information for an idea and route the idea for approval. The user has two options:

- Click Submit for Approval.
- Change Status to Submit for Approval.

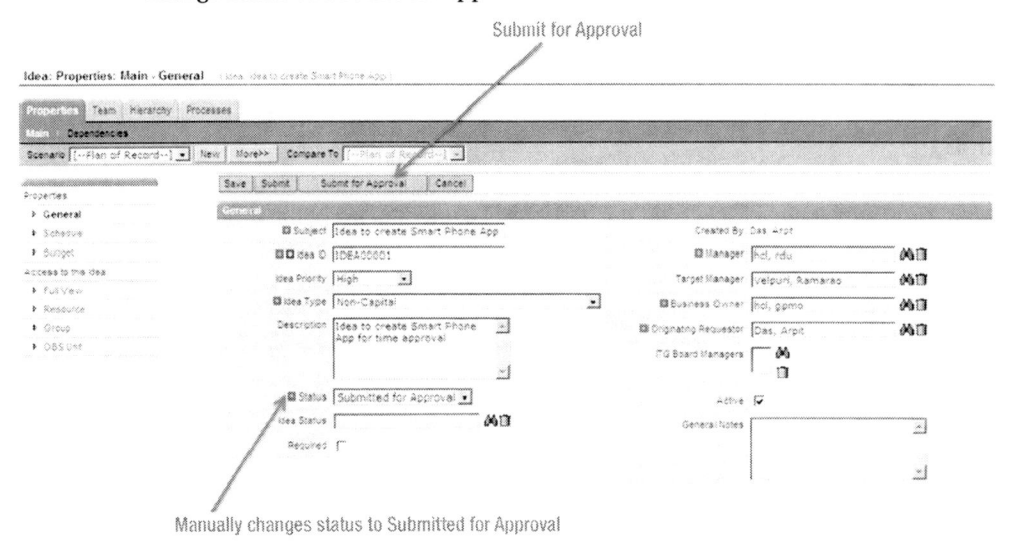

Figure 8-3. Submit for Approval button

Once the idea is submitted for approval, the Submit for Approval button does not appear, as shown in Figure 8-4.

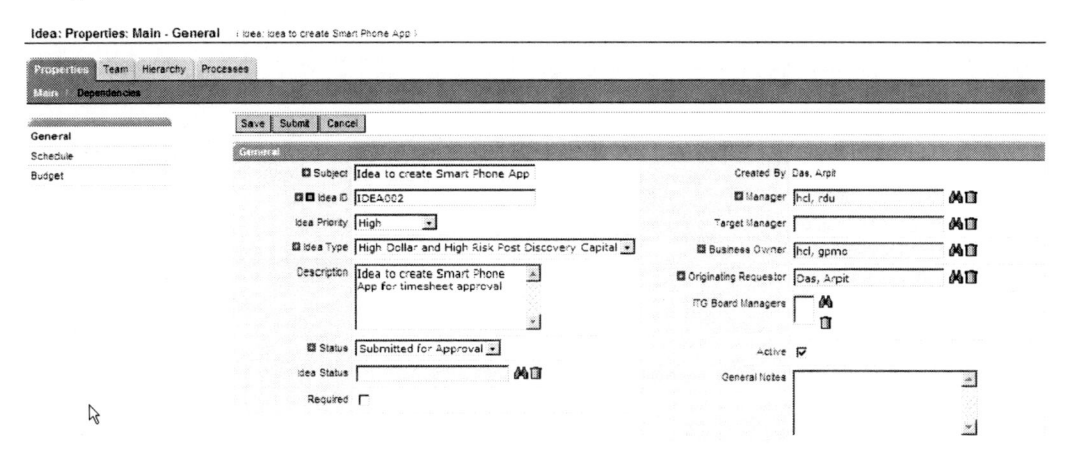

Figure 8-4. Screen after submitting for approval

The ideas can be approved in the following ways:

- By a user with appropriate idea approval rights. The users having idea approval rights will see the Approve button.

- From the ideas list page by selecting the check box next to an idea that has been submitted for approval and then clicking the Approve button.

- By selecting Approved from the Status field on the Properties: Main – General page or through the action items distributed to appropriate managers by an activated idea approval process.

Idea Rejection

Only ideas with a status of Submitted for Approval, Approved, or Incomplete can be rejected. Ideas can be rejected from the ideas list page (in edit mode). Figure 8-5 shows the list of ideas in edit mode. The Status drop-down shows the valid options when an idea is submitted for approval.

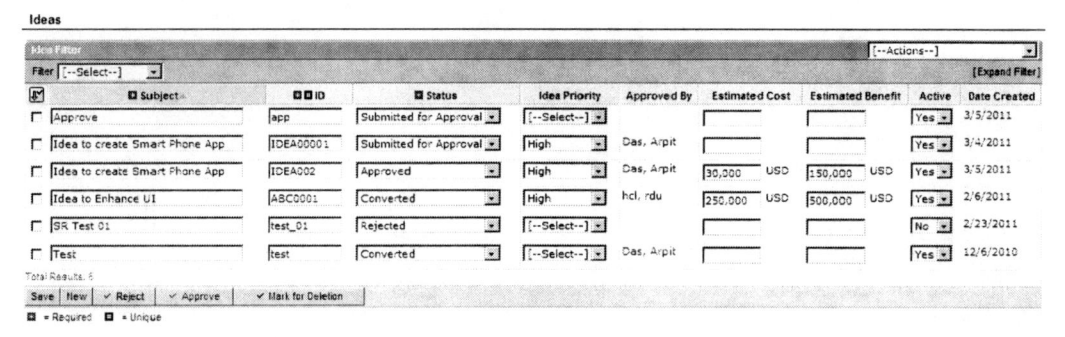

Figure 8-5. Ideas list page

Select an idea on the list page and click the Reject button. Figure 8-6 shows the list of ideas with their status. The user can select multiple ideas with the status Submitted for Approval, Approved, or Incomplete and then click Reject to reject the ideas.

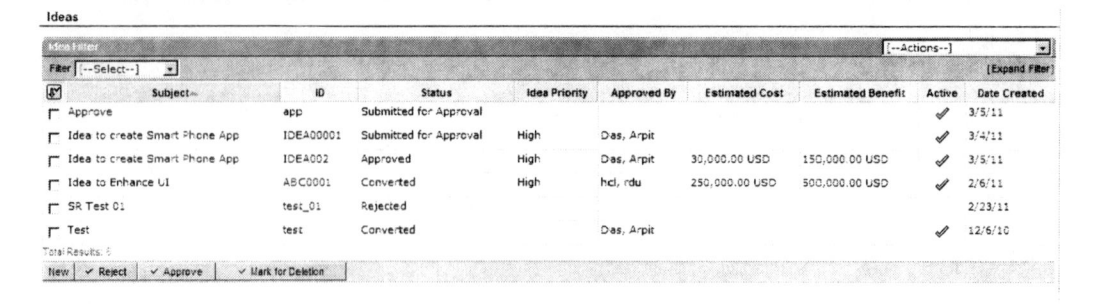

Figure 8-6. Rejecting an idea

CHAPTER 8 ■ DEMAND MANAGEMENT

A user can also reject an individual idea:

- From the Idea: Properties: Main – General page, as shown in Figure 8-7

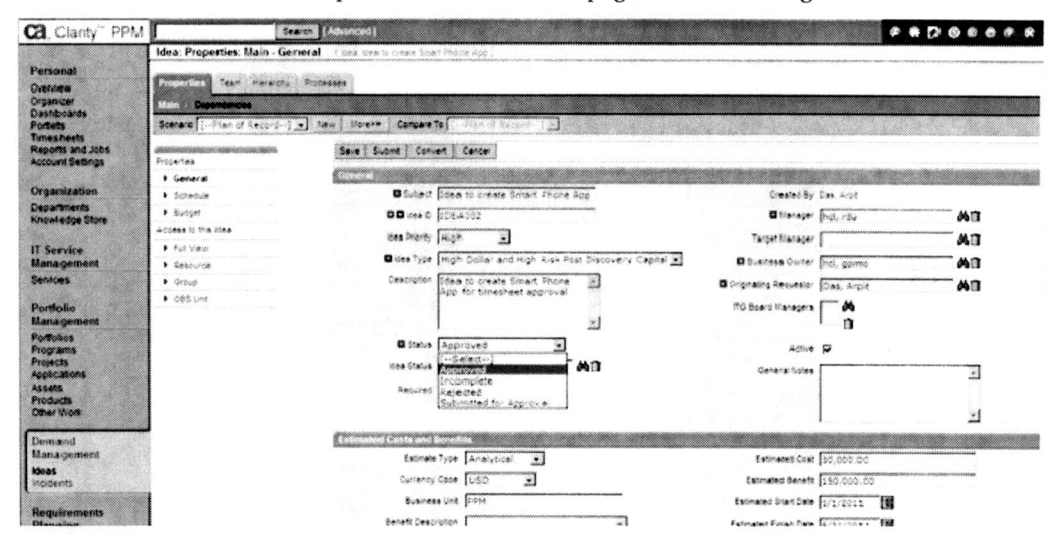

Figure 8-7. Rejecting an individual idea

- Via automated approval process

Converting Ideas

A Convert button appears when an idea is approved, as shown in Figure 8-8.

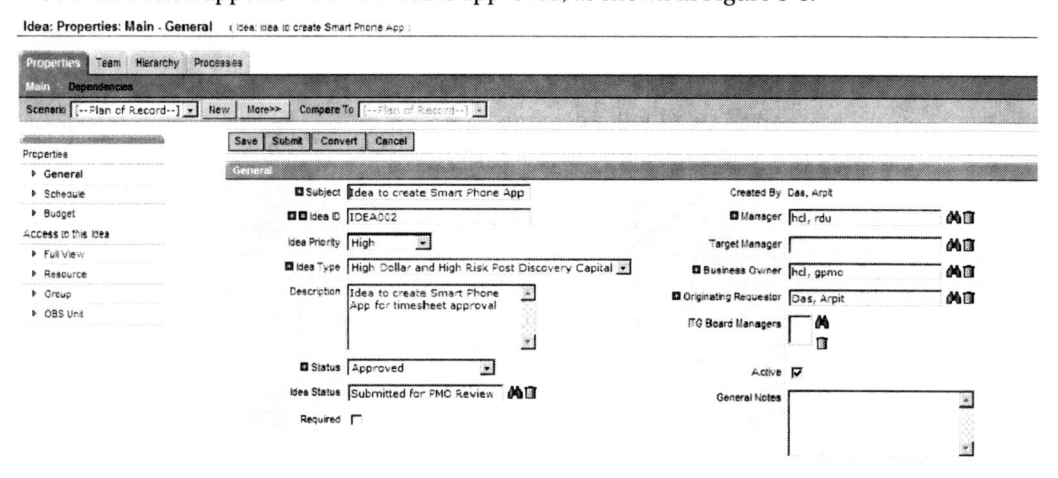

Figure 8-8. Converting ideas

197

After the idea is approved, a manager will have the ability to convert the idea into one of the following, as shown in Figure 8-9:

- Project
- Project from template
- Application
- Asset
- Product
- Service
- Other work

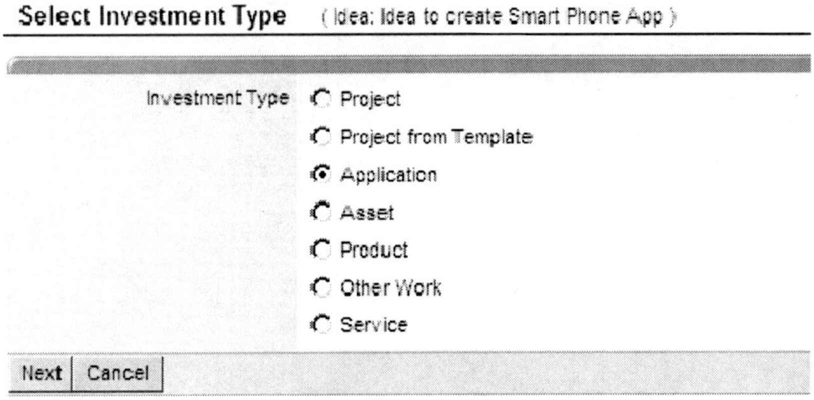

Figure 8-9. Investment types

The investment type options shown the Figure 8-9 are based on the manager's (who is converting the idea) access rights. The user should have the Investment create right(a global right) to see the investment type. For example, users with the Application create right will see only the Application radio button.

Tips

The following are some tips related to idea functionalities:

- After conversion, the idea subject will display as the originating idea (a read-only reference).
- The target manager is the resource who will receive an action item identifying them as the new investment's project manager. If this field is left undefined at conversion, the idea manager becomes the project manager.
- The idea's high-level schedule and budget data are mapped as the investment's Start Date, Finish Date, Planned Cost, and Benefit fields.

- Ideas cannot be financially enabled, meaning you cannot have detailed financial plans, post transactions, enable chargebacks, and billing.
- You can move data from custom attributes from an idea to a converted investment in the following ways:
    - Custom attributes are created at the investment object level and then moved to views for ideas and investments. In this case, if attributes are in views, the data gets mapped after idea conversion.
    - Custom attributes are created with the same attribute IDs. For example, a business requirement is to create an attribute for Business Goals at the idea level and then move it to a converted project. Then create a Business Goals attribute with the same attribute ID as the idea object and project object levels.
    - Use XML mapping to map target and destination object attributes and use the Convert Idea to Project or Convert Object system action in the process.
    - Use a GEL script to copy/update data from idea to investment attributes within the process.
    - OBS information, idea subobjects, and their instances and team information from the idea are not copied to a converted investment. CA Services Global Delivery has prebuilt scripts to accomplish this task. Please contact CA Services via your account manager for more details.

Introduction to Incident Management

Incidents are another type of unplanned work. An *incident* is any event that is not part of the standard operation of a service. Incidents can involve hardware or software but can also include *service requests* (request for support, delivery, information, documentation, and so on).

With Demand Management, you can create incidents to capture these *service requests* and the associated information regarding the assignment, discussion topics, resolution, and time spent to resolve.

Incidents can be created directly in Clarity or through integrations with other systems that already capture help-desk tickets, incidents, and service requests. Requestors will be able to view and edit only the incidents they created; these are listed on the Reported by Me tab. IT workers, on the other hand, will be able to view a list of all incidents associated with the incident category to which they are assigned; these are listed on the Assigned to Me tab. Figure 8-10 shows the Incident List screen with the three tabs. Table 8-1 gives a brief description of the three tabs.

CHAPTER 8 ■ DEMAND MANAGEMENT

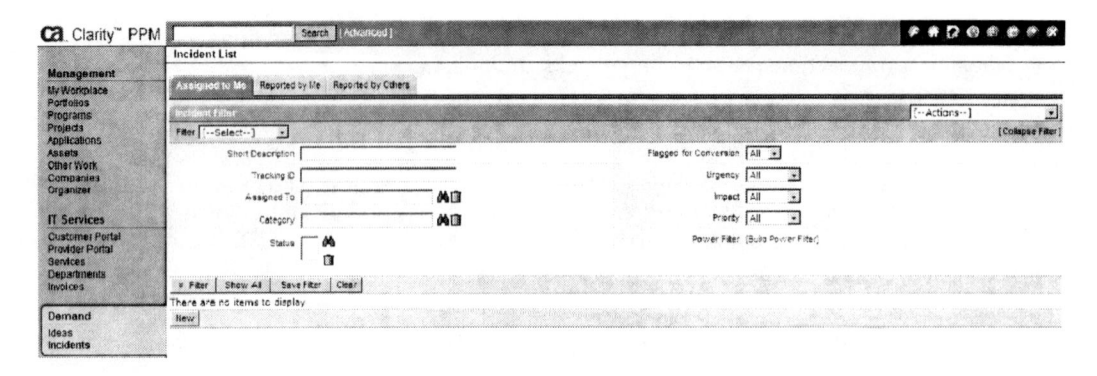

Figure 8-10. Incident List Screen

Table 8-1. Description of the Three Tabs

Tab	Description
Assigned to Me	This tab displays a list of incidents to which you have been assigned. This tab displays IT workers by default when viewing the Incident List screen. This tab also displays requestors when one or more incidents are assigned to the requestor. This tab appears only if you have the Incidents – Manage Category Incidents access right for incidents belonging to incident categories to which you have access rights.
Reported by Me	This tab displays a list of incidents that you reported or any incidents that have been assigned to you. This tab displays requestors and IT managers.
Reported by Others	This tab displays a list of incidents reported by other resources. This list includes incidents mapped to incident categories to which you have access rights, either directly or by association to a group. This list also includes any incidents that have been assigned to you and that have been reported to you. This tab appears only if you have either the Incidents – Create/Edit All access right or the Incidents – Manage Category Incidents access right for incidents belonging to incident categories to which you have access rights.

Each resource can see only those incidents mapped to categories that they have access rights to. Generally, a combination of global and instance rights are required to access, create, and manage the incidents by category.

Incident categories *must* be set up (on administration side, as shown in Figure 8-11) before new incidents can be created. Once categories are set up, a new incident can be created via the Incidents link on the left navigation bar.

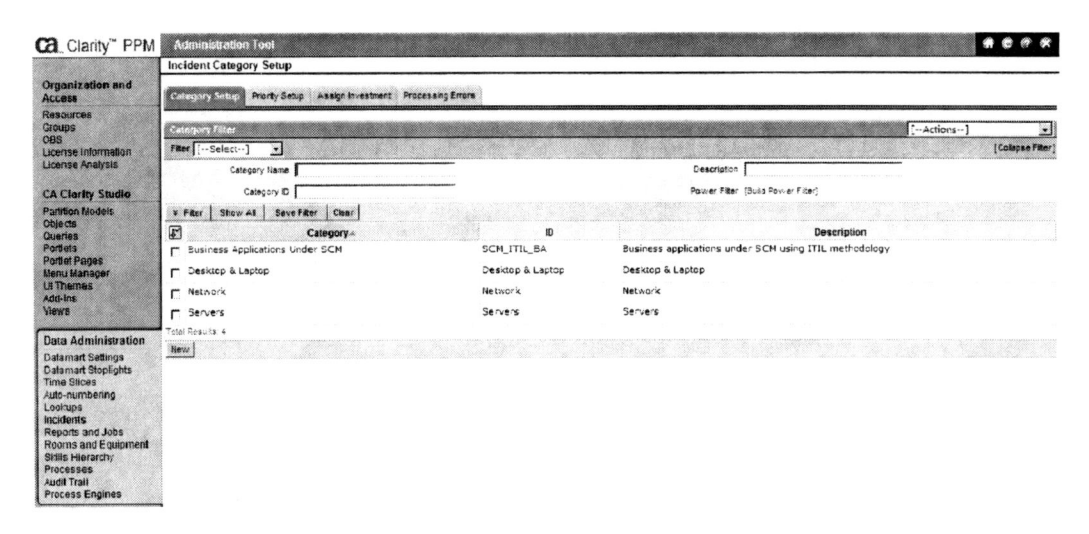

Figure 8-11. Incident category setup

If incident categories are not set up and the user tries to access incidents from the application side, an error will appear, as shown in Figure 8-12.

Figure 8-12. Incident nonconfiguration error

Creating an Incident

Figure 8-13 shows the Create Incident page. It contains specific information about the incident, including several required fields:

- The following fields are shown: Short Description, Tracking ID, Category, Status, Urgency, Impact, and Primary Contact Name.

- The Primary Contact portlet will pull valid information from the resources profile and populate respective fields.
- IT workers may receive notifications when an IT manager assigns work on an incident. These notifications will appear on the Overview: General screen under the Notifications portlet.

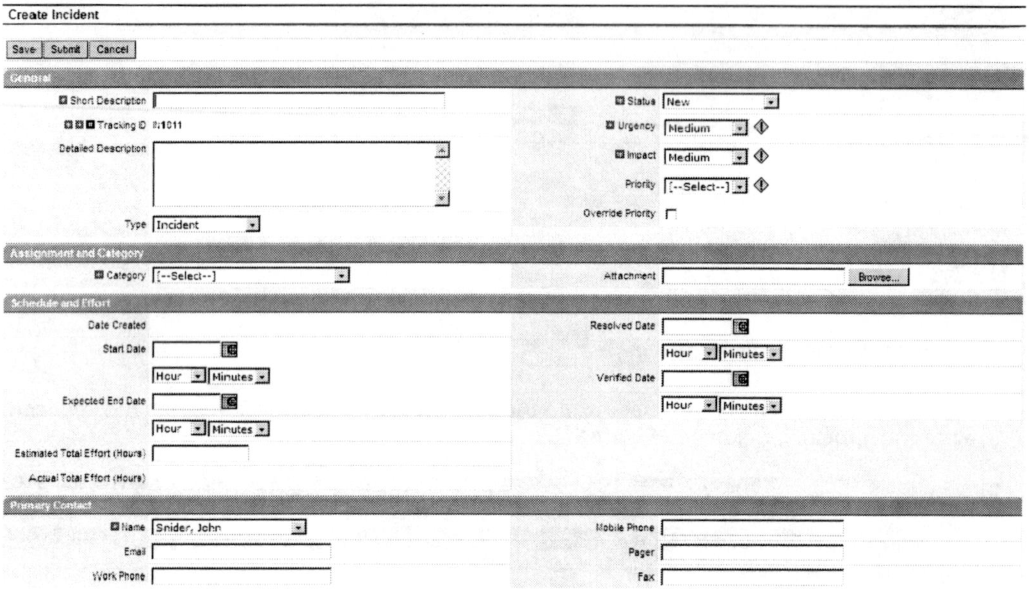

Figure 8-13. Incident creation page

Incident Effort

Resources can enter time against an incident in two ways:

- By using the Enter Time button that appears on the Incident Effort page or on the Incident Properties page. Figure 8-14 shows the Enter Time button.

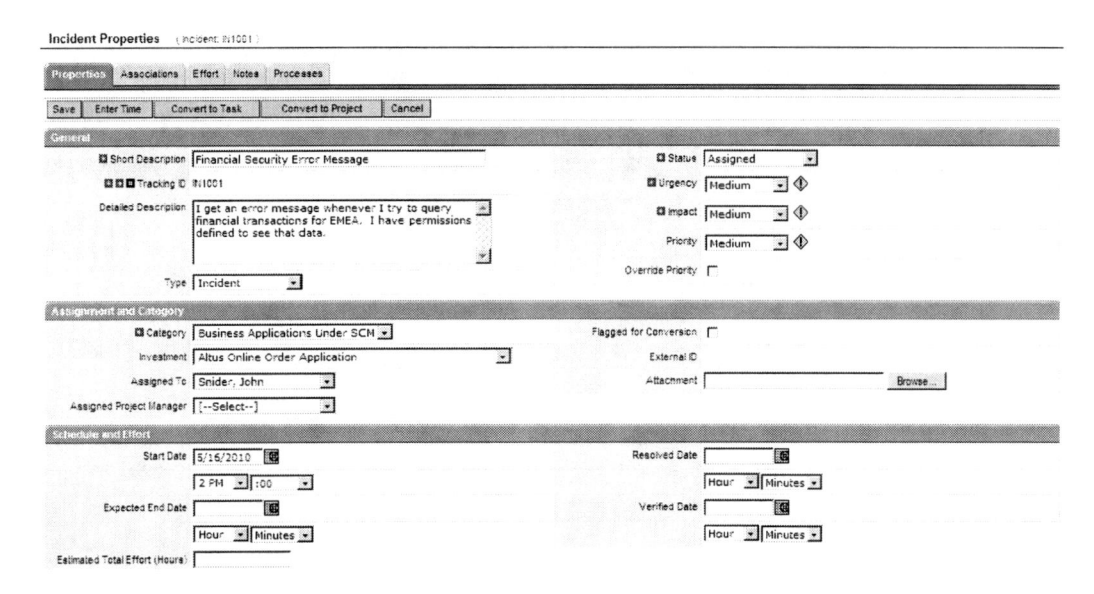

Figure 8-14. Incident Properties page

- By entering directly from a Clarity timesheet, as shown in Figure 8-15.

Figure 8-15. Entering effort through Clarity timesheet

Tips

The following are some tips related to incident functionalities:

- The time entered for the incident does not get carried forward when the incident is converted either to a task on an existing project or to a new project. The incident's effort and the new project's or task's effort represent separate activities and are time-tracked separately.

CHAPTER 8 ■ DEMAND MANAGEMENT

- The Incidents link on the associated application shows all the linked incidents with effort rollup, as shown in Figure 8-16.

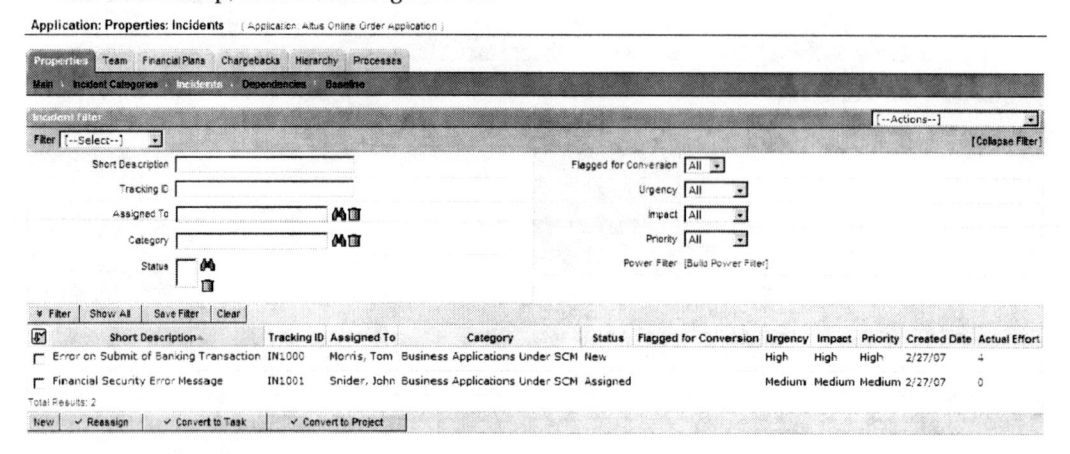

Figure 8-16. Effort rollup of incidents

- The resource picker lookup for the Assigned To field on the incident's properties page lists all resources that have incidents edit rights. Figure 8-17 shows the Assigned To field in the Incident Properties page.

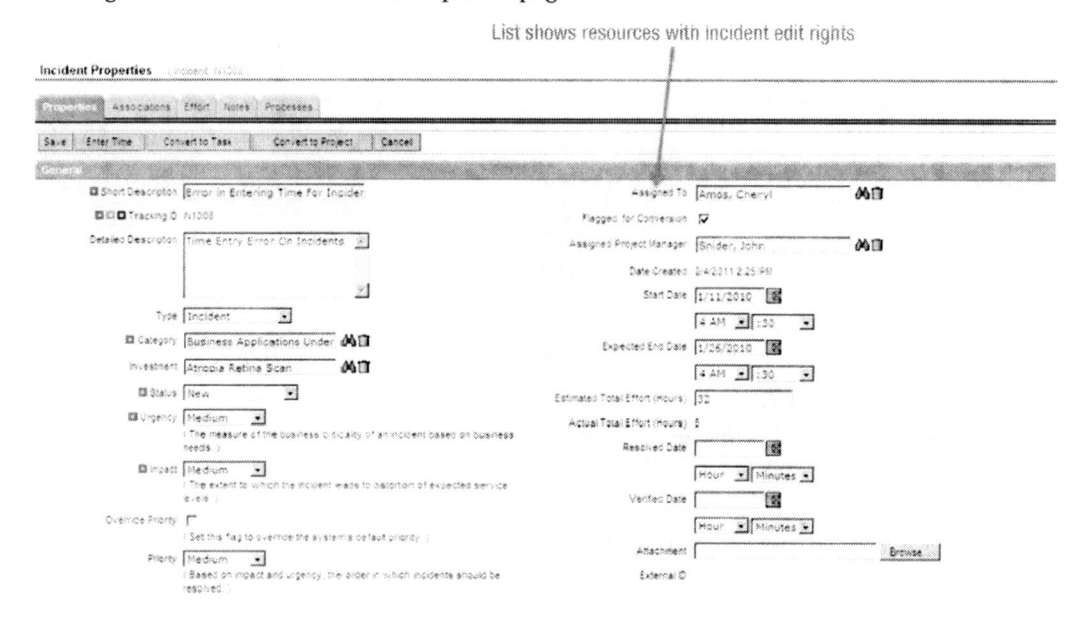

Figure 8-17. The Incident Properties page shows resources with edit rights for the incident.

204

Converting an Incident

When an incident's scope reaches a point where it needs to be handled as a project or as a task, the resource assigned to work on the incident flags the incident for conversion and then assigns the incident to a project manager. The project manager can then convert the incident into a project or task.

Converting an incident or service request into a project or task is the process of converting unplanned work into planned work. In CA Clarity PPM, when incidents become planned work, they are converted into either projects or tasks. Once an incident is converted into either a project or a task, you can use the Incident: See Associations page to view a list of the projects and tasks associated to the incident. There is no link from the project or task to see the incident association.

Before an incident can be converted into a project or task, it must be flagged on the properties page for the incident. Once it is flagged for conversion, a project manager must be assigned, and then it can be converted by the project manager. If the incident is not flagged for conversion, an error message is shown when the Convert to Task or Convert to Project option is selected, as shown in Figure 8-18.

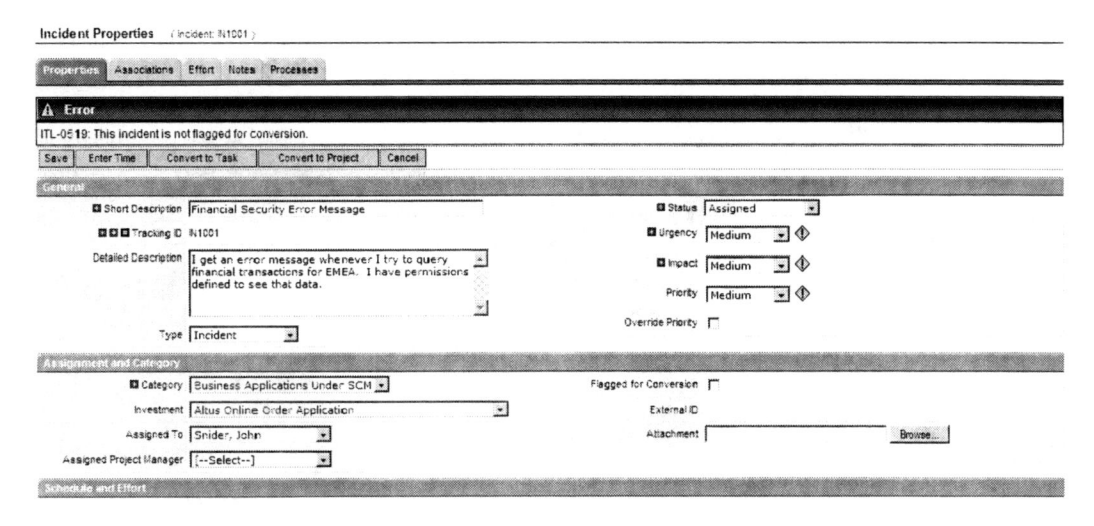

Figure 8-18. Error reporting during incident conversion

Once it's set to Flagged for Conversion, a project manager must be assigned. Only the assigned project manager can convert the flagged incident to a project or a task; otherwise, an error message will appear, as shown in Figure 8-19. Also, the assigned project manager should have the appropriate rights to create a project or convert to a task.

CHAPTER 8 ■ DEMAND MANAGEMENT

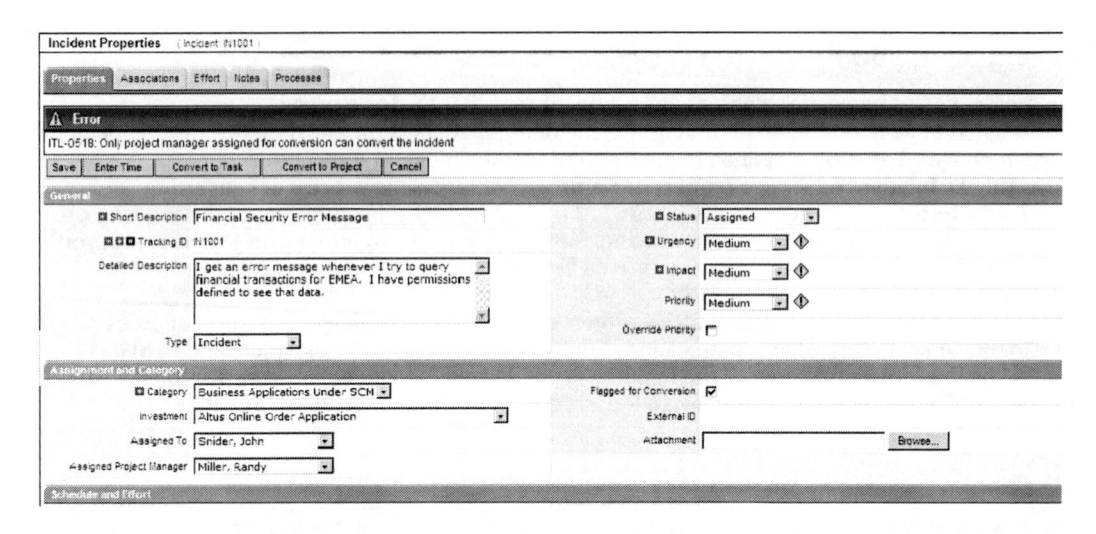

Figure 8-19. Error reporting

The project manager can convert an incident if the incident is *flagged* and is *assigned* to the project manager. The assigned project manager will receive a notification that the incident needs to be converted. The notification links directly to the incident.

Converting an incident or service request into a task is the process of associating unplanned work with a task. Only the project manager assigned to the incident can convert the incident into a task, and only if the following is true:

- The project to which the task is associated exists
- The project is active

An incident can be converted by using either the Incident List page or the Incident Properties page. Each new task is added to the bottom of the hierarchy of the WBS within the project.

Data Mapping

When an incident is converted into a project or task, the incident data is carried forward. Since the resource assigned as the contact for the incident may not be a team member on the project, contact information is *not* carried forward to the project. When an incident is converted into a project or task, a one-way link exists from the incident to the converted project or task.

Table 8-2 shows the data mapping between the Incident data field and the Project or Task data field when an incident is converted.

Table 8-2. Data Mapping During a Conversion

Incident Data Field	Project Data Field	Task Field
Short Description	Project Name	Name
Tracking ID	Project ID	ID
Status	Status (Unapproved)	Status (Not Started)
Detailed description	Description	N/A
Assigned Project Manager	Manager	N/A
Start Date	Start Date	Start (date)
Expected End Date	Finish Date	Finish (date)

CHAPTER 9

Portfolio Management

Businesses surviving and remaining competitive in today's globalized world appears to be an overwhelming challenge. Think about the constant threats—innovative competitors, technology turning obsolete, lines of businesses becoming redundant, and laws and regulations. How do executives steer their businesses in the right direction and stay ahead of these challenges?

Defining organizational goals and strategies to achieve those goals is certainly the first step. But, how do executives ensure that the strategies are implemented? Management teams or senior executives responsible for achieving organizational goals require the ability to monitor the various portfolios of projects/investments/initiatives. What are the growth and profitability measures for existing initiatives? What is the likely ROI for new initiatives? Could some loss-making initiatives be cut down or completely terminated? What is the likely cost for nondiscretionary projects (such as any initiative to comply with a regulatory directive)? Portfolio management helps address some of these questions and could be simply described as a process for deciding which investments to start, continue, discontinue, or postpone. Remember that no organization possesses unlimited funds or resources at their disposal. The ability to "balance" the different portfolios is the key to efficiently allocating funds and deploying resources.

There are four recommended stages for portfolio management:

- *Stage 1: Inventory (construct the portfolio)*: Create a detailed inventory of your investments with attributes that your company uses to measure its performance—budget, actual costs, resource requirements, ROI, and so on. The portfolios could be categorized on certain investment attributes. For example, all investments that are meant to "reduce costs" could be grouped together.

- *Stage 2: Evaluate (executives have a view of the projects organized across portfolios)*: Study all present and possible investments, and provide business cases and estimated costs to your company's steering committee. The committee then determines which investments are aligned with the overall company objectives by evaluating their risk with respect to technology, change management, and resources. Those investments that meet the committee's investment criteria are implemented.

- *Stage 3: Categorize and score (understand gaps)*: Find the best combination of investments by categorizing and scoring them according to their alignment with your company's objectives. First, establish the right metrics and models. Then, take steps to minimize errors and biases in inputs provided to those models. This will help you prioritize initiatives, add people to understaffed projects, make changes to budgetary allocation by business unit, and help decision making on projects that need to be shelved/discontinued. By doing this, your company has a greater chance of estimating the value that would be added by doing any proposed project portfolio.

- *Stage 4: Implement (allocate funds and resources to get the best mix of investments)*: Implement all of the decisions made to add, continue, or cease investments. Actively manage the portfolio by monitoring and evaluating the projects and incoming demands, tracking project and portfolio-level metrics, managing risks, and responding to "what-if" scenarios. By doing so, your company can make timely decisions regarding ongoing investments and potential new investments.

Investments are closely aligned to organizational strategy, and there is greater likelihood of achieving organizational goals.

Clarity's Portfolio Management module provides the tools that portfolio managers need to scope, plan, limit, and distribute funds by thoroughly and carefully allocating money and time to high-priority initiatives. Using this feature, portfolio managers can create a detailed inventory of their projects, programs, services, applications, assets, products, and other work and then add these investments along with ideas to their portfolios.

Within a portfolio, portfolio managers can view and analyze each project and investment, apply different scenarios, create reports, and apply processes.

The portfolio's details include the investment name, length, remaining life, ROI, estimated cost, business objective, number of users, and benefits.

Investments in Clarity

Investments make up a portfolio's inventory. Collectively, they are the investments under analysis. In Clarity, there are eight possible investment types:

- Project
- Program
- Application
- Asset
- Product
- Idea
- Service
- Other Work

Table 9-1 describes the Clarity investments.

Table 9-1. Clarity Investments

Project	**Used to capture data specific to the existing projects or future projects within your organization. For details, see the Clarity Project Management User Guide.**
Program	Used to capture data specific to the existing programs or future programs within your organization. A program is a top-level project that serves as the parent or "umbrella" project to one or more child projects. For details, see the Clarity Project Management User Guide.
Application	Used to capture data specific to the applications running or being implemented within your organization.
Asset	Used to capture data specific to the assets that incur costs and the benefits for your organization.
Product	Used to capture data specific to the products produced or owned by your organization.
Idea	Used to capture data specific to the ideas being considered for implementation by your organization.
Service	Used to capture data specific to the services provided by your organization.
Other Work	Used to capture data specific to steady-state work performed by Clarity resources. Other work can represent overhead tasks such as management and maintenance. Use this investment type to catalog the investments that are incurring costs and benefits and are not projects, assets, applications, ideas, services, or products but that need to be included in your investment portfolio.

Excepting the Project type, all other investments are called nonproject investment objects (NPIOs). Table 9-2 compares projects to NPIOs.

Table 9-2. Projects to NPIOs

Item	Project	NPIO
Tasks	A project can have one or more tasks visible on the WBS tab.	There is one automatic task that is hidden, but it permits time entry.
Time entry	Time can be entered.	Time can be entered.
Incidents	Incidents can be associated.	Incidents can be associated, except ideas.
Incident conversion	Incidents can be converted to a project or task.	Incidents cannot be converted to an NPIO.

Table 9-2 cont.

Allocations	Estimate from allocations and allocation from estimates are available.	These options are not available because allocation and estimates will always be the same.
Start and End dates	Start and End dates are required.	Start and End dates are not required.
Requisitions	Requisitions are available.	Requisitions are not available.
Participants	Participants are available.	Participants are not available.
Resource Planning/ Capacity	Work can be displayed in portlets and aggregated for display.	Work can be displayed in portlets and aggregated for display.
Resource Finder	Resource Finder helps find resources that can be booked to projects.	Resource Finder shows a list of all investments to permit resources to be booked.
Role replacement	Roles can be replaced with resources using Resource Finder.	Roles can be replaced with resources using Resource Finder.

Using Portfolios

The Portfolios page in Figure 9-1 lists all the parent and child portfolios you have access rights to view and modify. The Portfolios list provides three options:

- Filter on specific criteria to narrow search
- View or edit an existing portfolio
- Create a new portfolio

CHAPTER 9 ■ PORTFOLIO MANAGEMENT

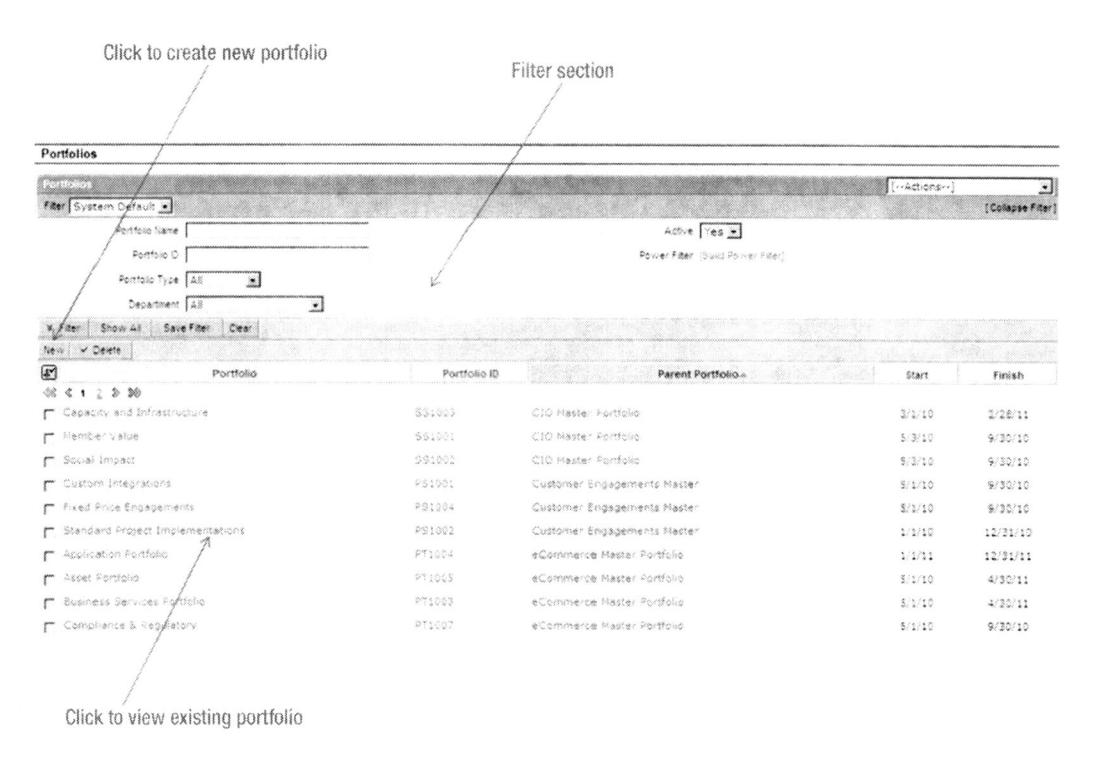

Figure 9-1. List of portfolios

The Portfolios list enables you to monitor and analyze grouped investments to improve decision making in business processes.

Creating a new portfolio lets a user apply different scenarios to predict outcomes, create reports, and apply processes as needed. Building parent-child relationships lets user group portfolios logically summarize and analyze data and help in decision making. Figure 9-2 shows the Portfolio: Properties screen.

CHAPTER 9 ■ PORTFOLIO MANAGEMENT

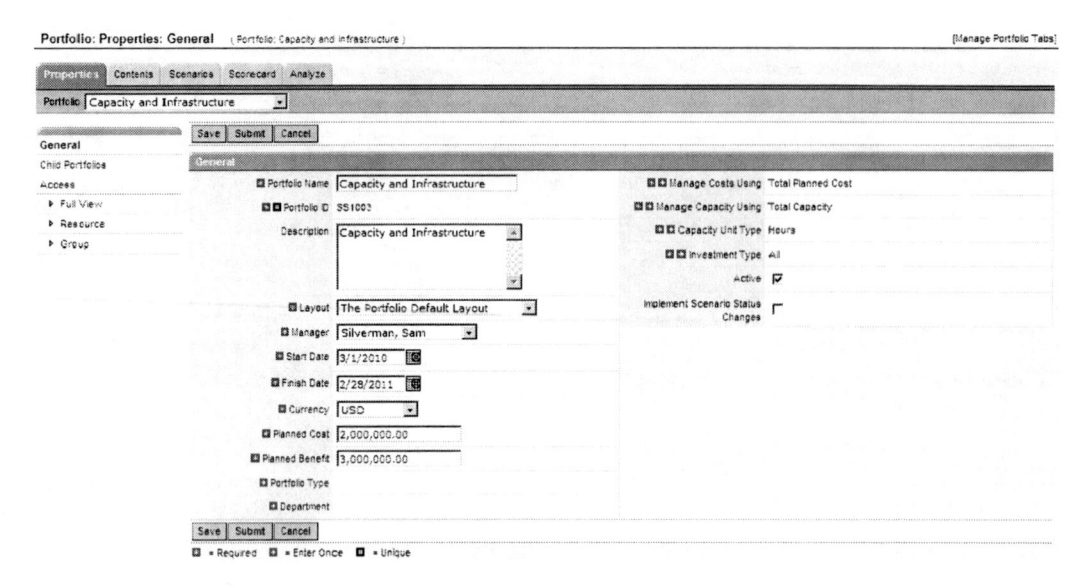

Figure 9-2. Portfolio: Properties screen

You can use the following tabs, as shown in Figure 9-3, to view and edit a portfolio:

- *Properties*: General information
- *Contents*: Investments included
- *Scenarios*: What-if scenarios
- *Scorecard*: Investments to rank and prioritize
- *Analyze*: Charts and graphs to organize and display results for analysis

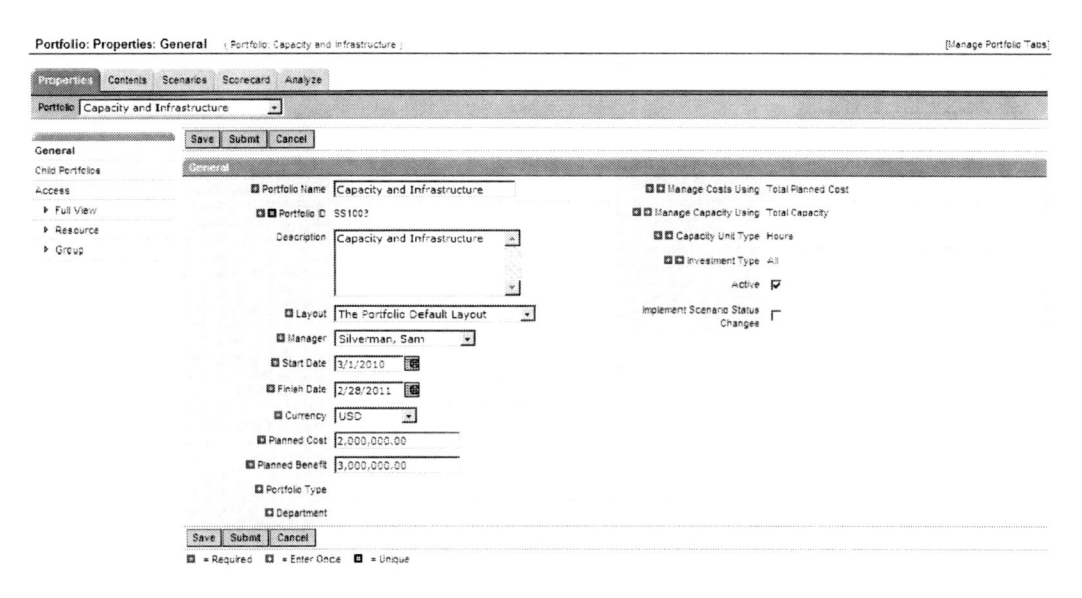

Figure 9-3. Screen to view and edit portfolios

Create a Portfolio

The Portfolio – Navigate security access right enables users to click the Portfolios link in the left navigation menu. Figure 9-4 shows this link. Additional security rights must be assigned to the user to create, edit, and view portfolios. The edit right includes the rights to delete portfolios and to create, edit, and delete scenarios.

Figure 9-4. The navigation menu

    The Portfolios: Properties: General page contains specific fields that define the scope of the portfolio. Figure 9-5 shows the screen to create a portfolio. The key fields in this screen are described next.

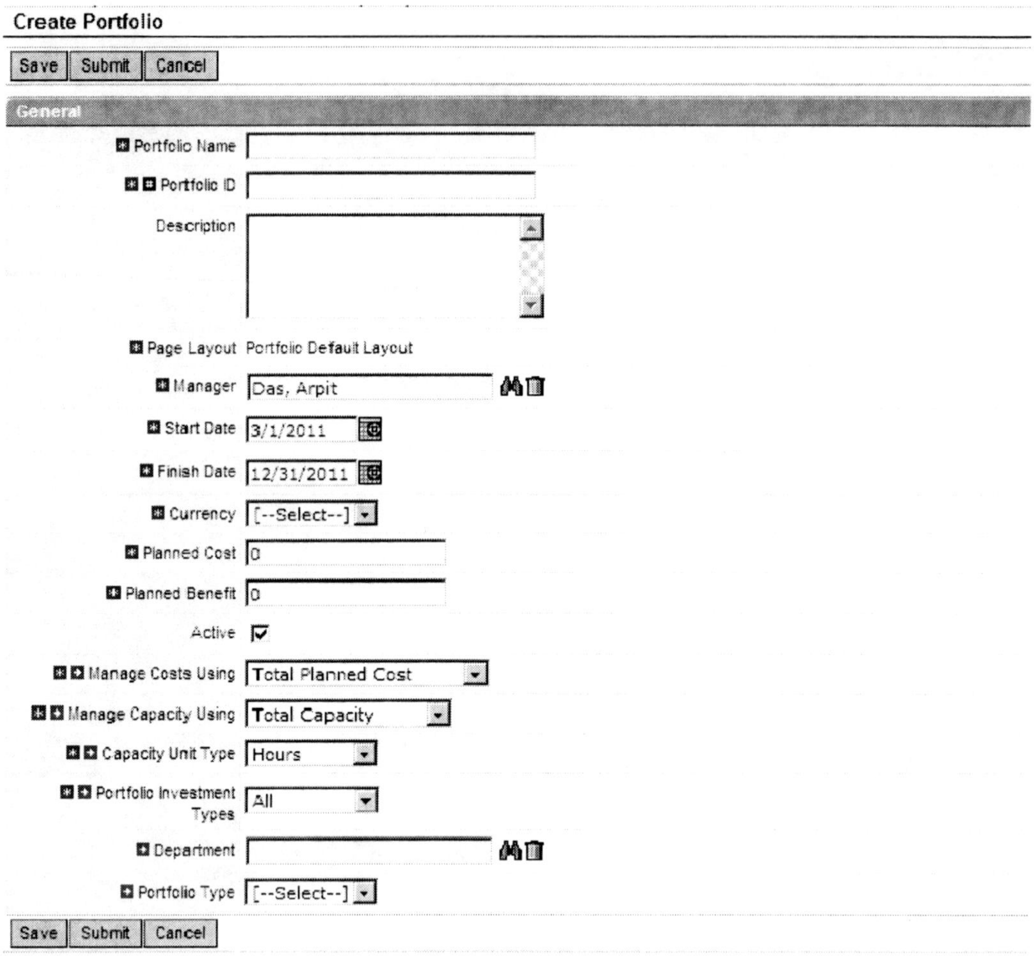

CHAPTER 9 ■ PORTFOLIO MANAGEMENT

Figure 9-5. Screen to create a portfolio

- *Portfolio ID*: The Portfolio ID field is autopopulated if autonumbering is enabled for the portfolio object.

- *Page Layout*: In the Page Layout field, you can define what tabs and pages the user will see. Other page layouts may be available from add-ins or user-defined pages.

- *Start or Finish Date*: The start and finish dates constrain portfolio data.

- *Currency*: Select the currency here. A currency code to display data can be selected from a list of active codes when CA Clarity Project & Portfolio Manager (CA Clarity PPM) is configured for multicurrency and when more than one currency code is active.

- *Planned Cost or Benefit:* When creating a parent portfolio, Planned Cost and Planned Benefit can be set to zero, if child portfolios are used to roll up values. Clarity supports this strategy with the parent-child portfolio strategy. Define a set of portfolios linked to a master portfolio, and then allocate a percent of total investment to each child portfolio. Each child will then take the allocation and optimize their individual investments to that budget.

- *Manage Costs or Capacity:* The portfolio manager can manage the portfolio using total values instead of remaining values for planned cost and for capacity. This will affect the fields that are visible on the portfolio portlets. These fields cannot be altered after they are saved.

- *Portfolio Investment Types:* Portfolio Investment Types can be set to One or All. The view of the Portfolio: Contents tab will change based on the selected investment type. The advantage of selecting only one specific investment type is that the attribute field list will contain all the attributes for that investment object. The list of attributes available when selecting all investment types is reduced because it provides a list only of common attributes across all investment types.

- *Department:* A portfolio can be defined for managing the investments associated with a specific department. When selecting a department unit, Portfolio Type must be set to Provider or Customer. After making these selections and saving, they cannot be altered. Creating a department portfolio will affect the list of available investments for analysis within the portfolio; only investments associated with the selected department will be available.

Define Portfolio Content

Portfolio contents can be selected in two ways:

- Indirectly, using the Include and Filter investments
- Directly, using the individual investments

Adding portfolio roles allows for capacity analysis. The Contents tab has nothing included by default. Figure 9-6 shows the Portfolio: Contents tab.

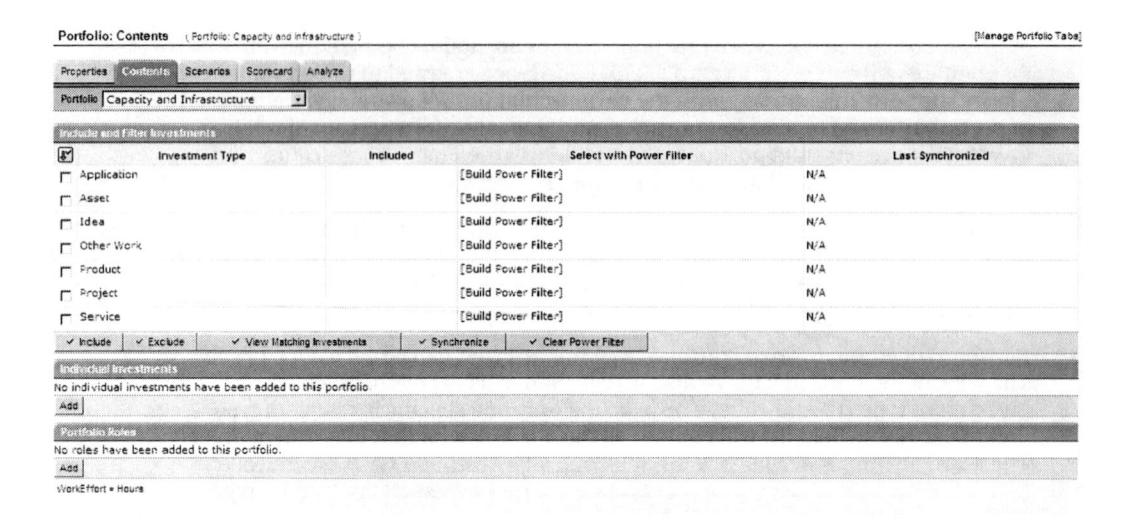

Figure 9-6. The Contents tab

Including and Excluding Portfolio Investments

When you first create a portfolio, its contents are empty. Investment types, although marked as Included by default, do not automatically add investments to the portfolio. For an investment to be added in the portfolio content, its investment type must be marked as Included, and the investment must meet the conditions of the built power filter. Only those investments to which the user has access rights are available to add to a portfolio.

Use the Include and Filter section of the Portfolio: Contents tab to include and exclude investment types before adding portfolio investments. To view this page, open the portfolio, and then select the Contents tab.

Excluding Investment Types

To leave out investments of a particular type from the portfolio's content, in the Include and Filter section of the Portfolio: Contents page, check the box next to the investment type you want to exclude, and then click Exclude. Excluded investment types do not have a yellow check mark in the Included column.

Including Investment Types

By default, all investment types are included in the portfolio's content. Included investments have a yellow check mark in the Included column. User can exclude an investment type to leave out investments of that type (see the "Excluding Investment Types" section in this chapter). Included investments can be considered as potential portfolio content.

To include investment types, in the Include and Filter section of the Portfolio: Contents page, check the box next to the name of the investment type you want to include, and click Include.

Building Power Filters to Add Portfolio Investments

The first step in adding investments to a portfolio using a power filter is building the power filter. Power filters allows the user to restrict which investments are added to a portfolio by specifying the conditions the investment must meet. Use Clarity's power filter functionality to include, for example, projects managed by a particular resource, assets associated to a particular OBS, applications with a budgeted cost under a particular amount, or any other criteria specific to investments you want to include in a portfolio.

The second step in adding investments to a portfolio using a power filter is synchronizing investments. To learn how to do this, see the "Updating List of Investments" section.

Use the Power Filter page to build expressions. This page is a standard expression builder page. To view this page, from the Include and Filter section of the Portfolio: Contents page, and select the Build Power Filter link next to the investment type to which you want to add an expression.

You can build only one power filter per investment type. Each expression build applies only to that investment type. If you build a power filter for an included investment type, the portfolio includes only those investments that meet the conditions of the power filter. Without a power filter, all instances of the included investment type are included as portfolio content.

Viewing Matching Investments

Once a power filter is built for an investment type, you can choose to view the results of the expression before deciding to add them to the portfolio. The investments that match the selected investment type and meet the conditions of the power filter display in the Current Matching Investments section of the View Matching Investments page.

Note: This page only lists the investments to which users have access rights and that are not also marked for deletion. This page displays investments of only one type at any given time.

To view this page, on the Portfolio: Contents page, check the box next to the investment type, and click View Matching Investments.

To view a list of investments that have been added to Clarity since the user last synchronized matching investments, click Synchronize. For more information about synchronizing matching investments and the actions the user can take on the Synchronize Matching Investments page, see the "Updating our List of Investments" section.

Updating List of Investments

Synchronizing an investment type ensures that all investments added to Clarity and that meet the conditions of the power filter are also added as content in the portfolio. It also ensures that investments that no longer meet the conditions of the power filter are removed from the portfolio.

Once you have decided which investment types to include in your portfolio and have built a power filter, you will need to periodically use the Synchronize button to bring the list of investments up-to-date. The complete list of matching investments display is on the Synchronize Matching Investments page. Use this page to view the list of investments that now match the power filter before adding them as content to a portfolio.

To view this page, on the Portfolio: Contents page, check the box next to the included investment type, and click Synchronize. Newly added investments that match the power filter and investments that no longer match the power filter are displayed in the Investments section of the Synchronize Matching Investments page. To bring the list up-to-date, click Synchronize.

Note: Only those investments that meet the conditions specified in the power filter and that are not already included in the portfolio are displayed in the list.

Adding and Removing Individual Portfolio Investments

You can manually add investments of any type individually to a portfolio, regardless of its state. You can individually add investments before or after using power filters or instead of using power filters. By default, the portfolio contents consist of all investments to which a user has *view* access rights. Once added, these investments display in the Individual Investments section of the Portfolio: Contents page.

Adding Individual Investments to Your Portfolio

To add an individual investment to a portfolio, follow these steps:

1. From the main menu, under Portfolio Management, select Portfolios. The Portfolios page appears.
2. Click the name of the portfolio to which you want to add an investment. The Portfolio Scorecard page appears by default.
3. Click the Contents tab. The Portfolio: Contents tab appears.
4. In the Individual Investments section, click Add. The Select Investments window opens. Only those investments to which the user has view access rights is displayed in the list.
5. To filter for investments:
    a. In the Investments filter, choose an investment type from the Investments Type pull-down. (The choices are Projects, Products, Applications, Assets, or Other.)

Note: You can filter for investments of only one type at any given time.

---

   b. Click Filter.
6. Select the investment you want to add to the portfolio.
7. Do one of the following:
    a. Click Add.

CHAPTER 9 ■ PORTFOLIO MANAGEMENT

b. Alternatively, click Add and Select More until all of the selected investments are added. Click Close when finished.

The Select Investments window closes. The selected investment is displayed in the list on the Portfolio: Contents page.

Removing Individual Investments from Your Portfolio

The investments that are added individually to a portfolio display in the Individual Investments section of the Portfolio: Contents page. To remove an investment, check the box next to the name of the investment, and click Remove.

Analyze a Portfolio

Tabs contain the information needed to analyze portfolios and make comparisons between different sets of data.

The Scorecard tab provides a snapshot view of the status of investments and supports the decisions the user makes about investments that should be added to or removed from the portfolio. Figure 9-7 shows the Scorecard tab in the Portfolio screen.

The Scorecard tab provides a balance bubble graph measuring how the portfolio investments align with corporate objectives. The Scorecard tab provides a listing of the investments with their risk scores and stage progress indicators. The Gantt and Financial views of the same investments display net present value (NPV), ROI, and other metrics.

Investment Portlet

The Investment portlet displays a summarized rollup of all investment financial values that are within the portfolio start and finish dates. The Investment portlet is useful for tracking the status of investments in the portfolio and provides a quick snapshot of objects that align to the business without posing excessive risk and cost to the organization. The Investment portlet requires that the investment objects be associated to organizational goals, scored for alignment to the business, scored for risk, tracked through the investment life cycle, and budgeted for cost. Figure 9-7 shows the Investment portlet.

The user can configure the grid and search by status, priority, goal, and planned cost.

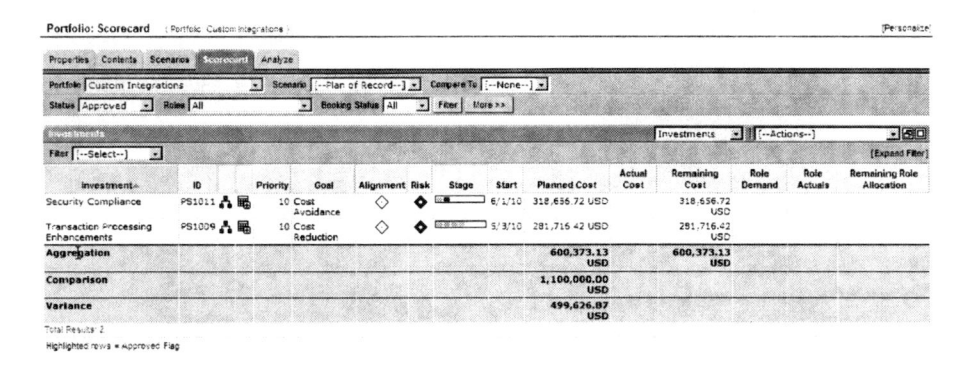

Figure 9-7. The Scorecard tab and the Investment portlet

221

Balance Portlet

The Balance portlet displays a bubble chart in which each bubble represents an investment. This portlet identifies the planned investments and investments in progress that are aligned to the organizational goals without posing excessive risk or cost to the organization.

The chart can also be used to assess supply and demand for labor and financial resources required to deliver the work. At the portlet level, the user can use the standard filter to configure the priority and planned cost. The Balance portlet requires that each investment object be scored for risk and business alignment. The investment objects should also be budgeted for cost. Figure 9-8 shows the Balance portlet.

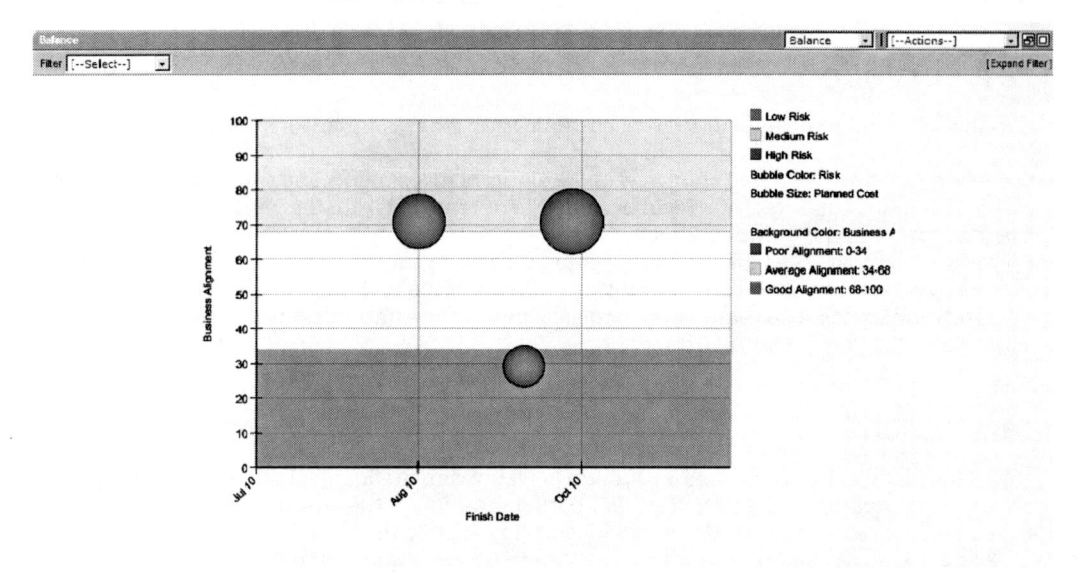

Figure 9-8. The Balance portlet

Gantt Portlet

The Gantt portlet shows the progress of the investments. Useful for understanding the status or progression for each investment, the Gantt portlet identifies which investments may not be on track or need assistance. The Gantt portlet contains investment type and stage, which is the process within the investment life cycle and the stage within the process. The Gantt portlet is useful for tracking the progress of investments and requires that the investment be tracked through the investment life cycle and be updated with a status score. The Gantt portlet can be used to determine that investments that are not being managed well might require management intervention to cease funding or provide assistance to get the investment back on track. Figure 9-9 shows the Gantt portlet.

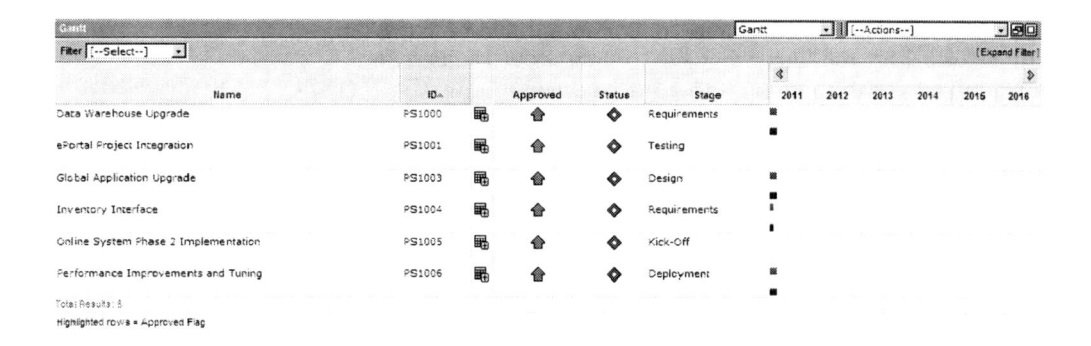

Figure 9-9. The Gantt portlet

Financials Portlet

The Financials portlet provides a snapshot to identify which projects expect to yield the greatest financial benefit to the organization. This portlet contains budgeted and forecast ROI and budgeted and forecast NPV. The Financials portlet requires the investment object to be budgeted with cost and benefits for ROI, NPV, and break-even calculations. Figure 9-10 shows the Financials portlet.

Figure 9-10. The Financials portlet

Scenarios

Creating hypothetical scenarios enables you to plan the allocation of resources across investments, decide on the correct set of investments for the portfolio, or make adjustments to the portfolio budget. Figure 9-11 shows the Scenarios screen.

The Scenarios screen displays all the existing scenarios for a chosen portfolio that the user has access rights to view, edit, or delete.

Select the portfolio in the Portfolio drop-down list on the Scenario tab toolbar. In Figure 9-11 we have selected scenarios for a portfolio called Compliance & Regulatory.

Existing scenarios can be copied, deleted, or communicated from this tab.

The Portfolio values are red-lined when the scenario value is different.

The Communicate Scenario option uses a process to inform stakeholders when a scenario will be implemented.

Click New to create a new scenario.

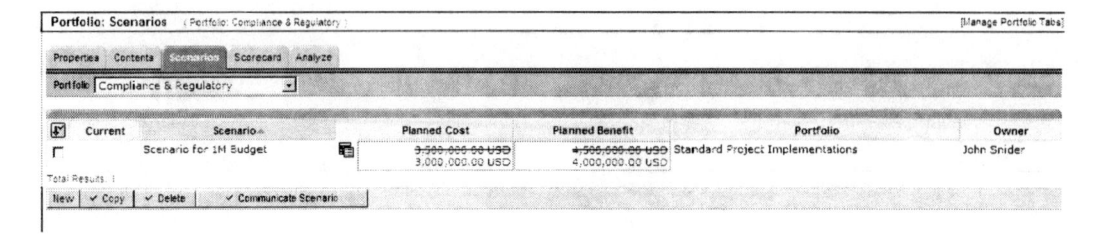

Figure 9-11. The Scenarios screen

Best Practices

These are some best practices related to implementing a portfolio management solution.

First, use scenarios for organizations with mature portfolio management processes. After reviewing the baseline and performance of portfolios, generate a scenario to change which investments should appear in the portfolio, aligning them with the budgeted benefit and cost goals.

Second, generating a scenario does not alter the actual details of investments:

- Generate "what-if" scenarios that can then be communicated to the investment managers.
- Have investment managers meet the required scenario metrics to see how they might rebudget or replan investments.

Finally, when generating scenarios, answer the following questions:

- Do I need to commit my approved investments so that they must appear in the portfolio?
- Do I need to commit my started investments so that they must appear in the portfolio?
- What other criteria should I use to place portfolios?
- Are there other investments that I should manually commit to my portfolio, such as compliance investments?

Summary

Portfolio management is an important consideration for an organization of any size so that projects within the portfolio can be monitored and evaluated for many factors to improve the allocation of resources within the organization and the effectiveness of their spends and results. The Clarity Portfolio Management module allows the organization to inventory and monitor their entire portfolio of projects.

CHAPTER 10

■ ■ ■

Process Management

A business flow has a series of sequential and repetitive steps often called *process flow* that need to be performed to accomplish the business needs. Keeping track of all the sequential steps manually at times becomes very difficult, especially in the case of very complex process flows. The need for an automated system to help accomplish the repetitive tasks and to guide the users through the sequence of steps becomes eminent.

An effective and well-defined business process, executed in a structured way, can help in increased process adoption, improved user/understanding of processes, and faster and more efficient work. Processes, once formalized, can be automated, which can reduce manual effort, improve communication, reduce delivery time, improve quality of deliverables, and hence result in greater customer satisfaction.

The Process Manager module of CA Clarity PPM reaches across all other application-side modules to help tie them together into an integrated whole. In this example, the Process Manager module works with the Demand Management, Portfolio Management, Project Management, and Resource Management modules. This combination provides for a unified, cohesive management of demand, from initiation to selection to implementation. Demand for IT services is initiated by business users who create ideas. The Process Manager module routes the ideas for feasibility study, vetting, and inclusion in the associated portfolio based on the business rules of the organization. After the portfolio is balanced against business priorities, the management of selected projects and the planning of resource requirements begins.

Process management in CA Clarity PPM refers to the creation and use of defined, structured workflows, or processes, to automate and formalize knowledge-based business processes.

These processes can

- Be initiated on demand by a user or can be autostarted based on some system event, such as the creation of a new project

- Act upon and interact with a variety of CA Clarity PPM objects to obtain information from the object and update information about the object

- Interact with a variety of CA Clarity PPM users to request action, solicit approval, or notify

- Be executed by a sophisticated, event-driven process engine that typically runs on the CA Clarity PPM background service

Using CA Clarity PPM Process Manager can produce some very important benefits:

- Improved consistency of business processes

- Implemented in a structured workflow
- Increased process adoption, improved use/understanding of processes, and faster, more efficient work
- Improved consistency of data
- Automation of manual processes
- The ability to act upon objects directly
- Reduced manual effort
- Improved communication
- Creation of Alerts like: notifications, action items, escalations, proxies
- Reduced communication efforts
- Reduced delivery time
- Higher-quality deliverables
- Greater customer satisfaction

CA Clarity PPM is used for a number of business processes, including the following:

- *Project life-cycle governance*: Helps ensure that project managers follow the approved project governance model for the life cycle of projects
- *Project funding*: Manages the initial and subsequent funding of a project
- *Demand management*: Manages the initiation, routing, approval, and fulfillment of demand from business users
- *Regulatory compliance*: Ensures compliance with Sarbanes-Oxley and other regulations
- *Vacation approval*: Manages the request, approval, and booking of vacation time
- *Risk and issue escalation*: Ensures that high-priority risks and issues are escalated in a timely manner to the appropriate parties for mitigation
- *Change request approval*: Manages the initiation, scoping, and approval of project change requests, including the subsequent impact on budget, baseline, and schedule
- *Timesheet approval*: Manages the routing and approval of timesheets based on specific business rules

Flow of CA Clarity PPM Workflow Process

Figure 10-1 shows the basic flow of a process in CA Clarity PPM.

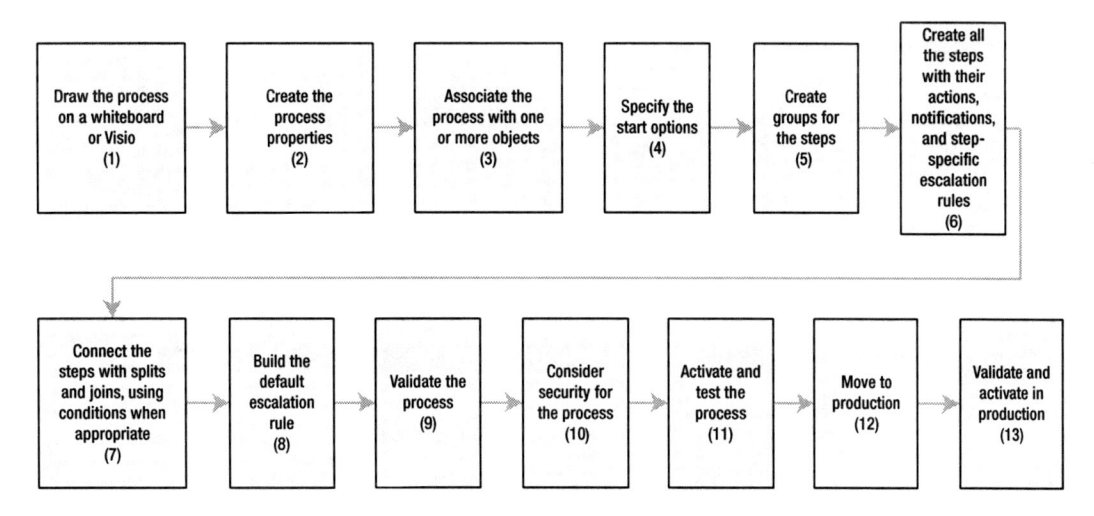

Figure 10-1. Flow of process

Create a Process

You can access the Processes link from the Administration Tool in Clarity under Data Administration. A user should have process create rights to create a new process. Figure 10-2 shows the list of processes available.

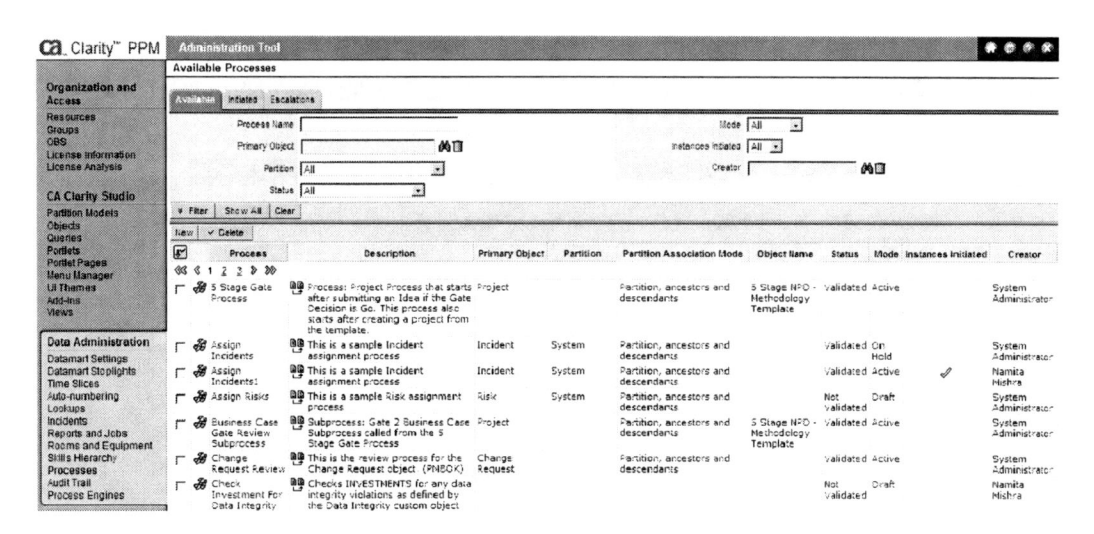

Figure 10-2. List of processes

Steps to Create a Process

Acme Data Systems (ADS) has a business requirement to notify the Project Manager group whenever a new project is created in the CA Clarity PPM system. They want to automate this process in CA Clarity PPM to notify all members of the Project Manager group.

Figure 10-3 shows the screen that the system administrator at ADS uses to create a process. The steps are as follows:

1. Click New.
2. Fill in the required information and save.

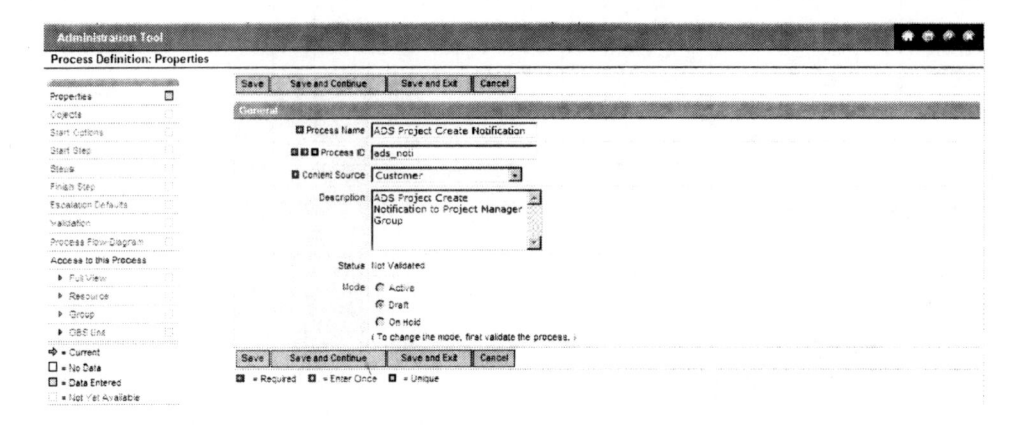

Figure 10-3. Screen to create a process

Figure 10-4 shows the screen where the ADS system admin can associate a primary object to a process.

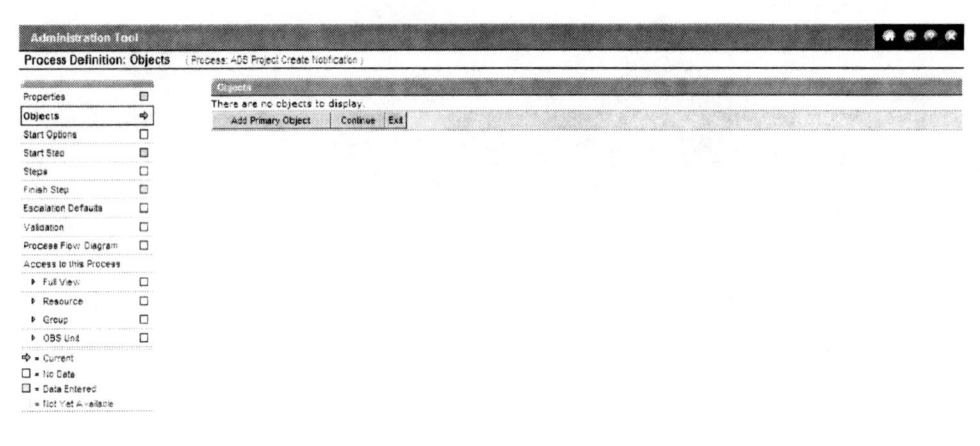

Figure 10-4. Adding a primary object

CHAPTER 10 ■ PROCESS MANAGEMENT

Figure 10-5 shows the screen to select the object type from the drop-down list. The system admin also has an option to associate the project template if the object type is Project. If this process is kicked off for a project that was created based on a template, then you select the appropriate template.

Figure 10-5. Selecting the object type

Figure 10-6 shows the screen where the project object is associated with the process.

Figure 10-6. Associating the project object

Figure 10-7 shows the screen where the system admin can specify a start condition of the process. The start condition can be Create or Update.

229

CHAPTER 10 ■ PROCESS MANAGEMENT

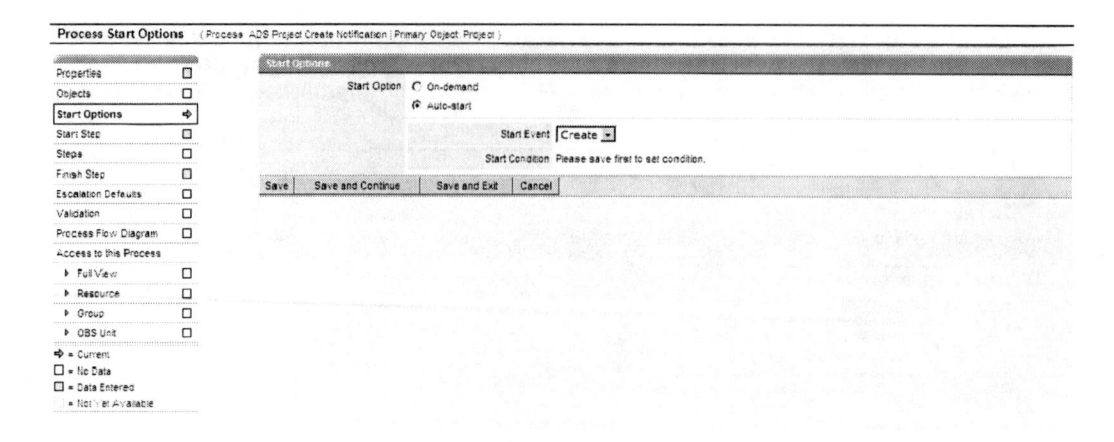

Figure 10-7. Defining a start condition of the process

Figure 10-8 shows the screen to create new steps in the process. A user can create new steps or groups.

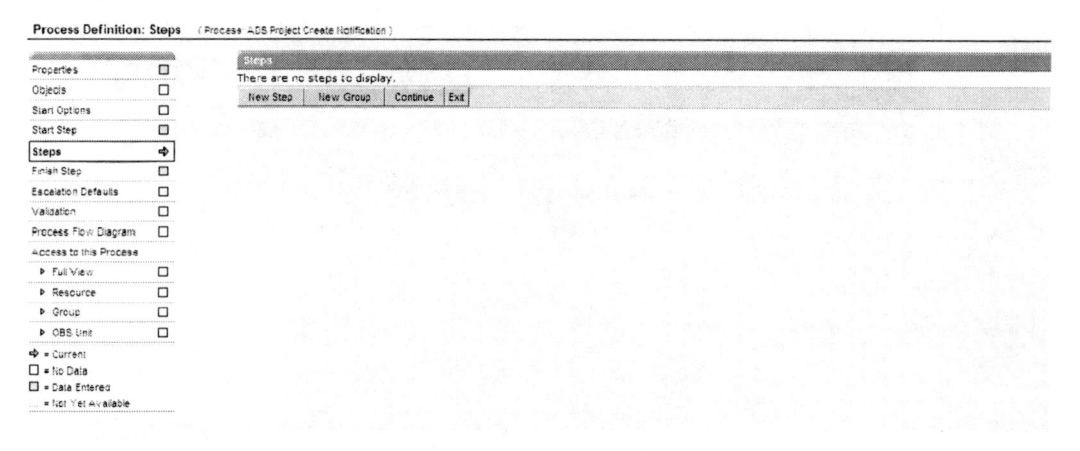

Figure 10-8. Defining the process steps

Figure 10-9 shows the properties page of a step in the workflow.

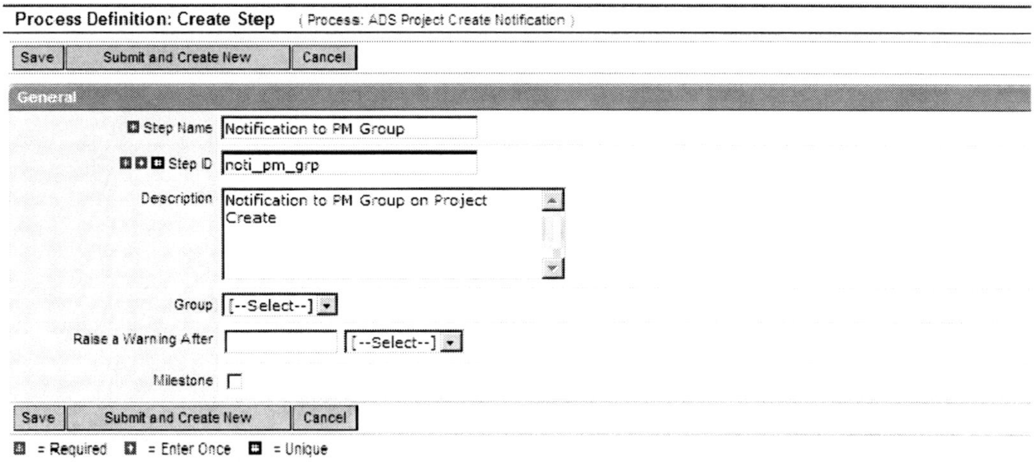

Figure 10-9. Creating a step in the process

Figure 10-10 shows the step properties screen where the ADS system admin can create new action items, specify pre- and postconditions, set escalations, and set step notifications. Here the system admin can create a new manual action item.

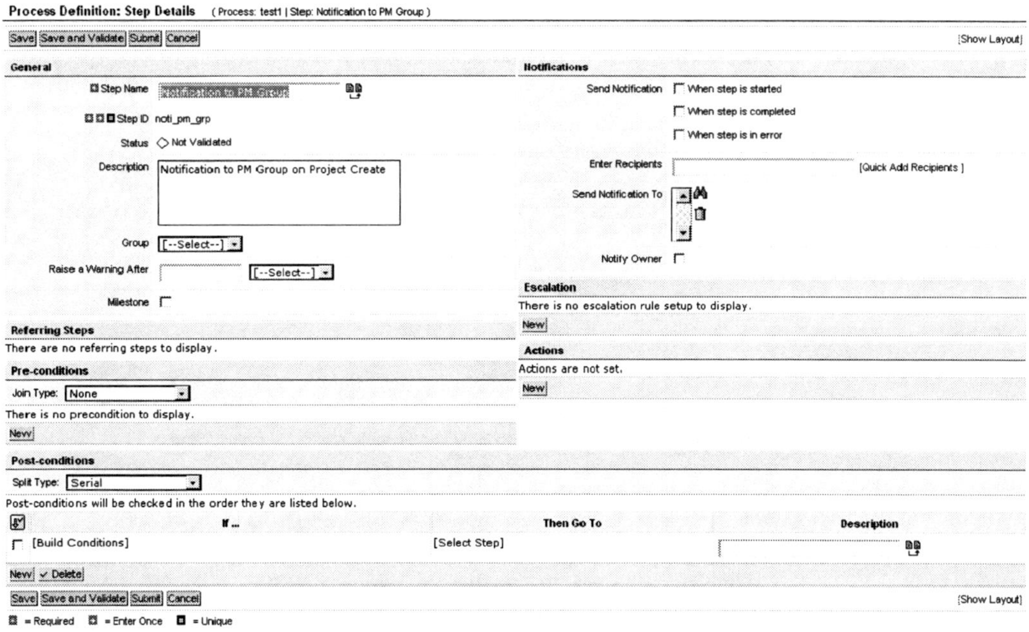

Figure 10-10. Step details screen

CHAPTER 10 ■ PROCESS MANAGEMENT

Figure 10-11 shows the properties page of manual action items. Fill in properties of the action item and select the Project Manager group that will receive notifications.

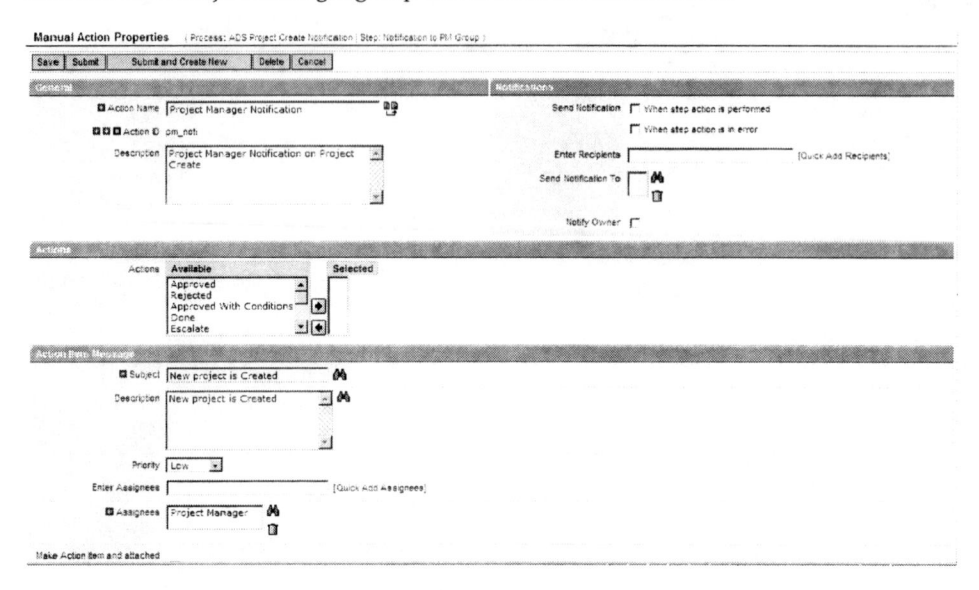

Figure 10-11. Properties screen of manual action items

Figure 10-12 shows the step properties page where postconditions and step linking can be specified. In this example, the system admin will link the Start step to the Notification to PM Group step and then the Finish step.

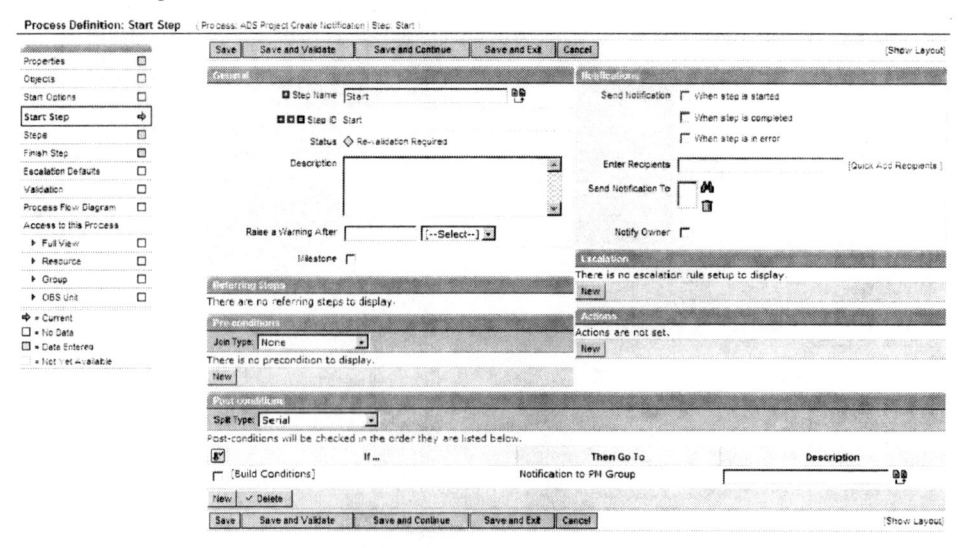

Figure 10-12. Step Definition: Start Step screen

232

Figure 10-13 shows the screen of step properties where the system admin has created a manual action item and then links the step to the next logical step.

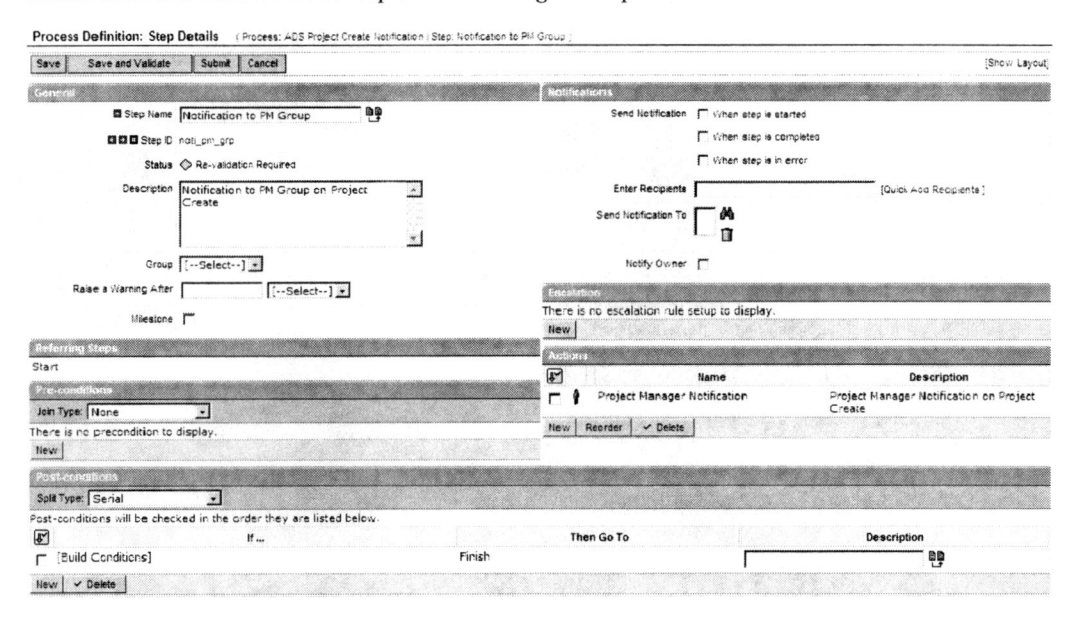

Figure 10-13. Step Definition: Step Details screen

Figure 10-14 shows the final process flow diagram with all the steps linked.

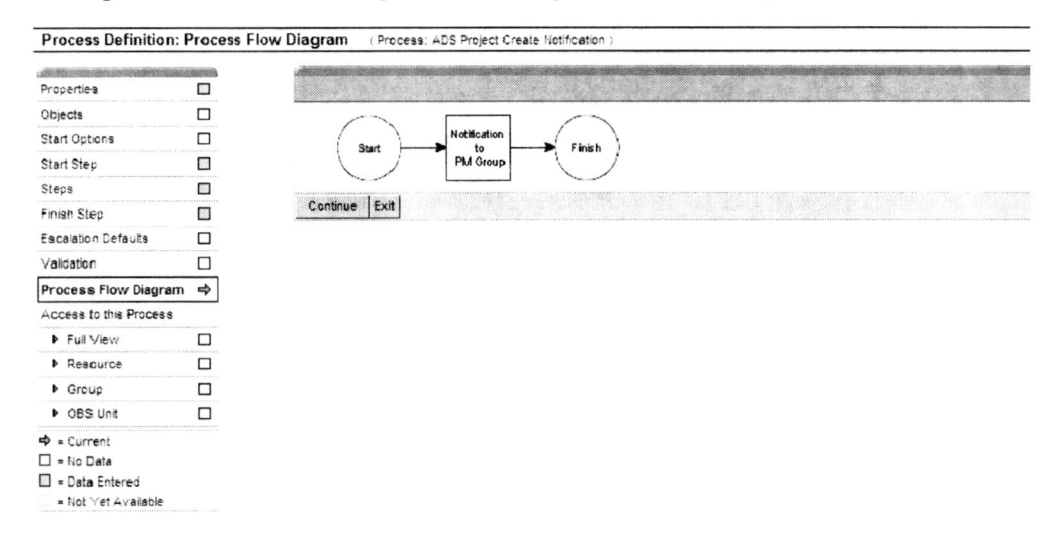

Figure 10-14. Final process flow diagram

CHAPTER 10 ■ PROCESS MANAGEMENT

Figure 10-15 shows the screen to validate the steps and activate the process. The process needs to be validated before it can be activated.

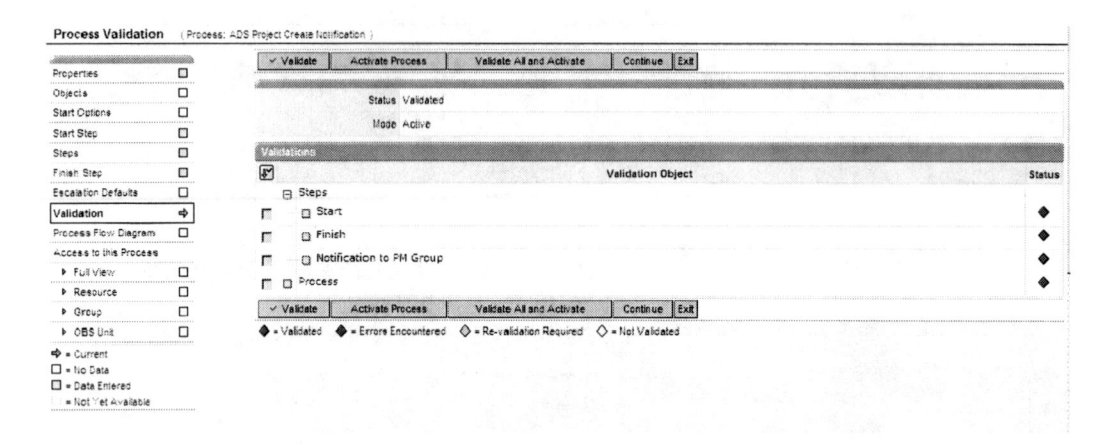

Figure 10-15. Validation and activation of process

Figure 10-16 shows the screen to specify security access to a process.

ADS wants only the Project Manager group to start the process because they are the ones who will create the projects. So, we set up security rights for the process.

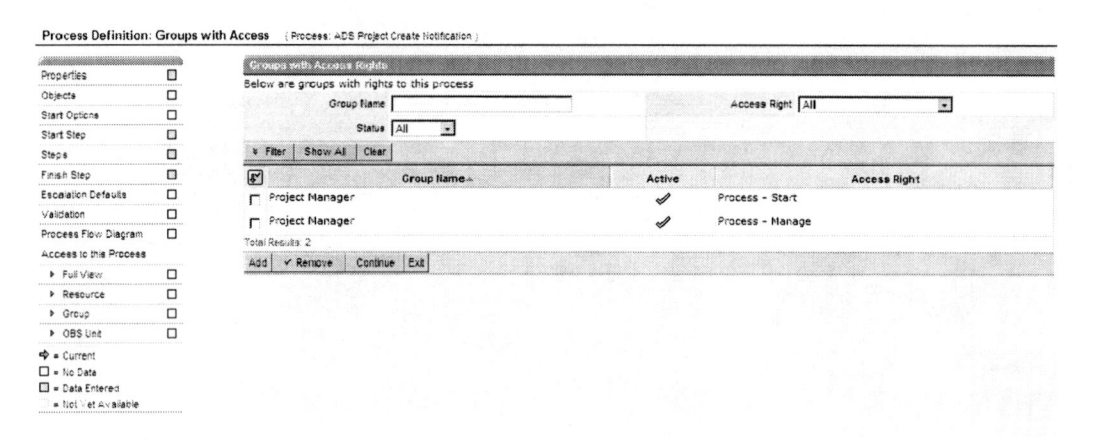

Figure 10-16. Setting up security rights

Now the process is all ready to kick off when a Project Manager group member creates a project.

234

Execute a Process

The process starts when a project is created in the system by a Project Manager group member. John Snider is a part of the Project Manager group and creates a new project. Once the project is created, the process kicks off and sends a notification to the members of the Project Manager group.

Figure 10-17 shows the Processes tab from within a project where a user can view the processes that are initiated based on their security rights.

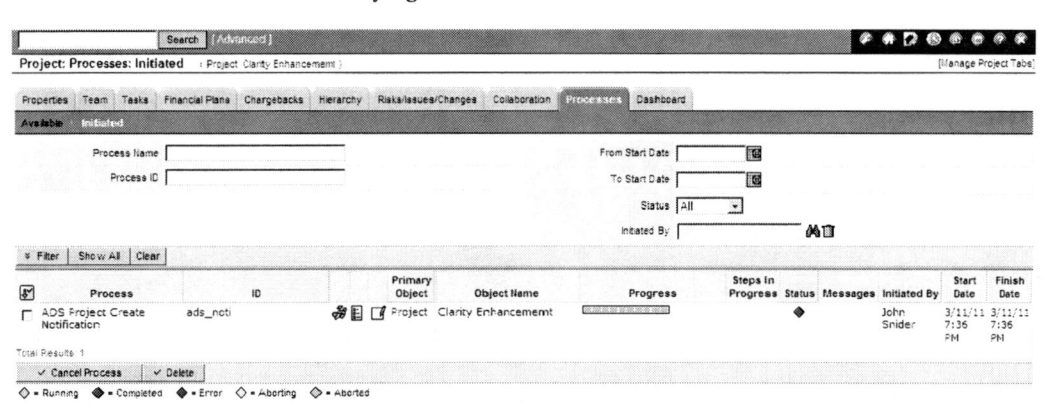

Figure 10-17. Processes within the project

Figure 10-18 shows the running process with color, indicating the status of the steps. Green color indicates that the step is successfully executed.

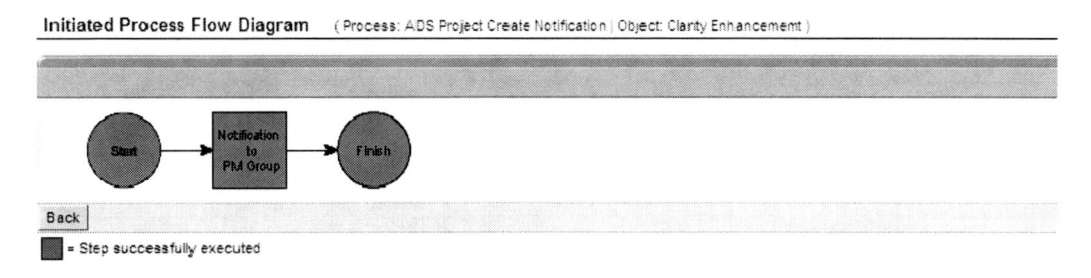

Figure 10-18. Execution of a process

Figure 10-19 shows the action item initiated from the process for a user. A member of the Project Manager group receives a notification about the project creation.

Figure 10-19. Action items of the process

Summary

This chapter described how a simple process is created and executed in CA Clarity PPM. Hence, an organization can use the Process Management module in Clarity to automate their business processes for efficient operations and business functions.

PART 3

CA Clarity PPM Utilities

This part gives you an introduction to the basics of CA Clarity PPM Organizational Breakdown Structure, Clarity security and Clarity Components (the Pre-Packaged Work Products that are available for Clarity PPM).

CHAPTER 11

■ ■ ■

CA Clarity PPM Organizational Breakdown Structure

An organizational breakdown structure (OBS) is a hierarchical representation of the way a company is organized for various operational or business purposes such as managing multiple divisions, managing resources, supporting the financial setup, and representing different geographical locations.

An OBS could be used to represent the following:

- Locations of different stores of a retail giant
- Reporting structure of resources in the IT division of a large company
- Locations of different manufacturing plants for a pharmaceutical company
- Cost centers within an organization

Therefore, OBS lends itself very well to reporting needs such as resources, projects, or any investments that could be associated with different levels of an OBS.

The OBS could also be used in terms of defining access controls.

Acme Data Systems (ADS) is rolling out a CA Clarity PPM Portfolio Management solution for its Global Supply Chain/Global Quality Operations business units. These business units are spread across Europe, the Asia-Pacific, and the Americas, and there are multiple sub-business units that require cross-business unit rollups of the projects and other investments in the parent portfolio. ADS wants to explore using CA Clarity PPM partitioning and OBSs to effectively implement a portfolio management solution.

Organization Structure

An OBS is a hierarchical structure used to view the framework of an organization from a visual functional perspective for aggregation, drill down, and resource searching. An OBS may include org charts, department charts, location charts, and so on. OBSs can be used for both reporting and security. OBS security operates in two ways:

- Security can be given to a portion of the OBS in order to perform the same security functions.
- Access can be given to a group, OBS unit, or individual to perform a function on a specific portion of an OBS.

Figure 11-1 shows the organizational and operations layout of the Global Supply Chain and Global Quality Operations business units.

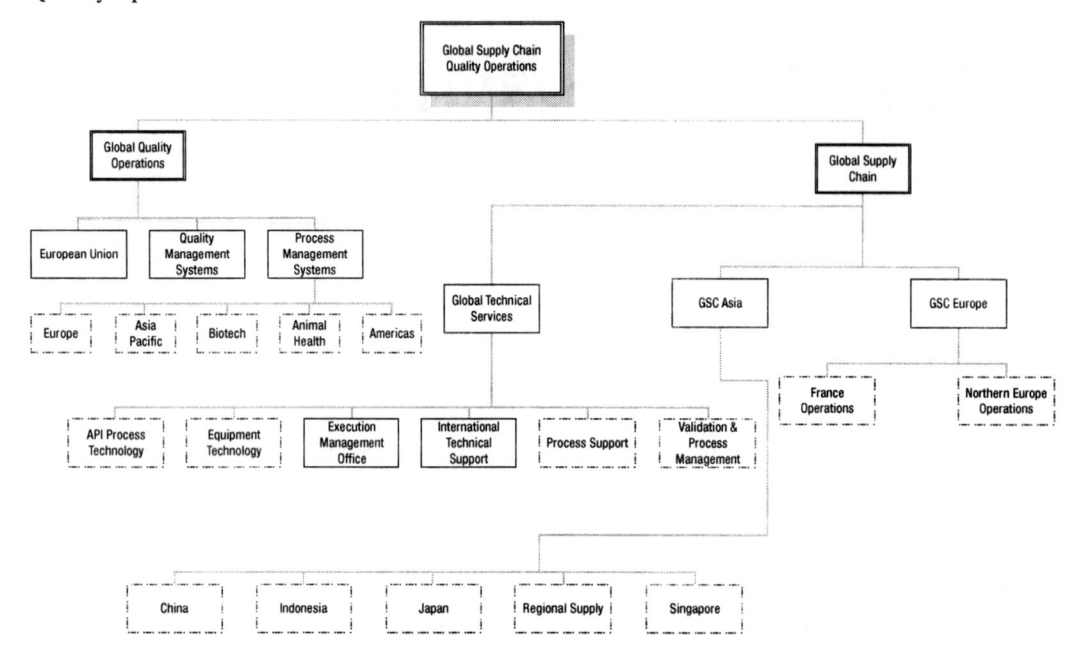

Figure 11-1. The organizational layout of the Global Supply Chain and Global Quality Operations business units

ADS has a business requirement to report its projects based on the particular department that provides project funding. Also, it wants to align its resources and reports based on its resource reporting hierarchy. An OBS can help ADS align projects, investments, resources, and most objects to an OBS.

ADS also has a business requirement that each business unit should be able to access its own investments. For example, resources under Global Technical Services should be able to access investments that are tied to the Global Technical Services business unit. The CA Clarity PPM OBS functionality helps grant resources access to their object instances based on their OBS unit associations.

CA Clarity PPM OBS functionality also helps ADS use the department and location OBS to enable and support Clarity financial setup. It also helps categorize objects for filtering and reporting.

OBS Definition

An OBS's structure is defined from the Clarity Administration side under Organization and Access, as shown in Figure 11-2. The user needs to have appropriate rights to access, create, and edit the OBS information from the admin side.

CHAPTER 11 ■ CA CLARITY PMM ORGANIZATIONAL BREAKDOWN STRUCTURE

Figure 11-2. Defining OBS

A user needs to have the following rights to access the OBS section from the Administration side.

Administration - Application Setup — Allows user to edit Clarity options and settings, including OBS, Time, Data Administration and General Settings. Includes the Administration - Navigate right.

An OBS has three components: OBS type, OBS levels, and OBS units.

OBS type: Types are used by the OBS to categorize the company's geographical office locations, organizational chart, project types, and resource pool and are defined in the OBS type, as shown in Figure 11-3.

Figure 11-3. OBS type

OBS levels: An OBS level defines the depth of the OBS hierarchy. The levels of the OBS should have a logical name based on the OBS type. For example, if the OBS type is ADS's office locations, then level names can be the company, country, and city or county. In CA Clarity PPM, ADS can define a maximum of ten levels for any OBS type. Figure 11-4 shows four levels for the OBS type defined.

241

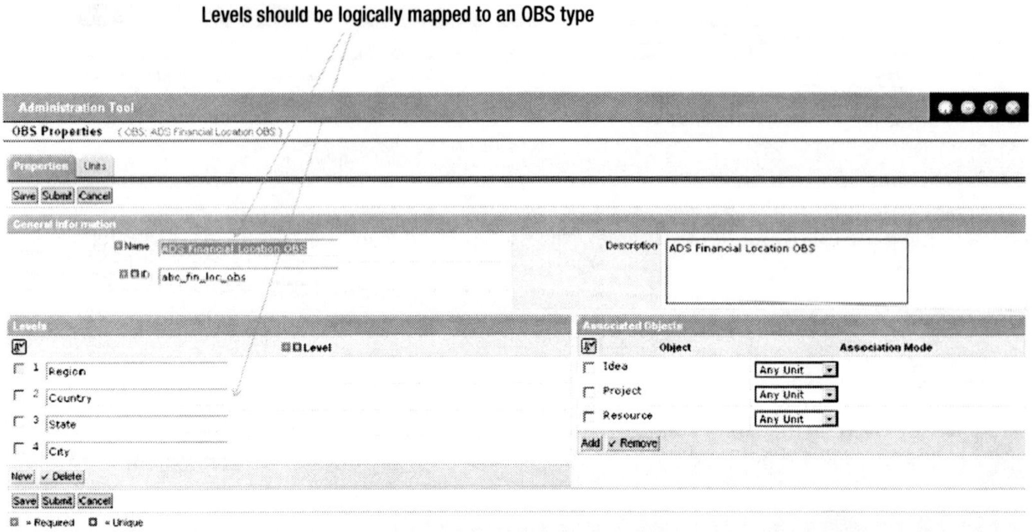

CHAPTER 11 ■ CA CLARITY PPM ORGANIZATIONAL BREAKDOWN STRUCTURE

Figure 11-4. OBS levels

OBS units: OBS units are units or divisions in the hierarchy based on the OBS type. For example, if the OBS type is ADS's corporate OBS, then units can be different business units such as IT, Marketing, Finance, and so on, as shown in Figure 11-5.

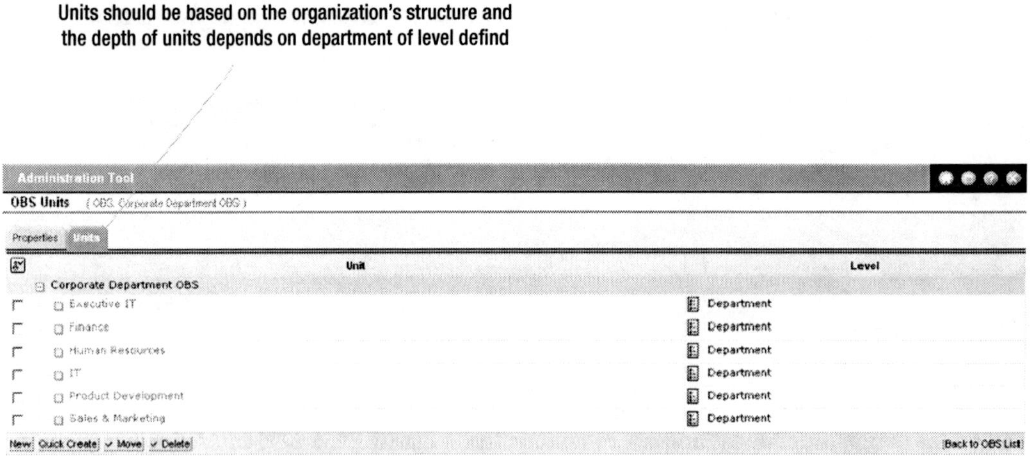

Figure 11-5. OBS units

Tips on OBS

- There is no limit to the number of OBSs in a system.

- Each OBS is limited to ten levels.

- OBSs can be created for security, reporting, financials, and categorizing objects, such as projects, resources, and so on.

- Each OBS can be associated with one or more objects.

- Resources are assigned a default OBS in the Administration Tool under OBS and Partitions upon creation.

- A default OBS is assigned to the project in the Main Properties page.

OBS Properties

You can use an OBS to define the organizational models by geographic location, industry, department, or any other model that suits your specific informational needs. OBS offers similar functionality to groups with respect to user rights. Unlike groups, an OBS can also be used to group together objects, such as projects and resources, for reporting and analysis.

Once an OBS model is created, you can edit the properties, manage the levels, and associate objects. You can also delete levels. However, any resources or investments associated with that level will have to be removed prior to removing the level.

OBS units are added from the OBS Properties page. You can add units in bulk to the same level using the Quick Create button. When adding units in bulk (also known as *bulk adding* units), you can units associate them with a parent OBS unit. After bulk adding OBS units, you can edit attributes such as the unique ID. OBS units can also be moved to a different level within a given OBS.

Tips

- When using Quick Create to create a department OBS, make sure to add unique IDs to avoid any errors when adding the OBS to an entity.

- It is recommended that you use unique IDs for an OBS unit because it can be helpful during the XOG process.

OBS Object Association

Objects must be associated with an OBS to enable OBS capabilities. OBS object capabilities include security and reporting on those objects. Objects associated with the OBS can apply to all OBS units, or only units at the lowest level.

- *Any unit:* You can associate an object with any unit of the OBS.
- *Lowest unit:* You associate an object with the lowest level of the OBS.

You can add or delete an object association from the OBS at any time, as shown in Figure 11-6.

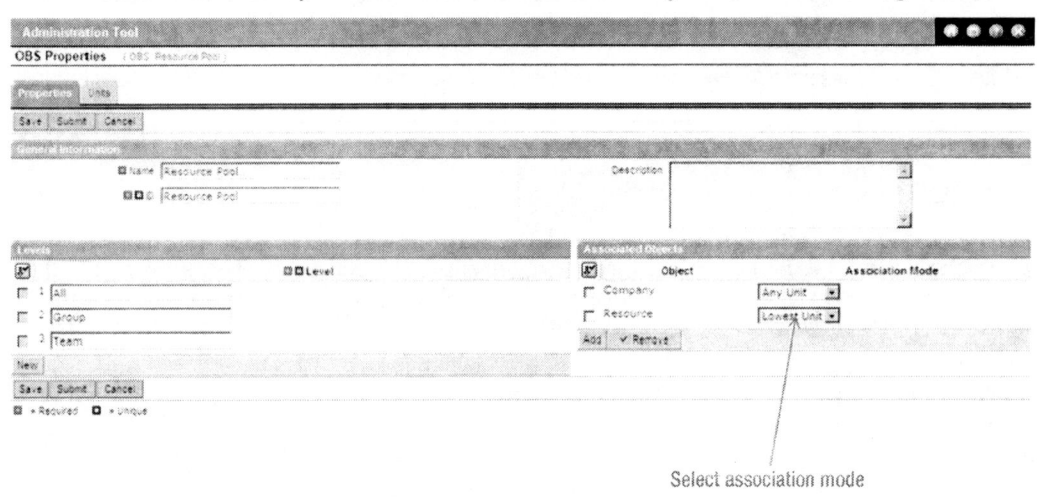

Figure 11-6. Adding object associations

OBS and Financial Entities

A department OBS type and location OBS type are required for each financial entity. Once you associate a department OBS and location OBS with an entity, these OBSs are automatically enabled for access rights, as shown in Figure 11-7.

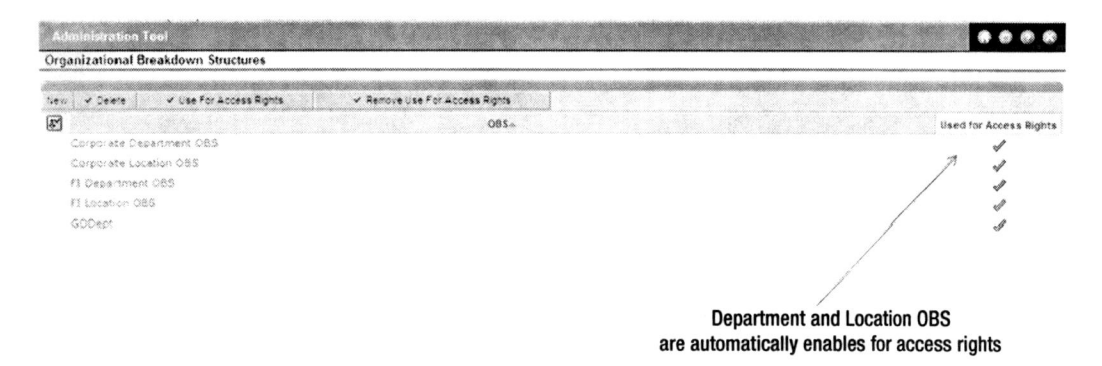

CHAPTER 11 ■ CA CLARITY PMM ORGANIZATIONAL BREAKDOWN STRUCTURE

Figure 11-7. OBS and financial entities

Also, they cannot be deleted, and their structure cannot be edited directly from the OBS. Once the department OBS is mapped to an entity for Clarity financial setup, it can be edited only from Departments on the Application side, as shown in Figure 11-8.

Figure 11-8. Editing department OBS

Once the location OBS is mapped to an entity for financial setup, it can be edited only from Locations under the financial organization structure, as shown in Figure 11-9.

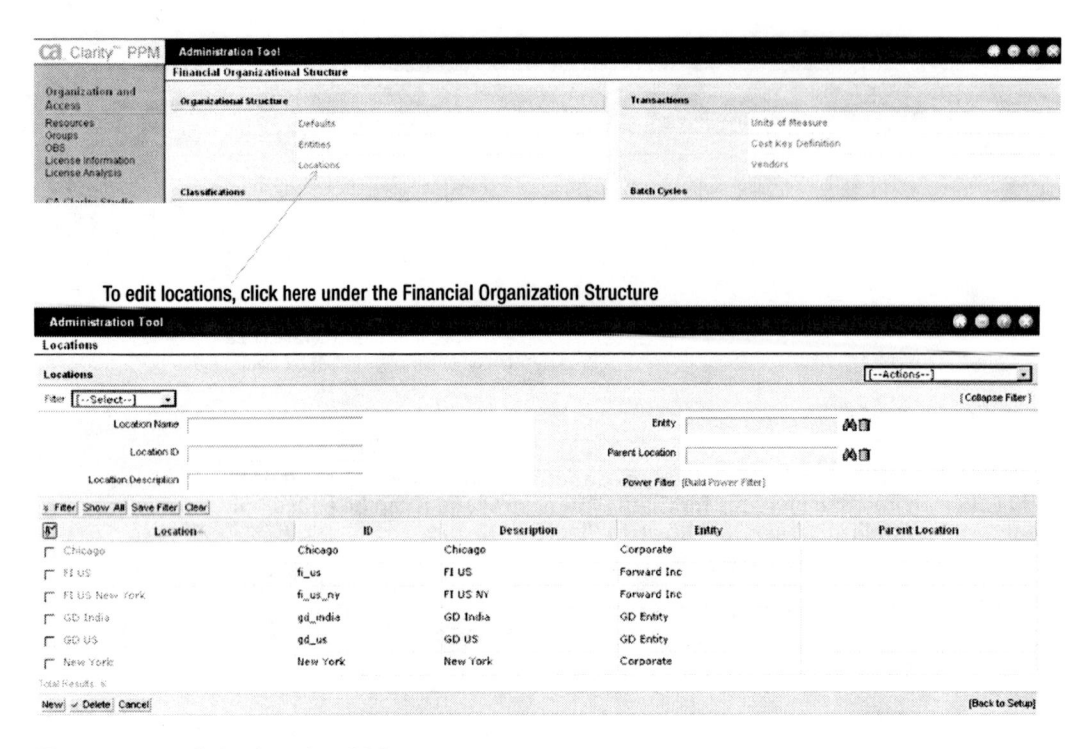

CHAPTER 11 ■ CA CLARITY PPM ORGANIZATIONAL BREAKDOWN STRUCTURE

Figure 11-9. Editing location OBS

Department and location OBSs can be associated to a financial entity from the Setup option under the Finance menu in the Administration Tool, as shown in Figure 11-10.

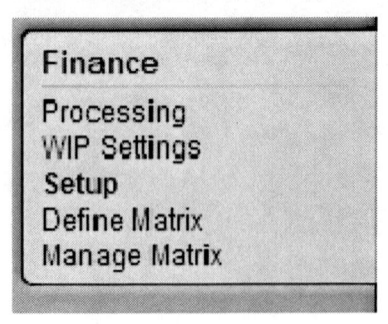

Figure 11-10. Finance menu in the Administration Tool

This is easily accomplished. On the Entities screen, select an entity to access its properties, as shown in Figure 11-11.

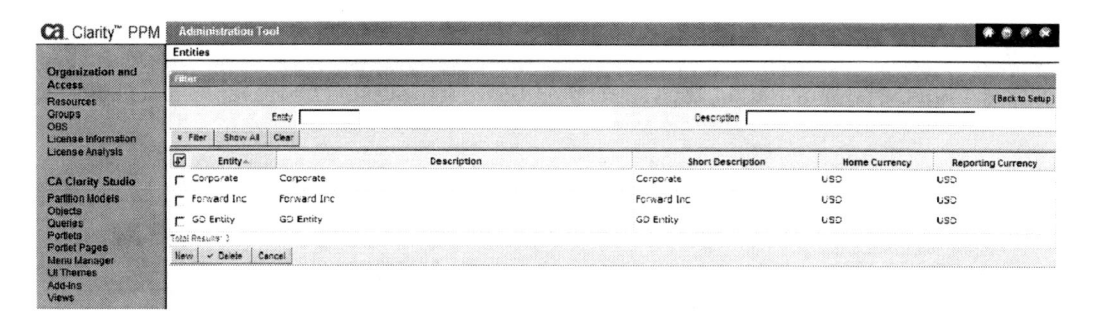

CHAPTER 11 ■ CA CLARITY PMM ORGANIZATIONAL BREAKDOWN STRUCTURE

Figure 11-11. Entities screen in the Administration Tool

On the Entity Properties screen, you associate department and location OBSs, as shown in Figure 11-12.

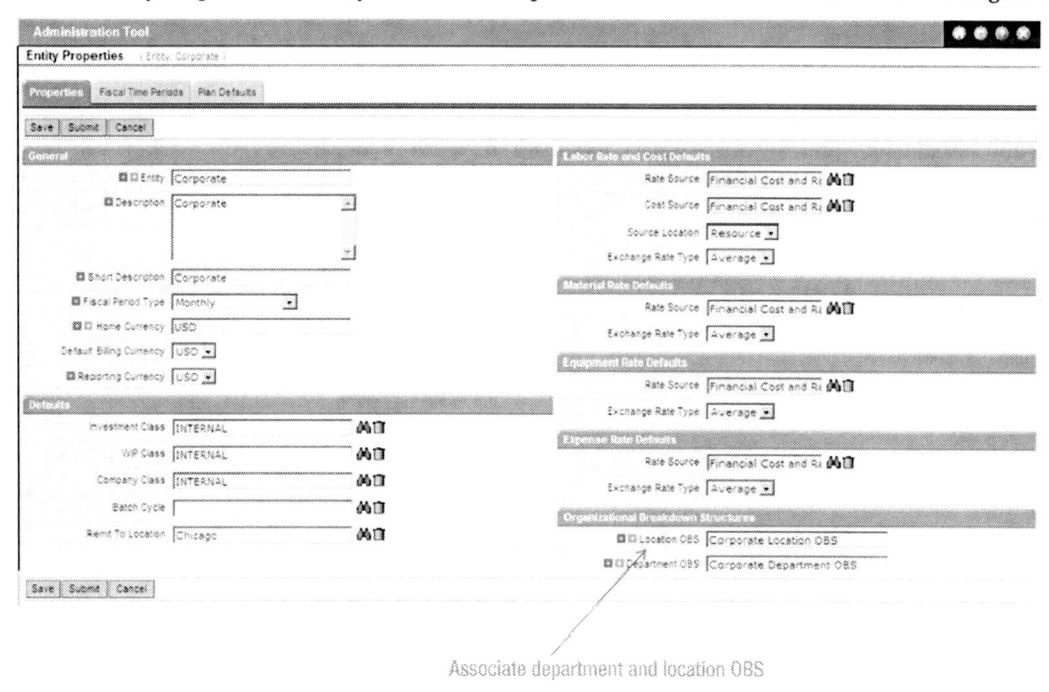

Figure 11-12. Associating department and location OBSs

Associating a Resource with the OBS

Once the OBS is defined, you can start to attach relevant instances to build up the reporting and access right structures. You can associate a resource with an OBS unit in three ways, as discussed next.

247

CHAPTER 11 ■ CA CLARITY PPM ORGANIZATIONAL BREAKDOWN STRUCTURE

Directly from OBS Unit Properties

In this method, from the Administration Tool, select the OBS from the list of OBSs, as shown in Figure 11-13. Then click the Resource Pool OBS.

Click on OBS on Administration tool to see list of OBS

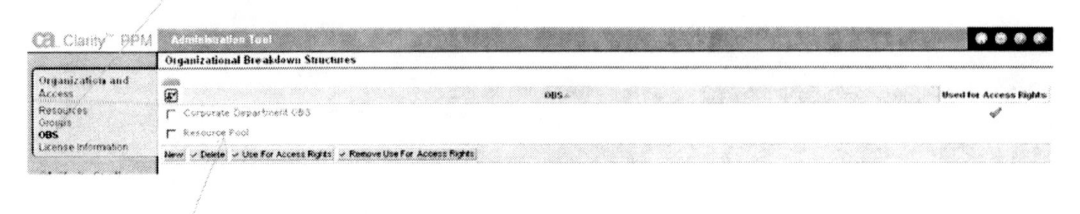

Click on Resource Pool OBS to access OBS properties

Figure 11-13. Select list of OBSs

The selected OBS should be associated with a Resource object for it to assign a resource instance. Click the OBS and associate it with a Resource object, as shown in Figure 11-14.

Click on Units to access OBS units

OBS is associated with Resource object

Figure 11-14. Selecting OBS units to associate with a Resource object

Now drill down to the OBS unit that you want and attach the resource instance, as shown in Figure 11-15.

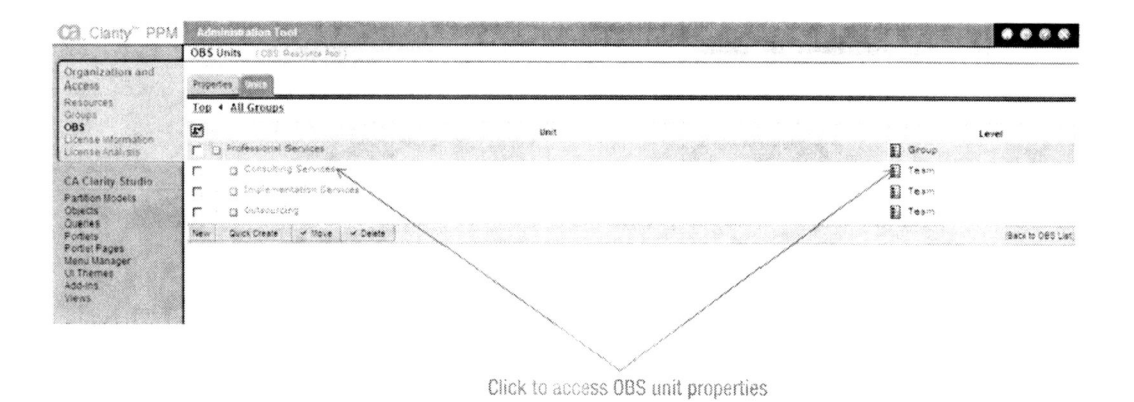

CHAPTER 11 ■ CA CLARITY PMM ORGANIZATIONAL BREAKDOWN STRUCTURE

Figure 11-15. OBS unit properties

In the OBS properties, click Attached Instances and select Resource from the list of objects. The list shows the objects that are associated with the OBS, as shown in Figure 11-16. Click Add and select the resource that you want to associate with the OBS unit.

■ **Note:** If a resource is already associated with another OBS unit within the same OBS type, then adding the resource will change the OBS association.

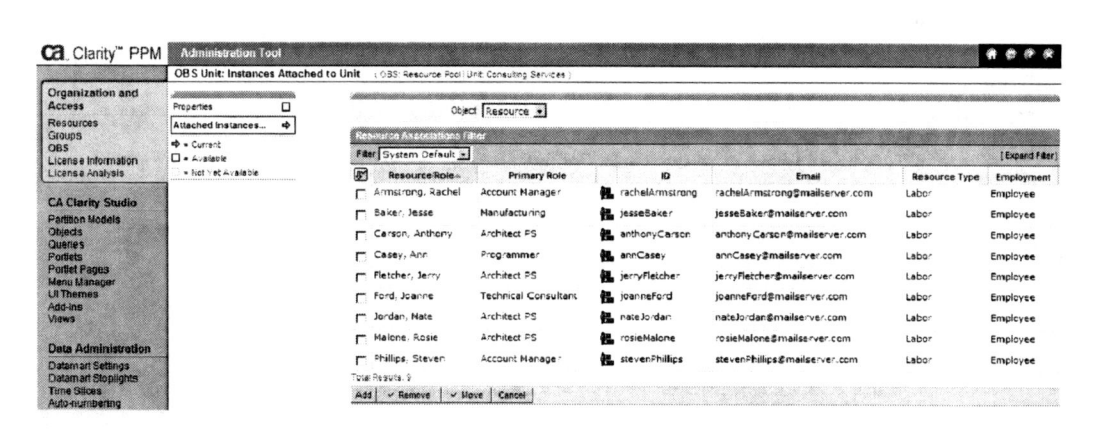

Figure 11-16. Objects associated with the OBS

CHAPTER 11 ■ CA CLARITY PPM ORGANIZATIONAL BREAKDOWN STRUCTURE

Directly from OBS Section in User Properties

In the second method, the OBS unit can be associated to a resource from the OBS section via the user properties on the administration side, as shown in Figure 11-17. The resource needs to have administration access to access user properties.

Figure 11-17. Resource screen from Administration Tool

Directly from Resource Properties

In the third method, the OBS unit can be associated with a resource from the resource properties on the application side, as shown in Figure 11-18. The resource needs to have resource edit rights or has to be a resource manager to edit the OBS information.

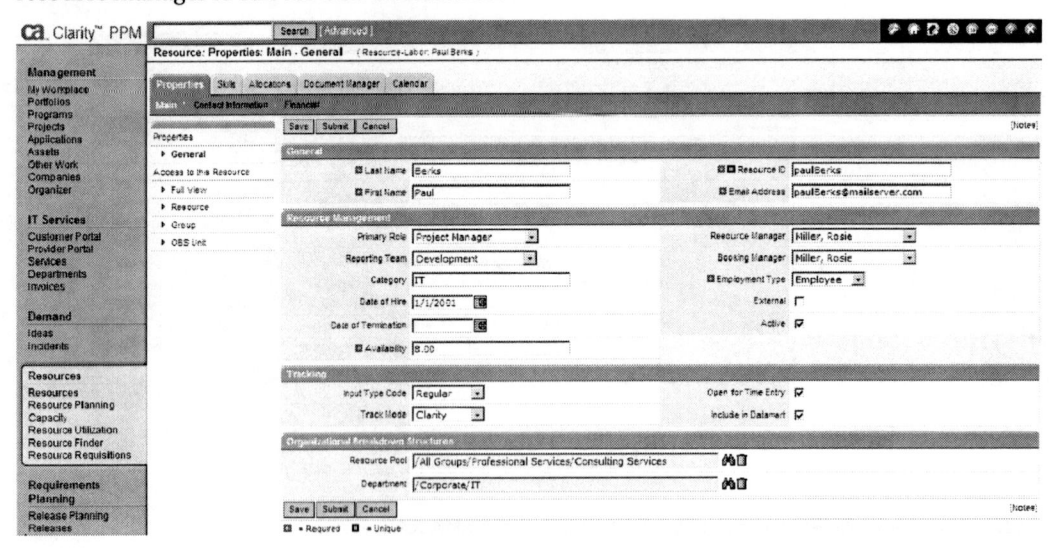

Figure 11-18. Resource properties from the application side

Granting Access Rights via OBS

You can use an OBS for reporting and/or security access rights. To use an OBS for security access, check the Used for Access Rights column, as shown in Figure 11-19.

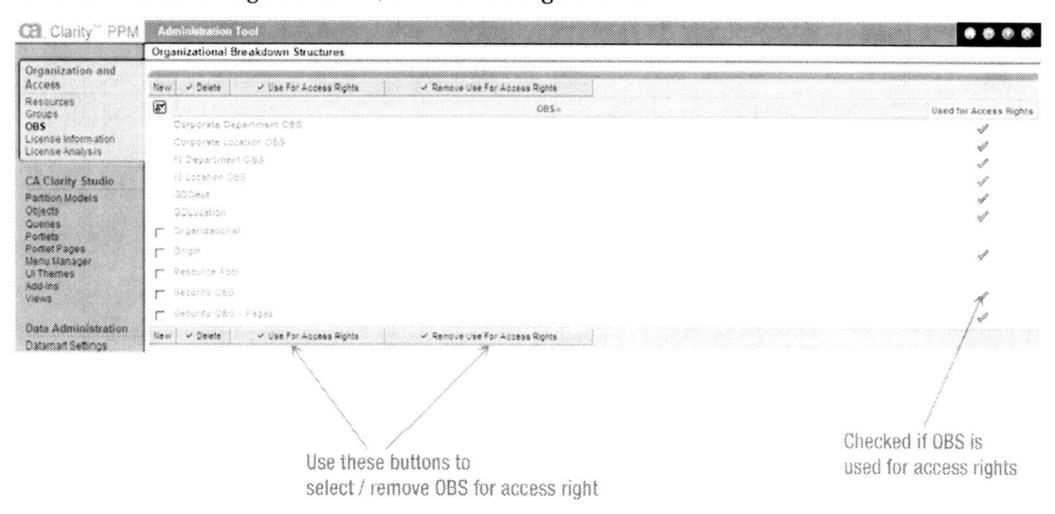

Figure 11-19. Selecting an OBS for access rights

Once the OBS is selected for access rights, the OBS units have security information associated with the OBS unit. Figure 11-20 shows the OBS used for access rights.

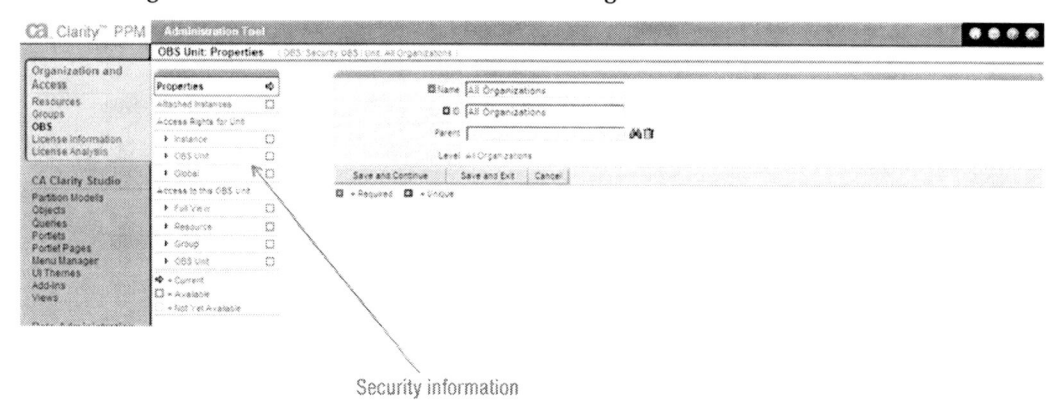

Figure 11-20. OBS with access rights

Similarly, Figure 11-21 shows the OBS that is not used for access rights.

CHAPTER 11 ■ CA CLARITY PPM ORGANIZATIONAL BREAKDOWN STRUCTURE

Figure 11-21. OBS with no access rights

OBS and Datamart

OBSs are assigned in Datamart Settings under Data Administration on the administration side, as shown in Figure 11-22. The datamart settings specify a default OBS for each OBS type in order for them to be used in the datamart extraction.

- *Project OBS mapping type*: Limited to 5 OBSs
- *Resource OBS mapping type*: Limited to 5 OBSs

The OBS acts as a holding bucket for projects and resources that have not been assigned to an OBS type when you set the default project and resource OBSs.

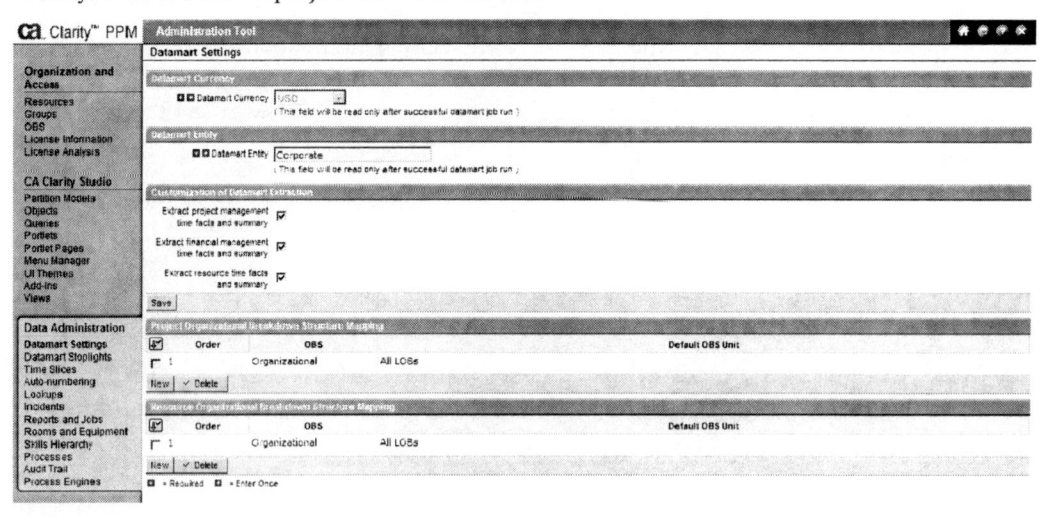

Figure 11-22. OBS and datamart settings

Partitions and Views

A CA Clarity PPM *partition* is a functionality that allows an organization to partition the configuration of a single instance of Clarity. It is a feature that is configured using Clarity Studio and is used in user views across the Studio configuration. Partitions are similar to an OBS but are not used to control security or reporting structures; they are used to control how objects are managed within Clarity.

A partition is a classification of users. Certain items in CA Clarity can be partitioned such that one partition of users "sees" the item one way and another partition of users "sees" the item a different way.

Partitions dictate what you see for an instance but do not provide security to that instance; whether or not you see a particular instance is still dictated by normal security.

The Partition Model

Partition models organize partitions into a hierarchical model. When you create partitions, you use this hierarchical model to assign user-defined attributes at any level and make them available (or required) at lower-level partitions. A default system partition exists in each Clarity enterprise installation. Any partitions you create become children to the system partition.

Figure 11-23 shows an example of a geographical partition model.

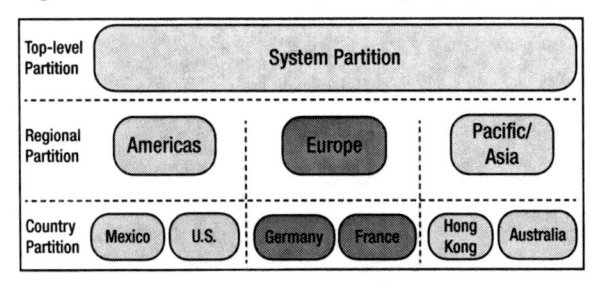

Figure 11-23. Geographical partition model

Partition models are similar to OBSs except for the following:

- OBSs are often used to control security and drive reporting.
- Partition models control how objects (in other words, projects, resources, investments, incidents, and so on) are managed in Clarity.
- Partition models support resource memberships that are based upon groups or OBS units and thus are a way of grouping resources.

An organization can set up multiple partition models; however, a business object can be assigned to only one partition model at a time. As a Clarity Studio user, one can be a member of more than one partition within a partition model. However, when new objects are created, it is required to select the partition to use. Clarity users who are members of one partition need not select a partition. Users who are not members of any partition will see the System Partition (default) view. You will see the Default Partitions link in the Account Settings page if partitions are being used, as shown in Figure 11-24.

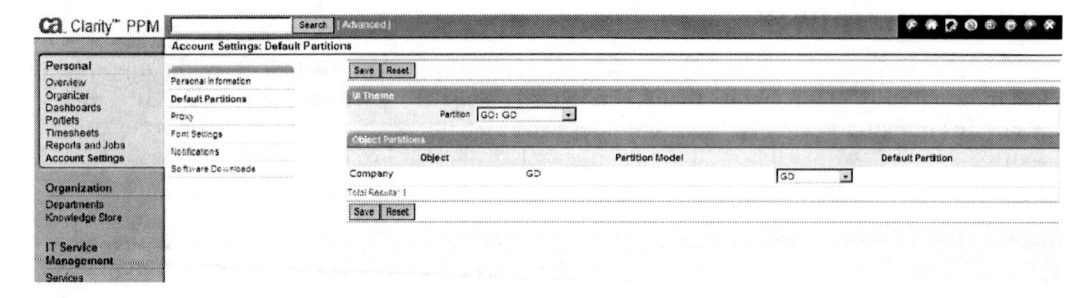

Figure 11-24. Default partitions

Users with access to multiple partitions can use the Actions drop-down on the List/Filter page to toggle between partitions, as shown in Figure 11-25.

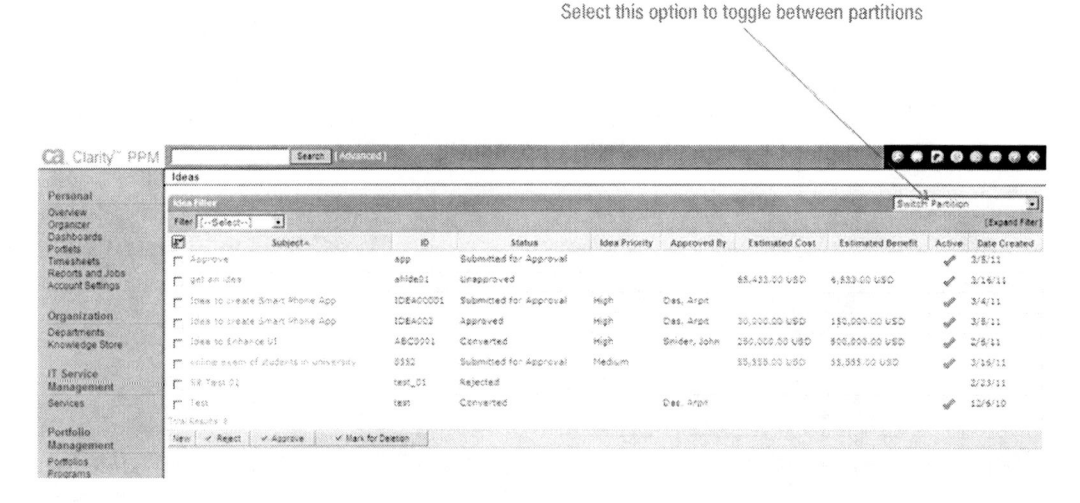

Figure 11-25. Swiching between partitions

The user has an option to select partitions that they are a member of, as shown in Figure 11-26.

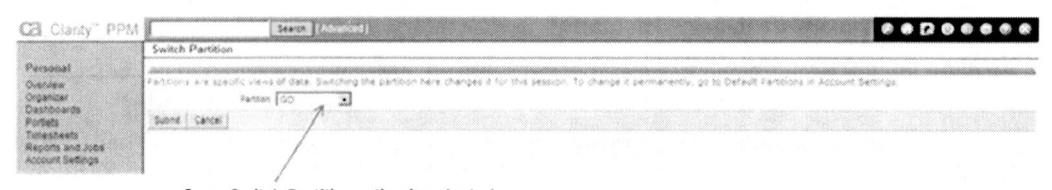

Figure 11-26. Selecting a partition

The choice of desired partitions will be provided upon creation of a new object. The object properties page (Edit) will display in the current partition view when the object instance is created. With partitions, organizations can implement and see Clarity (pages, processes, user interface themes) in different ways. Certain items in Clarity can be partitioned such that one partition of users sees items one way and another partition of users sees those items in a different way. An example would be object attributes and lookup values.

OBS vs. Partitioning

In CA Clarity PPM, OBSs control security and drive reporting, whereas partitions control how objects are managed and appear in Clarity, for instance as projects, resources, investments, and incidents.

Access Rights vs. Partitions

In CA Clarity PPM, access rights determine what users can see and the functions they can perform. Partitions affect how objects appear once users have access to them. However, partitions work with access rights; they don't replace them.

Define Partition Model

A partition model organizes partitions into a hierarchy. This hierarchy is very similar to an OBS. The hierarchy has levels and units, which are the partitions themselves. Figure 11-27 shows the model that Acme Data Systems (ADS) uses.

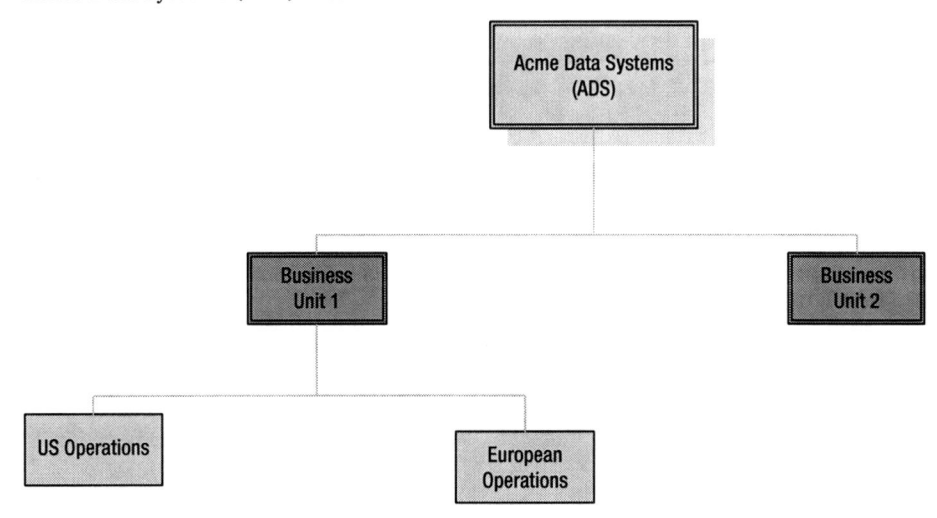

Figure 11-27. ADS partition model

In this model, Business Unit 1, Business Unit 2, U.S. Operations, and European Operations are separate partitions.

Partition models support resource memberships. They assign users to partitions within a model:

- Individually
- By group
- By OBS

Figure 11-28 shows the relationship between partitions, objects, and attributes. If a master object is added to a partition, any subobjects of the master objects are automatically associated with the same partition.

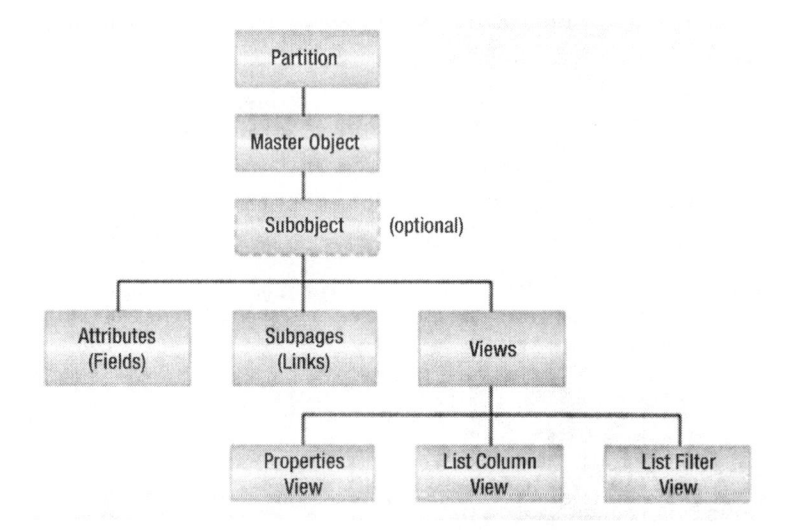

Figure 11-28. Relationship between partitions, objects, and attributes

The partition model can be created from the Partition Models link under CA Clarity Studio in the administration part of CA Clarity PPM, as shown in Figure 11-29.

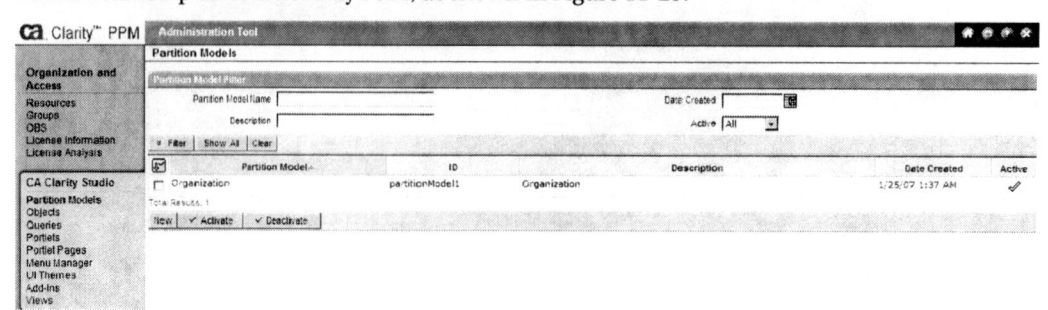

Figure 11-29. Creating a partition model

Figure 11-30 shows the *rights* the user needs to manage and administer partition models on the administration side.

Access Right	Description	Granted Through
Administration - Partition Models	Allows user to manage Partition Models. Does not include the Administration - Navigate right.	Resource
System Partition - Administer	Enables administration of the System Partition	Resource

Total Results: 2

Figure 11-30. Rights to manage the administration partition model

Association Mode

There are four association modes to choose from when associating objects to partitions. Partitions lower than a given partition in a hierarchy are called *descendents*. Partitions higher than a given partition in a hierarchy are called *ancestors*.

Association modes for attributes and lookup values include the following:

- *Partition only*: Members of this partition can see this object.
- *Partition, ancestors, and descendents*: Members of this partition, its ancestors, and descendents can see this object.
- *Partition and ancestors*: Members of this partition and its ancestors can see this object.
- *Partition and descendents*: Members of this partition and its descendents can see this object.

Partition Configuration

The following items may be partitioned in CA Clarity.

User Interface Themes (Logos and Colors)

UI themes are associated to partitions to allow branding of the application by business units. Figure 11-31 shows the UI themes.

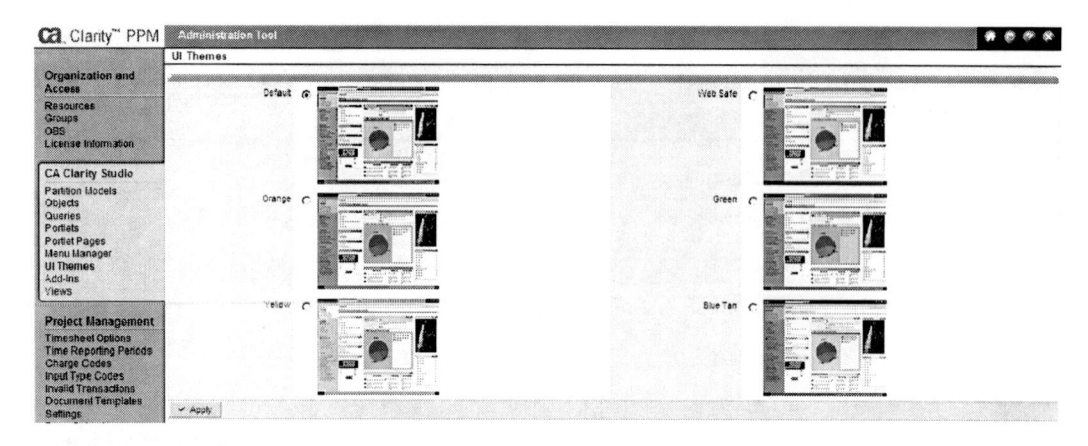

Figure 11-31. UI themes

Object Fields (Attributes)

Partition models may be associated to one or many objects. After this association, the fields and views on the object may be partitioned. That is, the look and feel of the object may be tailored according to the organization hierarchy defined in the partition model, as shown in Figure 11-32.

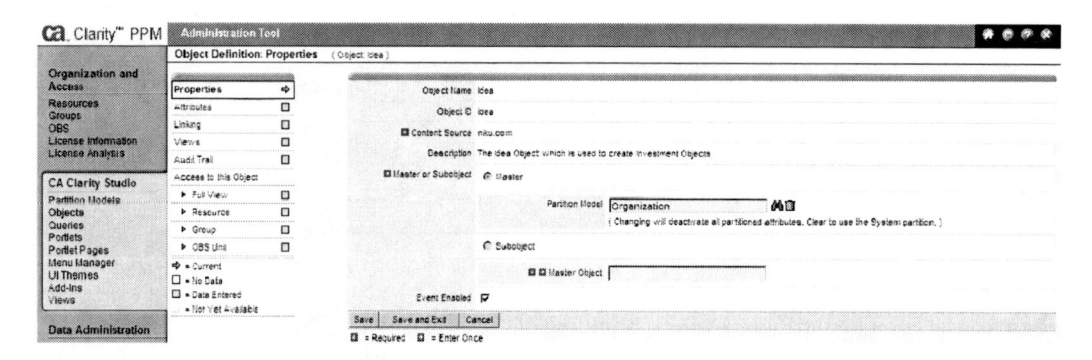

Figure 11-32. Object fields and partitioning

Partitioning fields on an attribute is accomplished by selecting a partition and the association mode in the CA Clarity Administration Tool, as shown in Figure 11-33.

CHAPTER 11 ■ CA CLARITY PMM ORGANIZATIONAL BREAKDOWN STRUCTURE

Figure 11-33. Partitioning fields

Autonumbering Schemas

Autonumbering schemas on attributes of an object can be partitioned. This enables an organization to create schemas based on their business units, as shown in Figure 11-34.

Figure 11-34. Autonumbering schemas

259

Object Lists, Filters, and Property Pages

In CA Clarity PPM, views may be defined for each *partition*. Views in Clarity include property page layouts, lists, and filters, as shown in Figure 11-35.

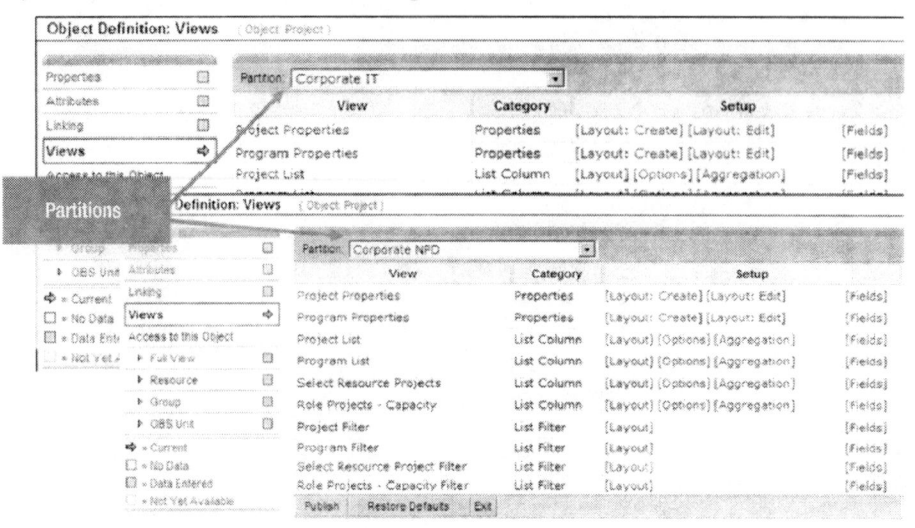

Figure 11-35. Object lists, filters, and property pages

Lookup Values

Partitioning lookups is accomplished by selecting a partition and the association mode in the CA Clarity Administration Tool. The partition is defined in the properties of the lookup values, as shown in Figure 11-36.

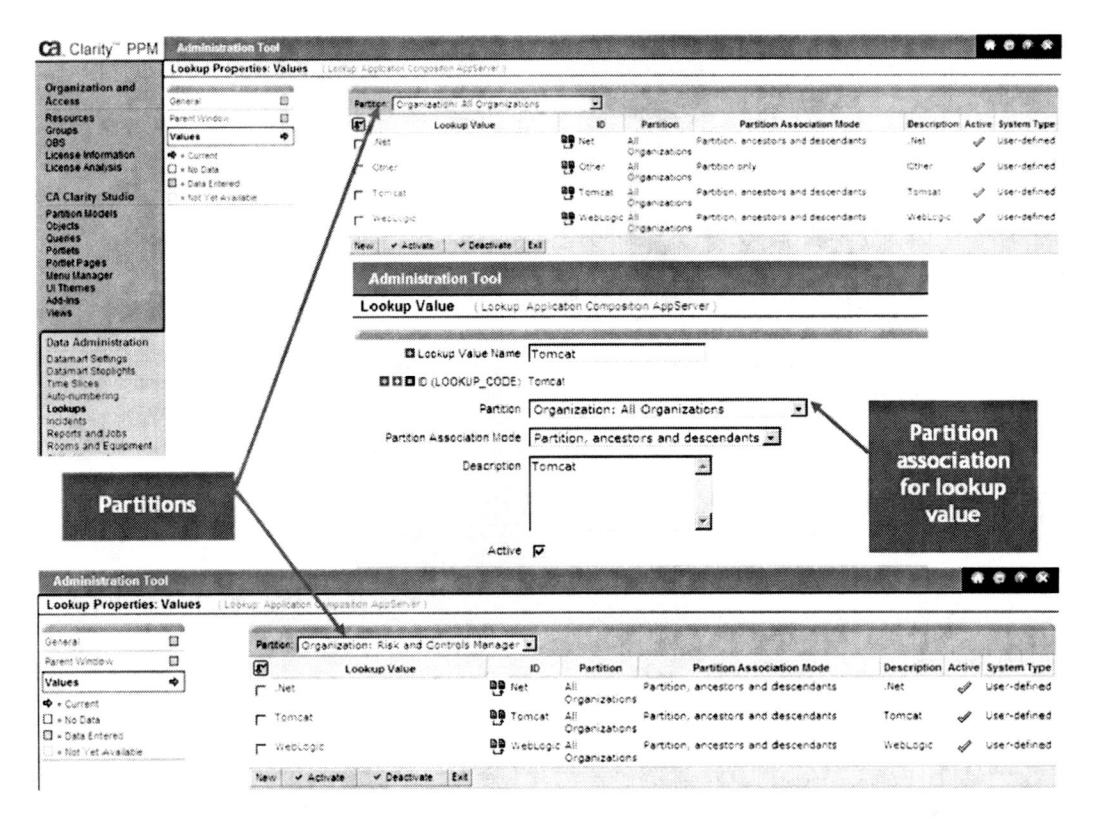

CHAPTER 11 ■ CA CLARITY PMM ORGANIZATIONAL BREAKDOWN STRUCTURE

Figure 11-36. Lookup values

Object-Based Portlets

A portlet can be partitioned based on an object partition. Figure 11-37 shows a sample portlet.

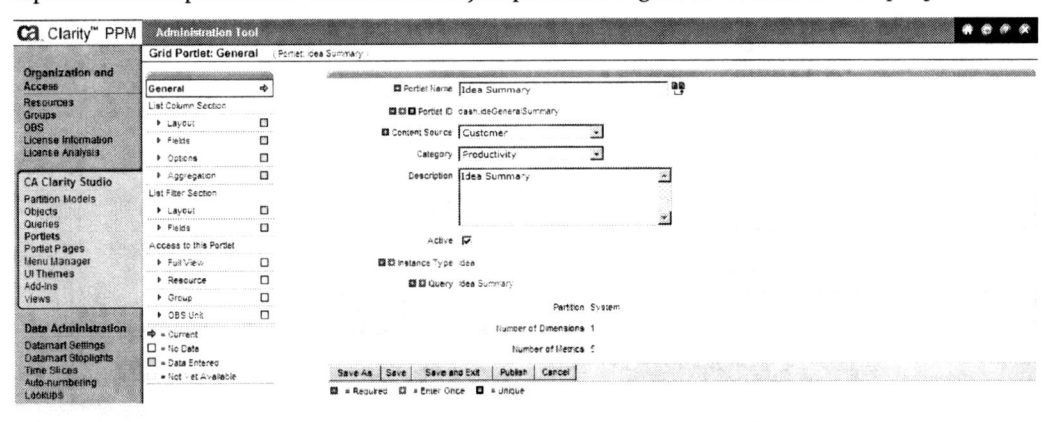

Figure 11-37. Portlets

261

■ **Tip** NSQL queries cannot be partitioned.

Processes

Processes can be partitioned when a partitioned object is associated with the process, as shown in Figure 11-38.

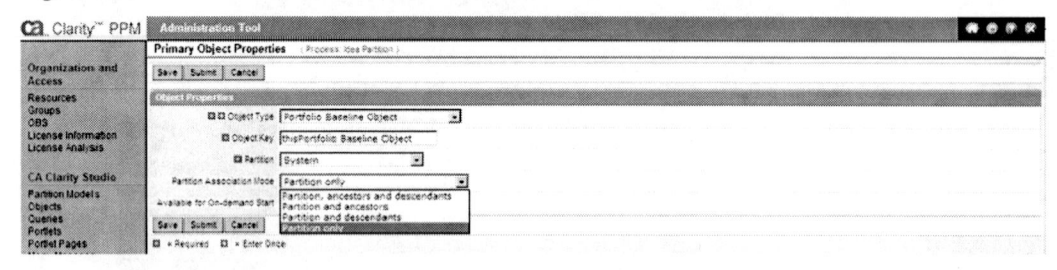

Figure 11-38. Processes and partitioning

For example, if an idea object is partitioned and you create a process based on the idea object, then you see valid partitions with the association mode. This means that the user whose partition matches the one in the process will have access to the process. Figure 11-39 shows how the same project is viewed differently in two partitions.

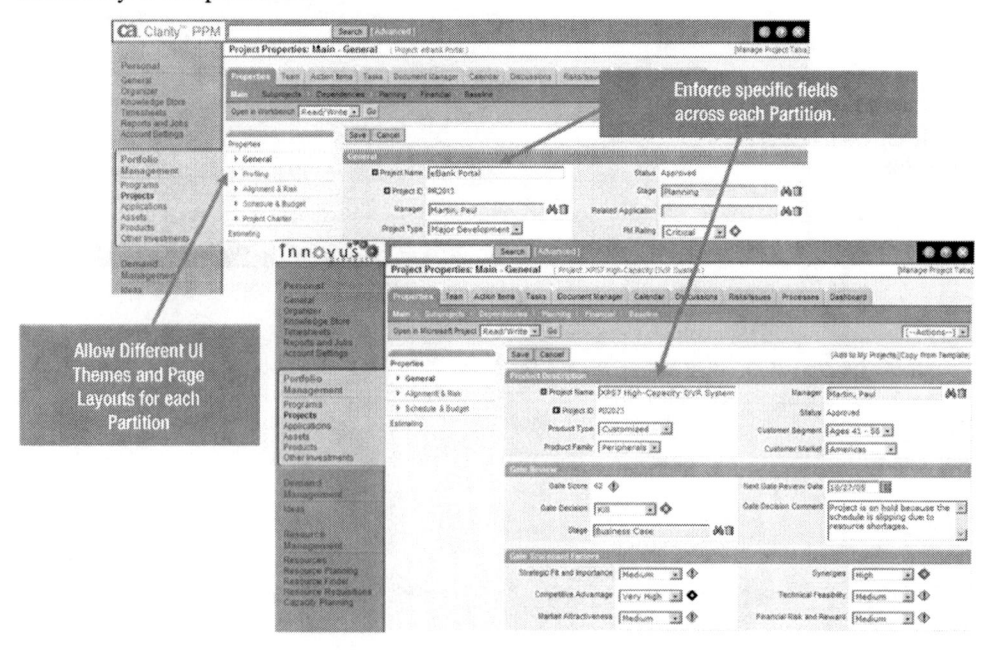

Figure 11-39. Project view and partitions example

Nonpartitionable Configuration

The following cannot be partitioned in CA Clarity PPM.

Financial Setup

All organizations using Clarity are required to leverage the same financial account codes as reflective of the organization's ledger systems. (A slight caveat is that different legal entities can have different fiscal time periods and relationships to department and location OBSs.)

Timesheet Options

All organizations are subject to the same view of timesheet details. Figure 11-40 shows a sample timesheet and its options.

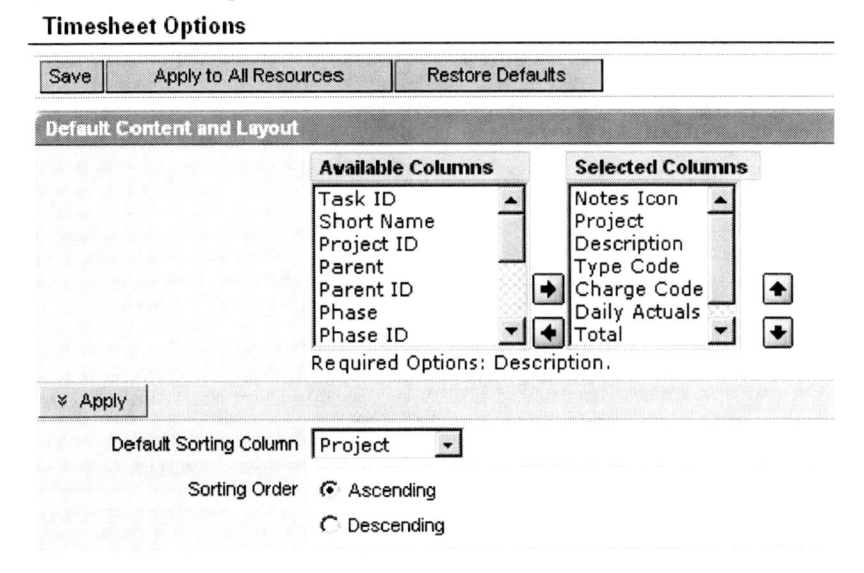

Figure 11-40. Timesheets options cannot be partitioned.

> **Tip** NSQL queries and thus NSQL-based lookups and portlets cannot be partitioned.
>
> Reports and jobs cannot be partitioned.

Best Practices

In this section, we will discuss some best practices and tips that CA Services teams have found to be most effective when using the functionality.

Organizational Breakdown Structure (OBS)

The following are best practices for OBSs:

- An OBS can represent an organizational resource reporting structure.
- You can have multiple OBSs in the system based on organizational business needs such as resource OBS, project OBS, location OBS, department OBS, and security OBS.
- An OBS can be used for reporting as well as for security access.
- All OBSs should not be marked for the use of security access unless it's very clear that they will be used for security.
- OBS security can be very efficient but can also become a maintenance nightmare, so consult CA Services before designing it.
- OBS can have a maximum of ten levels.

Partitioning

The following are best practices for partitioning:

- A resource should have appropriate CA Clarity PPM Studio access rights to work with partitioning.
- Proper understanding of an organization's methodology is necessary to develop successful partition models and to create effective partitions.
- The following considerations can be applied when creating partition models:
    - It is possible to set up more than one partition model in CA Clarity PPM Studio.
    - Once created, partition models cannot be deleted; they can only be deactivated.
    - Once a partition is set up, it cannot be moved, not even within the same level.
    - An object can be assigned to only one partition model.
- It is recommended that you define partition views at the top of the partition model. It is not required that you define object views for each partition in a partition model. If a partition has no view, it inherits the view from the nearest ancestor partition. For example, in Figure 11-41,

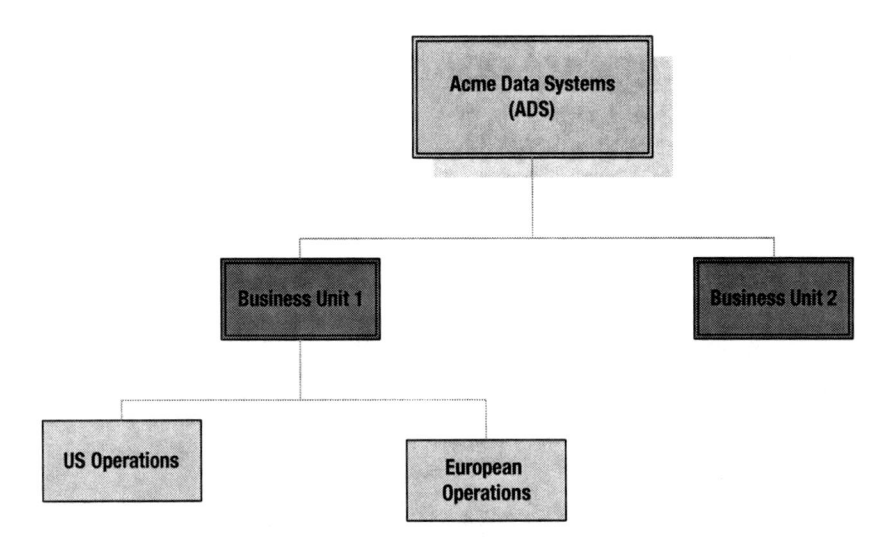

Figure 11-41. ADS partition model

Views applicable to Business Unit 1 should be associated with the Business 1 partition unit. Views applicable to U.S. Operations should be associated with the U.S. Operations partition unit only.

Partitions are *not* security. Security is *what data* we see. Security controls the level of access (edit/view) you have to the data in the application. Partitions are *how* data is seen. Partitions allow you to present forms and data to business units in a format that supports your unique processes.

For example, when viewing project lists, security determines which projects one can see (and edit), while each project's partition determines the data collected for that project, as shown in Figure 11-42.

Figure 11-42. Partitions vs. security

Partition Value

The following example shows how a partition in CA Clarity PPM can add value to an organization.

Example Use of Partitions: An ERP Provider in Higher Education

The following implementation scope is used in this example:

- Global time and financial management for approximately 2,500 users across the enterprise with integration of financial management systems for projects and the general ledger accounting
- A local release of opportunity, project, and resource management for an 800-person professional services organization.

- A flexible design to support future releases of Clarity to information technology, marketing, and product development needs to be considered in the design

Enterprisewide projects needed to be modeled to support global time management. Professional services had local requirements that needed to be supported with a more robust design and configuration for projects and resources. The solution required an organizational partition.

Partition Caveats

The following explains the caveats of using partitions in CA Clarity PPM.

Additional Administration

A more complex configuration can result in greater administration overhead: resources need to be associated to the partitions for which they will need to create objects so that, for instance, they can create the object in the correct partition. Configuration changes need to be managed for each partition. Partition models cannot be deleted, only deactivated. In CA Clarity PPM, an organization cannot share configuration across two partitions in two different branches of a partition model, as shown in Figure 11-43.

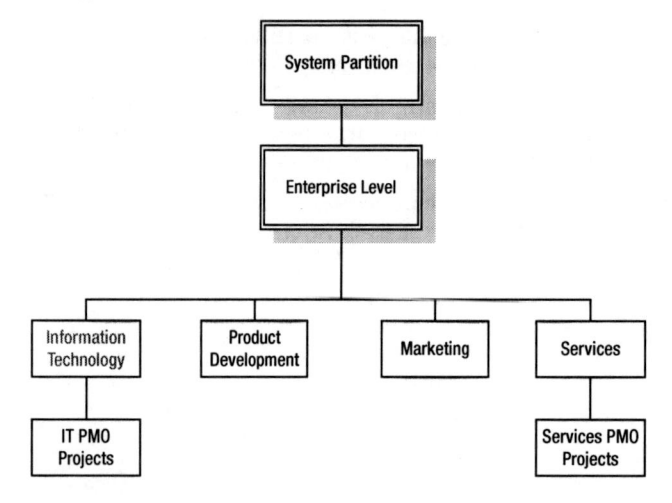

Figure 11-43. Configuration complexity and partitioning

Reporting

When defining reporting requirements and design, care must be taken to understand how the data elements are defined in each partition. Figure 11-44 shows a sample report.

Annual Forecast Generated by IT Owner				
	Stage (Not in ESS Partition)	Work Type (Not in EPM Partition)	Current Year Forecast	Next Year Forecast
Active Projects				
EPM Project 1	Initiation		$2,000,000.00	$1,200,000.00
ESS Project 2		Enhancement	$125,000.00	$80,000.00
EPM Project 3	Analysis		$450,000.00	$675,000.00
Active Project Total			**$2,575,000.00**	**$1,955,000.00**

Figure 11-44. Sample report

Case Study

The following is an example of where partitions in CA Clarity PPM can create maintenance overhead and can be avoided.

Example Use of Partitions: Healthcare Services Provider

The implementation scope included project, resource, and financial management functionality for a healthcare services provider. The organization needed to distinguish between internal strategic/tactical projects, client projects, maintenance, and administrative work. The solution did not warrant the use of Clarity partitions. The use of other Clarity features such as dynamic subpages supported the ability to capture different data depending on the project type, which results in less maintenance overhead.

Summary

This chapter was a brief overview of the organizational breakdown structure and partitioning in CA Clarity PPM. Also, it included a few best practices and tips when implementing partitioning and configuring OBS.

CHAPTER 12

■ ■ ■

CA Clarity PPM Security

Would organizations like their sensitive financial data to be visible to everyone within the organization? Would users appreciate application screens with a lot of unnecessary information? Would project managers like that anybody with access to their projects could change and update data? How do organizations segregate the use of an application by multiple divisions? How do companies ensure that approval rights rest with chosen managers? Security setups in applications help address these concerns.

Enterprise applications usually require access controls to be in place. Access controls and security operate at multiple levels, and they need to do the following:

- Protect data when there is communication from server to browser (SSL)

- Have access to company intranet web sites through features such as single sign-on and LDAP integration

- Have role-based access within the application

Role-based access helps application users access relevant screens within an application perform tasks such as entering data, viewing dashboards, and so on. In addition to an individual's role, their department, location, or team could also play an important role in determining the areas or modules of the application that are available.

Security within the application could also be granted at multiple levels:

- *Global*: All employees in an organization can view telephone numbers in the corporate directory.

- *Divisional/unit based*: Only HR team members can see appraisal comments of all employees in an organization.

- *Instance based*: Managers can see time entry details of their direct reports.

Security also helps restrict the access to specific and relevant modules. For example, resource managers will be the primary users of the resource management features in an application.

Lastly, it is imperative to define who needs to be granted access:

- *A role*: All project managers have certain common application privileges.

- *A division*: Accountants who belong to the finance department can generate invoices.

- *Resource*: Business unit heads can provide an exception approval for leave.

Acme Data Systems (ADS) wants to organize resources and groups with similar responsibilities and grant them access rights. ADS wants the Clarity PPM users to see only the data needed to do their jobs. This chapter describes the security features of Clarity PPM. We discuss the Clarity security model, which includes organizational, financial, and object-level access rights. Then we present some best practices that are followed by Clarity users in the industry.

Introduction to Clarity PPM Security

CA Clarity PPM Security determines which objects a user or group of users can access and the actions they can take on them, such as create, edit, view, and approve. Security user rights can be offered at a number of levels and work in conjunction with an organization breakdown structure (OBS). This section describes the CA Clarity PPM Security model.

Figure 12-1 shows different levels of access and who to grant these access rights to. The left side shows what levels of access users or groups need in CA Clarity PPM, and the right side shows who in an organization needs the access. They could be a group of users or resources belonging to an OBS unit or an individual resource.

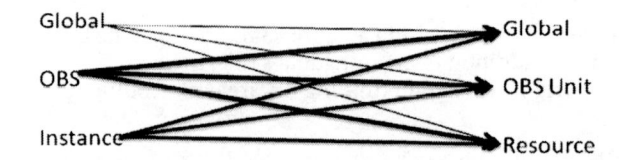

Figure 12-1. Level of access(left) and who to grant access to (right)

Security can be administered from the Clarity PPM administration tool. Figure 12-2 shows the access rights a user must have in order to manage security in CA Clarity PPM.

| ☐ Administration - Authorization | Allows user to manage resources and groups. Includes the Administration - Navigate right. | Resource |

Figure 12-2. Global rights required to manage security from the CA Clarity administration tool

CHAPTER 12 ■ CA CLARITY PPM SECURITY

Clarity Security Model

The CA Clarity PPM security model consists of three main types of security to control access to data and different features of the application:

- Organizational access rights
- Financial/entity-based access rights
- Object-level access rights

Organization Access Rights

Rights in CA Clarity PPM can be assigned in the admin tool and on the application side. To manage security rights from the admin tool, the user needs to have administration-authorization rights, as shown in Figure 12-2. Figure 12-3 shows the admin tool view where the security rights can be managed.

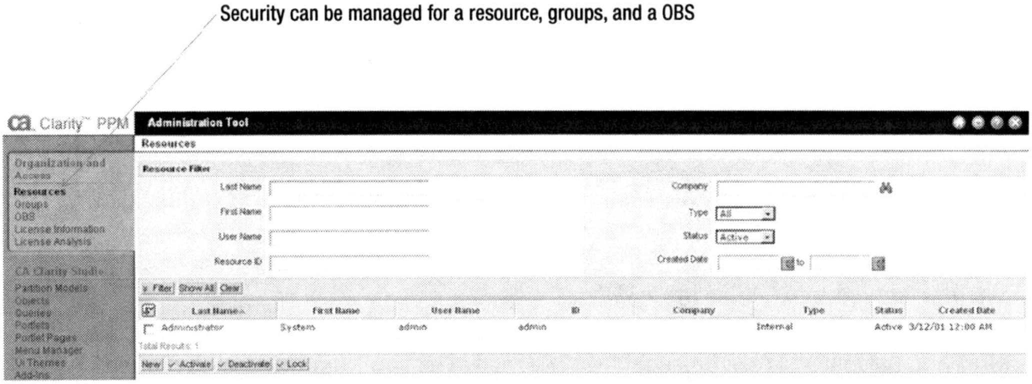

Figure 12-3. CA Clarity PPM admin tool used to manage security for resource, groups, and an OBS

Inherited Rights

Inherited rights are provided when a resource's name is associated with a particular field or screen in the application. For example, once a resource is named, the project manager and resource's name are populated in the field that gives the user inherited rights.

Figure 12-4 shows the few inherent rights in the system.

271

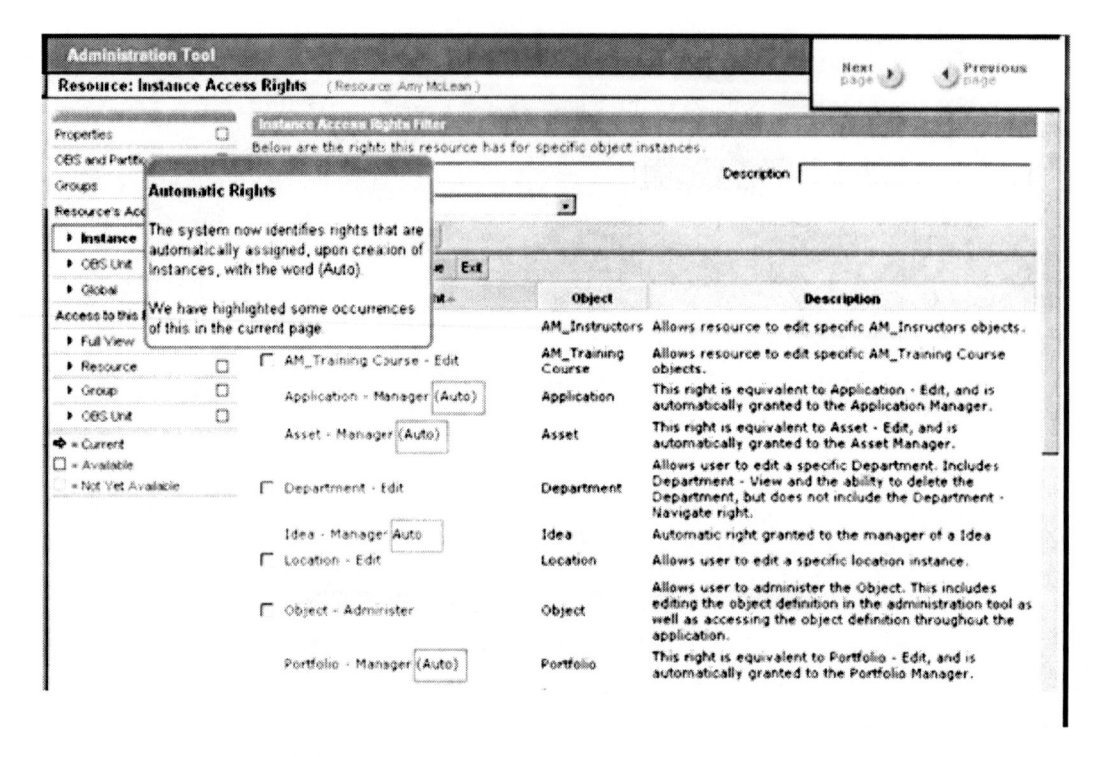

Figure 12-4. Inherent rights in CA Clarity PPM

In CA Clarity PPM, the following security rights are assigned in an application and are inherited.

User Added as a Collaboration Manager

Figure 12-5 shows a participant as the collaboration manager on a project. A project participant becomes the collaboration manager and inherits the collaboration manager rights when a resource does the following:

- When the participant creates a project
- When the existing collaboration manager makes another participant the collaboration manager

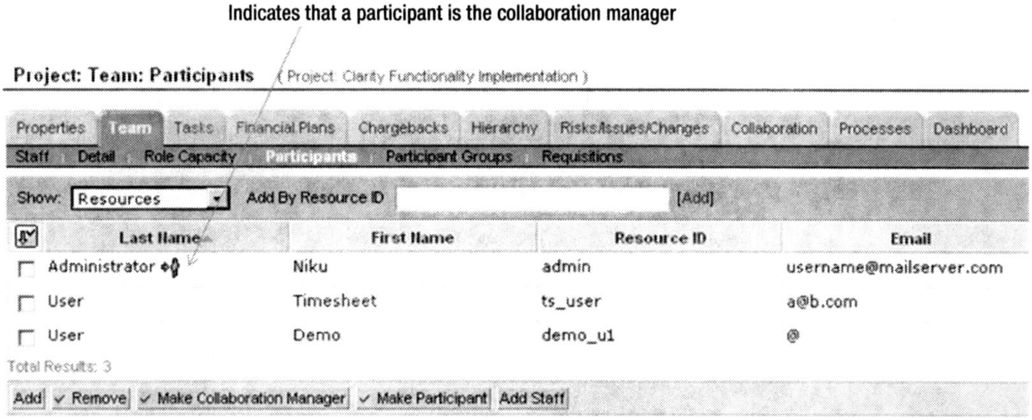

CHAPTER 12 ■ CA CLARITY PPM SECURITY

Figure 12-5. The collaboration manager is shown by the arrow on this project

A collaboration manager can exclusively perform the following tasks:
- Add or remove participants to the project
- Add or remove a participant as a collaboration manager to the project
- Initiate a discussion

User Added as a Collaboration Participant

When a resource is added as a participant on a project, certain rights are inherited such as the following:

- Read access to the projects and subprojects
- Collaboration features such as action items, discussions, documents, and the calendar

Figure 12-6 shows the list of participants on a project.

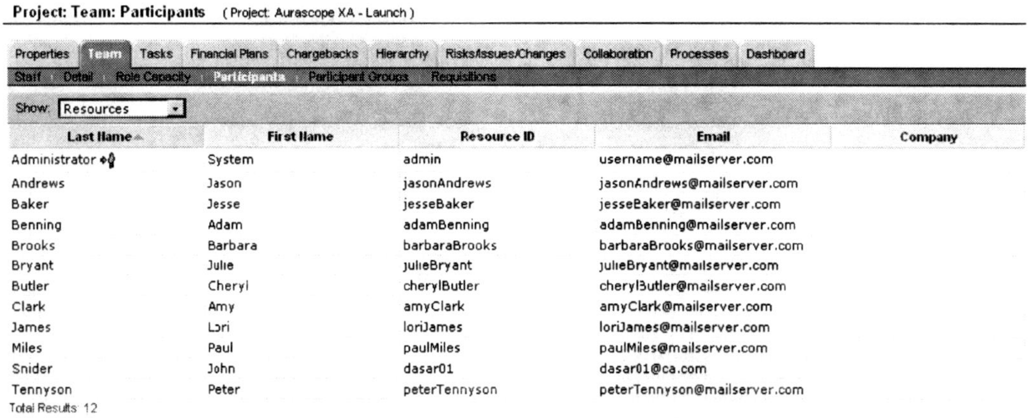

Figure 12-6. Participants on a project

273

User Added as a Staff Member

A resource allocated to a project as staff can be assigned tasks and can enter time on a project. Figure 12-7 shows the view showing staff members on a project.

Figure 12-7. Staff members on a project

User Added as a Project Manager

A user added as a project manager on a project inherits the view and edit rights from the general and management properties of the project. Figure 12-8 shows the inherited rights when a user, Michael Angelo, becomes a project manager on a project.

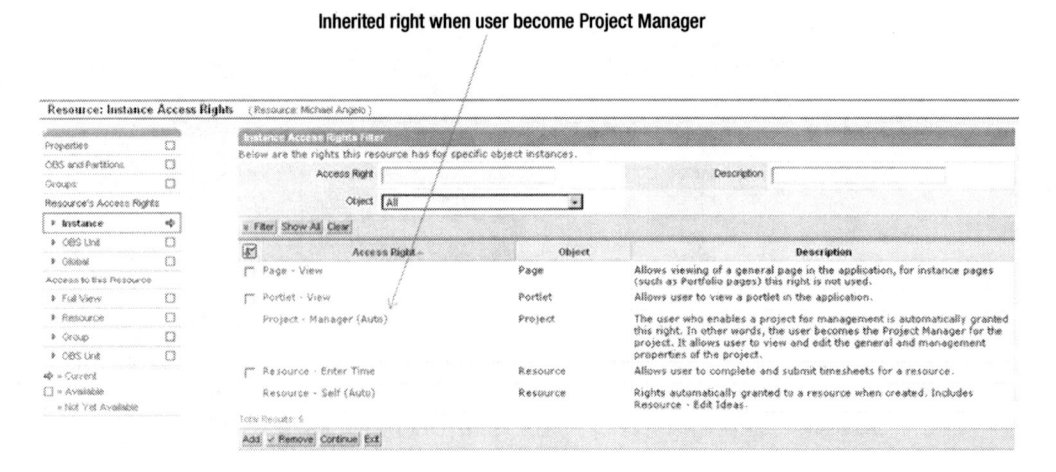

Figure 12-8. Project Manager inherited right

Making a user the project manager on a project does *not* automatically give them all rights. Here are some limitations that will need to be addressed if the project manager needs these rights:

- The user has to be added as staff and/or participant on a project to access the collaboration features (via the Collaboration tab).
- The user has to be granted rights to view/create/edit risks, issues, and changes.

Figure 12-9 shows a screen where a user is a project manager on a project and does not have access to the Collaboration tab and to risks, issues, and changes.

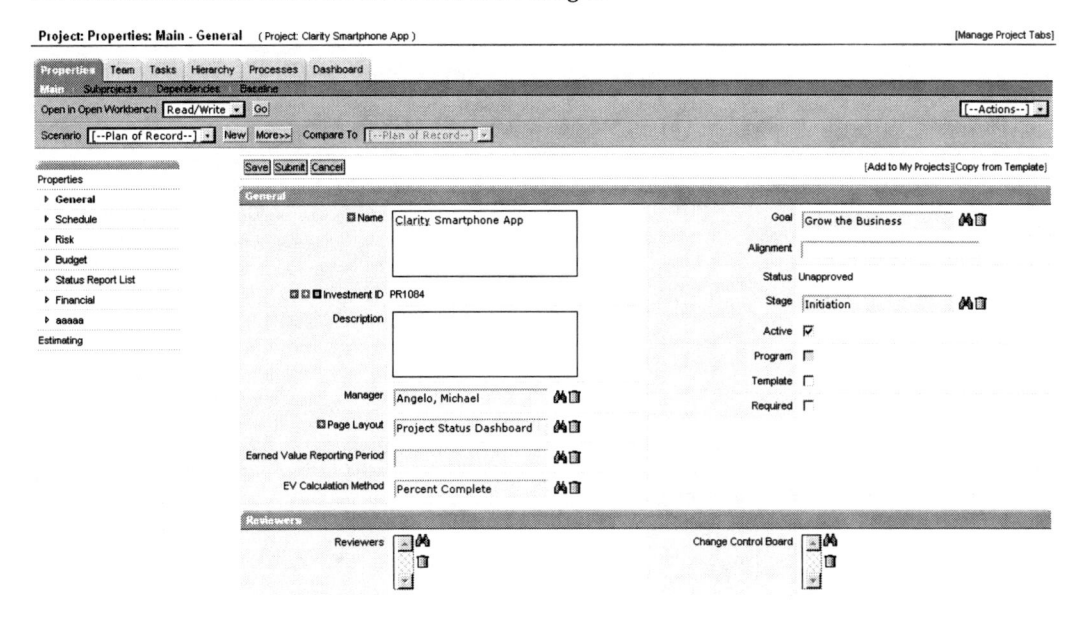

Figure 12-9. View of project for a project manager

User Added as a Resource Manager

When a resource becomes a resource manager for another resource, it allows the resource manager to view and edit general resource properties. Figure 12-10 shows the inherited rights for a resource manager.

CHAPTER 12 ■ CA CLARITY PPM SECURITY

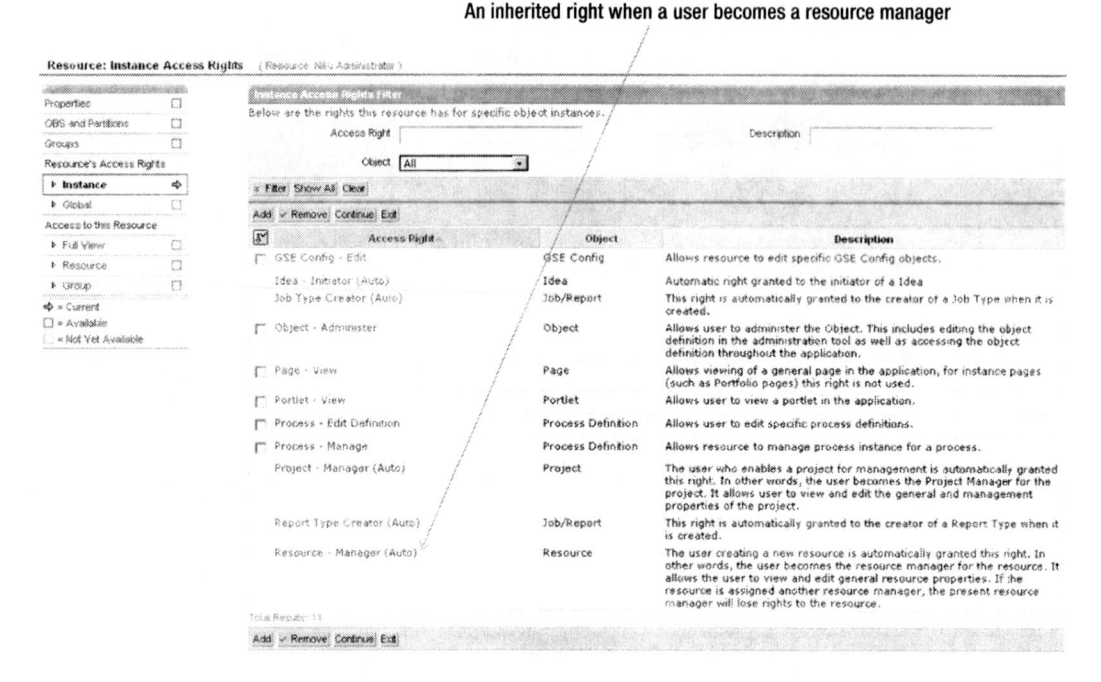

Figure 12-10. Resource manager inherited rights

The resource manager does not automatically get rights to enter or approve timesheets for their direct reports. These rights have to be explicitly granted.

Types of Security in CA Clarity PPM

To implement security in CA Clarity PPM, the following must be created and configured in the system:

- Resources must exist.
- Groups must be created with resources.
- The OBS should exist with security enabled.

Global Rights

Global rights in CA Clarity PPM provide access to all instances of a particular object. Global rights can be assigned to a group, to an OBS unit, or to an individual user. Global rights supersede OBS or instance rights.

Here's an example: Acme Data Systems (ADS) wants to provide global rights to John to view all resources in the system. ADS also wants all resources in the IT department OBS to be able to view all projects in the system. In addition, resources in the Executive IT group at ADS should be able to view all portlets in the in the CA Clarity PPM system.

In this example, the following scenario needs to be implemented. We have to grant global rights to a resource, an OBS, and a group.

Figure 12-11 shows John is granted global rights to view all resources in the system.

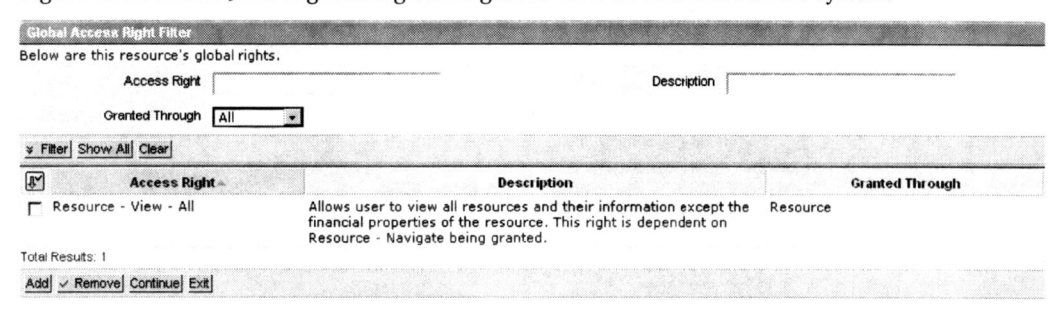

Figure 12-11. Global rights granted to a resource

Now we will grant the IT OBS unit OBS global rights to view all projects. From the OBS list, we select the Corporate Department OBS. To use an OBS for the security access rights, we check Used for Access Rights.

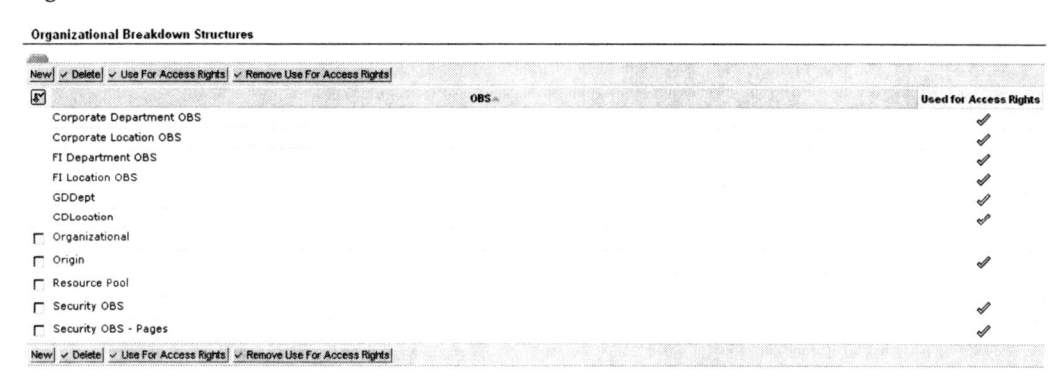

Figure 12-12. List of OBSs in CA Clarity PPM system

In the Corporate Department OBS, we select IT from the Units tab, as shown in Figure 12-13.

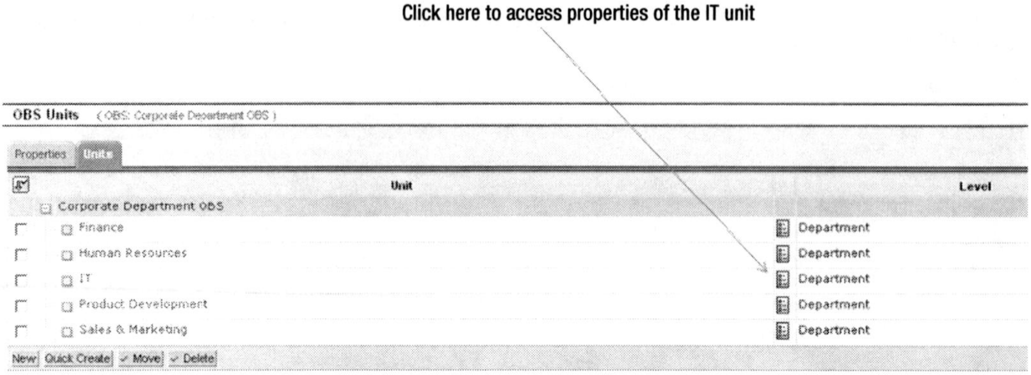

CHAPTER 12 ■ CA CLARITY PPM SECURITY

Figure 12-13. List of units under the Corporate Department OBS

In the properties of the IT unit, we add global rights as the next step, as shown in Figure 12-14.

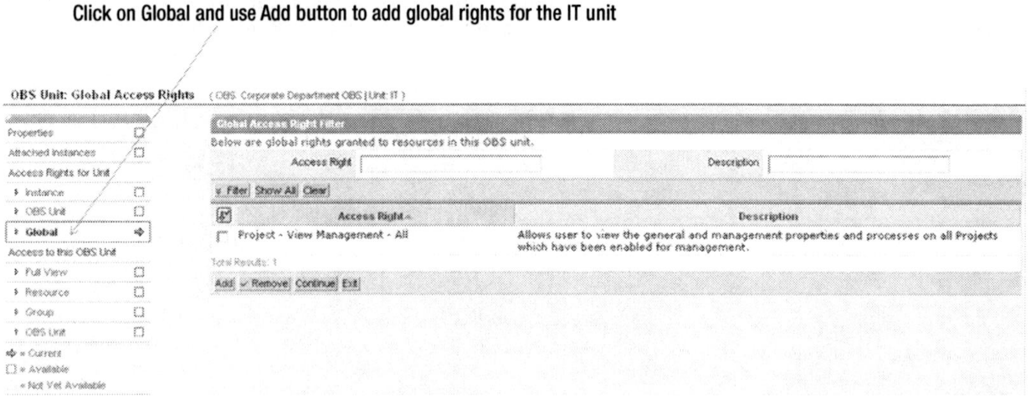

Figure 12-14. Adding global rights for IT unit

Now as shown in Figure 12-15, we have to add global rights for the Executive IT group to view all the portlets in the CA Clarity PPM system at ADS. To grant global rights to view all the portlets, we select the Executive IT group from the list of groups, and under Global in the group properties, we add the Portlet Viewer – All right.

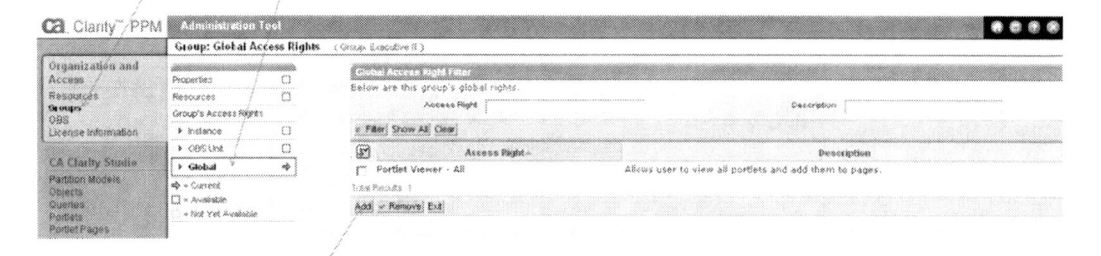

CHAPTER 12 ■ CA CLARITY PPM SECURITY

Figure 12-15. Adding global rights for the Executive IT group

OBS Rights

OBS rights provide a user or a group with access rights to a level of the OBS. Also, OBS rights provide a unit of the OBS with a particular right. So, OBS rights can be assigned to a group, to an OBS unit, or to an individual user. An OBS must be established as a security OBS and assigned appropriately to objects. Figure 12-16 shows how an OBS can be established as a security OBS.

Figure 12-16. Enabling and disabling an OBS for security access

Here's an example: ADS want to implement a security model where Adam Benning should approve the time for all internal IT resources under the Resource Pool OBS. Also, ADS wants resources in the IT OBS under the Corporate Department OBS to be able to view all ideas under the Product Development business units. Further, the Executive IT group in ADS should be able to view all projects under the IT unit for the Corporate Department OBS.

To implement this, first we set up a model where Adam should approve time for all internal IT resources under the Resource Pool OBS. We select the resource Adam Benning from the resource list in the admin tool and then go to the OBS Unit properties of Adam, as shown in Figure 12-17.

Click on Resources and select Adam

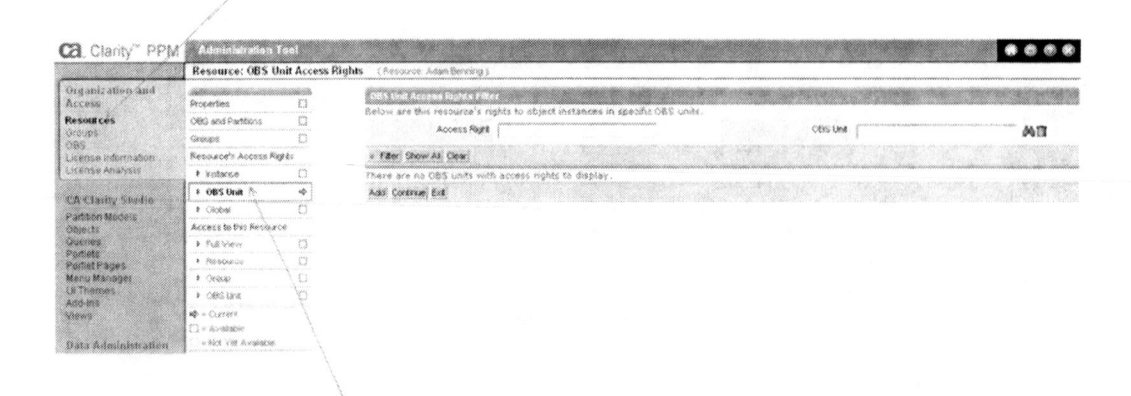

Figure 12-17. Granting OBS rights to Adam

Next, select Resource – Approve Time from the list of rights, as shown in Figure 12-18.

Select the right and click here

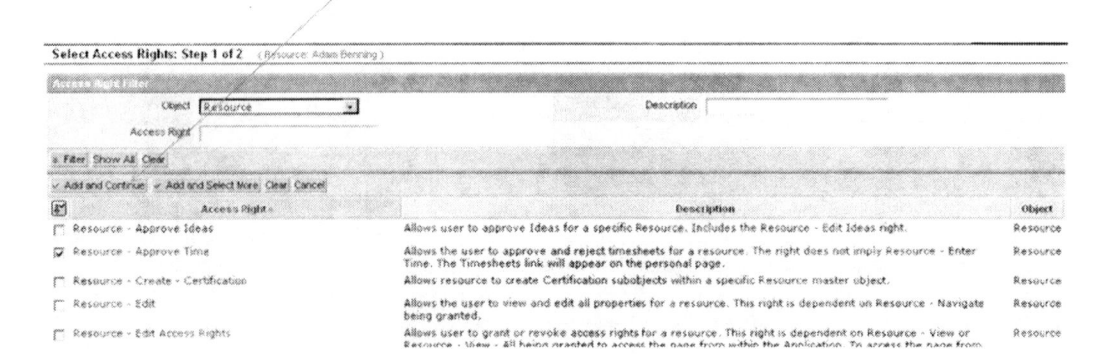

Figure 12-18. Filtering on the required right

The next step is to select the appropriate OBS unit, as shown in Figure 12-19. Select the OBS from the OBS drop-down, select IT unit, and click Add.

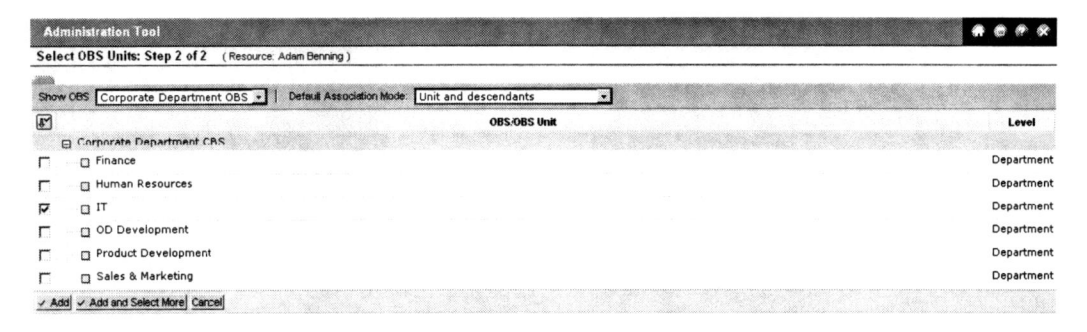

Figure 12-19. Selecting the appropriate OBS unit

Figure 12-20 shows that Adam is granted OBS rights for the IT department. The required security right is added for the IT department and any child units under IT.

Association mode specifies that
Adam can approve time for the IT OBS unit and units under IT

Figure 12-20. Adam is granted OBS rights for the IT department.

Now we will implement security where resources in the IT OBS under the Corporate Department OBS should be able to view all ideas under the Product Development business units. Figure 12-21 shows the units of the Corporate Department OBS and how we navigate to the properties of the IT unit.

CHAPTER 12 ■ CA CLARITY PPM SECURITY

Figure 12-21. Corporate Department OBS units

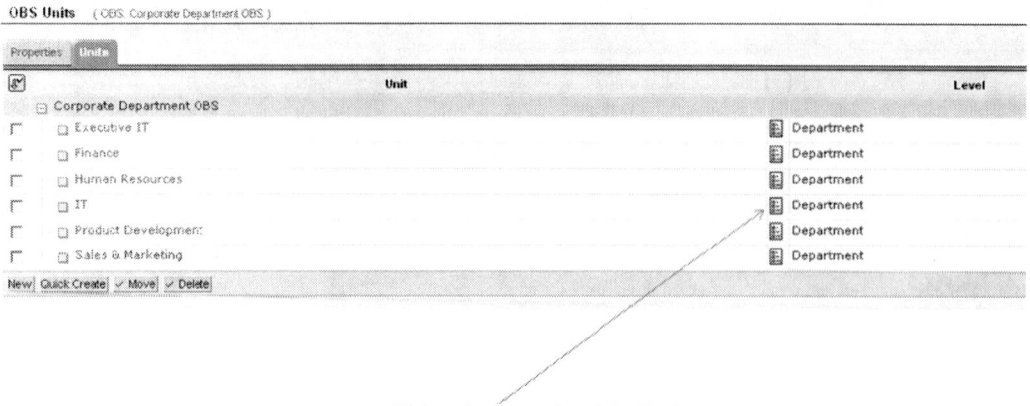

Next, navigate to properties of the IT unit and select the OBS unit link to add security rights, as shown in Figure 12-22.

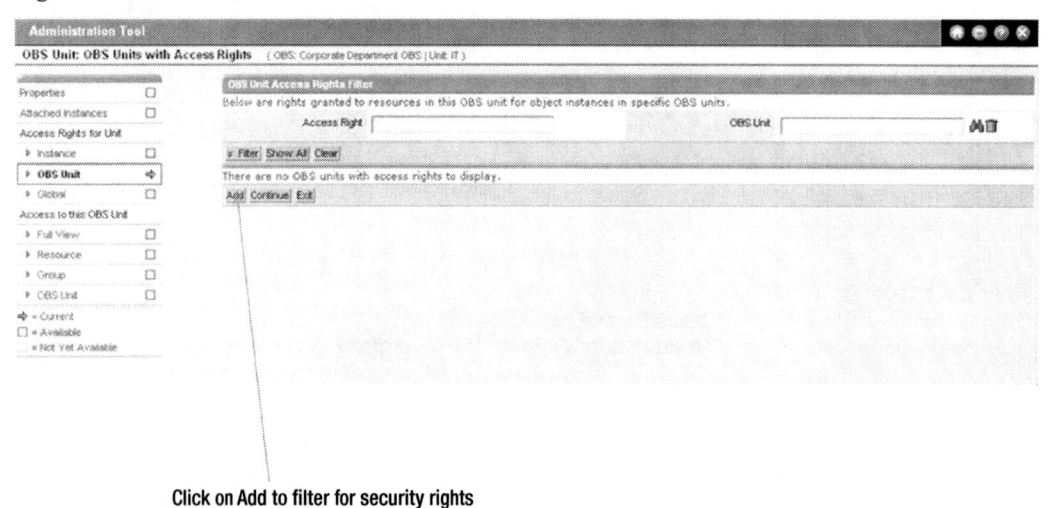

Figure 12-22. IT unit properties

Figure 12-23 shows the filtered list of the security rights, and we select the Idea – View right.

CHAPTER 12 ■ CA CLARITY PPM SECURITY

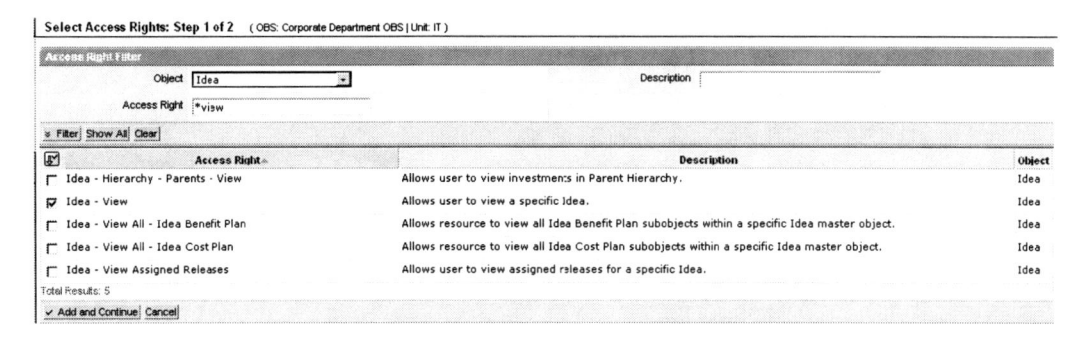

Figure 12-23. Filtering for the required security right

Once we select the rights, choose the appropriate department, such as Product Development, as shown in Figure 12-24, because ADS's requirement is to view ideas in the Product Development department.

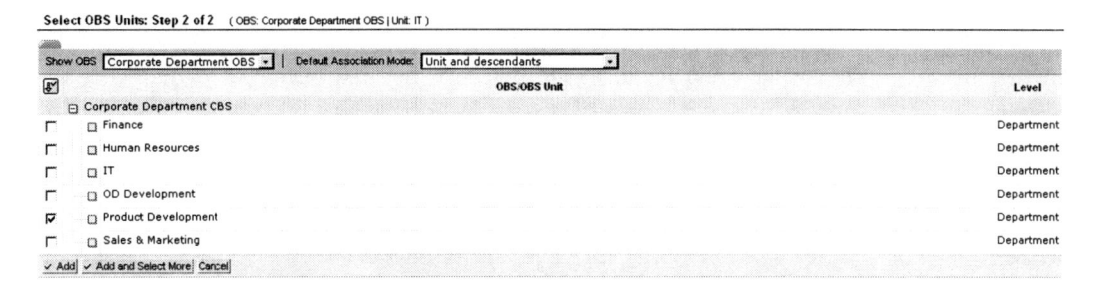

Figure 12-24. Selecting the appropriate department (which is Product Development)

Figure 12-25 shows security rights added wherein resources in the IT department can view all ideas under the Product Development department.

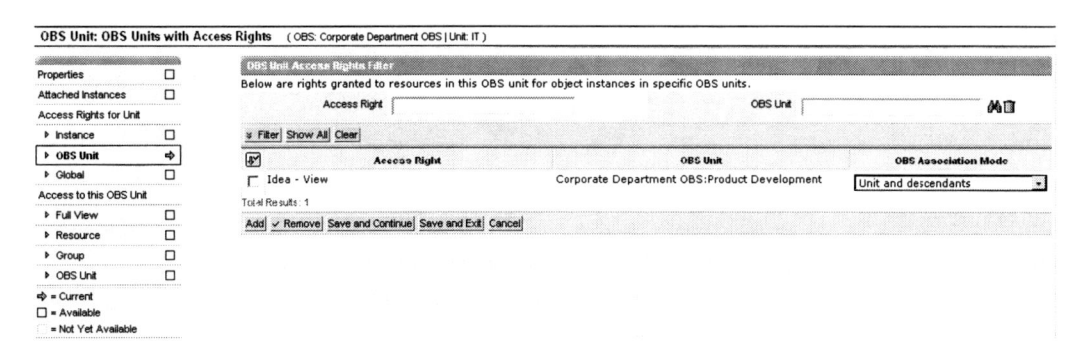

Figure 12-25. Configuring OBS security rights

Now we want to implement security so that the Executive IT group in ADS is able to view all the projects under the IT unit for the Corporate Department OBS. Figure 12-26 shows the properties of the Executive

IT group and a link to the OBS unit where we configure the security to view all projects under the IT department (including child units of the IT department).

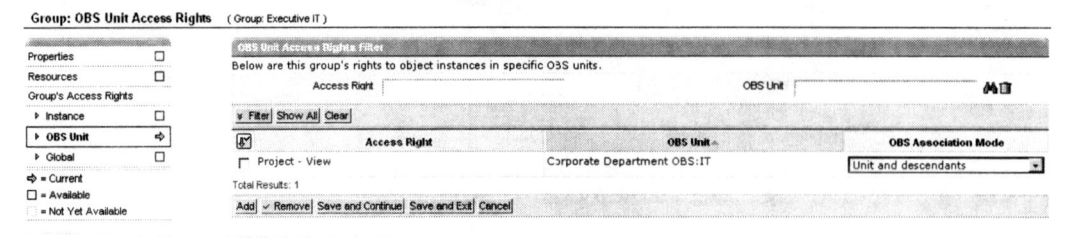

Figure 12-26. OBS security rights for Executive IT group

Instance Rights

Instance rights provide access to individual instances of a particular object. They can be assigned to a group, to an OBS unit, or to an individual user. Instance rights are very granular. You should be very careful in designing the system when using instance rights because they may become a maintenance nightmare.

Here's an example: ADS wants to implement the following security scenario. Julie should be able to approve timesheets for Jason and Peyton. Also, the Sales & Marketing OBS unit should be able to view the Benefits and Costs by Stage portlet. Finally, the Executive IT group should be able to view a few strategic projects.

Figure 12-27 shows the instance rights for Julie to approve time for Jason and Peyton.

CHAPTER 12 ■ CA CLARITY PPM SECURITY

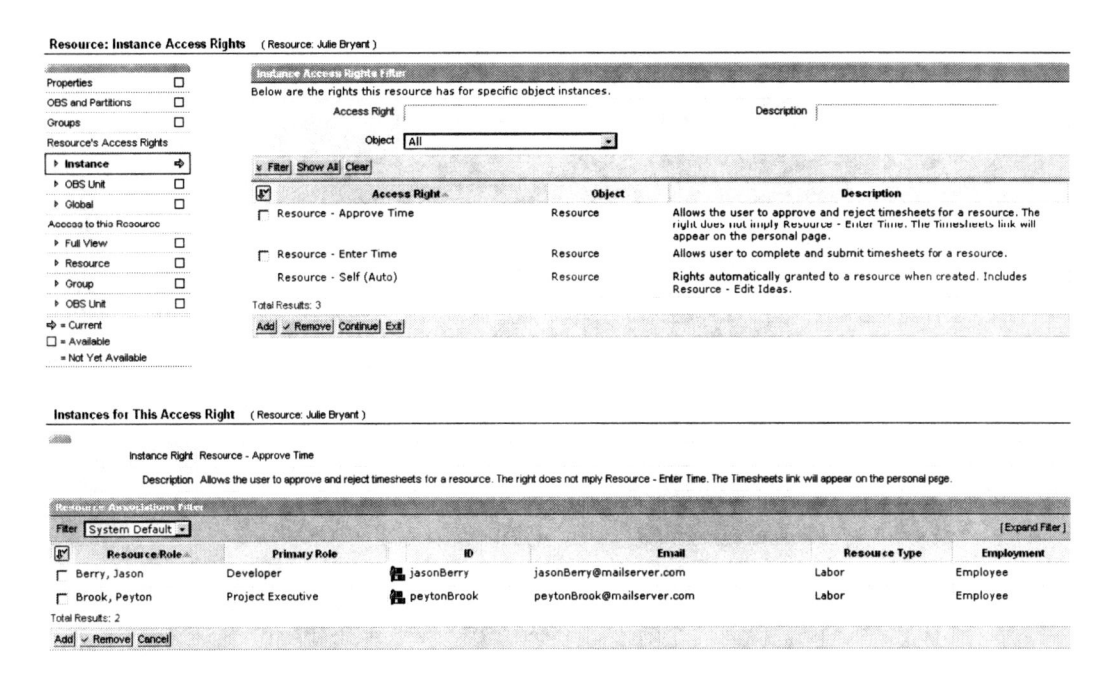

Figure 12-27. Instance rights for Julie

Now we want to grant instance-level Portlet – View rights to the Sales & Marketing OBS. Figure 12-28 shows the portlet instance rights to the Sales & Marketing OBS.

Figure 12-28. Instance-level rights for the Sales & Marketing OBS

285

ADS wants its Executive IT group to view all strategic projects. In ADS there are few projects that are classified as strategic. Figure 12-29 shows the Executive IT group having Project View instance rights on strategic projects.

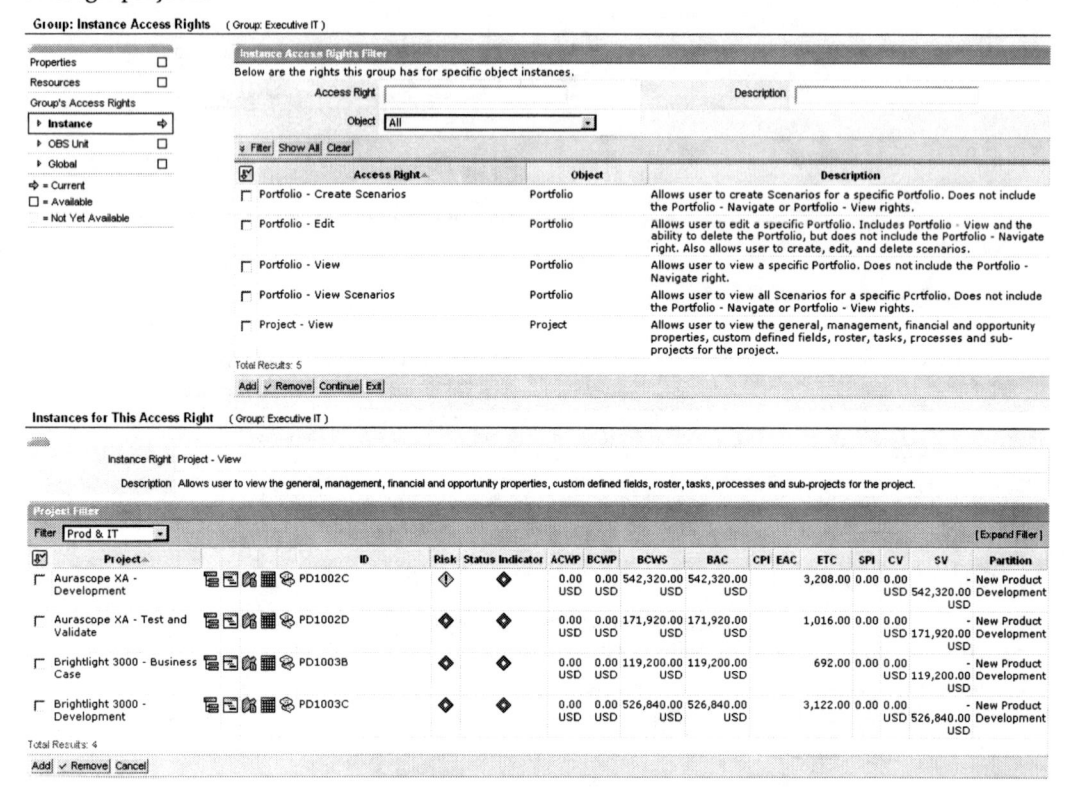

Figure 12-29. Instance-level rights for the Executive IT group

Financial/Entity-Based Access Rights

Entities establish financial boundaries and are the first step to financial management. They allow users to create financial plans, chargebacks, rates, and cost matrices. Once the Clarity Financial module is implemented, additional security rights become available. Resources in one financial entity are blocked from seeing data in another financial entity. Each resource is assigned to a financial entity within their resource profile.

For example, resources in the entity named USA cannot see projects that are attached to the entity named APJ.

These rights may be required if financial transactions are tracked in the system. Every project, resource, and company in the organization must be assigned to an entity, which is the highest level of financial organization; thus, access can be granted via the entity. The cost and rate matrices can be restricted so as to limit viewing by the resources in a particular entity-location combination. In the entity-based security processing, there are three options:

- *None*

- *Strict*: If Strict is specified, resources are able to see only applicable information for the entity they work for.

- *Parent*: If Parent is specified, resources can see only their entity information *unless* they belong to the parent entity, in which case they can see the information they have been granted access to, regardless of the entity.

Figure 12-30 shows the screen for entity-based security in CA Clarity PPM.

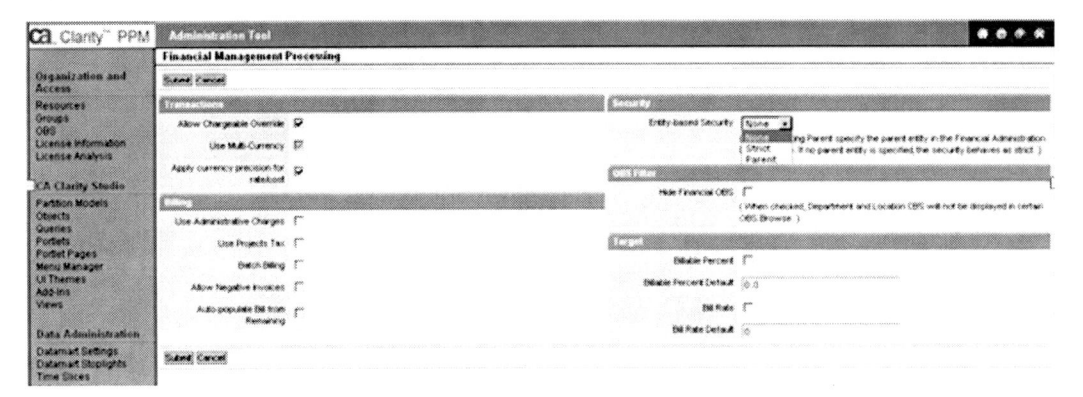

Figure 12-30. Entity-based security settings

When a user enters the financials for a project, the entity defaults to the user who is enabling the financial properties that are used for the WIP class, project class, client class, and bill cycle. Once the entity is defined for the user, they see only those values within their entity.

Object-Level Access Rights

Most objects in the application allow the owner of the object to assign additional view and edit rights for a particular instance of the object. Object-level access is defined within the edit pages by the object managers on the application side and provides control over who is able to see and update the object. It provides access via the access rights without having to always get access rights to their objects from the administrator. It also gives the manager a level of control within their workspace.

Object-level access can also be defined within the Access to this Object pages by administrators on the admin tool side. Figure 12-31 shows how to set object-level access rights from the application side.

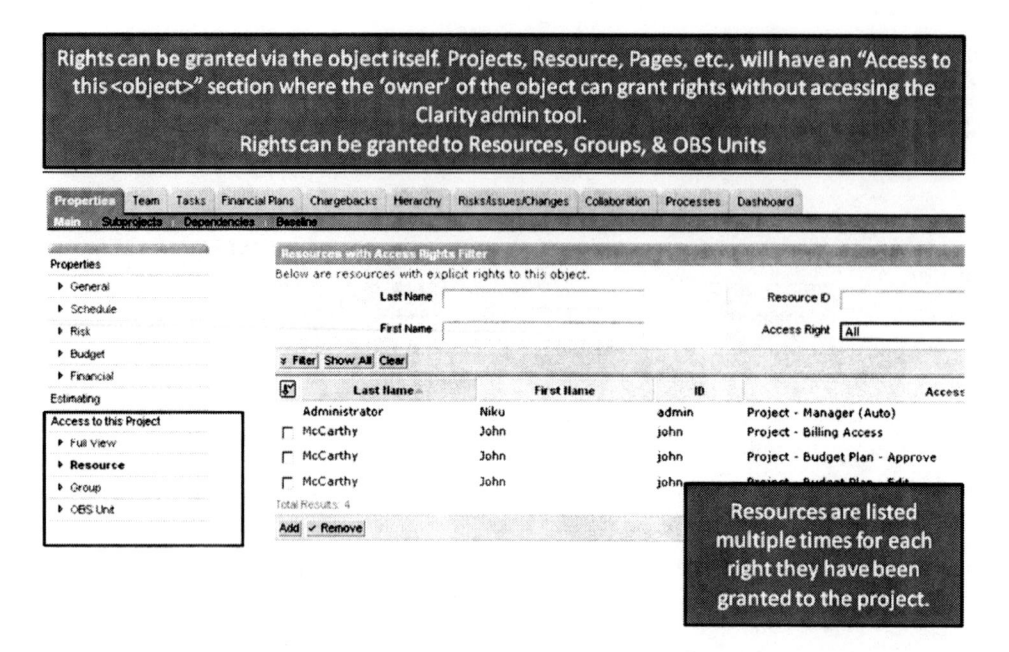

Figure 12-31. Object-level access rights from application side

Figure 12-32 shows that access is granted from the admin tool side to control the access to an object.

Figure 12-32. Object-level access rights from the admin tool side

Best Practices

The following are best practices to implement CA Clarity PPM security based on a CA services consultant's experience in the field:

- It is recommended that you don't make changes to the out-of-the-box groups. Instead, create a new group and assign applicable rights.
- When two or more resources have identical rights, the best practice is to create a group and then assign the resources to the group.
- OBS models must be created and designated as Use as Access Rights before OBS rights can be assigned to users or OBS units.
- Inherent rights are not always visible from the instance screen.
- OBS models are not necessarily based on the organization structure. OBS models should be based on what the organization's users can access.
- When rights are assigned to an OBS unit, all users who are assigned to the unit will automatically obtain the OBS unit rights.
- Create a spreadsheet listing all the instance/OBS/global rights, and then assign each user within the organization to the appropriate rights. This will help when creating the OBS organization chart. This, in turn, helps define groups that have common user rights and can access the common departments within the organization.
- Instance rights are very granular and maintenance intensive.

CA Clarity PPM Security Audit Report Prepackaged Work Product

CA Services Global Delivery has developed security audit reports that provide comprehensive information on the security model for any Clarity setup. Three reports cater to different access levels of the Clarity security model: User, Group, and OBS. The following are the reports that are part of this package.

- Access Rights by Users Report
- Access Rights by Groups Report
- Access Rights by OBS Units Report

The reports list access rights based on three different levels of security: instance, OBS, and global. The contents of the reports will be helpful to the following groups:

- *Audit team*: Significantly reduces time and effort involved in determining the security set up
- *Clarity administrators*: Enables quicker resolution of user access issues as part of routine support

- *Upgrade assessment:* Helps determine the access rights that are likely to be impacted on upgrade

Summary

In this chapter, we briefly described CA Clarity PPM's security model setup and how you can use different levels and types of security to successfully implement the security model with the Clarity solution. Security, a major part of Clarity solution, requires a thorough understanding of the business process and then must map to the solution to be implemented.

CHAPTER 13

■ ■ ■

CA Clarity PPM Components: Prepackaged Work Products

CA Clarity PPM provides a structured way for you to deploy and grow your PPM solution. CA offers a variety of modular service offerings, packaged accelerators, and prepackaged work products for CA Clarity PPM to speed up implementation time.

Both the CA Clarity PPM Rapid Implementation Service Offering (RISO) and the Clarity PPM Solution Implementation Service Offering (SISO) provide a fast on-ramp to a fully deployed CA Clarity PPM solution that leverages CA's PPM Best Practices Accelerator.

Customers are encouraged to leverage CA Services' catalog of CA accelerators and add-on services components (www.ca.com/us/collateral/licensing/na/ca-accelerators-and-add-on-services-components.aspx) to add further depth of functionality to their PPM implementations. These accelerators and components are preconfigured objects, reports, portlets, integrations, workflows, and jobs that can provide immediate value right out of the box. They are created to support industry-standard processes and represent the best practices across hundreds of existing CA Clarity PPM customers.

In this chapter, we describe some of the packaged accelerators and prepackaged work products. We describe how the accelerator or the package works, the benefits it provides you, and the technical prerequisites necessary for you to use it. This chapter should give you an idea of the type of benefits you can get from the other items in the catalog.

CA Clarity Smart Phone Time Management App Add-on Services Component

CA Clarity Smart Phone Time Management App extends the functionality of CA Clarity PPM to your mobile workforce. It provides users with functionality to create time entries directly from smartphones while enforcing business rules and data validation defined in CA Clarity PPM. It also provides managers with approval access to CA Clarity PPM time entries as well as action items to review and approve while working remotely—improving data currency, reporting, and analysis by reducing delays in time entry and approval.

The component provides three simple views:

- *Quick view.* The current reporting time period
- *Timesheet view.* All timesheets for all open time periods
- *Approval view.* All items in the approval queue for the logged-in user

The solution includes an installation package, documentation, and remote services to help install, set up, test, and verify successful deployment. CA Services can also offer mentoring of staff.

Benefits That Deliver Value

Smart phone time management for CA Clarity PPM offers the following benefits:

- Enables your mobile workforce with time entry capability and time and action item approvals

- Extends user adoption of CA Clarity PPM by providing a familiar user interface for mobile workers

- Drives consistent time entry and approval governance by removing data entry and workflow barriers for your mobile workforce

- Improves currency of CA Clarity PPM data for more accurate reporting and analysis

How It Works

The solution is comprised of three core technologies: the smartphone application that gets installed on the smartphone device, the middleware layer that acts as the content management system and enforces business rules and performs data validation, and the timesheet component that loads the time entries and approvals to CA Clarity PPM. Figure 13-3 gives the architectural diagram of Smart Phone Time Management for CA Clarity PPM.

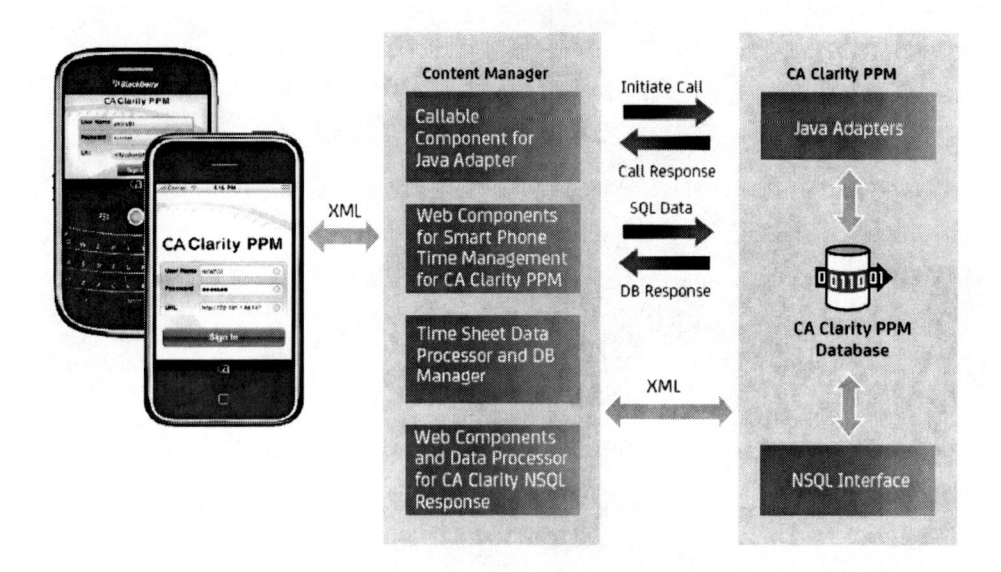

Figure 13-1. Three-tier system architecture for Smart Phone Time Management for CA Clarity PPM

Technical Prerequisites

The following are technical prerequisites.

- Mobile device support:
    - Apple: iPhone, iPad, iPod touch
    - Research In Motion: BlackBerry Bold: 9000; BlackBerry Curve: 8300, 8310, 8320, 8330; Blackberry Torch
    - Android
- OS support: Linux, Unix, AIX, Microsoft Windows
- Database support: Microsoft SQL Server, Oracle Server
- Java JDK 1.4.2 or newer
- CA Clarity PPM version 8.1fp03 or newer
- Language: English

CA Clarity Business Analytics Add-on Services Component

CA Clarity Business Analytics for Project & Portfolio Management (PPM) is a robust business intelligence and data analytics solution built on CA Clarity PPM. It extends the power for analyzing and reporting CA Clarity PPM data from traditional reports and portlets by enabling Online Analytical Processing (OLAP) reporting against CA Clarity PPM data using data cubes.

Business Analytics for CA Clarity PPM addresses the needs of analysts and executives for timely visibility into detailed business data. With this solution, users can easily analyze data, discover and depict trends, and assess patterns and relationships in ways not readily available to those relying on static data or traditional reports.

The solution includes an installation package, documentation, and remote services to help install, configure, test, and verify. Customers will also receive knowledge transfer for their staff.

Benefits That Deliver Value

Business Analytics for CA Clarity PPM offers the following benefits:

- Helps organizations obtain greater value from CA Clarity PPM data by delivering analysis and reports for multiple audiences (executives, managers, transactional users)
- Delivers clear, precise, and quick results from complex, multidimensional analytical queries using OLAP
- Supports trending analysis and reporting on historical data

CHAPTER 13 ■ CA CLARITY PPM COMPONENTS: PREPACKAGED WORK PRODUCTS

How It Works

The solution includes the following technologies, as shown in Figure 13-2:

- Data extraction: Pulls transactional data from CA Clarity PPM and populates the data warehouse
- Analytics processing: Processes the data from the data warehouse and creates a Microsoft Analysis Service Cube
- Data warehouse: A star schema data warehouse that enables fast, multidimensional relationships
- Microsoft Analysis Service Cube: Built from the data warehouse, provides the slice-and-dice capabilities for complex queries and multidimensional reporting
- Reporting: Integration supports reporting via third-party technologies including the following:
    - SAP Business Objects Voyager
    - SAP Business Objects Xcelcius
    - Microsoft Excel 2007 or newer
    - Google Analytics
    - Panorama NovaView and others

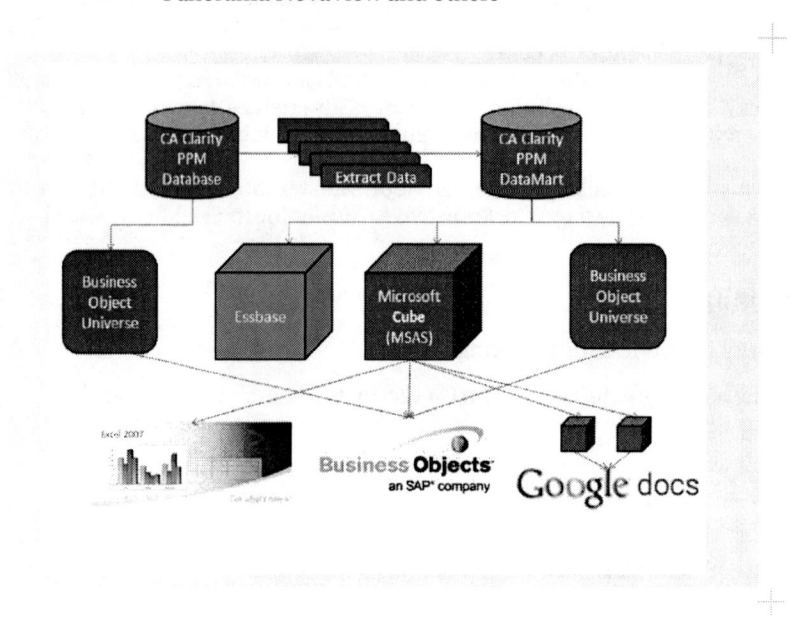

Figure 13-2: Architecture diagram that illustrates the logical three-tier design being used Business Analytics for CA Clarity PPM

Technical Prerequisites

The following are the technical prerequisites:

- OS support: Linux, Unix, AIX, Microsoft Windows
- Source database support: Microsoft SQL Server 2005 or newer, Oracle Server 10.2 or newer
- Cube technology: Microsoft SQL Server 2008 Analysis Service Analysis Services
- Java JDK 1.4.2 or newer
- CA Clarity PPM version 8.1fp03 or newer
- Language: English

CA Clarity KPI Monitor Add-on Services Component

CA Clarity KPI Monitor component helps CA Clarity PPM users including project managers and executives to monitor critical CA Clarity PPM data through defined business performance metrics and exceptions. With CA Clarity KPI Monitor, data is presented in a convenient dashboard as key performance indicators (KPIs) and exceptions to established thresholds. The KPIs and exception-based presentation of data allow users to proactively monitor business performance metrics and focus on high-priority issues that need attention. It also reduces the need to run reports and perform repetitive ad hoc data analysis, which can be time-consuming and prone to error.

The solution supports 25 KPIs that are defined by configurable business rules that can be activated or deactivated and modified to align to business requirements. KPI Monitor for CA Clarity PPM also includes predefined data consistency rules, many of which involve financial data attributes, to enforce data integrity.

KPI Monitor for CA Clarity PPM supports processes, business rules, and data integrity requirements. The solution does the following:

- Ensures that the proper project life cycle steps have been performed and completed in the proper sequence
- Validates that best practices such as project base lining and financial enablement are employed
- Enforces the proper charge code definition for projects so that timesheets are processed appropriately
- Ensures that the correct subset of resources is open for time entry
- Identifies active users mistakenly omitted from a certain required security group
- Ensures that all projects are present in a specified OBS definition and that active projects open for time entry have an approved budget plan

The solution includes a KPI object with 25 predefined configurable KPI rules (shown in Table 13-1), a stored procedure and a job to call the stored procedure, a workflow process to check project completeness based on rules stored in the object, two NSQL portlets, one business objects universe, installation files, documentation, a test plan that covers 20 specific use cases, and up to two hours of remote professional services related to installation, setup, testing, or use.

Benefits That Deliver Value

KPI Monitor for CA Clarity PPM offers the following benefits:

- Helps organizations derive greater value from CA Clarity PPM data by presenting it as KPIs and exceptions delivered in a context that is clear and consistent to users
- Enables users to proactively monitor critical data with less effort and risk of error to meet business objectives
- Controls who receives which KPI and exception data based on user role and login information

How It Works

Using a SQL stored procedure, a job is run by KPI Monitor for CA Clarity PPM that calculates the KPIs and checks the results for values that violate thresholds defined in the business rules. These business rules reside in the KPI object and can be modified to align to business requirements. Exceptions to thresholds are stored in a permanent data table that serves as an operational data store for two portlets:

- *The KPI Threshold portlet*: Displays KPI and exceptions data sorted by primary responsible party (used by CA Clarity PPM administrators and project teams)
- *The My KPI portlet*: Displays KPI and exception data specifically relevant for an individual active user

These portlets display a row for each instance of noncompliant data, a descriptive error message, a description of error symptoms, severity information, and detail about the object instance (KPI) that is in violation.

If enabled for a project, the workflow notifies project managers about missing data that requires remediation.

The job that supports KPI Monitor for CA Clarity PPM can be scheduled to run as often as needed to provide users with timely data with minimal impact to production systems

Table 13-1. Predefined KPIs

Assignments exceeding baseline hours	Late tasks	Projects exceeding baseline hours
Assignments with too many baseline hours	Overallocated resources (by month)	Projects not baselined
Change requests with high priority and an effect on cost	Overallocated team members (by month)	Project risk count
Incidents resolved with no resolution date	Overassigned resources (by month)	Projects started with open requisitions
Incidents with high urgency past expected end date	Portfolios active past finish date	Risks with a high impact and priority
Investments with no approved budget	Project change requests count	Tasks exceeding baseline hours
Issues with a high priority	Project issues count	Timesheets not approved yet
Late projects	Projects baselined too often	Timesheets not submitted yet
		Timesheets with excessive hours

Technical Prerequisites

The following are the technical prerequisites:

- OS support: Linux, Unix, AIX, Microsoft Windows
- Database support: Microsoft SQL Server, Oracle Server
- Java JDK 1.4.2 or newer
- CA Clarity PPM version 8.1 or newer
- Language: English

CA Clarity PPM Excel UI for Resource Management Add-on Services Component

The CA Clarity Excel UI for Resource Management prepackaged work product is for customers that would like to use Microsoft Excel as an interface to CA Clarity. The application consists of a core framework that enables the user to communicate directly with CA Clarity plus integration that allows for the extraction, editing, validation, and updating of data. The current interface for Resource Management provides resource allocations. This enables the user to extract a list of their projects and resources to Microsoft Excel, select project(s) for processing, edit and update FTE allocation information, and update CA Clarity with the updated values.

The prepackaged work product includes the code and installation information, documentation, and the services to install, set up, test, and verify the components. Customers will also receive knowledge transfer for their staff.

Benefits That Deliver Value

The CA Clarity Microsoft Excel Integrations Application prepackaged work product provides the following benefits:

- Improves your ability to identify over/underallocation of resources
- Easy data entry for allocation over a period of time for multiple resources on multiple projects
- Enables CA Clarity users who are more familiar or used to working in Excel the opportunity to continue to do so

How It Works

The CA Clarity Microsoft Excel Integrations Application provides an interface to extract information from the Clarity Application into Microsoft Excel. This data can then be viewed, manipulated, validated, and sent back to CA Clarity.

- This interface is developed using Microsoft Excel VBA and provides the capability to extract, edit, validate, and update CA Clarity.

- The VBA code will authenticate the user's login credentials to CA Clarity.
- Once authenticated, the user may then retrieve a list of projects/resources that they have CA Clarity user rights to.
- Once the projects are selected, the resource allocations (for the selected projects) are extracted and downloaded to the Microsoft Excel application.
- The user can then update this information and validate it for correctness.
- The data must be in the date range for the resource.
- The data must be valid.

Technical Prerequisites

The following are the technical prerequisites:

- OS support: Linux, Unix, AIX, Microsoft Windows
- Database support: Microsoft SQL Server, Oracle Server
- Microsoft Excel 2003 or newer
- CA Clarity version 8.1 or newer
- Language: English

CA Clarity PPM Excel UI for Risk, Issues and Change Requests Add-on Services Component

This component is designed to provide an interface to extract information from CA Clarity PPM into Microsoft Excel. Once the data is in Excel, users can modify the data and upload it to CA Clarity PPM. The component is designed to help simplify data entry for CA Clarity PPM users who are more familiar with an Excel front-end.

Description of Services

The following are the services included.

In Scope

The following are in scope:

- Electronically transmit installation files as identified in the Installation and User Guide.
- Installation and User Guide.
- Remote support consisting of up to one hour of the following:

- Installation, setup, and testing as described in the Installation and User Guide
- Mentoring on the use of the component
- The component will work only with the Product Architecture Stack identified in the Installation and User Guide.

Out of Scope

The following are out of scope:

- Component or database function customization
- Configuration or alteration of the component
- Development of custom code
- Any third-party product installation, the installation of third-party product interfaces, exit coding, or interfaces to customer systems and applications

CA Clarity PPM Grants Management Add-on Services Component

Grants Management for CA Clarity PPM assists organizations with managing the stages of the grants life cycle.

With this web-based solution, teams can research, compare, and select from available grants. Grants can then be managed as projects to streamline application processes, manage funding awards, and track performance objectives. The solution also provides automated "rollup" reporting to help address the American Recovery and Reinvestment Act (ARRA) requirements.

Grant management best practices (for both public and privately funded grants) built into the solution support collaboration across grant stakeholders including stimulus czars, grant reviewers and coordinators, grant developers, program managers, and finance officers.

Benefits That Deliver Value

The following are the benefits:

- Helps teams assess available grant opportunities in a structured system with built-in grant management best practices
- Helps develop an overall grants application strategy that is aligned with strategic goals and the mission of your organization
- Improves visibility of grants projects across numerous stakeholder groups for greater collaboration and better decision making
- Reduces reporting and compliance efforts and the potential for errors that can impact grants success

How It Works

This solution includes the following technologies:

- *Grant Opportunity Center*:
    - Provides a central forum for compiling grants information to rank and prioritize opportunities based on assigned values, ability to execute, and organizational goals
    - Supports "what if" scenarios to assess impact of attaining different levels of funding, from multiple sources and with a variety of grant types
- *Support for Adobe LiveCycle Forms ES2*: Facilitates online application submissions using customizable forms and defined workflows
- *Grants Repository*: Stores resource, task, and milestone data mapped to individual grants to help monitor and manage budgets, deliverables, and requirements attainment
- *Grants Management Dashboards*: Provide grantees with a view to track performance and financial details such as grant contributions and allocations for one or multiple funding sources or funding rounds

Figure 13-3 shows the view of the grants that are ranked and prioritized based on different criteria.

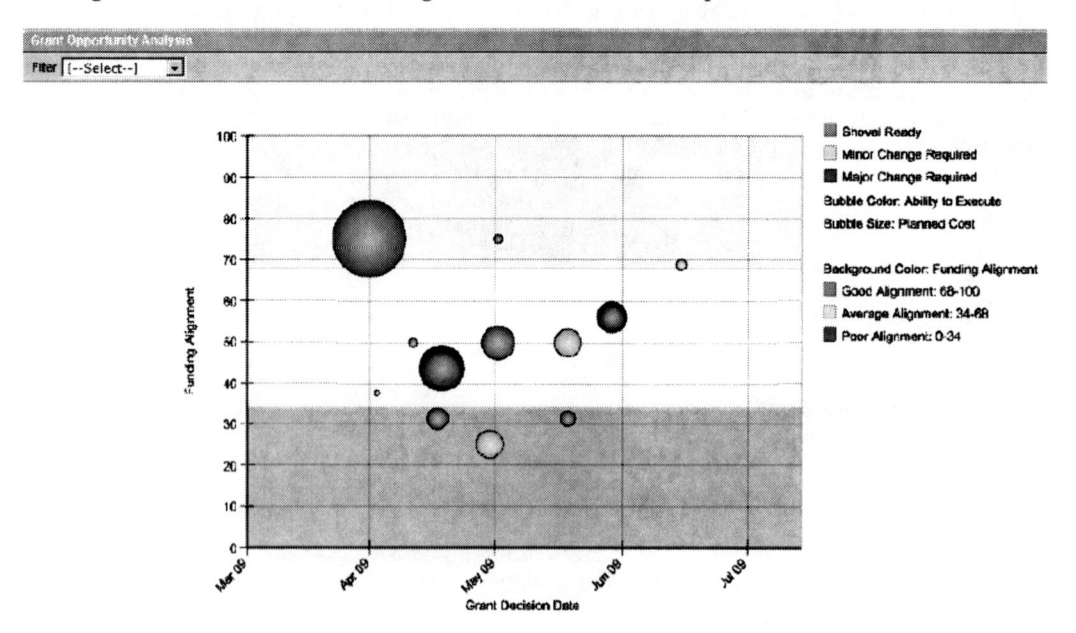

Figure 13-3: Bubble charts in Grants Management for CA Clarity PPM enable users to quickly rank and prioritize "shovel ready" grants based on merit, ability to execute, and goals.

Technical Prerequisites

The following are the technical prerequisites:

- OS support: Linux, Unix, AIX, Microsoft Windows
- Source database support: Microsoft SQL Server 2005 or newer, Oracle Server 10.2 or newer
- CA Clarity PPM version 12 or newer
    - CA Clarity PPM On Demand
- Language: English

CA Clarity PPM CPIC Add-on Services Component

The following sections cover the CA Clarity PPM CPIC Add-on Services component.

Description of Services

The CA Clarity PPM Capital Planning and Investment Control (CPIC) prepackaged work product is designed to help enable U.S. federal agencies to submit accurate and timely funding requests to the Office of Management and Budget (OMB) by using Studio configuration and CA Clarity PPM processes. This component also includes reports to support adherence to many OMB Exhibit 300 and Exhibit 53 requirements.

In Scope

The following is in scope:

- Electronically transmit installation files as identified in the Installation and User Guide.
- Installation and User Guide.
- Remote support consisting of up to one hour of the following:
    - Installation, setup, and testing as described in the Installation and User Guide
    - Mentoring on the use of the component
- The component will work only with the Product Architecture Stack identified in the Installation and User Guide.

Out of Scope

The following is out of scope:

- Component or database function customization

- Configuration or alteration of the component
- Development of custom code
- Any third-party product installation, the installation of third-party product interfaces, exit coding, or interfaces to customer systems and applications

CA Clarity Idea Vision Integration Add-on Services Component

Idea Vision Integration for CA Clarity Project and Portfolio Management (CA Clarity PPM) enables data exchange between CA Idea Vision and CA Clarity PPM. CA Idea Vision provides an idea management workspace whereby a community can generate, share, vote on, and offer commentary on ideas in an easy-to-use portal. Idea Vision Integration for CA Clarity PPM allows the promotion of ideas from CA Idea Vision to CA Clarity PPM, which provides greater control for tracking, managing, and elevating ideas to project status.

CA Clarity PPM enables the idea-to-project life cycle. Once an idea is migrated to CA Clarity PPM, data can flow to the originating idea portal so that there is continuity throughout the idea and project management life cycles. Specifically, if the status changes, it will be communicated back to the originating community.

An idea that has been moved to CA Clarity PPM always maintains links back to the ideas in CA Idea Vision, so as the idea moves through the idea-to-project life cycle, an active community remains linked to the idea.

Idea Vision Integration for CA Clarity PPM includes an installation package, documentation, and remote services to help install, set up, test, and verify solution deployment. Customers will also receive knowledge transfer for their staff.

Benefits That Deliver Value

The following are benefits:

- Provides an interactive, dynamic workspace that fosters idea creation, exchange, and debate with low process overhead
- Enables user communities to keep track of ideas and their status from the idea portal as the idea is assessed and developed prior to elevation to a CA Clarity PPM project
- Allows for extended idea management and idea conversion into CA Clarity PPM projects
- Maintains the relationship between the community, the idea, and the CA Clarity PPM project

How It Works

The solution is comprised of two core components:

- *CA Clarity PPM inbound process*: This is a workflow that can be scheduled or executed in real time to pull data from CA Idea Vision, which houses the idea portal.

- *CA Clarity PPM outbound process*: This is a workflow that can be scheduled or executed in real time to push data back to the originating idea portal.

The stock attributes that can move from CA Idea Vision to CA Clarity PPM include the following:

- Title
- Body
- ID
- URL
- Vote Total
- Vote Score
- Status
- Parent Idea ID
- Number of Comments

Five additional custom attributes may be added during implementation.

Technical Prerequisites

The following is the only technical prerequisite: CA Clarity PPM version 12.

CA Clarity Integration Accelerator

Integration Accelerator for CA Clarity PPM provides a comprehensive vision into disparate project, resource, finance, and support systems within an organization. It enables a 360-degree view and the financial alignment necessary to more effectively manage projects, budgets, and resources for immediate and measurable results.

Supporting Business

The CA Clarity Integration Accelerator gives resource managers, project managers, and executives the ability to automate the sharing of data between other business systems and CA Clarity, providing up-to-date cross-system data for better decision making. This set of powerful adapters integrates HR, accounting, ERP, time entry, and other processes for improved project alignment and greater synchronization between projects and finance.

Delivering Business Value

The CA Clarity Integration Adapters Accelerator does the following:

- Integrates project, resource, finance, and support systems with the CA Clarity Project Portfolio Management (PPM) solution

- Provides data from disparate systems to enhance decision making

Base Data Extraction for CA Clarity PPM

The CA Clarity PPM Data Extraction component is used to extract data from Clarity and also can be used as an outbound interface to send data to other systems such as SAP, Oracle, SharePoint, and so on.

This component provides the following functionality:

- *Configuration object:* This holds the configurable parameters (Delimiter, output file path, SQL, header labels, GUI required, and record count).

- *Configuration sub object:* Data Extraction File Labels is a subobject that allows the user to configure the file header labels that need to appear in final extracted output files.

- *Data Extraction UI:* The Data Extract HTML portlet navigates the user to a page where the user can see the list of extraction files and provides a facility to download/delete the files.

This component can be configured and executed via a Clarity job and scheduled to run at the desired interval. The solution includes an installation package, documentation, and remote services to assist with installation, configuration, and overall deployment.

Benefits That Deliver Value

The Data Extraction component for CA Clarity PPM does the following:

- Enables self-service outbound interfaces for Clarity.
- Fully configurable via the Clarity UI.
- Enables the export of data from multiple objects at the same time.
- Provides on-demand customers with a scalable and proven solution for extracting and accessing their data.
- Handles large data volumes through multiple file generation and efficient threading.
- Each extract can have its own configuration settings.
- Fully integrates with Clarity and enforces the security configuration.
- Multiple file download options via Clarity UI/SFTP.

How It Works

The following is how it works:

- Java-based extraction engine.
- Runs within the BG engine in Clarity.

- Extraction jobs are scheduled and executed from the standard Reports and Jobs menu.
- Extraction portlet provides visibility for users to manage and maintain the files manually as needed.

Architecture

Figure 13-4 shows the architecture diagram of the data extraction component.

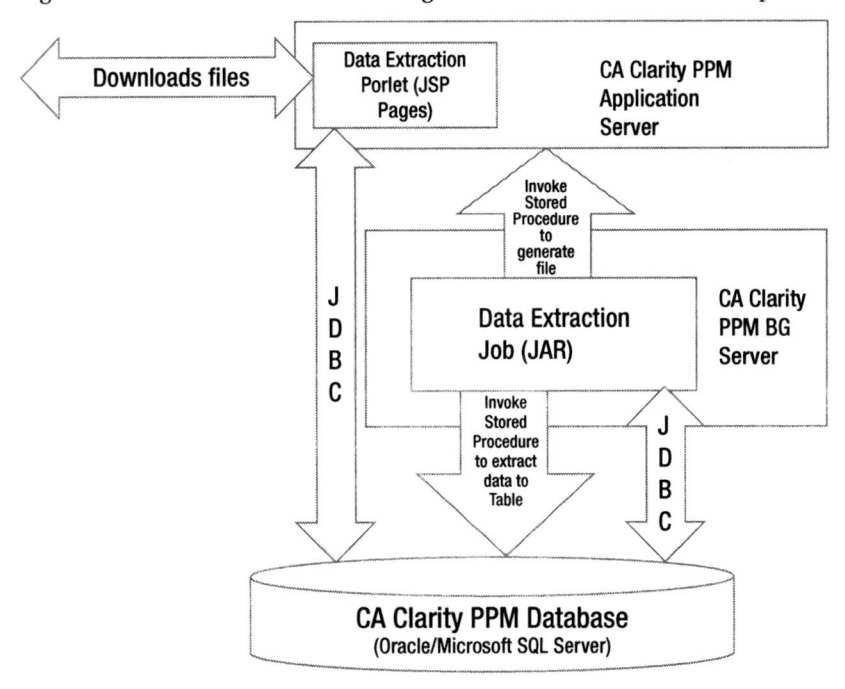

Figure 13-4. Architecture diagram of the data extraction component

Technical Prerequisites

The following are the technical prerequisites:

- Database support: Oracle Server/Microsoft SQL Server
- CA Clarity version 8 and newer
- Language support: All languages supported by the Clarity product

CA Clarity PPM Cost and Rate Matrix Adapter Add-on Services Component

The CA Clarity PPM Cost and Rate Matrix Adapter prepackaged work product (the *adapter*) is a connector that keeps standard costs and billing rates synchronized between CA Clarity and your accounting systems to support consistency in the financial information in all systems. This adapter can support importing costs and rates into CA Clarity to the extent that variables are supported in CA Clarity.

This adapter includes code and installation files, documentation, and remote services to help install, set up, test, and verify the adapter.

How It Works

Synchronizing costs and billing rate information from an external system on a user-definable basis requires extracting the relevant costs and billing rate attributes from the external system, loading adapter staging tables with this information, and importing the data into CA Clarity. This can be achieved via automated scripts.

Adapter staging tables are defined to map attributes from the source system to appropriate fields in the staging tables. Each field in a staging table equates to a field related to costs and billing rate information in CA Clarity.

- Scripts are defined to automate the process of populating information from the external system into the staging tables.

- A job is defined in CA Clarity that sets a schedule for the adapter synchronization process between CA Clarity and the target accounting systems so data is maintained automatically.

- The adapter is installed using the standard ClarityConnect wizard.

- Three portlets are configured to monitor and diagnose errors during operation:

    - XIF Activity Tracker

    - Processed Transactions

    - Error Logs

Technical Prerequisites

The following are the technical prerequisites:

- OS support: Linux, Unix, AIX, Microsoft Windows

- Database support: Microsoft SQL Server, Oracle Server

- Java JDK 1.4.2

- CA Clarity version 7.5.3 or newer with no XY_HOME path variable defined in the target environment

- Language: English

CA Clarity PPM Financial Transactions Adapter Add-on Services Component

The CA Clarity PPM Financial Transactions Adapter prepackaged work product (the *adapter*) is a connector that links finance and accounting systems with CA Clarity to support the transmission of financial transactions that may be required to do the following:

- Capture complete project costs

- Import expenses, write-ups, write-downs, project credits, material and equipment costs, and other financial transactions that can impact a project cost

The adapter includes code and installation files, documentation, and remote services to help install, set up, test, and verify the adapter. You also receive mentoring for your staff.

How It Works

Synchronizing financial transaction information from an external system on a user-definable basis requires extracting the relevant financial transaction attributes from the external system, loading the adapter staging tables with this information, and importing the data into CA Clarity. This can be achieved via automated scripts.

- Adapter staging tables are defined to map attributes from the source system to appropriate fields in the staging table(s). Each field in a staging table equates to a field related to financial transaction information in CA Clarity.

- Scripts are defined to automate the process of populating information from the external system into the staging tables.

- A job is defined in CA Clarity that sets a schedule for the adapter synchronization process between CA Clarity and the target finance and accounting systems so data is maintained automatically.

- The adapter is installed using the standard ClarityConnect wizard.

- Three portlets are configured to monitor and diagnose errors during operation:

    - XIF Activity Tracker

    - Processed Transactions

    - Error Logs

Technical Prerequisites

The following are the technical prerequisites:

- OS support: Linux, Unix, AIX, Microsoft Windows

- Database support: Microsoft SQL Server, Oracle Server

- Java JDK 1.4.2

- CA Clarity version 7.5.3 or newer with no XY_HOME path variable defined in the target environment
- Language: English

CA Clarity PPM Projects Adapter Add-on Services Component

The CA Clarity PPM Projects Adapter prepackaged work product (the *adapter*) is a connector that bidirectionally synchronizes external project accounting systems with CA Clarity to keep work breakdown structures (WBSs) and resource assignments coordinated and updated between CA Clarity and other project management systems.

The adapter includes code and installation files, documentation, and remote services to help install, set up, test, and verify the adapter.

How It Works

Synchronizing project accounting information from an external system on a user-definable basis requires extracting the relevant project accounting attributes from the external system, loading adapter staging tables with this information, and importing the data into CA Clarity. This can be achieved via automated scripts.

- Adapter staging tables are defined to map attributes from the source system to appropriate fields in the staging tables. Each field in a staging table equates to a field related to project accounting information in CA Clarity.
- Scripts are defined to automate the process of populating information from the external system into the staging tables.
- A job is defined in CA Clarity that sets a schedule for the adapter synchronization process between CA Clarity and the target project accounting systems so data is maintained automatically.
- The adapter is installed using the standard ClarityConnect wizard.
- Three portlets are configured to monitor and diagnose errors during operation:
  - XIF Activity Tracker
  - Processed Transactions
  - Error Logs

Technical Prerequisites

The following are the technical prerequisites:

- OS support: Linux, Unix, AIX, Microsoft Windows
- Database support: Microsoft SQL Server, Oracle Server
- Java JDK 1.4.2

- CA Clarity version 7.5.3 or newer with no XY_HOME path variable defined in the target environment
- Language: English

CA Clarity PPM Resources Adapter Add-on Services Components

The CA Clarity PPM Resources Adapter prepackaged work product (the *adapter*) is a connector that imports resource information from various HR and ERP systems into the CA Clarity Resource and User modules to do the following:

- Facilitate keeping your resource relationship structures current
- Help with appropriate Resource Capacity management processes
- Handle cascading updates to resource information

The adapter includes code and installation files, documentation, and remote services to help install, set up, test, and verify the adapter.

How It Works

Synchronizing resource information from an external system on a user-definable basis requires extracting the relevant resource attributes from the external system, loading adapter staging tables with this information, and importing the data into CA Clarity. This can be achieved via automated scripts.

- Adapter staging tables are defined to map attributes from the source system to appropriate fields in the staging table(s). Each field in a staging table equates to a field related to resource information in CA Clarity.
- Scripts are defined to automate the process of populating information from the external system into the staging tables.
- A job is defined in CA Clarity that sets a schedule for the adapter synchronization process between CA Clarity and the target HR and ERP systems so data is maintained automatically.
- The adapter is installed using the standard ClarityConnect wizard.
- Three portlets are configured to monitor and diagnose errors during operation:
    - XIF Activity Tracker
    - Processed Transactions
    - Error Logs

Technical Prerequisites

The following are the technical prerequisites:

- OS support: Linux, Unix, AIX, Microsoft Windows

- Database support: Microsoft SQL Server, Oracle Server
- Java JDK 1.4.2
- CA Clarity version 7.5.3 or newer with no `XY_HOME` path variable defined in the target environment
- Language: English

CA Clarity PPM Time Actuals Adapter Add-on Services Component

The CA Clarity PPM Time Actuals Adapter prepackaged work product (the *adapter*) is a connector that integrates with external time entry systems when CA Clarity is not the only timesheet system in use so that complete employee time details can be associated with your projects and support chargebacks or billings.

The adapter includes code and installation files, documentation, and remote services to help install, set up, test, and verify the adapter. You also receive mentoring for your staff.

How It Works

Synchronizing timesheet information from an external system on a user-definable basis requires extracting the relevant timesheet attributes from the external system, loading adapter staging tables with this information, and importing the data into CA Clarity. This can be achieved via automated scripts.

- Adapter staging tables are defined to map attributes from the source system to appropriate fields in the staging table(s). Each field in a staging table equates to a field related to timesheet information in CA Clarity.
- Scripts are defined to automate the process of populating information from the external system into the staging tables.
- A job is defined in CA Clarity that sets a schedule for the adapter synchronization process between CA Clarity and the target time entry systems so data is maintained automatically.
- The adapter is installed using the standard ClarityConnect wizard.
- Three portlets are configured to provide to monitor and diagnose errors during operation:
  - XIF Activity Tracker
  - Processed Transactions
  - Error Logs

Technical Prerequisites

The following are the technical prerequisites:

- OS support: Linux, Unix, AIX, Microsoft Windows

- Database support: Microsoft SQL Server, Oracle Server
- Java JDK 1.4.2
- CA Clarity version 7.5.3 or newer with no XY_HOME path variable defined in the target environment
- Language: English

CA Clarity PPM Data Management Accelerator

The CA Clarity Data Management Accelerator gives resource managers, project managers, and executives the insight to improve project management, optimize resource utilization, and increase the quality of project management. The portlets and utilities help ensure completeness of data, improve accuracy and consistency, and enhance the performance of CA Clarity.

Benefits That Deliver Value

The CA Clarity Data Management Accelerator provides the following benefits:

- Improves your ability to identify process bottlenecks
- Quickly identifies missing and inaccurate data
- Promotes the use of automated processes and enforces compliance requirements

What You Get

The CA Clarity Data Management Accelerator includes the preconfigured prepackaged work products listed in Table 13-2 and the services required to install, set up, test, and verify the accelerator. You also receive mentoring on how to best utilize the components as well as the supporting documentation and code.

Data Management Accelerator Components and Reports' Descriptions

Table 13-2 gives details on the various components of the Data Management Accelerator and the kind of report each component generates.

Table 13-2. Data Management Accelerator Components and Reports' Descriptions

CA Clarity™ Project & Portfolio Manager (PPM) Data Integrity Add-On Services Component	Utility that checks the accuracy and consistency of the data within CA Clarity and generates reports for administrators and users
CA Clarity™ PPM User Notification Manager Add-On Services Component	Utility that sets the notification preferences in each of 15 categories for all current and future users and can be configured to prevent users from changing their notification preferences or to enforce compliance requirements
CA Clarity™ PPM User Allocations Portlet Add-On Services Component	Shows all investments that the current user is allocated to work on over the next 12 weeks (including current week) along with the number of hours allocated to each investment for each week
CA Clarity™ PPM Multi-Value Lookups Add-On Services Component	Utility that flattens a multi-value lookup attribute by concatenating its constituent elements together with a user selected delimiter
Process Bottlenecks Portlet	General instance portlet that displays initiated processes with how long an assigned resource took before action was taken, identifying if any actions took longer than the required time
Resource Profile Portlet	General instance portlet that displays the full name of the currently logged-in user, helping administrators who log into multiple CA Clarity instances using different user names, and also links to user profile and shows current work assignments
CA Clarity PPM™ Investment Process Portlets Add-On Services Component	Three portlets that support tracking of the current status, action items, process times and bottlenecks for any investment process and
	For compliance auditing: lets users quickly substantiate the approval of production software deployment
	For financial accounting auditing: lets users quickly substantiate the funding approval for a number of investments from a single portlet

CA Clarity PPM Advanced Project Management Accelerator

The CA Clarity Advanced Project Management Accelerator is a set of reports, portlets, and workflows that show project performance to help project managers improve project success rates. By providing detailed project tasks, financials, resources, status reports, and informational portlets, CA Clarity Advanced Project Management Accelerator helps in enhancing decision making to realize positive business results.

Delivering Business Value

The CA Clarity Advanced Project Management Accelerator does the following:

- Provides accelerated ability to improve resource utilization
- Enables quick identification of project tasks and costs
- Delivers a comprehensive overview of project and financial status

What You Get

The CA Clarity Advanced Project Management Accelerator includes the preconfigured prepackaged work products, portlets, reports, workflows, and dashboards listed next, as well as the services to install, set up, test, and verify the accelerator. You also receive mentoring on how to best utilize the reports and portlets, as well as the supporting user documentation and code.

- Automate Open/Close Time Periods Job
- Monthly Project Status Summary Report
- Overdue Timesheet Approver Notification Job
- Overdue Timesheet Notification Job
- Pending Actuals Report
- Project Actuals Report
- Project Financial Summary Report
- Project Hours by OBS Portlet
- Project Performance by Manager Report
- Project Summary Report
- Project Task Dependencies Report
- Project Timesheet Details Report
- Timesheet Compliance Report
- Timesheet Data Extractor Report
- Timesheet Detail with Notes Portlet
- Timesheet Summary By Time Period Report

CA Clarity PPM Earned Value Management Accelerator

The CA Clarity PPM Earned Value Management Accelerator (the *accelerator*) delivers the insight your project managers need to easily understand which programs, projects, and tasks are meeting expectations and which ones are at risk for exceeding planned budgets and time frames. Reports can be manipulated by 15 key metrics and are presented in pie, chart, graph, and table formats.

In your CA Clarity 7.5.2 (or newer) environment, where the Resource Management and Project modules are fully implemented and operational, CA Clarity services experts deploy the accelerator through this service offering.

Benefits That Deliver Value

The CA Clarity Earned Value Management Accelerator provides the following benefits:

- Provides you with the insights to understand and resolve project performance issues
- Helps save costs by quickly identifying tasks that are exceeding budgets
- Gives the ability to maintain better control of programs, projects, and tasks

What You Get

The CA Clarity PPM Earned Value Management Accelerator includes the preconfigured reports and portlets listed in Table 13-3 and the services to install, set up, test, and verify this accelerator. It includes up to two hours of mentoring for two people on how to best utilize the reports and portlets, as well as the supporting user documentation and code.

CA Clarity PPM Advanced Resource Management Accelerator

The CA Clarity Advanced Resource Management Accelerator gives resource managers, project managers, and executives the insight to easily understand resource efficiency, availability, allocation, utilization, distribution, workload, and performance. Reports can be presented in pie, chart, graph, and table formats.

The accelerator is designed to be deployed in on CA Clarity 8.1 (or newer) environment—where the Resource Management module is fully implemented and operational—to provide reports and portlets that expand the capabilities of the Resource Management module.

Delivering Business Value

The CA Clarity Advanced Resource Management Accelerator does the following:

- Provides insight to easily understand and properly allocate resource capabilities
- Helps you improve project performance and best utilize your resources for maximum ROI
- Presents reports in many different formats

What You Get

The CA Clarity Advanced Resource Management Accelerator includes the preconfigured reports and portlets listed next and the services to install, set up, test, and verify this accelerator. It includes mentoring on how to best utilize the reports and portlets, as well as the supporting user documentation and code.

- Direct vs. indirect time report
- Project actuals by resource OBS report
- Employee performance report by month
- Labor distribution by project OBS
- Resource remaining availability
- Resource utilization comparison portlet
- Resource efficiency based on finished tasks
- Resource contact information portlet
- Resource head-count distribution
- Resource demand by project portlet
- Resource over or underallocation
- Project resource actual summary by date range report
- Resource utilization comparison
- Resource demand by goal bar chart portlet
- Resource work distribution
- Resource demand by goal pie chart
- Resource workload
- Resource supply vs. demand portlet
- Monthly resource productivity report
- User allocation portlet
- Resource actuals report

CA Clarity PPM Advanced Financial Management Accelerator

The CA Clarity Advanced Financial Management Accelerator provides resource managers, project managers, and executives with insight into the financial status and risk associated with projects and detailed comparisons of performance to budgets and forecasts. By using a comprehensive set of financial tools, CA Clarity Advanced Financial Management Accelerator provides a broad set of financial tools that enable superior project financial management.

Delivering Business Value

The CA Clarity Advanced Financial Management Accelerator does the following:

- Eases comparisons of project performance to budgets and forecasts
- Enables improved project financial management
- Presents a wide variety of financial reports and dashboards in different formats

What You Get

The CA Clarity Advanced Financial Management Accelerator includes the preconfigured reports and portlets listed next and the services to install, set up, test, and verify this accelerator. It includes mentoring on how to best utilize the reports and portlets, as well as the supporting user documentation and code.

- CA Clarity Fiscal Focus Actionable Dashboard prepackaged work product
- Investment Financials portlets
- Investment Process portlets
- Month and Year-to-Date Financial Variance Report
- Monthly Fiscal Finance Report
- Project Phase and Resource Actuals Report
- Quarterly Financial Variance Report

CA Clarity PPM Fiscal Focus Actionable Dashboard Add-on Services Component

The CA Clarity Fiscal Focus Actionable Dashboard prepackaged work product is a set of portlets that provide a consolidated dashboard of portlets for administration of financials in CA Clarity; it is most beneficial where timesheets and financials have evolved to provide chargebacks. This prepackaged work product is a convenient oversight and control set for your entire financial cycle within Clarity. It supplies exceptionally clear visibility into financial transactions as they progress to completion (work in progress [WIP] or chargeback). Of particular importance is that Fiscal Focus identifies exactly where transactions are and what to do next in logical sequence.

Because Fiscal Focus easily reveals the position of financial transactions, it also reveals whether transactions are not moving forward. It then pinpoints how to resolve problems that are causing these issues. The major benefit of Fiscal Focus is that financial data is more complete, and therefore transactions are not "missed." Closing of financial periods is typically achieved faster with greater confidence than before while users save time and effort.

The prepackaged work product includes the code and installation files, as well as the documentation and remote services to help install, set up, test, and verify the component. You also receive mentoring for your staff.

How It Works

Through CA Clarity Studio, the user selects the data to display in the portlet and where obtain this information from within CA Clarity or from other databases within the enterprise.

Portlets are embedded into pages and can populate grids or graphs to show a snapshot of the data in real time without the need to run reports.

Users can run the portlet by selecting parameters and hitting the "submit" button, and the results will be created in HTML.

The XOG script is used to install the portlet into the Clarity system.

Technical Prerequisites

The following are the technical prerequisites:

- Database support: Microsoft SQL Server, Oracle Server
- CA Clarity version 8.1 Financial Management module with financial planning
- Language: English

Index

A
ABC Music Corporation
    benefits, 23–24
    challenges, 22
    corporate structure, 22
    implementation, 22
    layout, 23
Acme Data Systems Inc. (ADS), 59, 102, 192, 228, 239, 270
    partition model, 255
Advanced Project Management Accelerator, 312–313
Advanced Resource Management Accelerator, 314–315
Analytics processing, 294

B
Balance portlet, 222
Bubble charts, 300
Business analytics
    benefits, 293
    description, 293
    technical prerequisites, 295
    three-tier design, 294
Business processes, 226
Business Relationship Manager (BRM), 6

C
CA clarity PPM tool
    Acme Data Systems Inc. (ADS), 59
    basic navigation
        application *vs.* administration tool, 65–66
        expand and collapse filter, 67–70
        filtering criteria, 70
        list pages and filters, 67
        manage and save filters, 74–75
        power filter, 71–73
    configurable and nonconfigurable items, 97–98
    customization vs. configuration, 95
    customized List pages, 97
    customized logos, 96
    customized navigation bar, 96
    document manager, 86–87
    Jobs tab, 95
    knowledge store, 84–86
    organizer
        action items, 75–76
        calendar, 77–80
        notifications, 81–84
        output display, 75
        processes, 80–81
        tasks, 76–77
    personalization
        account settings, 87
        default partitions, 88–89
        font settings, 90
        link, 92–94
        Manage My Tabs, 94
        notifications, 90–91
        Overview page, 92
        personal settings, 88
        proxy, 89
        Software Downloads page, 91
    Reports and Jobs link, 94
    Reports tab, 95
    user interface
        clarity toolbar, 64
        John's home page, 65
        login screen, 59

INDEX

main menu and navigation bar, 61–63
personal overview home page, 60
CA Clarity project and portfolio manager (PPM)
    ABC Music Corporation
        benefits, 23–24
        challenges, 22
        corporate structure, 22
        implementation, 22
        layout, 23
    benefits, 7, 17
    BRM, 6
    challenges, 10–11
        federal government, 12–13
        IT management and governance, 11
        new product development, 12
        professional services automation, 12
    critical success factors, 3
    Demand Manager, 8–9
    description, 3–4, 25
    effective project management, 13
        description, 13
        executive analytics, 15
        quantifiable metrics, 16
        resource utilization, 13–14
        risk mitigation, 15–16
    entertainment industry, 21–24
    features, 7
    financial sector companies, 20
    IT Financial Manager, 6
    IT governance, 28
        business transformation, 30
        description, 29
        models, 30
        problem statement, 29
        statistics, 30
    IT Portfolio Manager, 5–6
    modules, 4–5
    oil and gas industry, 21
    portfolio management
        business investment planning, 31–32
        IT governance (*see* Information technology (IT) governance)
        origins, 31
    Process Manager, 9
    Project Financial Manager, 9
    project life cycle management
        closure phase, 27
        description, 25
        execution and controlling phase, 27
        initiation phase, 26
        planning phase, 26
        stages, 25–26
    Project Manager, 8
    public sector and utilities companies, 17–19
    Resource Manager, 7
    road map and maturity assessment
        ABC Pharmaceutical Company, 54–57
        assessing organizational readiness, 53–54
        projects failure, 50–53
    standard enterprise application landscape, 10
    successful project systems
        collaboration, 28
        integration, 28
        management, 27
    tool (*see* CA clarity PPM tool)
    value proposition, 4
Calendar
    event, 77–78
    project, 80
    resource, 78–79
Capital Planning and Investment Control (CPIC), 301
Case study, Healthcare Services Provider, 267
Cost and Rate Matrix Adapter
    description, 306
    staging tables, 306
    technical prerequisites, 306

D

Dashboards, 122, 300
Data Extraction, 294
    architecture, 305
    benefits, 304
    description, 304
    technical prerequisites, 305
    working procedure, 304
Data Management Accelerator
    benefits, 311
    components and reports descriptions, 311–312
    description, 311
Data mapping, incident management, 206
Data warehouse, 294
Demand management
    ABC Corp
        approval process, 39–42
        idea approval, 37–39
        idea creation, 37

INDEX

ADS, 192
description, 191
idea management
    approval, 195–196
    conversion, 197–198
    creation, 193–194
    functionalities, 198–199
    life cycle, 192–193
    rejection, 196–197
incident management
    category setup, 200–201
    conversion, 205–206
    creation, 201–202
    data mapping, 206
    effort, 202–203
    functionalities, 203–204
    list, 199
    nonconfiguration error, 201
    three tabs, 200
module, 191

E

Earned Value Management Accelerator, 313–314
Effective project management
    description, 13
    executive analytics, 15
    resource utilization, 13–14
        actual, 14
        forecasted, 14
        what-if scenarios, 13
Estimated time of completion (ETC)
    customer scenario, 158–159
    editing, 157–158
    posting, 156–157
Event calendar, 77–78
Excel UI
    resource management
        benefits, 297
        data extraction, 297
        description, 297
        technical prerequisites, 298
    risk, issues and change requests, 298–299

F

Financial data setup
    charge codes, 169
    company class, 167
    cost and rate matrices, 170
    departments, 165–166
    entity, 164
    exchange rates, 168
    GL accounts, 166–167
    input type codes, 169
    investment class, 168
    location, 165
    resource class, 167
    transaction class, 168
    twelve step process, 163
    WIP
        class, 168
        settings, 169
Financial management
    clarity invoices, 185–187
    corrections
        guidelines, 183–184
        invalid transactions, 181–182
        review and reverse charges, 184–185
        WIP adjustments, 182–184
    financial enabling objects
        chargebacks, 172–173
        projects, 172
        resources, 170–171
    financial processing flow
        financial data setup (*see* Financial data setup)
        flowchart, 162–163
    financial transaction creation, 174
    IT
        description, 161
        goals, 162
    IT chargeback recovery
        description, 188
        statement details, 189–190
        statement summary, 188–189
    manual transaction entry functionality, 175–177
    module, 161
    reviewing invoice details, 187–188
    transaction processing
        actual cost, 179
        flow through clarity, 177
        transaction movement, 178–179
        WIP, 179–80
    vouchers creation, 174–175
Financial Transactions Adapter
    description, 307
    staging tables, 307
    technical prerequisites, 307

321

INDEX

Financial/entity-based access rights, 286–287
Financials portlet, 223
Fiscal Focus Actionable Dashboard
    description, 316
    technical prerequisites, 317
    working procedure, 317

G, H

Gantt portlet, 222–223
Grants management
    Adobe LiveCycle Forms ES2, 300
    benefits, 299
    bubble charts, 300
    dashboards, 300
    description, 299
    opportunity center, 300
    repository, 300
    technical prerequisites, 301

I, J

Idea management
    approval, 195–196
    conversion, 197–198
    creation, 193–194
    description, 192
    functionalities, 198–199
    life cycle, 192–193
    rejection, 196–197
Idea Vision integration
    benefits, 302
    description, 302
    inbound process, 302
    outbound process, 303
    stock attributes, 303
    technical prerequisites, 303
Incident management
    category setup, 200–201
    conversion, 205–206
    creation, 201–202
    data mapping, 206
    description, 199
    effort, 202–203
    functionalities, 203–204
    list, 199
    nonconfiguration error, 201
    three tabs, 200
Information technology (IT) governance, 28, 32
    ABC Corp case study
        automated processes, 42–47
        business drivers, 33–34
        business requirements and goals, 33
        chargeback, 50
        customer request life cycle, 35–36
        demand management, 37–42
        executive summary, 32
        project execution, 47–48
        project reporting, 48–49
        solution requirements, 34–35
    business transformation, 30
    description, 29, 32
    models, 30
    problem statement, 29
    statistics, 30
Integration Accelerator, 303–304
Investment portlet, 221
Investments, portfolio
    adding and removing individual portfolio, 220–221
    excluding investment types, 218
    including investment types, 218
    power filters, 219
    updating list, 219
    viewing matching investments, 219
IT Financial Manager, 6
IT Portfolio Manager, 5–6

K, L

Key project indicators (KPIs), 16
KPI monitor
    benefits, 296
    description, 295
    My KPI portlet, 296
    predefined KPIs, 296
    technical prerequisites, 297
    threshold portlet, 296

M

Microsoft Analysis Service Cube, 294
Microsoft Excel Integrations Application. *See* Excel UI

INDEX

N

Net Present Value (NPV)
    collaboration, 119–120
    dashboard, 122
    data elements and terms, 114–115
    interest rate, 114
    participant group, 118–119
    participants, 116–117
    program, 123
    project staff, 115–116
    resource plan functionality, 115
    risk/issues/changes tab, 121–122
    task tab, 120–121
Nonpartitionable configuration
    financial setup, 263
    NSQL-based lookups and portlets, 263
    NSQL queries, 263
    timesheet options, 263
Nonproject investment objects (NPIOs), 211–212

O

Object-based portlets, 261
Object-level access rights
    description, 287
    from admin tool side, 288
    from application side, 287
OBS. *See* Organizational Breakdown Structure (OBS)
Organizational access rights
    admin tool, security management, 271
    global rights
        corporate department OBS, 277
        description, 276
        executive IT group, 278–279
        granted rights, resource, 277
        IT unit, 278
        OBSs list, 277
    inherited rights
        description, 271
        user as collaboration manager, 272
        user as collaboration participant, 273
        user as project manager, 274–275
        user as resource manager, 275–276
        user as staff member, 274
    instance rights, 284–286
    OBS rights
        corporate department OBS unit, 281–282
        department selection, 283
        description, 279
        enabling and disabling, 279
        executive IT group, 283–284
        filtering, 280, 283
        granting OBS rights, 279–281
        IT unit properties, 282
        security rights configuration, 283
        unit selection, 280
Organizational Breakdown Structure (OBS)
    access rights, 279–284
    best practices
        configuration complexity and partitioning, 266
        partition caveats, administration, 266
        partitioning, 264–265
        partition value, 265
        reporting, 266
        sample report, 267
    global supply chain and global quality operations business units layout
        access rights, 251–252
        Datamart, 252
        financial entities, 244–247
        levels, 241, 242
        object associations, 244
        properties (*see* Properties, Organizational Breakdown Structure (OBS))
        types, 241
        units, 242
    Healthcare Services Provider case study, 267
    investment aggregation portlet, 137
    partitions and views, 253
        model (*see* Partition model)
    resource aggregation portlet, 136
Organizer
    action items, 75–76
    event calendar, 77–78
    notifications, 81–84
    output display, 75
    processes, 80–81
    project calendar, 80
    resource calendar, 78–79
    tasks, 76–77

P, Q

Partition model
    access rights *vs.* partitions, 255
    Acme Data Systems (ADS), 255
    administration model management rights, 257
    configuration
        autonumbering schemas, 259
        lookup values, 260, 261
        nonpartitionable (*see* Nonpartitionable configuration)
        object fields (attributes), 258, 259
        object-based portlets, 261
        object lists, filters, and property pages, 260
        processes, 262
        project view, 262
        user interface themes (logos and colors), 257
    creating, 256
    default, 254
    geographical, 253
    OBS *vs.* partitioning, 255
    partition and ancestors association mode, 257
    partition, ancestors, and descendents association mode, 257
    partition only association mode, 257
    relationship between partitions, objects, and attributes, 256
    selecting partitions, 254
    switching between partitions, 254
Portfolio management
    analysis
        Balance portlet, 222
        Financials portlet, 223
        Gantt portlet, 222–223
        Investment portlet, 221
        scorecard tab, 221
    best practices, 224
    clarity investments, 210–212
    content selection
        adding investments, 219
        adding and removing individual investments, 220–221
        excluding investment types, 218
        including investment types, 218
        investments updating list, 219–220
        power filters, 219
        viewing matching investments, 219
    contents tab, 217–218
    creation, 215–217
    description, 224
    lists, 212–213
    NPIOs projects, 211–212
    properties screen, 213–214
    scenarios screen, 223
    stages for, 209–210
    view and edit screen, 214–215
Portlets
    balance, 222
    financials, 223
    Gantt, 222–223
    investment, 221
Power filter, 71–73
Prepackaged work products
    Advanced Financial Management Accelerator, 315–316
    Advanced Project Management Accelerator, 312–313
    Advanced Resource Management Accelerator, 314–315
    business analytics
        benefits, 293
        description, 293
        technical prerequisites, 295
        three-tier design, 294
    Cost and Rate Matrix Adapter
        description, 306
        staging tables, 306
        technical prerequisites, 306
    CPIC, 301
    Data Extraction
        architecture, 305
        benefits, 304
        description, 304
        technical prerequisites, 305
        working procedure, 304
    Data Management Accelerator
        benefits, 311
        components and reports descriptions, 311–312
        description, 311
    Earned Value Management Accelerator, 313–314
    Excel UI
        resource management, 297–298
        risk, issues and change requests, 298–299
    Financial Transactions Adapter
        description, 307

staging tables, 307
technical prerequisites, 307
Fiscal Focus Actionable Dashboard
   description, 316
   technical prerequisites, 317
   working procedure, 317
grants management
   Adobe LiveCycle Forms ES2, 300
   benefits, 299
   bubble charts, 300
   dashboards, 300
   description, 299
   opportunity center, 300
   repository, 300
   technical prerequisites, 301
Idea Vision integration
   benefits, 302
   description, 302
   inbound process, 302
   outbound process, 303
   stock attributes, 303
   technical prerequisites, 303
Integration Accelerator, 303–304
KPI monitor
   benefits, 296
   description, 295
   My KPI portlet, 296
   predefined KPIs, 296
   technical prerequisites, 297
   threshold portlet, 296
Projects Adapter
   description, 308
   staging tables, 308
   technical prerequisites, 308
Resources Adapter
   description, 309
   staging tables, 309
   technical prerequisites, 309
smart phone time management
   approval view, 291
   benefits, 292
   description, 291
   quick view, 291
   technical prerequisites, 293
   three-tier system architecture, 292
   timesheet view, 291
Time Actuals Adapter
   description, 310
   staging tables, 310
   technical prerequisites, 310
Process management

business processes, 226
description, 225–226
flow of process, 226–227
manager module, 225
process creation
   ADS, 228
   execution, 235–236
   flow diagram, 233
   initial stage, 229
   list, 227
   manual action items, 232
   object type, 229
   postconditions and step linking, 232
   primary object, 228
   process manager benefits, 225–226
   project object, 229
   properties page, 230–231
   security access, 234
   step properties, 233
   step properties screen, 231
   validation and activation, 234
process flow, 225
Process Manager, 9
Project calendar, 80
Project Financial Manager, 9
Project life cycle management
   closure phase, 27
   description, 25
   execution and controlling phase, 27
   initiation phase, 26
   planning phase, 26
   stages, 25–26
Project Management Body of Knowledge
   (PMBOK), 101
Project Management module
   ADS, 102
   booking, 118
      hard booking, 119
      mixed booking, 119
      soft booking, 119
   description, 102
   financial plans, 113
   initial stage, 103
   key project parameters, 101–102
   NPV
      collaboration, 119–120
      dashboard, 122
      data elements and terms, 114–115
      interest rate, 114
      participant group, 118–119
      participants, 116–117

INDEX

program, 123
project staff, 115–116
resource plan functionality, 115
risk/issues/changes tab, 121–122
task tab, 120–21
PMBOK, 101
project creation
    idea conversion, 105
    projects list page, 103–105
    XML Open Gateway (XOG), 106
project properties
    budget, 112–123
    general, 106–107
    risk, 110–112
    schedule, 107–110
staffing options, 118
strategic goals, 101
Project Manager, 8
Projects Adapter
    description, 308
    staging tables, 308
    technical prerequisites, 308
Properties, Organizational Breakdown Structure (OBS)
    resource properties, 250
    unit properties, 248–249
    user properties, 250

R

Resource calendar, 78–79
Resource finder
    booking manager (BK), 139
    description, 137
    Out-of-the-Box requisition notifications, 142
    requisition creator (RC), 139
    resource requisitions, 138–139
    staffing resources
        direct staffing, 141–142
        resource requisitioning, 139–141
Resource management, 30
    benefits, 297
    capacity, 135
        OBS resource aggregation portlet, 136
        role capacity portlet, 135
    data extraction, 297
    description, 125, 297
    equipment resource, 126
    expense resource, 126
    labor resource, 126
    material resource, 126
    module, 126
    OBS investment aggregation portlet, 137
    resource creation
        adapter add-on services component, 129
        administration tool, 127–128
        application administration, 128–129
    resource finder
        description, 137
        resource requisitions, 138–139
        staffing resources, 139–142
    resource planning
        allocations, 132–135
        features, 130–131
        workloads, 131–132
    roles, 127
    technical prerequisites, 298
Resource Manager, 7
Resource planning
    allocations
        allocation discrepancy lists, 135
        booking status portlet, 134
        unfilled requirements, 133–134
        weekly detail portlet, 132–133
    features, 130–131
    workloads, 131–132
Resource utilization, 13–14
Risk management, 30
Risk mitigation, 15–16
Road map and maturity assessment, 50
    ABC Pharmaceutical Company, 54–57
    assessing organizational readiness, 53–54
    projects failure
        control, 52
        definition, 51
        evaluation, 51
        goals and objectives, 51
        improvement, 52
        measure, 52
        monitor, 52
        resources, 51

S

Security, CA Clarity PPM
    access controls, 269–270
    ADS, 270
    audit report prepackaged work product, 289

best practices, 289
description, 270
entity-based security settings, 287
financial/entity-based access rights, 286–287
global rights required, 270
levels of access, 270
object-level access rights, 287–288
organizational access rights (*see* Organizational access rights)
Smart phone time management
    approval view, 291
    benefits, 292
    description, 291
    quick view, 291
    technical prerequisites, 293
    three-tier system architecture, 292
    timesheet view, 291

T, U, V

Time Actuals Adapter
    description, 310
    staging tables, 310
    technical prerequisites, 310
Time management
    aspects of, 143
    fixed task, 158
    front task, 158
    timesheet
        approval, 151–153

ETC, 156–159
modification, 153–155
set up, 144–150
Timesheet
    adjustment timesheet, 155
    approval, 151–153
    ETC
        customer scenario, 158–159
        editing, 157–158
        posting, 156–157
    modification, 153–155
    set up
        access, 144
        autopopulated timesheets, 150
        default populate time range setting, 149
        investment properties, 147
        populate, 148–149
        resource properties, 146
        security rights, 145–146
        tasks setting, 150
        time reporting period, 144–145, 149
        timesheet filter, 147

W, X, Y, Z

Work in process (WIP)
    and actual cost, 179
    corrections, adjustments, 182–184
    financial data setup
        class, 168
        settings, 169

CPSIA information can be obtained at www.ICGtesting.com
Printed in the USA
LVOW120256240112

265293LV00003B/42/P

9 781430 235576